Lord Brougham
and the
Whig Party

Lord Brougham
and the
Whig Party

ARTHUR ASPINALL

NONSUCH

First published 1927
Copyright © in this edition 2005
Nonsuch Publishing Ltd

Nonsuch Publishing Limited
The Mill, Brimscombe Port, Stroud, Gloucestershire, GL5 2QG
www.nonsuch-publishing.com

British Library Cataloguing in Publication Data.
A catalogue record for this book is available from the British Library.

ISBN 1-84588-033-1

Typesetting and origination by Nonsuch Publishing Limited
Printed in Great Britain by Oaklands Book Services Limited

Contents

Introduction to the Modern Edition

HENRY PETER BROUGHAM, later 1st Baron Brougham and Vaux, was one of the foremost political figures of the nineteenth century. Born in Edinburgh on 19 September 1778, at the age of fourteen he was sent to be educated at Edinburgh University, and it was here that his friendship with a group of staunch Whigs set him on the road to a political career that would span the first half of the nineteenth century.

During the early nineteenth century the British political system was dominated by two factions, the conservative Tories and the more liberal Whigs, although a third, grouped under the heading of 'Radicals', was beginning to make its presence felt. The Whig party had evolved during the crises of the reign of Charles II. Its members were considered to be the equivalent of the Roundheads, intent on decreasing the power of the monarchy in favour of Parliament. Indeed the name Whig was originally a disparaging nickname awarded to the party by their opponents, a short-ened version of Whiggamore, the name of a group of Scottish Presbyterians who had marched on Edinburgh in 1648 to oppose Charles I.

Although the Whigs had enjoyed a long period of ascendancy, with the governments of Robert Walpole and Henry Pelham in power for the majority of the period 1721–1756, with the accession of the conservative-minded George III to the throne in 1760 the party entered a period of decline. Not only did the King's opposition prevent them from having any chance of forming a government without a massive popular mandate, something they failed to achieve, but the party also fragmented into different factions, some more, some less liberal in their thinking, which crippled them as an effective opposition party. In the early nineteenth century Charles James Fox's friendship with Prince George seemed to offer some hope to the party for future advancement, but Fox died in 1806 and the Prince grew more conservative over time, breaking with the Whigs entirely in 1811. It was not until 1830, after George IV's death, that the Whigs were called upon by the new King, William IV, to form a government.

Not only was the early nineteenth century a troubled time for the Whigs, it was also a troubled time for the country in general. The ideas propagated by the French Revolution and the economic depression following the Napoleonic Wars contributed to general unrest within Britain. In Ireland, the Act of Union in 1801 had failed to end the unrest there; the Catholic emancipation promised in the Act had been opposed by George III. Although this eventually came in 1829, it failed to satisfy the Irish dissenters, who now sought the repeal of the Act of Union itself.

Furthermore, Britain was now in the middle of the Industrial Revolution. The advent of steam-powered machinery destroyed traditional cottage industries, forcing many people out of work. This, coupled with the migration of the population from rural to urban areas, fuelled yet more civil unrest, epitomised in the disturbances led by the Luddites and later in the 'Swing Riots'.

While the Tory government had suppressed the more vocal and extreme supporters of reform, sometimes ruthlessly, as at 'Peterloo' in 1819, this failed to stem the growing tide of dissent and, in 1832, Britain seemed to be, superficially at least, on the verge of revolution.

At least this was what was claimed by some supporters of the 1832 Reform Act.

It was in these turbulent social and political times that Brougham carved himself a niche in British politics. Despite what appears to be a Tory bias on his entry to university, it was to the Whig party that Brougham affiliated himself throughout his career. However, his unwillingness to support all Whig policy unquestioningly, and his occasional support of Tory and Radical policies, led to conflict with his fellow Whigs and was, perhaps, the principal reason he failed to reach even higher political office.

Despite this, as will be seen, his achievements were significant, particularly in the areas of the abolition of slavery, educational reform and law reform. A brilliant but difficult man, whose own personality was perhaps the biggest constraint on his career, Brougham pursued his goals with a passion and energy rarely seen in today's political world.

Preface

LORD BROUGHAM was assuredly one of the most remarkable men who have lived in modern times. Few have attempted to play, and fewer still have succeeded in playing, so many parts on the stage of life. He began his career as a briefless barrister on the Scottish Southern Circuit; he rose to be Lord High Chancellor of England. But though he so greatly distinguished himself as a lawyer, it was as a politician that he became really eminent. For many years he was the most popular parliamentarian in the country, and the most powerful orator in the House of Commons. As a member of the Cabinet during the Reform Bill days, he helped to guide the nation through one of the most serious crises that it had to face during the nineteenth century. Possessing great mental and physical powers, he was a man of extraordinary vitality. He was a man, too, whose ambition was boundless. His thirst for fame and notoriety was far from being satisfied by his success at the bar and by his brilliant achievements as a politician. He sought to win renown as an historian and as a man of letters. The tracts and pamphlets that came from his pen filled many volumes; and the number of his articles in the *Edinburgh Review*, to which he was one of the original contributors, far exceeded that of any other writer of his time. He even attempted to shine as a novelist, for in his old age he wrote and published (but immediately suppressed) a romance in three volumes. He did more than any other man to found the London University, and to set on foot the movement for juvenile and adult education in this country. He was one of the most prominent advocates of the abolition of the slave trade and of slavery itself. He was a great traveller, and a man of fashion. Kemble declared that he would have made his fortune had he gone on the stage, so excellent was his mimicry. He became a convert to spiritualism, and attended séances in the company of Robert Owen. Like most men of genius, he was somewhat eccentric in his manners; and contemporaries, who failed to understand him, mistook his eccentricity for madness. He went to the races in a sedan chair, dressed in his wig and gown. He compelled his coachman to ride down the Horse Guards because he was "in a hurry". He took a hot-water bottle with him to the Court of Chancery and the House of Lords. The peculiarity of his features and the oddity of his dress added to the eccentricity of his appearance; and his long, prominent nose and his famous plaid trousers proved an inexhaustible source of inspiration and merriment to the caricaturists and the ballad-mongers.

Two "Lives" of Lord Brougham have so far been published. The first, by Lord Campbell, appeared in 1869 in the last of the eight volumes in which he sketched the careers of the Lord Chancellors and Keepers of the Great Seal of England. It had some of the merits and all the defects of a contemporary biography. On the one hand, Campbell had an intimate knowledge of the subject of his Memoir, having, indeed, been on familiar terms with him for over forty years. On the other hand, for a long period, the two had been keen rivals, and their rivalry had produced an abundance of private as well as public quarrels. Campbell, indeed, warned his readers that they must not expect him to be impartial, and that they might reasonably regard his narrative with suspicion. The warning was amply justified by the event; for the biography, though highly entertaining, is utterly untrustworthy.

In 1906 J.B. Atlay included a biography of Brougham in his two volumes on the Victorian Chancellors. It was ably written, but was not based on any original research, nor did the author even make full use of the abundant material that had been printed since the appearance of Campbell's book.

During the closing years of his life, Brougham wrote his auto-biography, which appeared as a posthumous work in three volumes in 1871. But he wrote it when he was over eighty years of age, and for years his memory had been failing. His inaccuracies of statement are, therefore, many and glaring, and his Memoirs are as untrustworthy as Campbell's biography. But they are valuable because they contain a good deal of private correspondence; and although, as has been pointed out, errors have crept even into the original documents, it by no means follows that on this account the Autobiography is so valueless as Sir Spencer Walpole declared it to be.

The present volume is not intended as a biography of Brougham; and many events in his life that would have to be dealt with in such a volume have not been touched upon at all. An attempt has been made to sketch his career as a statesman, with special reference to the history of that political party with which he was most closely con-nected during his public life.

Few statesmen's letters reveal so much of the personality of the writers as do those of Brougham. I make no apology, therefore, for having, in the following pages, inserted on so generous a scale excerpts from Brougham's hitherto unpublished correspondence. I have been exceedingly fortunate in gaining access to private manu-scripts, and it is a pleasing duty I have to perform in thanking their owners for allowing me to make use of their collections. I am deeply indebted in this connection to His Grace the Duke of Devonshire, the Marquess of Lansdowne and the Earl of Kerry, Earl Spencer, the Earl of Ilchester, the Earl of Durham, and Lord Hatherton. Unfortunately, I was not allowed to see the family papers at Brougham Hall, but Lord Brougham informs me that he has seen none of any value.

The present book is an elaboration of a thesis which was approved for the degree of Doctor of Philosophy in the University of Manchester in the summer of 1924. During the two years in which I was working on this theme, I had the good fortune to be able to study under the direction of Professor H.W.C. Davis. I owe to him more than I can well express. He suggested the subject to me; his assistance, his advice, his criticisms, constantly and generously given, were more than invaluable. From Professor Powicke and from Professor Tout, to whom all Manchester students of history owe so much, I have received much encouragement in a variety of ways. Professor Hilda Johnstone, Professor Veitch, and Mr. C.S.S. Higham have been good enough to read portions of the manuscript and to give me much valuable advice. Mr. Harold Cox, Editor of the *Edinburgh Review*, and Messrs. Longmans, Green & Co. Ltd., kindly supplied me with a list of Brougham's contributions to the *Edinburgh Review*. Mr. T.W. Mercer, of the Co-operative Union, was good enough to send me transcripts of letters that passed between Brougham and Robert Owen, the originals of which are now preserved at Holyoake House, Manchester. Dr. G.M. Trevelyan, Mr. J.R.M. Butler, Mr. F. Thompson, Librarian at Chatsworth House, and Dr. Guppy, Librarian of the John Rylands Library, have helped me in ways too numerous to mention. Messrs. Longmans, Green & Co. Ltd., and Mr. G.N. Clark and Mr. C.W. Previté-Orton, joint-Editors of the *English Historical Review,* were kind enough to allow me to make use of an article entitled, "The Westminster Election of 1814" which I contributed to the *Review* in October 1925. Finally I have to thank Mr. McKechnie for his help in seeing this book through the press.

A. ASPINALL

21 PROME COURT, RANGOON
December 1926

I

Early Years
1778–1810

HENRY BROUGHAM, afterwards Lord Brougham and Vaux, and Lord High Chancellor of England, was born in Edinburgh on September 19, 1778. Though in later years his vanity prompted him to claim descent from the ancient and noble house of Vaux in Normandy, competent genealogists have been unable to trace back his descent beyond the sixteenth-century Broughams who flourished in the Lake district. Brougham Hall, the family seat, prettily situated about two miles south of Penrith, near the river, is a fine old mansion, dating in parts from the Middle Ages. The care which has been lavished upon it during the last hundred years and more has saved it from the ruin with which time and neglect were at the end of the eighteenth century threatening it. The remains of Brougham's parents lie in the very small and very ancient church of St. Ninian, which stands close by the house. There is a tradition that a stairway which used to lead down from one of the rooms of the Hall, but the exit from which is now blocked up by a cupboard, gave access to a subterranean passage which was supposed to extend to Brougham Castle, the ruins of which lie half a mile away. Had Brougham's boyhood been spent in the family home instead of in the Scottish capital, he might well have played with Wordsworth amongst the remains of this ancient stronghold, and climbed

> The darksome windings of a broken stair,
> And crept along a ridge of fractured wall,
> Not without trembling
> Until they safely looked
> Forth from some Gothic window's open space,
> And gathered with one mind a rich reward
> From the stretching landscape.

It was in Edinburgh, however, that Brougham spent the first twenty-five years of his life. His mother, who, like himself, lived to a ripe old age, and to whom he remained to the last wholly devoted, was the niece of Robertson the famous Scottish historian and the Principal of the Edinburgh University.

At an early age young Brougham was sent to the High School in the town, and there he absorbed a mass of knowledge which would have put the erudition of one of Macaulay's famous schoolboys completely into the shade. At the University, to which he proceeded at the age of fourteen, he developed a decided penchant for classics and mathematics; and before he was nineteen he had had two papers on scientific subjects read by the Royal Society and printed in their *Transactions*.[1] No wonder that the Edinburgh mathematicians were astonished by such precociousness! But his success did not turn his head. When, more than ten years later, Lady Holland congratulated him on his first great speech as a lawyer, and warned him of the dangers attending success, he replied:

> Pray don't be afraid about my *fate*. I am not so silly as not
> to know that every first speech of a certain length and
> loudness is much talked of. . . .Besides, I do really assure
> you that when I was sixteen I got such a dose of flattery
> from the Royal Society here and some such men abroad
> as effectually cured me of vanity for life.[2]

His papers met, indeed, with some criticism; but, as Brougham said, they were of sufficient importance to attract the attention of foreign scholars, and, in especial, of Professor Prevost of Geneva.

Brougham's education was exclusively Scottish, but it had the advantage of throwing him into the midst of an undergraduate society more distinguished for its light and learning than that of which any other University in the kingdom could then boast. The most remarkable were Jeffrey, the future editor of the *Edinburgh Review*; Sydney Smith, the famous wit; Henry Cockburn, destined for the Lord Chief Justiceship of England; Francis Homer, whose premature death in 1817 deprived the Whig party of its most distinguished economist; and Lord Henry Petty, who, as Marquis of Lansdowne, played a leading part in the politics of the first thirty years of the nineteenth century. All these young men were staunch Whigs; they were reformers at a time when progressive opinions were not only distinctly unpopular, but an almost fatal bar to advancement in any branch of the public service, the Church, or the law. Though Brougham was said to have entered the University with a bias towards Toryism, his intimate association with such liberal-minded friends did much to crystallise his own political opinions in a liberal mould. In the debates of the famous Speculative Society of the University he took a leading part. It was then that he developed and trained his debating and oratorical powers, which were speedily to win him fame when he was launched into public life. Choosing the law for a profession, in 1795 he began his legal studies, to which he applied himself with an energy which he maintained throughout his active career, and which never failed to astonish all those with whom he came in contact.

In 1798 he paid his first visit to London, where we find him vastly interested in politics. At that time England had been at war with Revolutionary France for five years, and was passing through one of the most terrible crises in her history. Financial ruin was apparently staring her in the face; Ireland was in rebellion; the fleets that alone protected our shores from invasion had recently mutinied; the military genius of Napoleon had broken the resistance of all our allies.

Political reaction, engendered by the fears of the governing class that the revolutionary movement in Europe would spread to England, reigned supreme. The agitation for sweeping social and political change had been crushed, and the liberty of the subject had been seriously curtailed. The little band of Whig reformers, headed by Charles Fox, alone dared to challenge the policy of repression pursued by the Pitt Ministry and tacitly accepted by public opinion. Regarding the disheartening struggle against a triumphant and reactionary Toryism as hopeless, the Opposition had just seceded as a body from the House of Commons, thereby abdicating its functions.

Brougham, gaining first-hand knowledge of the political situation, affected to be greatly concerned about the gloomy prospects of the Whigs and of the cause for which they vainly fought. He condemned the recent secession as a bad measure, "ill-carried on, half done, worse than useless"; and there can be no doubt that he was right. "Indeed, I begin to fear for the cause," he went on. "God grant that we may not live and die under the present system of things—but I am much afraid."[3]

In 1800 he was called to the Scottish Bar, and at once proceeded to go the Southern Circuit. He was sanguine of success, but for the moment his achievements lagged far behind his expectations; and practically the only briefs he could obtain were from poor prisoners who could not afford to pay him any fees. Lord Cockburn has left on record a trustworthy account of Brougham's eccentric conduct in court, where he acquired a certain notoriety by badgering the senile judge unmercifully.

> Brougham tormented him, and sat on his skirts wher-
> ever he went, for above a year. The Justice liked passive
> counsel who let him dawdle on with culprits and juries
> in his own way; and consequently he hated the talent, the
> eloquence, the energy, and all the discomposing qualities
> of Brougham. At last it seemed as if a court day was to be
> blessed by his absence, and the poor Justice was delighting
> himself with the prospect of being allowed to deal with

things as he chose, when, lo! his enemy appeared—tall, cool, and resolute. "I declare," said the Justice, "that man Broom or Brougham is the torment of my life." His revenge, as usual, consisted in sneering at Brougham's eloquence by calling it or him *the Harangue*.[4]

His indifferent success keenly disappointed him; by the end of the year he was "disgusted with law", and instead of attempting the Circuit a second time, he went off to the Ayr races.

Despairing of any great success in Scotland, and desiring to escape from the humiliations that await a briefless barrister, Brougham began to turn his thoughts in other directions. He would gladly have accepted a secretaryship in the East or West Indies, and would have jumped at the offer of a place under Government at home; but he rightly feared that lack of influence in official circles would be a fatal bar to his chances of employment. After the return of peace in 1802 he even thought of trying his luck on the continent, and requested a cousin who was staying in Paris to inquire "what encouragement is given to strangers in France".

But in spite of occasional fits of despondency he persevered with his studies and burned a good deal of midnight oil. From very early days he had successfully striven to pose as a prodigy, and with a weakness for exaggeration that became characteristic, he asserted that he was actually studying nineteen hours a day, and still finding time to enjoy the charms of female society. He also found time for a good deal of boisterous but harmless amusement; with Jeffrey and his friends he would be found rollicking in taverns, diverting himself in the evenings by smashing street lamps and pulling off door-knockers, or at that famous social institution of Edinburgh, the Friday Club, making punch for supper.

It was during one of the suppers, wrote Cockburn, that the memorable attack was made on Galen's head. An apothecary called Gardiner had a shop (which his son still continues) in the house immediately to the east of

the Assembly Rooms in George Street. Over the door
was a head of the Greek doctor (was he a Greek?), which
certain of our more intellectual members had long felt
an itch to possess. But it stood high and was evidently
well secured. However, one night Playfair, Thomas
Thomson, and Sydney Smith could resist no longer; they
mounted the iron railing, and one of them got on the
back of another and had almost reached the prize when
Brougham, who had eagerly encouraged them to the
exploit but had retired, was detected in the dim distance
of the oil lamps, stealing up with the watch, for which he
had wickedly gone. The assailants had just time to escape,
and the gilded philosopher smiles a gracious defiance at
this day.[5]

Brougham had already won a reputation for cleverness, and his versatile gifts excited general admiration; but no confidence was placed
in his character, in which there was neither steadiness nor simplicity.
His conceit and arrogance were unpleasant even when they were not
profoundly irritating. Even in his professional capacity he thought
much more of achieving notoriety by making a long, argumentative,
and eloquent harangue to the jury in the Court of Session than of
getting a verdict for his clients. It is well known that his friends Jeffrey,
Horner, and Sydney Smith, who were responsible for the founding of
that greatest of all periodicals, the *Edinburgh Review*, in 1802, fearing
that his unsteadiness and unreliability would be more dangerous than
his gifts would be serviceable, did not at first invite his co-operation. But it was soon thought politic to bring him in, partly, said
Campbell, his biographer, "from a dread of his enmity if he should be
excluded".

Not without reason was Brougham characterised as "the surest and
most voluminous among the sons of men".[6] For he was by far the
most frequent contributor to the new review. Neither the story of
his writing a whole number unaided, nor his own assertion that

he contributed eighty articles to the first twenty numbers, can be regarded as anything but apocryphal; but during the first five years of the *Edinburgh's* existence (October 1802-July 1807) he wrote an amazing number of articles (fifty-eight) on an extraordinary variety of topics.[7] With equal facility and confidence he dealt with such diverse subjects as the slave trade, prismatic reflection, Herschel's astronomical discoveries, Dr. Black's lectures on chemistry, the liquidation of the national debt, Dr. Hill's Latin synonyms, Lord Lauderdale's excursions into economic theory, the state of Turkey, the condition of Poland, and a life of Dr. Johnson. By this time, indeed, he had assimilated a vast and imposing amount of knowledge, but it was diffuse rather than exact and profound, and his articles were by no means of a uniformly high standard of excellence. But, written as most of them were with an exasperating cocksureness, and appearing in a periodical which at once acquired an authoritative character, they did, in one or two instances, completely ruin an author's reputation. Dr. Young's case was one of the most notorious. He had just propounded the new 'undulation' theory of light, which Brougham covered with ridicule and most unjustly condemned; and so great was the *Edinburgh's* reputation for infallibility that the unfortunate Professor's second and explanatory tract never left the booksellers. Lord Lauderdale's painstaking work, *An Enquiry into the nature and origin of public wealth and into the means and causes of its increase*, was summarily dismissed as one which, "excepting where it refutes some errors of former writers, cannot be considered as an investigation merely tinctured with doubtful or erroneous theory, but as a collection of positions all of them either self-evident or obviously false, and founded upon errors which the slightest attention is sufficient to detect".[8]

During the early years of the *Review* Brougham wrote little on political subjects, but his references to current politics are highly significant. They show that not all the intercourse with Jeffrey and other Whig friends had completely exorcised the evil spirit of Toryism. For Pitt, the Tory Prime Minister who in 1794 and succeeding years had gone far to destroy the political liberties of the people, he had nothing but praise. In October 1802 he wrote:

> We rejoiced to see, in the last session of Parliament, a disposition to renew the momentous question of the slave trade. We sincerely hope once more to behold the same splendid talents marshalled in the cause of humanity and sound policy which formerly almost rendered it triumphant; and we expect to find that great statesman, who so eminently distinguished himself upon all the former discussions of the question, in opposition to his own personal interest, now dedicate a part of his leisure to a contest in every way so worthy of his powers.[9]

In 1798 Dr. Watson, Bishop of Llandaff, had revived a plan originally proposed in 1716 by a member of Parliament named Archibald Hutcheson, to pay off the national debt by means of a general levy on all the capital in the country; and in 1803 the Bishop explained his proposals at greater length, in second pamphlet, which Brougham reviewed in the *Edinburgh* and unsparingly condemned.[10] One of his objections to the scheme bore upon it the distinct mark of Toryism. The liquidation of the debt would, he complained, diminish enormously the influence of the Crown by doing away with the expenses of management.

> We confess that, sincere as our attachment is to the ancient privileges of the people, we cannot contemplate without some alarm so sudden a shock as the power of the Crown must necessarily receive by the change. We can call the projected reduction of patronage by no other name than a violent change in the balance of the Constitution; and this consideration alone should have no small weight with us, in these times, when the unhappy experience of our neighbours has so strongly recommended to practical statesmen that predilection, which every wholesome

theory had long before encouraged, for the most gradual alterations in political systems.[11]

The results of his recent researches on the subject of the political and economic future of the West Indian Islands appeared in 1803 in his two-volume publication, *An Inquiry into the Colonial Policy of the European Powers*. The book has long since ceased to possess any but an historical interest, and, years before the death of its author, it had been consigned to the dead limbo of forgotten controversial literature. It was an extraordinary production running to well over a thousand pages, which might with advantage have been compressed into half that number. But the arrangement was worse than the prolixity. The volumes were divided and subdivided into a bewildering number of parts, sections, divisions and subdivisions, with obscurely-worded titles. Seldom, indeed, do we meet with a book less skilfully and more defectively arranged.

The book is remarkable, too, for the vast number of subjects that are discussed in its many pages. Brougham's main object was to refute the doctrines of economists like Turgot, who maintained the inutility of colonies to parent states. He denied that they were a source of expense to the mother country; that they were a fruitful cause of war; that the wars in which Great Britain had been engaged in the eighteenth century were essentially wars of commercial and colonial rivalry. On the contrary, he affirmed that "any influence which the circumstances of the colonies can exert on the dispositions of the parent state is much more likely to be of a nature favourable to the maintenance of peace".[12] He denied that the English Channel really made Britain independent of the continent; that the navy was a safe insurance against invasion; and that we ought to pursue a policy of 'splendid isolation'. He pinned his faith to the 'balance of power', and, whilst condemning that 'iniquitous transaction', the partition of Poland, denied that it afforded an example of the failure of that system of international control to preserve the independence of the small states of Europe from the aggressions of the Great Powers. He thought that Egypt would become one of the most productive colonies in the world, but he dismissed as visionary the idea that a canal joining the Red Sea with either the Nile or the Mediterranean would shorten the voyage to India, or be anything but a route "extremely tedious and inconvenient for the course of mercantile transactions". "The same vessels," he explained, "which navigate the Mediterranean cannot ascend the Nile and cross the desert in the canal. The goods must therefore be all unloaded at Alexandria. The canal and river boats can never encounter the tempests and swell of the Red Sea and Indian Ocean. Another loading will therefore be necessary at Suez."[13]

In the second volume Brougham analysed the effects on the European colonial system in the West Indies of the recent establishment in St. Domingo of an independent negro republic. He was convinced that the continued existence of a free negro commonwealth in that part of the world would be a fearful menace to the security of the European settlements in the other islands:

> An universal earthquake or deluge which should at once blot out those fertile regions from the face of the physical globe is not so much to be deprecated as the lamentable catastrophe which should absorb them in negro dominion, and destroy their existence as a civilised quarter of the globe.[14]

Impressed with the magnitude of the threatened danger to the hegemony of the white man in the West Indies Brougham urged that Great Britain should co-operate with her traditional enemy, France, with whom she had just concluded a nine years' war, in order to destroy the newly-won freedom of the blacks:

> It is the interest of every Power possessing colonies to league with whatever parent State may be annoyed by colonial rebellion, and to assist its colonial neighbours, even if they should be its natural rivals or allies, in

crushing all revolt, and preventing the independence of
the colonial insurgents.[15]

After thus advocating a military expedition which would result in
the massacre of half the negro population of St. Domingo and the
reduction of the rest to a most horrible slavery, Brougham proceeded
to denounce and abuse those who felt qualms at the idea of countenancing such a barbarous and devilish plan:

> With the greatest sympathy for the unmerited sufferings
> of the unfortunate negroes, with unmingled detestation of
> the odious traffic to which they owe all their wrongs and
> the West Indian colonies their chief dangers, the consistent
> friend of humanity may be permitted to feel some
> tenderness for his European brethren, although they are
> white and civilised, and to deprecate that inconsistent spirit
> of canting philanthropy which in Europe is only excited
> by the injuries or miseries of the poor and the profligate
> and, on the other side of the Atlantic, is never warmed but
> towards the savage, the mulatto, and the slave.[16]

Brougham was strongly in favour of the abolition of the slave trade,
but was at this time opposed to the abolition of slavery itself. Such a
measure, he thought, could be urged only by 'fanatics', prompted by
an 'inexcusable thoughtlessness'.[17]

He endeavoured to make his book as politically colourless as possible, but, with the Tories, he defended the Pitt policy of intervention
in France in 1793:

> It has been denied that the total overthrow of all regular
> government in the greatest nation of Europe; the aboli-
> tion of every salutary restraint upon the operations of the
> multitude; the erection of a standard to which everything
> rebellious and unprincipled might repair; the open avowal

> of anarchy, atheism, and oppression as a public creed—it
> has been denied that the existence of this grand nuisance
> gave the vicinage . . . a right to interfere. Yet it is difficult
> to conceive what national changes, except the introduc-
> tion of the pestilence, could give a better right to the
> neighbourhood to reject all intercourse with so infected a
> mass as France then was.[18]

We have examined in some detail the main features of his book,
because it was his first considerable achievement; because he lived
to retract nearly all the opinions which he had expressed with such
a show of confidence and argument; and because it proved to be of
immediate personal advantage. Of its success he had professed to be
not very sanguine; but, though the sale was small except in Edinburgh,
the work attracted considerable attention in abolitionist circles. It
was praised, too, by German periodicals, and when its author was in
Holland (1804) he was gratified to discover that his volumes were well
known in that country.[19]

Although the *Colonial Policy* was adversely commented upon by one
or two men of note (by Gladstone, for instance, in 1834[20]) the general
verdict of competent people was certainly not unfavourable, and Sir
James Mackintosh even went so far as to say that there had been no
such book on political economy since the days of Adam Smith.[21]

But though his volumes received a good press, Brougham never
felt tempted to continue exclusively along the line upon which he
had begun in so promising a manner. He never aspired to be a mere
man of letters. The *Colonial Policy* was intended by its author to
promote his political advancement, and he judged its success from
that point of view alone. He disliked his legal work; he contributed
so frequently to the *Edinburgh* mainly because the pay was good;
and his sole ambition was to make a great name in politics. Even in
his University days he had never allowed his law books to interfere
with an intensive study of current political questions. He candidly
admitted that his only object in taking up the question of the West

Indian sugar colonies was to make himself known and to acquire a reputation *pour la politique.*[22]

Towards the end of 1803 Brougham, after having applied in vain to Lord Hawkesbury (afterwards Earl of Liverpool and Prime Minister), followed the example of a long line of illustrious Scotsmen who had sought and achieved fame in England. He left Edinburgh for London, and entered his name as a law student at Lincoln's Inn, with the idea of qualifying for the English Bar. A friend who gave him letters of introduction to people in London asked him what his politics were to be. "I do not know yet," he replied; adding, however, that he was "much pleased with Mr. Pitt".[23]

His book gave him the entrée into the society of Wilberforce and other notable abolitionists, who gladly welcomed him as a fellow-labourer in the same vineyard. He became a constant visitor at Wilberforce's house, and an untiring worker for the cause of the abolition of the slave trade. With characteristic energy he set to work almost immediately after his arrival in London, and in 1804, just before Wilberforce brought forward his motion for the first reading of an abolition Bill, Brougham rendered his first important service to the cause by writing a pamphlet on the subject. Entitled *A Concise Statement of the Question regarding the Abolition of the Slave Trade*, it was particularly intended to influence the votes of members of Parliament, and copies were sent to every leading member of both Houses.[24] Wilberforce freely acknowledged its merits, and, indeed, it attracted much attention. Pitt delivered his speech (June 7) with the pamphlet in his hand;[25] and on two occasions motions were made by Dent and George Rose, two opponents of abolition, for delaying the debate in consequence of the impression which the pamphlet produced.[26] On June 7, after Wilberforce had moved the order of the day for the second reading, Rose got up and said

> that a pamphlet had been just published, and had very widely circulated, which he knew had produced a strong impression upon the minds of the members of that House.

> This impression was such that he wished the House to decline coming to any immediate decision upon this important Bill.

Wilberforce at once rose to answer him. He

> thought that as the House had determined on the second reading of the Bill that evening, no sort of objection could be rationally taken to it on the ground of surprise. . . . As to the pamphlet alluded to, he had read it with great pleasure and approbation, but he could not see what improper effect it could have. Was the House to be supposed to be taken captive by that book so as to require another week to enable them to recover their judgement?[27]

A translation was widely read in Holland, where a strong disposition to abolish the slave trade had recently been manifested.[28]

A few months later Brougham himself went to Holland to obtain information from the Dutch Government about the possibilities of getting the traffic in slaves abolished. Lord Harrowby, the Foreign Secretary, provided him with letters of introduction. After spending two or three weeks in the Netherlands, and having reported that the Dutch were willing to abandon the slave trade if Pitt would restore their conquered colonies, Brougham proceeded leisurely up the Rhine and crossed the Alps into Italy.

Before going abroad, Brougham had prominently associated himself with a movement to establish an Edinburgh corps of Volunteers at the time of the invasion scare; and he was appointed Chairman of the Association. For some unexplained reason, the Volunteers, though encouraged by the military authorities in the town, were totally ignored by Lord Hobart, the Secretary for War. Brougham abandoned his earlier intention of raising a company in the West York militia, and threw himself into the work of enrolling an Edinburgh battalion of light infantry 588 strong. His efforts, however, were of no avail, and Lord Hobart's negligence effectively destroyed the project. In July 1804 Brougham wrote an indignant letter to Pitt, the Prime Minister:

> . . . It remains to mention the reception with which it pleased Lord Hobart to honour the hearty and unqualified offer of our most zealous and active services. He returned *no answer—he never even acknowledged the receipt of our papers*. We waited in Edinburgh to our utmost inconvenience the whole summer—many of us belonging to very distant parts of the island, and every post expected to be called out. The Lord Lieutenant wrote repeatedly in our favour and so did the commanding officer. They received no answer any more than we had done. In November I tried to set on foot a new corps, after Lord Moira's arrival—and so disgusted were those *hundreds* now whom I could have persuaded with a word to march to Land's End three months before, that only *eleven* would put down their names. This was the true way to encourage "*the volunteering system*" and "*call forth the energies of the country*". I am no advocate for that system nor for the militia system, except as subservient to the recruiting of the only defence of any modern, and civilised state—a regular army; on the contrary I hold every other means of defence to be barbarous in the extreme, and utterly repugnant to the whole principles of political science; and as for balloting, I think it is not a jot different from a *poll-tax* falling in the way of a *lottery*; while the principle of volunteering is worse than that of supporting the State or the poor by voluntary gifts. Therefore it is not as an advocate for the system that I feel the bad consequences of the above conduct, but as an enemy to gross inconsistency in great State affairs, and as a friend to conciliatory measures in great emergencies of the public fortunes. I have drawn up this narrative to satisfy those who did me

the honour of putting themselves and their zeal under my direction. It is a duty I owe them, and they will be more than recompensed for the *intolerable* insult which was formerly thrown upon them if their efforts are made known to those distinguished persons whom it is their first and best wish to please. [29]

Until 1806 Brougham succeeded in deluding Wilberforce with the idea that he was a loyal supporter of the Tory cause; and in this implicit belief Wilberforce in October 1805 recommended him for a diplomatic post. Writing to the Prime Minister, he said:

If in the course of any of your calls for proper men to be employed in any diplomatic business you should be at a loss for one, you perhaps could not in the whole kingdom find one in all respects so well qualified as the Mr. Brougham whom I formerly mentioned to you. He speaks French as well as English, and several other languages. But the great thing is that he is a man of uncommon talents and address, and for his age, twenty-six, knowledge also, and I told you of his being so long the advocate for your Government in Edinburgh.[30]

By this time all his friends were of the opinion that he would rise to eminence as a politician rather than as a lawyer. Horner wrote of him in 1804:

He was for the present wholly absorbed in political schemes, with the view of bringing himself into action; though I thought it not an improbable event, if he were disappointed in his immediate views, that he might bury himself for the remainder of his life in retirement, devoted to science and literature, and occupied with some vast scheme of literary ambition.[31]

In 1804 Brougham had attached himself to no political party. Had the Government had the discernment to put him into harness, he might have become permanently associated with the Tory party, and within a few years he might possibly have come to dispute with Canning for the leadership of the rising school of new Tories. It was due much more to the accidental circumstance that the Ministers did not appear to see his merits, rather than to any considered political opinions of his own, that threw him in 1806 into the arms of the Whigs.

He owed his introduction into Whig society to his friend Horner, who had settled in London some time before, and had become intimately acquainted with the leading members of the Opposition. Brougham made the most of the opportunity, and carefully cultivated friendships with Lord Grey, Lord Holland, and other Whig magnates. He now hoped that they would speedily recognise his abilities and bring him into Parliament; and in October 1805 he was anxiously inquiring of Wilberforce whether there was likely to be a dissolution.[32]

The death of Pitt and the downfall of the Tory ministry in January 1806, followed by the formation of a Whig government, excited in him new hopes of a seat if not of active employment to boot. At Lord Holland's suggestion[33] he took up the pen on behalf of the Whig party, and in that year published a pamphlet entitled, *An Inquiry into the State of the Nation at the Commencement of the Present Administration*. It consisted of a vigorous attack on Pitt's foreign policy since the rupture of the Peace of Amiens. Brougham had the bad taste to puff his own pamphlet in the *Edinburgh Review* (April 1806), where he complimented himself on having written something which had obtained "a very unusual share of the public attention", and which had gone through three editions in less than a week.

But though he was obviously becoming more and more identified with the Whigs, he thought it expedient to keep a footing in the Tory camp, lest his hopes from the other side should not be realised. Even as late as May 1806 he successfully represented himself to Wilberforce as a neutral politician with a Tory bias. In that month there occurred a notable incident in his life which has been noticed by none of his biographers. He asked Lord Lonsdale, through Wilberforce, to bring him into Parliament as one of the members for the county of Westmorland. The modest patrimony of the Brougham family bordered on the vast estates of the Lowthers, who sometimes complained that Brougham's younger brothers poached on their neighbours' land.[34] The Lowthers, too, were the greatest boroughmongers in the north of England, and returned nine members (the famous 'Ninepins') to the House of Commons.

At the beginning of 1806 the Lowther nominee for Westmorland, Sir Michael le Fleming, fell ill and died. Somewhat reluctantly Wilberforce agreed to write to the Earl and to press Brougham's claims to the vacant seat; and in his letter he recommended Brougham as "a man of very extraordinary talents and qualifications and knowledge for his time of life". He spoke of the publication of 1803 as being "for the years of the writer a wonderful production", and more than once he alluded to him as the champion, whilst at the University, of Pitt and the Tories.

Wilberforce, however, was obliged to confess that the language of Brougham's latest pamphlet was hardly such as one might expect from a warm admirer of the late Minister. "I ought, however," he added apologetically, "to do Mr. Brougham the justice to say that having been a good deal abroad last summer but one, he became deeply impressed with a sense of the mismanagement of our affairs on the continent, and spoke of several of our agents abroad in terms of strong censure." Wilberforce rightly suspected that Brougham's Tory sympathies had been to some extent alienated by the fact that the Ministers themselves had neglected him when his services might have been bought, and by the scarcely civil manners of the Tory Sir Michael, whose friendship Brougham had apparently tried to cultivate.

But the vacant seat had already been offered to and accepted by Lord Muncaster, a Pittite and a friend of the 'Saints'. Brougham's application, therefore, received scant attention, and Lord Lonsdale returned his note the very same day, "without answer or observation".[35]

Brougham was bitterly disappointed at his failure to secure a seat either from the Whigs or the Tories. Even when, in the following year, a vacancy was created by Lord Howick's accession to the peerage as Earl Grey, the Whigs made no sign of recognition. But Brougham was partially mollified by his appointment (1806) as secretary to Lord St. Vincent and Lord Rosslyn, who were sent on a mission to Lisbon with the object of negotiating with the court regarding the defence of Portugal, which, there was reason to believe, Napoleon was about to invade. The mission, however, proved abortive, for Napoleon's attention was for the moment distracted by events in central Europe; and Brougham returned home in December out of pocket and out of humour, in the belief that but for his absence from England he would have secured a seat in Parliament.[36]

Early in 1807 the short-lived Whig Ministry came to an end, and in the General Election that followed the formation of the Tory Government under the Duke of Portland, Brougham was put in charge of the press campaign organised by the Whigs. His thorough acquaintance with the most effective methods of appealing to public opinion through the medium of the Press made him peculiarly well fitted to play the part allotted him. Never was his amazing energy more fully displayed. His letters to Lord Holland and Allen show that Lord Holland's own account of Brougham's activities was not in the least exaggerated:

> His extensive knowledge and extraordinary readiness, his
> assiduity and habits of composition, enabled him to cor-
> rect some articles and to furnish a prodigious number
> himself. With partial and scanty assistance from Mr.
> Allen, myself, and two or three more, he in the course
> of ten days filled every bookseller's shop with pamphlets,
> most London newspapers and all country ones without
> exception with paragraphs, and supplied a large portion
> of the boroughs throughout the kingdom with handbills
> adapted to the local interests of the candidates, and all
> tending to enforce the principles, vindicate the conduct,

elucidate the measures, or expose the adversaries of the Whigs.[37]

"The great thing is that nothing should be lost from want of suggestion," said Brougham at the beginning of the campaign. Some extracts from a long letter to Allen reveal the fertility of his imagination:

> There are one or two things which strike me as worth attending to, and which I shall therefore note down in case they should not have already been considered.
>
> 1. Monk Lewis and poet Campbell should be put in requisition without delay—for they are poets and of course will be fanciful and plead 'shortness of notice'.
>
> 2. Different people should at their spare hours be reading Shakespeare and Swift, with a view to selecting passages suitable to the time, as, descriptions of base courtiers, particular characters of bad Ministers, hits at bishops (if safe), etc. These passages may be published in a kind of series, as quotations communicated by Jenksberry, Castlerogue, etc., on whomsoever they apply to. I mention this because the constancy and variety of the fire that is kept up is more material than its strength, and any one can do such mechanical tasks as the above.
>
> 3. Porson is an excellent hand at many things—at quotation, especially from the Bible, he greatly excels; he should be immediately applied to.
>
> 4. Little biographical sketches of the new Ministers— extremely concise—not very violent—exposing them rather to contempt—and that by leaving out whatever they have done of a serious or important kind, good or bad, dwelling on the laughable or trifling parts of their history.
>
> 7. Repeated allusions, and very plain ones, should be made to the former animosities of the Junto—Canning's speeches

against Jenky—his epigrams against Castlereagh, Jenky, and
many of the lower limbs of the Ministry, etc. . . .[38]

But in spite of these truly herculean efforts, the Whigs sustained
heavy casualties at the polls; some of their leading members, ejected
from popular constituencies, had to fall back on close boroughs; and
Brougham's hopes of coming in were once more dashed to the ground.

Nothing daunted, however, by the party's misfortunes, Brougham
in the following year (1808) again displayed his devotion to Whiggism
by writing another lengthy pamphlet, *An Enquiry into the Causes
and Consequences of Continental Alienation*, in which he defended
the Whig Ministry's foreign policy, and sought to discover why the
country was left without a single ally after the coming in of the Tories.
He ascribed the hostility of our former allies to the "inadequacy of
our diplomacy", and to the

> rigorous maintenance of what we assume to be our
> maritime rights, and to a system of policy the evident
> end and object of which were the attainment of our own
> immediate interests; an extravagant preference of ourselves
> and everything connected with us, and to a consequent
> relative and active contempt of the rights and interests
> of others.

Thus the emergence in 1808 of the vexed question of the Orders
in Council gave Brougham another opportunity of putting forth his
great powers as a pamphleteer, but it also gave him his first semi-
legal, semi-political case. Purporting to be issued "for the protection
of the trade and navigation of Great Britain", the Orders in Council
were threatening the commercial classes with ruin. The merchants of
Manchester, Liverpool, and London, began to agitate for the repeal of
the obnoxious Orders, prepared a petition to Parliament, and engaged
Brougham to state their case at the bar of both Houses. The task of
examining witnesses and delivering eloquent speeches to an admir-

ing audience occupied him for several weeks; and, though his efforts were at that time unavailing, they earned him the gratitude of the mercantile classes.

In November 1808 he was called to the Bar, and, anticipating that his connection with the Liverpool and Manchester merchants would bring him abundance of professional work, he attached himself to the Northern Circuit, declaring that he meant to devote all his energies to the law, and abandon politics. He stated that he had 'refused' Parliament,[39] but we may suspect that his 'refusal' was due more to necessity than to choice.

Ever since the General Election of 1807 he had continued to write for the Whig press (dirty work, like most works of necessity, he complained). Throughout 1808–9 he wrote copiously for the *Morning Chronicle*, and his temporary absence from London in October 1809 gave Lord Holland some concern. "We shall be a little gravelled for paragraphs for some days," he informed Lord Grenville. "Can you procure me any or give me sense for some? Hitherto the labour has fallen exclusively upon me."[40]

A month or two later Brougham was informed that his hopes of a seat were at last to be gratified. If we are to believe Campbell, Brougham had threatened to sever his connection with the Whigs because of their neglect of his interests. Alarmed at this intelligence, they came to the conclusion that such a formidable man had better be conciliated and provided for. The succession of his friend Lord Henry Petty to the Marquisate of Lansdowne paved the way for Brougham's introduction into the Commons as member for the close borough of Camelford, the property of the Duke of Bedford.

One pledge only was required of him. He had spoken so coldly of the Catholic question, said Lord Holland, that he was asked to state that he was not averse to concessions. His letter to Lord Holland of January 31, 1810,[41] removed all doubts and fears on that score:

> I beg you to offer my warmest acknowledgements to the
> Duke of Bedford for the proposition he has made me

through you, and for the very handsome terms in which he has made it. . . .

The consequence of my coming into Parliament will be the sacrifice of a very considerable professional income, and I feel it both to be consistent with my duty and to be in some sort also necessary that I should consult my father about this matter before I take my resolution. Unless, therefore, some circumstances should make it necessary for me to give an answer at once, I trust the Duke will increase the obligations under which he has already laid me by permitting me to wait a few days for the above purpose. At all events I feel the full effect of the kindness which he is disposed to do me.

With respect to the Catholic question, my opinions are exactly the same with your own, and in so far as anonymous writing in its behalf can be called a pledge I have repeatedly given one of my zeal for that cause. It is equally my conviction that great loss of character would result to the party from the slightest abatement of their efforts in this cause, and, indeed, I do not see the possibility of their withholding their warm support of the Catholic petition as often as it may be presented to Parliament, or of their ever taking office without clear explanations on this point. My only doubt is (and it relates to rather distant negotiations about office and not to parliamentary conduct) how far it would be wise or consistent with the former conduct of the party to insist upon the *whole question* being granted, as a *sine quâ non* of their giving the country the assistance of their services. This, however, is quite a separate question and need not be mooted at present.[42]

Nearly a fortnight elapsed before he sent his answer to Lord Holland (January 11, 1810):

I have received from my brother (who happened to be in Edinburgh) a communication of my father's sentiments by his direction. The substance of it is, that he cannot take upon himself the responsibility of giving any positive advice which might weigh with me. . . . I lose no time in requesting you to repeat my acknowledgements to the Duke of Bedford, and to inform him that I accept of his offer. . . .[43]

The reasons for Brougham's long exclusion from the House of Commons are fairly clear. Whilst, on the one hand, Lord Holland and Lord Grey, who, recognising his great abilities and extraordinary energy, went so far as to declare him to be the "first man this country has seen since Burke's time", were willing and even anxious to serve him, others questioned his loyalty to the party and feared that he could not be trusted. They were probably only too well aware of his recent flirtations with the Tories, and suspected that his attachment to Whiggism was much less strong than his anxiety to promote his own interests. And, indeed, the frankly opportunist character of his conduct was not at all calculated to inspire confidence and trust; and Horner's prediction that those with whom Brougham was politically connected would often have occasion to doubt his allegiance was soon to be verified.

Brougham, too, had frightened the more timid Whigs on account of the wholly new character he had given to the *Edinburgh Review*. In 1807 he had overcome Jeffrey's scruples and misgiving, and had caused the *Review* to be overwhelmed with politics. Jeffrey's article on Cobbett, written in that year entirely at Brougham's instigation, had, as Lord Holland observed, the effect of stamping the *Edinburgh* as a purely Whig journal.[44] To many leading Whigs that change was strongly distasteful, and to none more than to Lord Holland and Tierney, who were of the opinion that the influence of the *Review* was best maintained by preserving in its political discussions an independent and impartial tone. "The turn it has taken of late, by descending to questions between Ministry and Oppositions and even to individual crimination, has lowered its name, and given a prejudice against all its opinions and reasonings, even upon other occasions," complained Horner, who, however, was well aware that Brougham was too useful and powerful an ally to be thrown over and sacrificed.[45]

The climax came after the appearance of the famous 'Don Cevallos' article in October 1808. Had it appeared in a popular form in 1794 instead of in 1808, little short of a miracle would have saved the author from the hands of the hangman and his head from reposing on Temple Bar. The bulk of the article was written by Jeffrey himself, but Brougham, who was in Edinburgh at the time of its composition,[46] was responsible for some of the paragraphs that gave most offence.[47] It was an uncompromising denunciation of aristocratic government. Its effect throughout the country was enormous. It inspired Byron to write some famous iambics.[48] It called the Tory *Quarterly* into existence. It occasioned the publication of a pamphlet by a Tory member of Parliament, who lamented that the reviewers had abandoned the congenial occupation of mangling the carcasses of unfortunate literary authors for the much less entertaining and infinitely more dangerous pursuit of portraying all the diabolical features of Jacobinism and of reviving the language of anarchy.[49] Tory readers threw up their hands in pious horror at the sight of such execrable opinions in cold print. Lord Buchan, Lord Erskine's eccentric brother, kicked the offending volume out of his front door into the street. Sir Walter Scott, aghast at such Jacobinical outpourings, at once ordered his name to be struck off the list of subscribers. "You have no idea of the consternation which Brougham's attack upon the titled orders has produced. The *Review* not only discontinued by many, but returned to the bookseller from the very first volume: the library shelves fumigated, etc.," Sydney Smith humorously remarked.[50]

The passage which gave perhaps greatest offence, and which is so absolutely characteristic of Brougham's style that it can hardly be doubted that it came from his pen, was that which, alluding to the rising of the Spanish people against the French invader, said:

> Those who had so little of what is commonly termed
> *interest* in the country—those who had *no stake* in the
> community (to speak the technical language of the
> aristocracy)—the persons of *no consideration* in the
> state—they who could not pledge their fortunes, having
> only lives and liberties to lose—the bulk—the mass of
> the people—nay, the very odious, many-headed beast, the
> multitude—the mob itself—alone, uncalled, unaided by
> the higher classes—in despite of these higher classes, and
> in direct opposition to them . . . raised up the standard
> of insurrection. . . .

We know now that the article was mainly Jeffrey's work; but the important point is that it was universally attributed to Brougham, who incurred all the odium that it occasioned. It offended Lord Grey and the Holland House circle almost as much as it did the Tories.[51] Is it matter of wonder that the aristocratic Whig borough proprietors should have hesitated as long as they did to bring to the front a man, however talented, however industrious and active, who could propound views so shocking, so disgusting, so repugnant to their own aristocratic feelings?

1. "Experiments and Observations on the Inflection, Reflection, and Colours of Light", read Jan. 24, 1796; "Further Experiments and Observations on the Application and Properties of Light", read June 15, 1797.
2. Holland House MS.
3. *Brougham and his Early Friends*, i. 36.
4. *Cockburn's Memorials*, p.111.
5. *The Book of the Old Edinburgh Club*, iii. 110.
6. Horner, *Memoirs*, i. 278.

7. See Appendix A.

8. *Edin. Review*, July 1804, p.346.

9. *Ibid*. Oct. 1802, p.237.

10. The two pamphlets were entitled, (a) *An Address to the People of Great Britain* (1799); (b) *The Substance of a Speech intended to have been spoken in the House of Lords*, Nov. 22, 1803.

11. *Edin. Review*, Jan. 1804, p.477.

12. *Colonial Policy*. i. 120.

13. *Ibid*. ii. 340.

14. *Ibid*. ii. 304

15. *Ibid*. ii. 298.

16. *Ibid*. ii. 310.

17. *Ibid*. ii. 405.

18. *Ibid*. ii. 259.

19. *Brougham and his Early Friends*, ii. 198.

20. Morley's *Gladstone*, i. 117

21. *Memoir of Sydney Smith*, ii. 17.

22. Broughton, *Recollections*, i. 165.

23. *Ibid*. iii. 223.

24. *Correspondence of Wilberforce*, i. 328. The pamphlet was published anonymously.

25. Holland House MS.: Brougham to Allen, Saturday, 17/07.

26. *Parl. Deb.*, June 7, 1804, p.545; Holland House MS.

27. *Ibid*.

28. P.R.O., Pitt Papers, clxxxix.; Wilberforce to Pitt, 1805.

29. P.R.O., Pitt Papers, cxvi.

30. *Corr. of Wilberforce*, ii. 51.

31. Horner, *Memoirs*, i. 259.

32. *Corr. of Wilberforce*, ii. 46.

33. Holland, *Memoirs of the Whig Party*, ii. 228.

34. Hatherton MS., Diary, August 27, 1839.

35. *Hist. MS. Comm.*, 13th Report, xxvii. 182-84.

36. *Life and Times*, i. 367; Horner, *Memoirs*, i. 378; Holland House MS.

37. *Memoirs of the Whig Party*, ii. 228.

38. Holland House MS.

39. *Brougham and his Early Friends*, ii. 343.

40. *Hist. MS. Comm.*, Fortescue Papers, ix. 346.

41. Probably a mistake for December 31, 1809.

42. Holland House MS.

43. *Ibid.*

44. *Further Memoirs of the Whig Party*, p.387.

45. Horner, *Memoirs*, ii. 52.

46. *Life of Jeffrey*, ii. 125.

47. Napier, *Correspondence*, p.309.

48. *English Bards and Scotch Reviewers*, the most pungent of all his satires.

49. Wharton, *Jacobinical Tendency of the 'Edinburgh Review.'*

50. *Memoir of Sydney Smith*, ii. 49.

51. Napier, *Correspondence*, p.308.

II

First Years in Parliament

> There's a wild man at large doth roam,
> A giant wit!—they call him Brougham.
> And well methinks they may;
> He deals, whene'er he speaks or acts,
> With friends and foes and laws and facts
> In such a *sweeping* way
>
> Lord Holland

BROUGHAM embarked upon his parliamentary career at the age of thirty-one, with many advantages in his favour. He enjoyed the firm friendship of Earl Grey, the leader of the Whig party. His association with the *Edinburgh Review* had already brought him into prominence before the public. His connection with the mercantile classes had revealed the amplitude of his intellectual powers; and the combination of a gigantic brain with great physical strength enabled him to accomplish more than four or five active men of ordinary capacity could hope to achieve.

At the beginning of the session a new writ was issued for the borough of Camelford, and in accordance with the usual procedure

Brougham journeyed down to Cornwall. Under the circumstances, of course, neither canvassing nor speech-making was required, and on February 5 the *London Gazette* announced his election. It is said that, in order to prove to his incredulous friends that he could if necessary restrain his impetuosity and curb his impatience, he vowed not to open his mouth in the House for a whole month; and certain it is that his maiden speech was not delivered until March 5. In January he had written:

> I have really many more apprehensions about succeeding should I come into Parliament than you seem to entertain. Making a speech at the Bar of the House of Commons or House of Lords is in some respects more difficult, but *upon the whole* much easier than doing so in the House. I am moreover so much accustomed to writing that I shall infallibly get into a preaching, dissertating, *Edinburgh Review* kind of manner, if I do not look sharp. One thing you are, however, quite right about—if I come into Parliament, and try and fail, neither one nor two failures, be they ever so complete, will at all dishearten me—nay, I should feel much more comfortable were I in the predicament of having already failed and having my way to fight up again. Nothing can be worse than beginning with a sort of character formed.[1]

His maiden speech was only partially successful, and it satisfied neither his friends nor himself; and in a letter written immediately after the debate he declared that, so complete was his failure, he must turn to something else.[2] Nor did succeeding efforts at once erase the first unfavourable impression. J.W. Ward (afterwards Lord Dudley and Ward) wrote:

> I am sorry to find that people in general are not so well satisfied with his appearances in Parliament as the

> partiality of friendship and the desire of seeing my own
> predictions verified had at first induced me to be. He
> is not a favourite with the House, and there is a sort of
> hardness in his manner which does not take. It is very
> odd, for in private nobody is more popular.[3]

But in spite of this somewhat unpromising beginning, Brougham
contrived, before the end of his first session, to secure a commanding
position in the Commons. His rapid rise to power and influence
not unnaturally excited the jealousy of the occupants of the front
Opposition bench, and they endeavoured to keep him in the background as much as possible. He believed (and Lord Holland shared
his belief) that had the party leaders entrusted to him the management of the Walcheren inquiry,[4] the issue might have gone against
the Tories, the Whigs might have returned to power, and in that event
he would have been rewarded with office. But that pleasing prospect
was obscured at the outset of the inquiry by the unwillingness of
the Opposition leaders to abdicate their functions, and not only was
he not put in charge of the attack, but he was not even given a fair
opportunity of speaking in the debates.

The question which engaged most of his attention during his first
session was that of the slave trade, the abolition of which he had
already urged in his *Colonial Policy*, in his 1804 pamphlet, and in the
periodical press. That odious traffic had not been completely destroyed
by the Act of 1807, for its grossly inadequate penalties (forfeiture and
fine) had made its violation economically profitable. Numerous were
the consultations held in Palace Yard by Wilberforce and his friends,
who anxiously discussed ways and means both of putting an end to
the abuse, and of encouraging foreign governments to follow Great
Britain's example.

On June 15 Brougham made the first of a long series of parliamentary speeches which won for him the reputation of a great and powerful orator. He declared that the only effective means of abolishing
the slave trade was to make slave trading a felony, punishable with

fourteen years' transportation; and he pledged himself to bring in a Bill to strengthen the existing law, early in the following session.[5] He referred to this speech in an interesting letter to William Roscoe, a prominent Liverpool citizen, who had sat in the Parliament of 1806 as a supporter of Fox.

> The reports in the newspapers can give you no notion of the honest zeal and indignation manifested by the House of Commons upon the occasion, and I do assure you that all the abuse I lavished on slave traders (which was really very unmeasured and only flowed from my feelings towards them) was cheered the more warmly the more violently it was bestowed—nor did any one say a syllable in extenuation, so greatly is the feeling of Parliament improved since this question was first started! It had long been my settled conviction that not only consistency, but the necessities of the case, prescribe a law which shall make slave trading punishable as a felony—that, in short, you have no other way of effectually stopping it. My repeated conferences with able lawyers as well as with the chief abolitionists, strengthened this conviction. I was particularly encouraged by that excellent and most enlightened friend of everything that is right and just, Sir Samuel Romilly, and, if anything could confirm me still further in my views of the subject, it would be the knowledge I have since the debate received that after all, and although no man—not even George Rose[6]—ventured to deny the charge of being *suborners of mercenary murder*, which I brought against the traders in slaves—yet since that debate, and the unanimous and loud expression of those sentiments in the House, men have been found daring and base enough to purchase the *Comercio de Rio* after its condemnation, with the view of trying once more how far they can evade the law and fit her out again as a slave

trader. I am quite shocked to have to add that *members of Parliament* have actually been found engaging in such detestable practices—though I of course would keep this fact for the present carefully concealed.

I cannot help regretting that so little attention has been paid to this important subject even by the journals devoted to the party of the Methodists. One of these was shown to me t'other day in which Scott's poem[7] was reviewed in twenty pages, and a few lines only were devoted to the abolition. I confess my fear is lest that party may be jealous of any measure not coming from one of themselves—and I own that one great object of my motion is frustrated by the proposition of making slave trading a felony having received so little discussion out of doors. It was my wish to prepare men's minds for the Bill which I am to introduce—in order to give it the better chance of success and so disarm our adversaries of their pretext that we take them unawares. . . .[8]

But his fear that opinion out of doors had not been sufficiently organised to influence the votes of doubtful Tories proved to be groundless, for in the session of 1811 his Bill was carried rapidly through all its stages without encountering any real opposition.[9]

Acting for the most part with Whitbread, Creevey, and the rest of the more advanced section of the Whig party known as the 'Mountain', Brougham spoke frequently and at considerable length on many subjects in which they were specially interested. He took upon himself the task of ventilating all kinds of questions involving the liberty of the subject, the control of public moneys by Parliament, the restriction of the royal prerogative, the freedom of the press. All these questions were extremely popular in the country, and his advocacy of them was eminently calculated to increase his popularity and influence out of doors. His speeches were intended to serve a double purpose: they helped to give him the reputation of a zealous reformer, and they contributed to bring the Government into disrepute. Thus he strove hard to secure the abolition of the barbarous punishment of flogging in the army; he was indefatigable in exposing cases of cruelty to sailors and prisoners. He denounced a proposal to tax leather, as tending to press more heavily on the labouring classes than on the well-to-do. He cried out against the Preservation of the Peace Bill (1812), a stern measure of repression introduced into Parliament to cope with the Luddite riots in the north of England. At every opportunity he clamoured loudly against proposals that would increase the power of the Crown, and in this connection he thoroughly mastered the difficult question of the droits of Admiralty. He showed how the long continuance of the war had increased enormously the amount of prize-money derived from the sale of confiscated enemy ships, and pointed out the danger of allowing seven or eight million pounds to remain at the absolute disposal of the Crown. He stigmatised it as a "jobbing fund consisting of annuities and an immense capital to remunerate those vile minions whose claims to reward the Minister would not have the hardihood to bring under the cognisance of Parliament".

But that which raised him to the very pinnacle of parliamentary fame was his attack on the Orders in Council. Originally intended as a counterblast to Napoleon's Berlin and Milan decrees, they had had the wholly unlooked-for result of seriously crippling our own trade and creating a vast amount of unemployment. In the face of impending disaster the Government blindly persisted in continuing its policy, but daily increasing discontent amongst our manufacturers, and simmering rebellion amongst the starving operatives and pauperised unemployed, enabled Brougham to accomplish what he had failed to accomplish four years before.

Early in the session of 1812 he succeeded in securing the appointment of a committee of the House of Commons to inquire into the state of trade. Of this committee he became the life and soul. It sat for six weeks, examined over a hundred witnesses from thirty manufacturing towns, and laid before the House in record time an enormous mass of evidence. Brougham would not even allow the assassination of Perceval, the Prime Minister (May 8), to interfere with his inquiry. Said Lord Holland:

> He braved the censure of enemies and shocked the more timid and more gentle of his friends by resolutely insisting, without regard to the feelings of individuals or the convenience of the Government, on the immediate relinquishment of the Orders in Council, before Mr. Perceval was cold in his grave or the arrangements for a new Ministry in any forwardness at Court. To that wise and firm, but at the same time somewhat odious conduct, the country is indebted for a revision of a system unjust to other nations and ruinous to itself.[10]

Brougham's brilliant speech of June 16 was a damning and unanswerable indictment of the ruinous policy which the late Ministry had pursued. Conscious of its weakness, though steadfastly refusing to acknowledge its error, the new Government, of which Lord Liverpool became the head, reluctantly gave way and repealed the Orders. With a singular insight into the real significance of the Ministry's defeat, Castlereagh recognised that this was the first occasion on which the new industrial interests triumphed over the Government, and that further instances of their growing supremacy over the old landed aristocracy must soon be expected.[11] The Reform Bill was to be the second, the triumph of the Anti-Corn Law League the third.

Brougham's magnificent victory came too late to prevent war with America, but it increased enormously his already considerable reputation, and his popularity with the industrialists in the north. He himself always regarded it as his greatest achievement.[12] He was now universally regarded as one of the most important men in Parliament. Bentham, with whom he had recently become personally acquainted, pointed him out as "one of the first men in the House of Commons. He seems in a fair way of being very soon universally acknowledged to be the very first, even beyond my old and intimate friend Sir Samuel Romilly; many, indeed, say he is so now". His importance, indeed, was such that he was destined for office whenever the Whigs returned to power. In October 1809, when there was a serious likelihood of the coming in of the Opposition, Brougham was marked out for the Under-Secretaryship of State for Foreign Affairs.[13] Again, in 1810, when the king's illness necessitated the appointment of his son as regent, the Whigs were so confident of the succession that they planned out their Ministry; and Brougham was to have been Secretary of the Admiralty or else President of the Board of Trade. And in 1812, when Wellesley was preparing a coalition with Grey and Grenville, Brougham's name was included in a list of several who were to be employed in some undecided capacity.[14]

But not only were his hopes of office dissipated by the Opposition's failure to storm the citadel of power, but a more serious prospect opened before him in 1811 when the Duke of Bedford sold the borough of Camelford. Ill-natured people began to hint that the underlying motive for the sale was to get rid of an excessively active and turbulent nominee, but the truth was that the Duke was compelled by pecuniary embarrassment alone to sell the seat. Brougham wrote to Lord Holland on October 8:

> I lose no time in communicating to you the substance of a letter which I have this morning received from the Duke of Bedford, and which I please myself with imagining may be a matter of regret to you as well as myself, viz. that from unexpected circumstances our parliamentary connection is to close at the approaching dissolution. What those circumstances are I am not at liberty to mention, but this I may say, and it gives me the most hearty satisfaction—that it is owing to no difference whatever either of a personal or a political nature. The various reports and hints, *now* proved to be unfounded, which reached me both last session and the

session before, I never took the trouble of inquiring into. I never gave them the smallest credit, and, had they been all true, it would have made no change in my conduct. That they are now shown to be utterly groundless, I must say is less a surprise than a gratification to me, and it is impossible for any one to have a more thorough esteem for another's character both private and, what is of more consequence in these times, public also—than I entertain for the Duke of Bedford.

. . . In whatever respects you may have fancied, or rather been told, that I was not (in my little way) drawing with the party, you may depend upon it, you were misinformed, and I can most conscientiously declare that what I most invariably have kept in my view, has been an adherent to the true principles of the Whig party and Mr. Fox, which I considered to be the same. I am as sincerely attached to liberty and as hearty a detester of every kind and form of oppression as I believe any one can be—and if ever I may seem to have differed with the body of the party, it has been owing to the warmth with which I entertain those principles or feelings, a warmth which I well know you above all men will most readily excuse.[15]

Some time before Brougham received this 'fatal' intelligence, the Worcester reformers offered to bring him in for their city "upon the popular interest, in the most independent manner, and at small expense". But at that moment he had been in safe possession of Camelford, and he had declined the offer. He wrote to Lord Holland:

. . . You may possibly have heard of an offer made to me some time ago to stand for Worcester, and declined by me then. If it is not too late I shall now endeavour to renew that treaty. I can't afford to throw away money, but

> popular contests are of great use whether they succeed or
> not, and it would be absurd to give up Parliament so soon
> without having a run for it.[16]

To the request made by his Worcester friends for a statement of
his views on parliamentary reform, he had replied, "I am generally
friendly to reform, differing, however, with such reformers as will
only listen to wholesale plans; and preferring, chiefly on the score
of practicability, a more gradual change". Up to that time he had
fought extremely shy of that most important question. He had never
spoken on it in Parliament, but he had, indeed, broached the subject
under the mask of anonymity in the *Edinburgh Review*. His articles
on 'Erskine's Speeches' and 'Rose's Influence of the Crown' (April
1810) show how tepid were his opinions at that time. He desired
nothing more than the exclusion of a few placemen and the Welsh
judges from the House of Commons, the extension of the franchise
to English copy-holders, an improvement in the Scottish representation, and the substitution of triennial for septennial Parliaments.
Then, "A wise and prudent statesman would stop short at this point,
and be satisfied with having gone so far". He had nothing more to
propose regarding that most indefensible part of the representative
system, the close boroughs, than that a "*gradual* extinction of the
worst borough franchises, by the *voluntary surrender* of their existing
rights of election to such large towns as Manchester, Birmingham,
Leeds, and Sheffield, and to such of the larger counties as send too
few representatives . . . would be a most valuable improvement in
the representation. . . ."

It was as an advocate of such moderate proposals that Brougham
contested Liverpool at the General Election of October 1812. Creevey
was the second Whig candidate, whilst Canning, General Gascoigne,
and General Tarleton stood in the Tory interest. The contest lasted
from October 8 to 16, and throughout its course Brougham worked
like a horse. He afterwards wrote to Grey:

You can have no idea of the nature of a Liverpool election.
It is quite peculiar to the place. You have every night to go
to the different clubs, benefit societies, etc., which meet and
speechify. This is from half-past six to one in the morning
at least; and you have to speak to each man who polls, at
the bar, from *ten to five*. It lasted eight days. I began my
canvass three whole days before, and had nine nights of the
clubs, besides a regular speech each day at close of the poll.
I delivered in that time 160 speeches and odd. . . . You may
guess how exhausted I am.[17]

The election was memorable for Brougham's attack on the departed
statesman whom he had been wont to eulogise.

I stand up in this contest, he exclaimed, against the friends
and followers of Mr. Pitt, or, as they partially designate
him, the immortal statesman now no more. Immortal
in the miseries of his devoted country! Immortal in the
wounds of her bleeding liberties! Immortal in the cruel
wars which sprang from his cold, miscalculating ambition! Immortal in the intolerable taxes, the countless
loads of debts which these wars have flung upon us!
Immortal in the triumphs of our enemies and the ruin
of our allies, the costly purchase of so much blood and
treasure! Immortal in the afflictions of England, and the
humiliation of her friends, through the whole results of
his twenty years' reign, from the first rays of favour with
which a delighted court gilded his early apostasy to the
deadly glare which is at this moment cast upon his name
by the burning metropolis of our last ally![18] But may no
such immortality ever fall to my lot—let me rather live
innocent and inglorious, and when at last I cease to serve
you and to feel for your wrongs, may I have an humble
monument in some nameless stone, to tell that beneath

it there rests from his labours in your service, "an enemy
of the immortal statesman—a friend of peace and of the
people".[19]

But in spite of all Brougham's eloquence and superhuman exertions,
the poll closed with Canning and Gascoigne at its head. For the first
few days the Whigs had everything in their favour, and Canning was
not unwilling to compromise, so that he and Brougham should be
elected. We may suspect that Brougham too would not have scrupled
to throw over his friend Creevey, and that the latter's suspicions of his
good faith were excited precisely on that account. Creevey admired
him for his brilliant qualities, but could not like him. "He has always
some game or underplot out of sight—some mysterious correspondence—some extraordinary connection with persons quite opposite
to himself."[20]

The result of the election might well have given rise to ironical reflec-
tions. Though Liverpool had suffered severely from a trade depression
aggravated if not caused by the Orders in Council, the electors chose
as one of their representatives a man who had been largely instrumen-
tal in promoting that policy, and rejected him who had done more
than any one else to get that policy reversed. That seeming paradox is
to be explained by the nature of the constituency. Nominally an open
borough with a popular franchise, it was really controlled by a very
small number of merchants peculiarly interested in the West Indian
trade and the survival of the slave traffic. Brougham wrote:

> Of 100,000 people not 3000 have votes. . . . Think of such
> men as Roscoe having no vote, while every slave captain
> who served seven years' apprentice ship to that traffic of
> blood was enabled to vote against the person who made
> it a felony! If the *inhabitants* had voted, the good cause
> would have been supported by 99 voices in 100. As it
> was we ran them very near, but the fear of losing their
> bread made many a poor creature vote against us with

tears and protestations that his heart was with us. Every means of influence was exhausted and at last *gold* carried the day.[21]

Brougham was by no means the only prominent Whig who met with disaster at the polls, but to his intense mortification he found himself almost alone amongst the 'dead men' whom the powerful Whig borough owners failed to bring to life again. He hastily went north in a vain attempt to win a seat for the Inverkeithing group of Scottish boroughs, where he met with strenuous opposition from the Government;[22] and, in spite of Lord Grey's friendship and of his sincere desire to be of service, Brougham remained excluded from St. Stephen's until the beginning of 1816.

> These professors of party attachments, he wrote angrily, have no sort of scruple to dissolve the regular Whig interest, or leave it with one single leader in the House of Commons, rather than forego the gratification of giving some cousin or toadeater a power of franking letters! This is their love of the Whig cause, and the Constitution and party. When it costs them nothing, they can profess it; but any, even the smallest sacrifice, they do not care to have anything to do with it.[23]

When writing to Lord Grey, Brougham chose to attribute his exclusion from Parliament to the Whig aristocracy's dislike of his advocacy of parliamentary reform:

> I have no claims with those who abhor reform—which, by the way, I am so far from overrating, that I never yet have said anything about it.[24]

But on their side the leading Whigs had much to complain of, and we may be sure that they did not, without good and sufficient reasons, voluntarily deprive themselves of the aid of so powerful an ally. Brougham, in fact, gave his case against them completely away when he privately confessed to a friend (Leigh Hunt) that his exclusion was the result of his not having faithfully served his party. No other explanation is required than his own frank avowal: "They are not very likely to return a reformer, and one who has shown himself an indifferent[25] party man." "But I trust," he added, "I may do as much good to the great cause of liberty by being out of Parliament—for a while—as if I continued to share in the wranglings of that place."[26]

He believed that there was quite a serious possibility that his parliamentary career had terminated for ever. He told Creevey that he had received from all the party leaders except Grey regular letters of dismissal, with thanks for services rendered. All kinds of schemes flitted across his outraged mind whereby he might secure a deep revenge. At one moment he thought of joining the Tories and of ranging himself under the banner of Canning.[27] At another, he contemplated turning Radical, purchasing a seat, and re-entering the Commons as a free lance. Then, he said, he might "Enjoy the purest of all pleasures—at once do what I most approve of in politics, and give the black ones an infernal licking every other night!"[28]

Not the least of his regrets at his changed prospects was his forced abandonment of an imposing programme which he had drawn up for the following session. He was to have brought forward the question of popular education, of the income tax, which he strongly desired to see abolished; of tithe reform, of the American war in so far as it was connected with the manufacturing and mercantile interests of the country; and of a measure to increase the liberty of the press.[29]

The most striking thing about this projected programme is its essentially popular and non-party character. There can be no doubt that his energetic search for new lines of policy that would appeal to the sympathies and imagination of the nation as a whole was a serious cause of annoyance to the old-fashioned, steady-going, tradition-loving leaders of the Opposition. It was the ventilation in Parliament of such extra-party subjects, the open avowal of his intention to enlarge his appeal to the ear of the country, coupled with suspicions of his loyalty and sincerity, aroused by his contemptuous attitude towards the purely party politicians, that were the cause of his exclusion from Westminster until 1816.

The change in his prospects synchronised with a decided veer to the left of his political principles. He now meant to turn 'demagogue'. In October he secretly confessed that to be returned as a Radical member for Westminster, one of the most important constituencies in the country, was almost the height of his ambition.[30] Leigh Hunt had just informed him that all his friends in London were anxious that he should contest the city at the earliest opportunity. But it was not until the spring of 1814 that his ambition seemed likely to be gratified. On February 20 occurred that famous Stock Exchange hoax, in which Lord Cochrane, one of the members for Westminster, was implicated.[31] The possibility of developments arising from this episode caused a flutter of excitement amongst the Westminster electors. Cochrane's trial, conviction for fraud, and expulsion from Parliament were all anticipated before even preliminary inquiries had been made. With grossly indecent haste, both Whigs and Radicals at once began to prepare for a bye-election, and it was soon announced that Sheridan would come forward in the Whig interest, and Brougham in the Radical. On March 10 Byron wrote:

> Sherry means to stand for Westminster, as Cochrane (the stock-jobbing hoaxer) must vacate. Brougham is a candidate. I fear for poor dear Sherry. Both have talents of the highest order, but the younger has *yet* a character. We shall see, if he lives to Sherry's age, how he will pass over the red-hot ploughshares of public life.[32]

The Whigs were anxious to avoid a contest with a popular candidate, and on June 11 the Duke of Norfolk, whose great borough influence entitled him to some consideration, condescended to call on Samuel Brooks, the chairman of the Radical Election Committee, and urged him not to propose Brougham, but to accept the Whig nomination of

Sheridan. But the Radicals were confidently anticipating a repetition of their former triumphs, and the Duke's well-intentioned efforts met with not the slightest success.

By the end of June it was known that the Government had definitely decided not to put forward a candidate of their own, but to support the Whigs against the common enemy. The Radicals themselves, however, were by no means united in favour of Brougham, whose attitude towards the subject in which they were most interested was, not without reason, suspected. On June 10 Major Cartwright, the veteran reformer, intimated that he would stand as a second Radical candidate.

The first public meeting in connection with the expected election was held at the Crown and Anchor tavern on June 8 by the reformers. They passed a resolution that their candidate must subscribe to the three principles of reform which Sir Francis Burdett had asserted in Parliament in 1809: an extension of the franchise to all subject to direct taxation; equal electoral districts; and annual parliaments.[33] At their second meeting (June 16) the Radicals' disunion was publicly revealed, for both Brougham and Cartwright were nominated. An extraordinarily animated discussion ensued, and the merits and demerits of the two candidates were freely canvassed. Some speakers objected that Brougham's views on the great subject of reform were really unknown; and they pointed out that his opinions in 1810 had been distinctly opposed to those which the Westminster electors had at their last meeting regarded as indispensable.

On the very day of the public meeting, Brougham, aware that he would have to subscribe to Burdett's Radical reform programme, informed Francis Place, through Edward Wakefield, the father of the famous Edward Gibbon Wakefield, that he was willing to make the pledge. On the 23rd, two days after Cochrane had been sentenced to a long term of imprisonment, the Livery of London held its annual Parliamentary Reform dinner, at which Place had arranged for Brougham to make his public confession of faith. As it happened, another subject of much more universal interest was being discussed that very night. The affairs of the Princess of Wales, who was at that time exciting a vast amount of attention, were being debated in the House of Commons; all the regular reporters were in attendance there, with the result that the press accounts of the proceedings at the dinner, and especially of Brougham's speech, were extraordinarily poor and unsatisfactory. At Place's instigation, therefore, the Radicals requested Brougham to write out his speech afresh, so that it might be printed in their own papers. It appeared in the *Sunday Review*, which had been supporting Brougham's candidature. The autograph copy of the speech, in Brougham's own hand, was carefully preserved in Place's library, and, as will be seen, was used on a memorable future occasion.

But all Place's efforts to induce Cartwright to withdraw failed, and the schism in the Radical party remained. Brougham, however, had powerful backing. Place himself was a host; Brooks, the chairman of the Radical committee, strongly supported him, and so did James Mill and other Benthamite Radicals. He was puffed in the *Sunday Review*, and Leigh Hunt, in his moderate Radical paper, the *Examiner*, sang his praises. Most of the advanced Whigs were on his, not on Sheridan's, side. Henry Grey Bennet promised financial assistance. Lord Tavistock volunteered his services.[34] Whitbread, Creevey, Bennet, Grattan, Lord Ossulston, and Lord William Hamilton would all have come to support Brougham at the Livery dinner but for the important business that detained them in Parliament.

It was not until July 5 that an election was made a certainty by Cochrane's expulsion from the Commons by a majority vote. The proceedings in the House, the support given to him by many of the Whigs, and his own vehement assertion of his innocence, caused a rapid revulsion of feeling in his favour amongst the Westminster reformers who had been largely indifferent about his fate. It soon became evident that public feeling had been so much aroused that Brougham would not have the ghost of a chance of being returned. Within twenty-four hours of the debate in Parliament, Brooks and the rest of the members of the Westminster committee who had supported Brougham had come to the conclusion that Cochrane ought to be re-elected. Major Cartwright at once withdrew in favour of the expelled member. In his memorandum book there appears an illuminating reference to Brougham, written after the election:

> Very different would be my feelings on this occasion if, at the close of forty years' faithful service, and immediately after having stood in the gap against the treachery of an unprincipled intrigue, I were to be unceremoniously dropped and cast off as a worn-out garment to clear the way for some reformist whose patriotism, like some gay flower, expands only in the sunshine and is shrivelled up at night or in apprehension of a storm.[35]

July 11 was nomination day, and at the meeting in Palace Yard a further proof of the almost universal change of opinion that had so quickly taken place was evinced by the reading of a letter from Sheridan, who also waived his pretensions. Burdett's two resolutions declaratory of Cochrane's innocence and of his fitness to be a representative for Westminster, were carried with the utmost enthusiasm. The nomination of but one candidate made the election, on July 18, a mere formality. Fortunately, perhaps, for its reputation, the House of Commons declined to provoke a storm similar to that which had burst upon it in the Wilkes affair half a century earlier, and no objection was raised when Cochrane took his seat. Francis Place shrewdly observed that one possible reason for the Government's acquiescence was that the contaminated lord was infinitely to be preferred as an opponent, to Brougham, from whose onslaughts the Ministry had so severely suffered.[36] Place was, in fact, disappointed at the tame attitude of the Commons. He had hoped that they would re-expel their convicted member without declaring his ineligibility to sit. Had that course been followed, the reformers would have been under no moral obligation to return Cochrane again, and the way would have been open for the election of Brougham.[37]

A few weeks after the termination of the crisis at Westminster, Brougham was informed that Canning intended to retire from the representation of Liverpool. Brougham, however, did not relish another contest in that quarter. He wrote to Grey:

> I have many communications on the subject from Liverpool, but decline doing anything. I am sick of Liverpool elections, and won't put myself up against his canine majesty on any account, even if sure of beating him. I shall let some other member of the party take a turn at it this time, having done quite as much as falls to my share already, and in return been kept out of Parliament—a whole Parliament—and lost almost all the practice I had in this county owing to the election.[38]

Though foiled at Westminster in July 1814, Brougham had an opportunity six months later of contesting the neighbouring borough of Southwark, where a vacancy was occasioned by the death of Henry Thornton, one of the most prominent of the 'Saints'. But though on January 18, 1815, Brougham was asked by a leading Southwark reformer to stand, there was little prospect of securing in that constituency the 'walk-over' that he had missed in Westminster, for in Southwark the Society of Friends had a strong footing and a candidate of their own to whom they were prepared to give their whole-hearted support. Place described the situation in a letter to his friend Mill:

> Charles Barclay, the young man who attends the Lancasterian committee, has started, and has delivered cards requesting the votes and interests of the electors. He will carry all the Quakers with him. William Allen says he does not know his politics, but if he is not on the Liberal side he will not vote for him. When I was telling William Allen that Brougham might perhaps be proposed, Fox interrupted me by saying, "All the respectable people will vote for Mr. Barclay". All the

Bible people will be for Barclay, and I do not think the
people in the borough will have the energy to return
Brougham.[39]

On the following day Brougham informed Lord Grey that he had
declined to accept nomination, since a contest would have interfered
with his law business. "It would have been madness in the middle
of term to stand a contest, even if I had cared more for politics than
I probably ever shall again, after all I have seen of their dirtiness".[40]
Place, who also believed that Brougham's chances of success were
remote, did not regret his decision.[41]

Although his election troubles stand out prominently in the history
of these years, Brougham was at the same time making a great name
at the Bar, as well as in the House of Commons. At the end of 1812
Horner declared that Brougham's success as a barrister had been much
more rapid and extensive than that of any other lawyer since the time
of Erskine's meteoric rise to fame in the 'nineties.

His first great legal case was his defence of the Hunts in 1811. In
that year John and Leigh Hunt, who had founded the *Examiner*
newspaper in 1808, were prosecuted for inserting and commenting upon an article condemning military flogging, which had first
appeared in the *Stamford News*, a Lincolnshire paper. Brougham,
who was retained for the defence, had little difficulty in disposing
of the Attorney-General's half-witted argument that the article had
been intended to provoke a French invasion. His speech was carefully prepared, for his own reputation depended on its success. His
method was to appeal to the intelligence of the jury with closely-
reasoned arguments—a method which contrasts strangely with his
later practice of descending to extravagant buffoonery as a means
of winning verdicts. Campbell, his biographer, and in later life his
rival, who had also recently begun his career at the Bar, was present
in court on this occasion, and was much impressed by Brougham's
address, which gained a verdict of 'Not Guilty'. That speech, he
declared, was the best that he had heard in the King's Bench for

seven years. To get a verdict from the Attorney-General in a criminal libel action was at that time thought a remarkable achievement; and Campbell said that Brougham was now a made man. "If he chooses to stick to the law, he is now sure of getting its highest honours," he added.[42]

That trial, indeed, established his reputation at the Bar; and when Drakard, the publisher of the *Stamford News*, was indicted at the Lincoln Assizes for publishing the same article, Brougham was specially retained for the defence. On this occasion, however, he was not so fortunate as to secure the verdict for his client, and the jury of Tory country gentlemen found Drakard guilty of publishing what was a libel in Lincolnshire but an innocent article in London.

Within two years of their triumphant acquittal, the Hunts were again prosecuted for a similar offence. Charged with libelling the Prince Regent, they were brought to trial on December 2, 1812, in the King's Bench, three weeks after Brougham had faced the same court on behalf of Daniel Lovell, the proprietor of the *Statesman* newspaper, who was convicted for publishing a libel upon the commissioners of

A suggestion for the new statue of Liberty, to be erected at Paris, from Punch, *1848*

the transport service.[43] But Brougham's spirited and able defence failed that time to save his clients from prison, where they were doomed to languish for two years.

In 1812, too, Brougham defended many of the Luddite rioters in the north of England. The most important trial in the Lancashire area of disturbance was that of thirty-eight working-class Manchester Radicals, who were charged with administering an unlawful oath to a certain Samuel Fleming, a spy under the orders of Nadin, the zealous deputy constable of the town. The case attracted the attention of Major Cartwright, who, judging that the conviction of these innocent men would seriously prejudice the progress of the reform movement, took upon himself the responsibility of engaging Brougham as one of the defending counsel. To the Major's great joy the prosecution failed and the prisoners were acquitted.

Brougham's motives in specialising in these semi-political cases are fairly clear. By taking what was called 'the sedition line' he could turn his professional business to political account. His speeches in defence of the Hunts, Drakard, and the rest, in addition to bringing him popularity out of doors as an ardent advocate of freedom of political discussion and of freedom of the press, were all calculated to damage the Government, which he could thus attack simultaneously on two sides—from within and from without the House of Commons—and to bring its stupid and reactionary policy into general disrepute.

1.   Holland House MS.: Brougham to Allen, n.d.

2.   *Life of Althorp*, p.137.

3.   *Letters to Ivy*, p.104.

4.   The disastrous failure of the expedition sent to capture Antwerp in 1809 led to a parliamentary inquiry in 1810.

5.   *Parl. Deb.* xvii. p.658.

6.   George Rose, the friend of Pitt, and a lifelong defender of the
     slave trade, was at this time Vice-President of the Board of Trade
     and Treasurer of the Navy.

7.   *The Lady of the Lake*, published in 1810.

8.   Add. MS. 34079, fol. 83.

9.   Brougham, *Speeches*, ii. 14.

10. Holland, *Further Memoirs*, p.132.

11. Hatherton MS., Diary, Dec. 15, 1845.

12. In his Memoirs, written more than half a century later, he said:
     "It was second to none of the many efforts made by me, and not
     altogether without success, to ameliorate the condition of my
     fellow-men. In these I had the sympathy and aid of others, but in
     the battle against the Orders in Council I fought alone" (vol. ii.
     p.1).

13. Dudley, *Letters to Ivy*, p.81.

14. Add. MS. 37297. fol. 166.

15   Holland House MS.: Brougham to Lord Holland, October 8, 1811.

16. *Ibid.*

17. *Life and Times*, ii. 62.

18. The burning of Moscow, September 1812.

19. *Speeches*, i. 486.

20. *Creevey Papers*, i. 172.

21. Add. MS. 38108, fol. 60.

22. Bentham, *Works*, x. 472.

23. *Life and Times*, ii. 50.

24. *Ibid.* 70.

25. Brougham crossed out the word 'bad'.

26. Add. MS. 38108, fol. 59.

27. *Corr. of Lord Granville*, ii. 464.

28. *Creevey Papers*, i. 174.

29. Holland House MS.; Add. MS. 38108, fol. 59.

30. *Corr. of Leigh Hunt*, i. 63.

31. A gentleman in French uniform suddenly arrived at Dover, posted
     to Cochrane's house in town, bringing the news that Napoleon was

dead, that the allies were marching on Paris, and that peace would follow almost at once. The Funds at once rose; Cochrane's uncle sold his stock, netting a big sum. The Funds fell again as soon as the news was proved to be false.

32. Moore, *Letters and Journals of Byron*, ii. 10.

33. Add. MS. 27850, fol. 278.

34. *Ibid.* fol. 283.

35. *Life of Cartwright*, ii. 78.

36. Add. MS. 27850, fol. 287.

37. Add. MS. 37949, fol. 18.

38. *Life and Times*, ii. 107. By 'his canine majesty' Brougham mean-Dent, who had invented the tax on dogs.

39. Add. MS. 35152, fol. 129.

40. *Life and Times*, ii. 278.

41. Add. MS. 35152, fol. 130.

42. Campbell, *Life*, i 267.

43. *Annual Register*, 1812, p.276.

III

The State of the Whig Party
1807–1815

The great thing that is wanted is resistance to the strides
that are making, in concurrence with the general tendency
of things throughout the world, to turn the country into
a democracy.   —Windham

AT the close of the Napoleonic war the Whig party, into the very
front rank of which Brougham's amazing energy and brilliant oratory
had, by the end of the session of 1812, placed him, was still pursuing its wearying and disheartening wanderings in the wilderness of
Opposition, whence it had been banished a generation before. From
the great conflict it had emerged despondent, discredited, and disunited. For the brief space of fifteen months, indeed, the Whigs had
tasted unexpectedly of the sweet fruits of office, but their short tenure
of power (1806–7) was a record of failure relieved only by one great
and splendid achievement. But though there had rarely been, in the
history of English ministries, so glaring a contrast between promise
and fulfilment, the failures of the Whig Government were largely due
to the open hostility of the king, lack of support from the nation, and
the inherent difficulty of the foreign situation.

After the abrupt termination of its brief régime, the position of the Whig party gradually worsened until, within three years of its dismissal from office, the Opposition, torn by internal dissensions, was threatened with complete disintegration and collapse.

During these years the Whig party was divided into three well-defined groups: the Grenville Whigs, the Foxite Whigs, and the 'Mountain'.

The Grenville *condottieri,* as they were contemptuously termed, consisted of Whigs who had seceded from Fox in 1794, and of Tories under the leadership of the first Marquis of Buckingham. Their numbers were comparatively small, a deficiency, however, which was more than counterbalanced by vast territorial and borough influence. Lord Grenville, the leader of the party, had played a conspicuous part in supporting Pitt's gagging bills in 1794, and throughout his life he ranged himself against all proposals calculated to increase the political power of the people at the expense of that of the aristocracy. His brother, the first Marquis of Buckingham, fully shared these reactionary views on the subject of parliamentary reform, and went further in advocating stern measures of repression by the sword and the bayonet in Ireland. "Systematic and vigorous coercion" was his specific for popular discontent in that unhappy country.

The Grenvillites in the Lower House were led by Grenville's elder brother, Thomas Grenville, and, later, by his nephew, Charles Wynn, whose ambition it was to sit in the Speaker's chair. He was described by Brougham as being skilled beyond all men in the history of the voluminous records of parliamentary precedents, and was popularly supposed to know the whole of the journals of the House by heart. And, added Brougham facetiously:

> His accuracy in everything connected with Parliament
> was so rigid that many persons imagined he really came
> down to the House every morning at 10 o'clock, the hour
> at which the House ought to assemble, according to the

strict letter of the adjournment; . . . whose devotion in this respect could only be equalled by that of a learned ancestor of his, who, having fainted from excessive toil and fatigue, a smelling bottle was called for, but one who knew much better the remedy adapted to the case of that gentleman, exclaimed, "For God's sake bring him an Act of Parliament, and let him smell at that"![1]

The leader of the Foxite Whigs was Earl Grey, Ponsonby being his chief lieutenant in the Commons. Increasing bodily infirmities, however, were making him more and more anxious to retire from public life, and to hand over the leadership of the party to Lord Holland. Grey's appearances in the Lords became more and more infrequent, and Holland himself, pursued by that relentless enemy the gout, was obliged to rely upon his younger friend Lord Lansdowne to represent the party in the Upper House.

Profoundly dissatisfied with the failures of the Whigs in office, and with the conventional and unenterprising character of their policy in opposition, a small but powerful group of Whigs, under the leadership of Samuel Whitbread, had been making itself increasingly felt since 1807. Whitbread, whose father had founded the famous brewery concern, had married Earl Grey's sister, and had entered Parliament in 1790 as a staunch supporter of Fox. In season and out of season he preached the doctrines of parliamentary reform and religious equality, and urged the abolition of the slave trade, at a time when some of these objects were shelved by many members of the Opposition. His followers became known as the 'Mountain', a name originally given to the French Jacobins, the most extreme section of the revolutionaries, who had occupied the highest benches on the left of the French Assembly.

The 'Mountain' represented the real driving force in the Whig movement. Whitbread and his friends were the most active and zealous exposers of the abuses that permeated every branch of the administrative system under the Tory régime. So extensive were their activities in this direction that Gifford, the first editor of the Tory *Quarterly Review*, could, with singular appropriateness, vent his unrivalled powers of sarcasm on their parliamentary conduct.

> If Mr. Whitbread and one or two others live, he declared, I do not despair of seeing the day when no country schoolmaster shall turn up a little brat's posterior without having a petition against him in that honourable House, which bas so wisely turned its attention to these things lately.[2]

Whitbread's chief friends were Bennet, Brougham, Creevey, and Romilly. Henry Grey Bennet, the second son of the fourth Earl of Tankerville, was the leader of the agitation for a more humane prison system; and he worked hard to organise public opinion in favour of the chimney-sweep boys. Creevey specialised in exposing ministerial jobbing, and in attacking the East India Company's trade monopoly. Brougham's amazing energy made his activities all-embracing. Whitbread was a pioneer in the movement in favour of popular education; he did his best to improve the lot of the agricultural labourers and to secure for them a minimum wage; and during these years no one worked more than he to make life less hard for the masses of the people.

The men of the 'Mountain' one and all detested the Grenvillites, the alliance with whom they regarded as a disastrous misfortune. They all, too, cried out against the incompetent leadership of George Ponsonby, and against the over-cautious and vacillating counsels of Tierney, Grey, and Holland. Only with the greatest difficulty was the breach between Whitbread and Lord Grey closed after 1809. The former's peace policy was as distasteful to the main body of the Whigs as were his reforming activities in the Commons.

One of the main causes of the impotence into which the Whigs had sunk during the long war was their inability to extend their influence beyond the narrow limits of their own class. They had nothing that could be called a programme with which they might win over the middle and lower orders of society. Their opposition to the war had caused them to be branded as an unpatriotic faction; their advocacy of Catholic emancipation was equally unpopular; they were as a party opposed to free trade; and they had practically abandoned the cause of parliamentary reform.

The Whigs were essentially an aristocratic party. Sir Walter Scott, himself a Pittite, admitted that the only difference between Whig and Tory was in words and personal predilections. "In principle, there is and can be none. No Whig will allow that it is his intention to break down the royal part of the Constitution, and no Pittite will call himself an enemy to legitimate freedom."[3] Hazlitt said that the two parties reminded him of rival stage coaches which bespattered each other with mud, but which both travelled along the same road and arrived at the same destination.

This theme was fully elaborated by James Mill in the *Westminster Review*, the famous organ of the Benthamite Radicals. Whigs and Tories, he said, were the two branches of the aristocracy, and by the term aristocracy he meant not merely the titled nobility and the wealthy families, but the whole governing class. Of this aristocracy the most influential and powerful part was that small number of great families, not more than two hundred in all, which returned a majority of the members of the House of Commons, and which, in virtue of that influence, was the real governing power in the country. This oligarchy of landowners had to share its power with a few able but less privileged men recruited from the moneyed interest, the Church, and the Law. The Whigs were as much pledged as the Tories to maintain the aristocratic form of government. The Whig creed and Whig practice were fashioned with a view to this ultimate end. Being in Opposition, it was indeed their object to discredit the Tories in the eyes of the country, to win the support of the people, and to become the 'Ins'. But in striving to effect this object they were careful to do nothing that would depress the power of the aristocracy and exalt that of the people. It was obviously not their interest to part with any portion of the inheritance they hoped some day to possess. Their programme, therefore, had a twofold aspect: to maintain intact the aristocratic monopoly of political power, and to hold out to the unprivileged and unpropertied masses hopes of reforms, the accomplishment of which would in no way endanger the existing social and political system, or disturb the balance of power. For good government they cared more than did the Tories, and they were prepared to secure it at less cost. In some degree they resembled the benevolent despots of the eighteenth century. An aristocracy was prepared to do what a monarchy under a Joseph or a Frederick had endeavoured to do: to reform abuses in the administrative machinery of government, to govern the country more economically, to win a reputation for enlightenment by repealing penal laws that savoured of religious intolerance, by mitigating the harshness of a barbarous penal code, and by abolishing the accursed slave trade. They were, for the most part, genuinely desirous of ameliorating the hard lot of the working classes, but they were comparatively ignorant of the real nature of the social problems that awaited solution; but proposals to alter the Constitution in a democratic direction were met with a hostility as uncompromising as that of the Tories. They then spoke of "our glorious constitution fashioned by the wisdom of our ancestors", and talked wildly of Jacobinism. In their view the aristocracy were the 'natural leaders' of the people, and popular agitation was only countenanced when directed by respectable men of property. Lord Erskine put the matter succinctly when he declared, "The mass of a people, when separated from those who, from the accidents of human life, are distinguished by property, or the privileges arising out of the constitution of a state, can no more exist for their own freedom, security, and happiness, than the limbs of a human body can have human action when separated from the trunk".[4] The petitions of the people, he further declared, ought to go for nothing when they ask what is ruinous to themselves.

Other old catchwords—preserving the 'balance' of the Constitution, and diminishing the 'influence of the Crown'—were employed just as they had been far back in the eighteenth century. The English

Constitution, as Whiggism interpreted it, was a mysterious and awe-inspiring blending of the three great principles of monarchy, aristocracy, and democracy, and its virtue depended on the continued maintenance of a balance between these three contending powers. The representative body was therefore originally intended as a check on the Crown and on the peers. In the course of time circumstances had destroyed the balance. The House of Commons had taken advantage of the weakness of the monarchy to swallow up the powers of king and lords, a process which had been immensely facilitated by the vast and rapid increase that had taken place in the wealth and importance of the country at large, and by the superiority of the elective over the hereditary principle as a means of securing men of talent and ambition to undertake political responsibilities. The legislative authority had become almost exclusively vested in the Lower House; for a century the Crown had never ventured to interpose its veto, and to popular legislation the Lords offered a still feebler barrier. How had the balance been redressed? It had been restored by the interference of the other two elements in the election of members of the House of Commons. In 1716 the number of office-holders appointed by the Crown who had seats in the Lower House was no less than 164; in 1807, indeed, the number had fallen to 74, but on the other hand, bloated war establishments had increased enormously the amount of patronage which could be used for election purposes.[5] Appointments to the army, the navy, the church, the law, the colonies and the home service, were said to number several hundred thousand, and the emoluments of these offices to approach the then enormous sum of twenty millions a year.[6] As for the influence exerted by the peerage, it was notorious that 300 members out of a total of 658 owed their seats to the aristocracy.

Thus the balance of the Constitution had been saved by the introduction into the House of Commons of the joint influence of the Crown and the peers. The new arrangement had striking advantages over the old:

> The collision and shock of the three rival principles is either prevented or prodigiously softened by this early mixture of their elements—that by converting those sudden and successive checks into one regulating and graduated pressure, their operation becomes infinitely more smooth and manageable, and no longer proceeds by jerks and bounds that might endanger the safety of the machine—while the movements, instead of being fractured and impeded by the irregular impulses of opposite forces, slide quietly to the mark, in the diagonal produced by their original combination.[7]

This system the Edinburgh reviewers not only defended, but declared that with its maintenance the welfare of the country and the safety of the Constitution were inextricably bound up.

> As for altering the composition of the House of Commons by excluding from it all who are sent there by the interest of the Ministry or of noble families, we can only say, that if we believed it at all likely to produce such an effect, we should think it our duty to strive against it, as against a measure which would deprive us of all the practical blessings of our Constitution.[8]

The doctrine of the balance was, then, essentially aristocratic in its nature. Destroy the balance, and bring the constitution of the House of Commons into accordance with the will of the people, they said, and a pure democracy will be the result. Once you get democratic government, they proceeded, the House of Lords will speedily be swept away as useless lumber; and, even if the monarchy were not quickly to meet with the same fate, the Government would nevertheless inevitably assume the form of a republic.

> If it be true that the whole force of the Government actually resides in the House of Commons, which we

take to be obvious . . . it follows that the nobility as
well as the Crown must either have something to say
in its deliberations or must have nothing to say in the
Government. We are perfectly satisfied that so long as
the administration retains any considerable share of its
present patronage, and so long as the great families retain
their popularity and riches, there will always be a due
proportion of their influence to prevent that omnipotent
assembly from being guided by the feelings of only one
class of the community.[9]

The Whig theory of representation is therefore a corollary of the
main doctrine that political power should be wielded by the property
owners of the country. To prevent the domination of any one class
in Parliament, the landed interest, the lawyers, the merchants and
manufacturers, the intellectuals, and the common people, ought all
to have separate representation in the Lower House.

One of the most characteristic features of English political theory is
that it has always tended to explain and justify political change, rather
than to be the stimulating cause of such change. The Whig philosophy of this period is obviously an elaborate apology for the existing
machinery of government. The tendency was to look back on the past
and to ruminate with satisfaction and even reverence on the glories of
the Constitution, which, before evil times had imparted some blemishes and defects, was regarded as a model of excellence and political
statecraft, upon which it was hardly possible to improve, affording,
as it did, a larger measure of liberty to the privileged governing class
than did that of any other country in the world.

We have attained a greater portion of happiness and
civil liberty than have ever before been enjoyed by any
other nation, and . . . the frame and administration of
our polity is, with all its defects, the most perfect and
beneficial of any that men have yet invented and reduced

> to practice. We have perfect liberty of person and security
> of property; we have an administration of law, both civil
> and criminal, that is not only impartial but unsuspected;
> we have freedom of speech and of publication beyond
> what any other people ever experienced; we have wealth
> and police and morality superior to any other country;
> and we have no privileged orders possessing a monopoly
> of the honours and dignities of the State.[10]

The most important question that was to be ventilated after 1815 was that of parliamentary reform. As a party the Whigs were without a policy, and the views of individual members were as wide asunder as the poles. The great Whig borough proprietors were not unnaturally of the same mind as the Tories in wishing to preserve that most distinctive feature of the unreformed Parliament, the close borough system. According to the *Black Book* published by the Radicals in 1820, the Duke of Bedford returned four members to the House of Commons, the Duke of Devonshire and Lord Darlington also four each; Lord Fitzwilliam five, the Marquis of Buckingham six, Lord Lansdowne two, and the Duke of Norfolk the astonishing number of eleven. All these great representatives of the aristocracy were at best but very lukewarm reformers; the Marquis of Buckingham was openly opposed to change, as was Lord Fitzwilliam until 1819.

Other leading Whigs necessarily fell in with the views of these influential personages. Fox declared in 1798 that until a radical reform of the representative system took place, he for one would never consent to hold office in any administration. But in 1806 the Whigs coalesced with the Tories and tacitly abandoned their pledges. As late as 1819 an Edinburgh reviewer declared:

> If [the Whigs] can carry the Catholic question and effect a
> wholesome and moderate reform of Parliament, the coun-
> try will gain so much the more; but no such point should
> ever be thought of as a condition *sine quâ non*.

In 1810 Grey, who had been in favour of household suffrage and triennial parliaments, confessed that "to go to the full extent of his original ideas would be too much".[11] That speech of his in the House of Lords was severely criticised by the Radicals; and it seems reasonable to suppose that their taunts made some impression on his proud, sensitive mind, for in March 1811 he wrote to Lord Holland: "The lesson that I have learnt is to pledge myself to as little as possible while in Opposition, and when in Government, if ever it should be my lot to be again in that station, to do as much as I can".[12]

To parliamentary reform the Grenville Whigs had as great an antipathy as had the Tories, and it is hardly surprising that their relations with Whitbread and his party were painfully strained. The principle upon which the Grenvillites acted was resistance to all popular movements, though they recognised that, to meet in some measure the views of their allies, resistance had to be tempered with discretion. What was particularly distressing to their excitable minds was the fact that the younger generation of Whigs, especially the sons of Whig peers, were reverting to the old principles of Fox in 1793, and were becoming infected with the fell plague of Jacobinism. The Grenvilles' extreme horror of such is well illustrated by the fact that amongst these young revolutionary firebrands they included Lord Fitzwilliam's eldest son, Lord Milton, who in Parliament opposed the extremely moderate proposal to enfranchise copyholders, for no other reason than that copyholders had never been given the vote. Lord Milton had further observed

> that his objections to change were radical, and were founded on a conviction that all measures of this sort did not go to reform but to alter the Constitution. . . . He would conjure the House to abstain from touching with sacrilegious hands an institution that had been raised by the wisdom of its ancestors.[13]

Lord Althorp and Coke of Norfolk were also instanced as young Whigs holding obnoxious and dangerous views. On several occasions we find Thomas Grenville writing to Earl Spencer, earnestly requesting him to use his influence to restrain his son's extravagant views. As for Coke,

> he has been holding very inflammatory language on these topics at Brooks', and has been talking about honest youth as contrasted with empty politicians; and has been dealing out his invectives against sinecures with the same abundance of nonsense which he generally reserves for the companions of his Norfolk dumplings at Holkham.[14]

The Whigs were but feebly supported by the Press, and they possessed only one daily newspaper of repute. But Perry, the editor of the *Morning Chronicle*, was not sufficiently imbued with the spirit of party thoroughly to suit the Whigs, who repeatedly complained that he neglected their interests. On several occasions after 1815 they seriously thought of setting up a morning and a weekly opposition paper of their own, but the project always fell to the ground.

Of far greater importance than the *Morning Chronicle* was the *Edinburgh Review*. By 1808—six years after its commencement—its circulation had risen to 9000 copies. As Sir Walter Scott remarked, no cultured family could pretend to do without it, for, quite apart from its politics, it gave the only valuable literary criticism that could then be obtained. Written from the beginning for the aristocracy, for some time it held the balance between the two contending parties, and Tory contributors like Scott aided Jeffrey and the Whigs. The first few volumes, indeed, consisted largely of literary articles and treatises on scientific and economic subjects. Politics occupied only a secondary position, and Brougham could eulogise the statesmanship of Pitt. It was not until 1809 that the *Review* finally abandoned its semi-neutral ground, and, inspired largely by Brougham, began to expound the Whig creed without restraint. He, more than any one else, was responsible for making the *Edinburgh* the peculiar organ of the Whig party. The result was the defection of Scott and the establishment of the Tory *Quarterly.*

When the services rendered by the *Edinburgh* in its early days to the cause of liberty are so often extolled, it is sometimes forgotten that the influence of the *Review* was not invariably exerted on the side of progress and enlightenment. Brougham's views on the rebellion of the Hayti negroes have already been quoted.[15] He pleaded, indeed, with great eloquence for the abolition of the slave trade, but on the question of the extinction of slavery itself he took the illiberal side. He wrote in July 1804:

> It is scarcely necessary to premise that the advocates for the abolition of the slave trade most cordially reprobate all idea of *emancipating* the slaves that are already in our plantations. Such a scheme, indeed, is sufficiently answered by the story of the galley slaves in *Don Quixote*; and, we are persuaded, never had any place in the minds of those enlightened and judicious persons who have contended for the abolition with so much meritorious perseverance. In this pamphlet, accordingly, we find none of that sentimental rant and sonorous philanthropy by which the cause of humanity has been so often exposed to ridicule. The argument, on the contrary, is conducted with the greatest moderation, sobriety, and good sense.[16]

The *Edinburgh's* obscurantism is equally strikingly displayed in its treatment of the subject of prison reform. A true description of the inhumanly wretched conditions under which prisoners still existed is to be found in the pages of *Hansard,* and in the recent survey by the Webbs. Life in those "diabolical dens of torment, mischief, and damnation", as Bernard Shaw describes our English prisons, was given a much more pleasant and rosy aspect by the imaginative reviewers:

Since the benevolent Howard attacked our prisons, incarceration has become not only healthy, but elegant; and a country jail is precisely the place to which any pauper might wish to retire to gratify his taste for magnificence, as well as for comfort. Upon the same principle, there is some risk that transportation will be considered as one of the surest roads to honour and to wealth; and that no felon will hear a verdict of 'Not guilty' without considering himself cut off in the fairest career of prosperity.[17]

Broadly speaking, the conception of Whiggism as expounded by Jeffrey and his coadjutors in the *Edinburgh* coincided with the doctrine of its political leaders. Based essentially on compromise, the Radicals denounced it as nothing better than a mere shuffle, and its exponents as selfish trimmers.[18] In December 1826 Jeffrey answered his Westminster critics and virtually admitted the charge.

We acknowledge that we are fairly chargeable with a fear of opposite excesses—a desire to compromise and reconcile the claims of all the great parties in the State. . . . But we are for authority as well as for freedom. We are for the natural and wholesome influence of wealth and

From Punch, *1848*

rank, and the veneration which belongs to old institutions, without which no Government has ever had either stability or respect; as well as for that vigilance of popular control, and that supremacy of public opinion, without which none could be long protected from abuse.[19]

1. *Parl. Deb.* xli. 225.

2. Scott, *Familiar Letters*, ii. 398.

3. *Ibid.* i. 170, 174.

4. *A Letter by Lord Erskine to an Elector of Westminster*, p.25.

5. *Parl. Deb* xxxv. 959.

6. *Edin. Review*, July 1809, p.285.

7. *Ibid.* July 1807, p.413.

8. *Ibid.* July 1809, p.300.

9. *Ibid.* pp.301, 303.

10. *Ibid.* July 1807, p.406.

11. *Parl. Deb.* xvii. 600.

12. G.M. Trevelyan, *Lord Grey*, p.183 n.

13. *Parl. Deb.* xxiii. 150.

14. *Hist. MS. Comm.*, Fortescue Papers, ix. 285.

15. The quotation was from his *Colonial Policy*, but the passage occurs almost word for word in his article in the Review on that subject.

16. *Edin. Review*, July 1804, p.477.

17. *Ibid.* April 1803, p.32.

18. Stephen, *English Utilitarians*, ii. 98.

19. Jeffrey, *Essays*, iv. 153.

IV

Riding the Radical Horse

He makes his mouth a puddled ditch for kings,
Bourbons and Brunswicks in the scum are stirr'd—
Indeed the Stuarts get a kinder word.
By him mean trifles are tremendous made;
A smuggler moves him more than stagnant trade.
Large seeds of lupin, thus, small growth are given,
While tiny mustard sends its tree to heaven.
Thus this ant-eater hunts not game that leaps,
But lolls his slimy tongue to catch what creeps.
The moment Br—m pronounces "something wrong",
"Hear!" shouts each Ex, the lobbies "Hear!" prolong.
Chop-houses clamour, newspapers indite,
And "something wrong" soon turns to "nothing right".
Pil'd Babels of petitions heaven ascend,
And call Reform from Hebrid to Land's-end.

The Talents Run Mad; or, 1816

ALTHOUGH he had, in his own opinion, been treated with extreme
shabbiness by the Whig aristocracy since the autumn of 1812, and

though he had been prepared to contest the city of Westminster as a full-fledged Radical, Brougham had thought it prudent not to sever his connection with a party which, after all, had given him the opportunity of entering upon a public career. That he had determined wisely in maintaining friendly relations with the leader of the Whig party was proved in the summer of 1815, when, at Lord Grey's earnest request, Lord Darlington, a wealthy Opposition peer, consented to provide Brougham with a seat.

Brougham re-entered Parliament as member for the borough of Whichelsea in February 1816 under circumstances profoundly different from those that had obtained when he had left it four years before. Since 1812 the situation both at home and abroad had undergone a complete transformation. The Waterloo campaign had been fought, the Congress of Vienna had given peace to a war-weary Europe, and Napoleon was an exile in St. Helena. At home the triumph of its war policy seemed to have given the Tory ministry a new lease of life, though it was soon to find that the problems of peace were no less testing and harassing than those of war. As for the Opposition, all its croakings had been most signally falsified; but still, in spite of their discomfiture, the Whigs, feeling that the game would soon be all in their hands, rejoiced at the return of peace. The standing argument of the Tories against all reform and innovation, that "nothing can be done while Hannibal is at the gates", was at last happily taken out of their mouths. The hurricane season had passed away, and the social and political fabric could now be overhauled and repaired. Day and night, said Brougham, the Opposition had been striving ineffectually to diminish the influence of the Crown by a mere ten or twenty thousand pounds; peace would at once bring down the expenditure by fifty or sixty millions.[1] The reduction of establishments to the peace level of 1792 would mean the dismissal of thousands of Government employees, and would engender a universal spirit of unrest; the Ministers would lose their prestige, and all the forces of discontent would seek political expression in opposition to the Government.[2]

On July 6, 1815, the Whig party lost in Whitbread one of its most useful leaders. Three days later Grey wrote to Lord Darlington about the borough of Winchelsea. To Brougham himself this seemed to be more than a coincidence, and he at once assumed that Lord Grey had marked him out for the leadership of the Whig party in the Commons. Henceforward, both in and out of the House, Brougham acted on this assumption. He determined that Whitbread's loss, grievous though it was, should not be irreparable, and that he himself was fully capable of filling the gap.

The next four years of his career have a unity of their own. During this period his great objects were to obtain official recognition from the party of his position as *de facto* leader in the Lower House; to bring the Whig programme up to date, and to make Whiggism more popular in the country; to create a personal following of his own, and to make himself the most popular political leader in the kingdom. With what success he attempted to effect these objects will be seen in the following chapters.

Before the opening of the parliamentary campaign in February 1816, Brougham, acting up to his new rôle, communicated to Lord Grey a detailed statement of the policy and tactics which he thought the party ought to adopt. Ponsonby, the titular leader in the Commons, being obviously incompetent, should be deposed, and a puppet should be put in his place. Lord George Cavendish, he thought, would be the very man for the job. His abilities were not too conspicuous; he hardly ever opened his mouth in the House; he had great family connections; and he possessed a house in town that would serve as a first-rate *rendezvous* for the Opposition. Unfortunately, however, Grey and Holland could not be persuaded to see the question in precisely the same light, and they were content to allow Ponsonby to retain the nominal lead until his death in the summer of 1817.

In the sphere of foreign policy the Opposition should, he thought, act with circumspection and moderation. A frontal attack was out of the question, since the Government had "won the war"; but the Whigs might well expose the Ministry's blunders in winning the peace. They might raise a debate on the damnable proceedings of Ferdinand of Spain, our late ally, who had erected a despotism over the ruins of the Liberal Constitution of 1812. They should attack the peace treaties for sanctioning the principle of intervention by the Great Powers in the internal affairs of other nations. They should condemn the doctrine of legitimacy, enthroned in France by the restoration of the Bourbons in despite of the wishes and feelings of the nation.[3] Our own foreign policy, said Brougham, should be based on the principle of non-intervention. The essential fact was that the country was staggering under a huge dead-weight of debt, all of which might have been avoided but for Pitt's proneness to unsheath the sword in 1793. He wrote:

> Must we always be so knit to the continent, even after our own dangers are terminated, that every quarrel of the German princes about territory or precedence shall draw us into a new war? Can't the people learn to hear of wars and rumours of wars without running out to fight, whether they have any concern in the business or not?[4]

But the main offensive against the Government was to be launched on matters of domestic concern. Retrenchment was to be the Whig rallying cry. Heaven and earth should be moved in order to get rid of the obnoxious income tax. Such popular objects as the reduction of the Royal Family's expenditure, the abolition of sinecures, the destruction of administrative abuses and of ministerial jobbing, should engage their close attention. An inquiry should be made into the distresses of the landed interest, and remedies should be diligently sought. All this, declared Brougham cynically, would open up the richest mine of attack in the world.

But the most interesting part of the new programme was that which comprised such diverse topics as prison reform, the education of the lower orders, the commutation of tithes, the slave trade, and the freedom of the Press. The significance of this third section of Brougham's programme, an outline of which had, as we have seen, long been in his mind, is that it consisted of reform questions which were for the most part dissociated with party: proposals which normally would never be brought forward by a regular Opposition for party purposes. If these extra-party objects could be secured, thought Brougham, they would not only be useful as a check on the power of the Crown, but would go far to increase his own and his party's reputation. Brougham was almost alone among the Whigs in perceiving the importance of appealing to the popular element, and, anxious to win a great name as a social reformer, he strove to model his programme accordingly.

During this session Brougham made a serious attempt to build up a new political connection of his own out of advanced Whigs and moderate Radicals. The parliamentary Radical party, led by Sir Francis Burdett, the senior member for Westminster, was as yet small in numbers, but powerful in debate and influential in the country. That Brougham should at this time be relying as much on the support of the Radicals as on the Whigs is hardly surprising when we remember that only two years before he had solemnly and publicly subscribed to the full Radical programme, and that he was still waiting patiently for an opportunity of exchanging for the open constituency of Westminster the seat which he held by the favour of a Whig peer. If only he could come in as the colleague of Sir Francis Burdett, his extraordinary energy, his great intellectual capacity, together with an ambition that knew no bounds, would all combine to make him the most powerful and formidable man in the House of Commons and the most popular in the country. With the new programme, which would make him the popular idol, he would verily be able to move mountains. Thus, whilst he was to get into his hands the control of the Whig party in the Commons, he was at the same time, and with an eye on the next Westminster contest, to expound the new creed which would win for him the support and active assistance of outdoor opinion.

It is not therefore surprising to find that he communicated his plans not merely to the Whig party leaders, but also to the most influential Radicals in London. Within a few weeks of the time when Lord Darlington had promised to provide him with a seat, Brougham was going over his programme with James Mill, the friend of Bentham, and the most powerful propagandist of the new philosophic Radicalism, and also with Francis Place, who could do more than any other man to secure his election for Westminster. Place was keenly anxious that the Radical party, which was just beginning to make a great impression on the country, should make its power increasingly felt in the unreformed House of Commons. Its numbers were small, and means had to be found to swell the ranks. It was his hope to detach Brougham completely from the Whig 'faction', which, he said, was in no respect to be preferred to the men in office. Though he had not yet come into close personal contact with Brougham, Place admired him for his wonderful talents and his seemingly disinterested and sincere advocacy of popular causes. He desired, therefore, to put Brougham at the head of the new reform movement.[5] Lord Dundonald, Cochrane's father, had long been in poor health and his death was almost daily expected, an event which would remove the junior member for Westminster to the House of Lords, and pave the way for Brougham's return for that great Radical constituency.

To the new programme Place gave his general assent. "Brougham will do well to press at such measures as you mention with his usual pertinacity—perseverance if you will," he wrote to Mill on August 29, 1815. He added:

> I do not know enough of him to make up my mind fully on his character. In political affairs I always fear for those who are not in all things republicans from principle. I think a man who is not so cannot know enough of himself to be able to trust to himself in all times and in all seasons.[6]

To ensure complete unity of action between the reforming Whigs and the Radicals, Place urged Brougham to discuss his proposals with Burdett, and to make arrangements for their parliamentary campaign. He wrote:

> If they and Bennet and a few others would pull cordially together and be incessant in attacking the enemy, I have no doubt that in a year or two a great sensation would be felt all over the country. Circumstances such as we have a right to expect to see will command attention, and if these men take their station now and do their duty, they will draw the best men and the strongest intellect of the country around them.[7]

On the ground of financial unsoundness, however, Place disapproved of the proposal to agitate for the abolition of the income tax. James Mill too concurred with his view that it would be a mere party attack on the Government, but nevertheless he urged his friend to do nothing to counteract it, since, he said,

> nothing is so good for all the wicked purposes of the Ministers as that they should be at their ease in regard to money—nothing so good for the people as that they should find it difficult to get money. The income tax will make all that prodigious difference.[8]

For several months before the opening of Parliament, strenuous efforts were being made to organise a party to carry out the new programme. From the ordinary Whig party man Brougham did not expect much help. The half-hearted tactics of Ponsonby, Tierney, Macdonald, Abercromby, and other prominent Whigs, disgusted him. "I am quite determined," he wrote "(though ready to meet them half-way for peace and union sake) that the game of the country and the people shall be played in good earnest—if not with their help, without it—by God's blessing."[9]

Thus it was clear that the actual fighting in the House would have to be done by the 'Mountaineers' and their Radical allies, although the Whigs might reasonably be expected to assist in the division lobby. The loss of such an able and persistent combatant as Whitbread was doubly disastrous at this critical moment. Brougham begged and prayed of friend Creevey, a very sound and trenchant Opposition man, who was dallying in Brussels, to come take part in the fray. In January Brougham sounded Lord Folkestone as to his willingness to enter the lists, and he had already made sure of the co-operation of Burdett, Bennet, and others. Place too had been active, and, through his friend Edward Wakefield, had made overtures to Western, the leading representative of the agricultural interest in the Commons, and a Whig party man. Western had shown a somewhat surprising but gratifying amount of enthusiasm, had declared himself anxious to become more intimately acquainted with Brougham, and had promised to go "any length" for reform "in any shape". Full of zeal, Western had taken the trouble to write to Lord Folkestone asking him to co-operate, and had succeeded in recruiting a Mr. Gordon, another Opposition man, "a curious-looking fellow—you will see something of him in the Mendicity Report", so Place informed Mill. "He is," he added, "described as a violent reformist; all this, except as before excepted, [10] looks well, and will I hope prosper to the extent of my prophecy in my last letter to you; this will be enough to satisfy any reasonable man for a year or two to come."[11]

Brougham had apparently achieved a considerable measure of success, not merely in working out the details of a programme, but in getting together a party with which to carry it out. A study of the parliamentary debates for the year 1816, however, shows that though the greater part of Brougham's imposing programme was duly carried out, it was accomplished mainly by Brougham himself. The party which he had taken such pains to rally melted away almost as soon as it had been formed, and its organiser found himself a general without an army. If the session of 1816 again afforded him an opportunity of displaying all his powers, it also revealed a weakness which he was destined never to overcome, an incapacity which perhaps alone prevented him from attaining to the highest of all political offices. It was his inability to lead a party and to retain the loyalty and goodwill of its members that caused him to have to fight the battle almost alone.

He himself had to bear all the heat and burden of the struggle, and all the glory too of the campaign was his own.

Brougham obtained a much larger amount of success with his proposals for social reform than with the other two groups of topics. He spoke in favour of a commutation of tithes, but, though he had made a complete study of the question, and had drawn up a Bill which, he said, was as plain sailing as a common Road Bill, he made no attempt to introduce it in this session. He had as much on his hands already as three or four ordinary mortals could have managed between them. His efforts to further the cause of popular education will be noticed in a subsequent chapter.

It was in this first year of his own return to Parliament that he made the first of a long series of endeavours to reform the law. On May 8 he applied for leave to bring in a Bill for securing the liberty of the Press. It proposed to bring the criminal law in cases of libel into conformity with the civil law, and to allow the truth to be given in evidence by the defence as matter of justification; to prevent further instances of newspaper proprietors and others being punished for libels inserted in their publications without their cognisance; to abolish the Attorney-General's privilege of filing *ex-officio* informations for libel;[12] and to abolish the privilege enjoyed by the Crown of having libel cases tried by specially selected juries.

The significance of Brougham's Bill is that it was highly calculated to increase his reputation in the country, and, in particular, amongst the Westminster Radicals, who were strongly opposed to the continuance of the restrictions on the freedom of the Press. But inside the House the great and sweeping changes which the Bill was intended to effect met with some opposition from the Tory benches. Discreetly enough, therefore, Brougham refrained from pressing his measure, and on June 14 he announced that in view of the approaching close of the session he would let the Bill stand over for the time being.[13]

Brougham carried out his intention of steering as clear as possible of inconvenient debates on the Government's foreign policy, and confined himself to such topics out of which party capital might be made. On February 9 he denounced the Holy Alliance, which he regarded as a sinister combination of the despots of Europe against the liberties of free peoples. On the 12th he urged the Ministers to make representations to the Austrian Government concerning the payment of the interest on its debt to Britain—a reasonable suggestion, since the Emperor had succeeded in restoring the finances of his dominions.[14] On the 15th he spoke on the situation in Spain. Though opposed in principle to the doctrine of intervention, he thought that the abominations practised by Ferdinand since his assumption of arbitrary power justified our interference. Lord John Russell concurred with his view, and supported the motion for an address to the Prince Regent, which, however, was negatived by an overwhelming majority.[15] The general principle seemed to be fading into the background when on May 22 Brougham supported Romilly in urging the Government to do something on behalf of the French Protestants, who were being cruelly persecuted. Finally on June 18 he denounced the sanction which the Ministers had given to the treaty concluded by Lord Exmouth in the name of the Neapolitan and Sardinian Governments with the Dey of Algiers. Whilst Castlereagh insisted on the enormous progress that had been made by securing the Dey's acknowledgement that European captives should be treated as ordinary prisoners of war rather than as slaves, Brougham assailed the clauses which provided a ransom for the slaves already in bondage. It was no less than a scandal, he thought, that a great civilised country and the greatest maritime Power in the world should have tolerated for so long and should continue to tolerate the existence in one of the great highways of trade, of a nation of pirates. His speech had peculiarly gratifying results, and at the beginning of the session of 1817 the Government was able to insert a congratulatory reference to the British fleet's victory over the Barbary corsairs, who were at last annihilated.

Brougham had made these attacks on the Government's foreign policy mainly to please the Radicals out of doors; and with the same object in view he concentrated his attention on the army and navy estimates. No member of the Opposition complained more loudly and effectually of the ministry's extravagance and disregard of the national demand for retrenchment. He urged that four out of the seven Lords of the Admiralty could be dispensed with[16] in a speech which was censured as being an "unnecessary as well as a very illiberal tirade", he furiously denounced the policy of increasing the salaries of the Scottish Commissioners of Excise and Customs, and contrasted it with the promise to reduce establishments to the lowest possible figure;[17] and he even went so far as to object (though reluctantly) to the purchasing on behalf of the nation of the Elgin marbles.[18]

He came to regard his attack on the army estimates as his most successful speech of the session. He demanded the withdrawal of our garrisons from Gibraltar and Malta (since they were no longer needed to protect us against a defeated and humbled France), and our abandonment of our newly-acquired West Indian colonies and of the Ionian islands, which he said were rich only in patronage. His explanation of the Government's policy of retaining the West Indian sugar islands has a peculiarly modern flavour. He attributed it to the sinister influence of Liverpool capitalists who had there invested a vast amount of capital, and who had successfully threatened and bullied our Foreign Office. He criticised, too, our unprogressive and unconciliatory Irish policy, which still necessitated the employment of 25,000 bayonets to keep that country quiet. As many before him had done, he declared that force could never be a remedy for Irish discontent.[19]

If Brougham was attempting to win the applause of the Radicals by fulminating against the Government's foreign policy and by dilating on its reckless extravagance, he tried to conciliate the Whigs by voicing the grievances of the landed interest.

The agriculturists had been the first to feel the effects of that economic depression that was to hang over the country throughout the remaining years of George III.'s reign. During the war, foreign supplies of corn had been largely shut out from our seaports; home production had been stimulated to an unprecedented extent, though at a heavy cost. Bumper harvests in 1812, 1813, and 1814 were followed by a cessation of army contracts, and a great depression had set in. The banks began to stop credit advances and to demand the repayment of their loans. Landowners found their situation threatening; farmers were suffering from high rents; the labourers' wages were forced down even faster than the fall in the cost of living, and though the markets were glutted with surplus corn the poor could hardly afford to purchase it. The unparalleled situation was threatening of the people being starved in the midst of plenty. The Corn Law of 1815, passed by a Parliament of landlords, had not made things any the easier for the poor, since its object was to force up once more the price of corn in order to relieve the farmer and the landowner.

Brougham made his great speech on agricultural distress on April 9. After drawing a lurid picture of the prevailing misery, he proceeded to propound his remedial measures. He insisted on the absolute necessity of a further reduction of the national expenditure and a substantial remission of taxation. He desired to see removed some of the special burdens which the landed interest had to bear: tithes, poor-rates, and general taxes. The landowner, he pointed out, had to meet the expense of almost all the public works in the neighbourhood, such as roads, bridges, and churches. Contrary to the intention of the statute of 1601, the chief burden of the poor-rates had fallen on the land, since merchants and manufacturers had to contribute only in proportion to the value of their real property. Thus a factory owner with an income of £10,000 a year, being rated on his small property, would pay no more than a farmer who made £500 a year out of his holding.

Brougham saw that the whole Poor Law system needed remodelling. Workmen's wages were totally inadequate for their bodily maintenance, and the practice had grown up whereby wages were systematically supplemented by parish relief. England was fast becoming a pauperised nation. Two drastic reforms, said Brougham, were necessary. Some means should be found to equalise the burden of poor-rates. Assessments should be made, not on property but on income. And after a certain period, parish relief should not be given on behalf of children under age (a remedy which Malthus had suggested in his famous treatise on population), but it should be reserved for aged and infirm persons. Brougham's proposals, based on a Malthusian's view of society, were largely embodied in the Poor Law Amendment Act of 1834.

Brougham's greatest triumph in this year was undoubtedly his defeat of the income tax. On the first day of the session, Vansittart, the Chancellor of the Exchequer, announced that the Government proposed to continue the tax (which had been imposed originally only for the duration of the war) at the reduced rate of 5 per cent. When further pressed, he acknowledged that it would be renewed for either two or three years, with the possibility of its continuance for an indefinite period.

For many months the Whigs, with Brougham as leader, had been organising opposition from without. The fruits of a carefully prepared campaign began to appear in the second week of the session, when petitions against what was described as an iniquitous and burdensome imposition began to flow in from all parts of the country. The Government, alarmed at the unanimity of public feeling, tried to settle the question before the agitation reached its height, but their miserable attempt was frustrated by Brougham, who organised long-winded discussions in the House, and who threatened to hold up the entire business of Parliament by making use of the privileges of the House.

After some four hundred petitions had been presented, the critical division took place between twelve and one in the morning of March 19, when, to the wild delight of the Opposition, the income tax was rejected by a majority of thirty-seven.[20] Brougham had gained no such victory since his defeat of the Orders in Council.

He had rendered a great service to his party, but none to the country. It relieved the moneyed and propertied classes of an oppressive amount (£7,500,000) of taxation, but for the impoverished poor, whose soap, candles, salt, leather, and other necessaries of life went unrelieved, it did nothing. It failed also in its object of forcing the Ministers to adopt a real policy of retrenchment, for Castlereagh blandly announced that the difficulty would be met by having further recourse to the money market.

The unexpected[21] defeat of the Government on such an important question created an enormous sensation not only in England but also on the continent. On March 25 Sir Robert Wilson, then confined in the prison of La Force in Paris for encompassing the escape of Lavalette, a French political prisoner, informed Lord Grey that the triumph of the Opposition had made a great impression on French public opinion;[22] and in Paris it was thought that the Whigs would come in and perhaps set Napoleon at liberty to rekindle another world-war.[23] Had later constitutional practice been in vogue, Lord Liverpool would have at once resigned. But the Ministers clung tenaciously to their offices, and determined to fight to the last ditch.

For some time they had been voyaging in smooth waters, but storms were now threatening to send them all to the bottom. Realising that a more experienced and able pilot was needed on board the ministerial vessel, the Prime Minister had, a day or two before the disastrous division, made overtures to Canning, who was still at Lisbon acting as our Ambassador to the absent Portuguese court. In spite of the unpromising prospects, Canning, who had been informed of the Government's embarrassing situation, accepted the office of President of the Board of Control. The greater the dangers, he thought, the more might his reputation increase if he were successful in surmounting them.

The Whigs, now jubilant beyond measure, expected to come in at any moment, and began to make their preparations accordingly. A few days before the debate on March 18, Castlereagh had sent round an urgent Whip to all Government supporters, requesting their continued attendance until the division on the income tax had taken place. He put the matter forcibly and bluntly. It was not a matter, he said, whether the present Ministers were to carry on the Government, but whether they were willing to throw it into the hands of Mr. Brougham.[24]

On the morning of the 19th, Brougham, on his way down to the House of Commons, called on Francis Place at his house in Charing

Cross, intensely elated at his triumph. Brougham explained that he had just come from a meeting at Brooks's Club of his Whig friends, who had been discussing the arrangements for a Whig ministry, and who had deputed him to consult the head of the Westminster Radicals. Brougham accordingly unfolded to the astonished tailor a most extraordinary design. He expected, he said, to get hold of a copy of Castlereagh's circular letter which he would read in the House of Commons. Then he would create a profound sensation in Parliament and astonish the whole country by declaring boldly, "*I am willing to take the charge of this Government, to reform the Parliament, and to change the whole of the present ruinous system*"![15]

But when he reached the House, either his courage or the opportunity failed him, and his friends were denied the promised thrill. That he could ever, at this time, have entertained the preposterous idea of forming a ministry, shows to what lengths his vanity and exultation led him. His friends too were infected with the same madness. Place wrote:

> The Whigs herded only with themselves, saw nothing beyond their wishes, from which they repeatedly drew conclusions so perfectly absurd that, if related as they occurred and stated as simple facts, they would be incredible to those who did not witness them.[26]

Ironically enough, the Government was saved by the very efforts of its greatest enemy to overthrow it. Not for the last time were Brougham's indiscretion and rashness to prove fatal to the hopes and expectations of his exultant party. Two days after the victory over the income tax, during the debate on the salaries of the two Secretaries of the Admiralty, he made a scathing attack on the personal character of the Prince Regent. The Prince's conduct, and that of his advisers and friends, was declared to be worse than that of the Stuarts.

Far otherwise, said Brougham, must those be estimated
who entertained no scruples of religion, who experienced
no tenderness of conscience; who, in utter disregard of
the feelings of an oppressed and insulted nation, proceeded from one wasteful expenditure to another; who
decorated and crowded their houses with the splendid
results of their extravagance; who associated with the most
profligate of human beings; who, when the gaols were
filled with wretches, could not suspend for a moment
their thoughtless amusements, to end the sad suspense
between life and death; who, alone, or surrounded only
by an establishment of mercenaries, and unable to trust to
the attachment of the nation for their security, yet desired
the House of Commons to enable them to lavish on their
favourites the money extracted from the pockets of the
suffering people of England.[27]

In itself it was not a very unfair estimate of the Prince's character,
but, publicly given, at the moment, too, when the Whigs were expecting to storm the Treasury benches, it made a deplorable impression.
Brougham blew himself up with his own petard. That speech, said
Romilly, would not have been too strong to have described the latter
days of the Emperor Tiberius.[28] The staid and sober Ponsonby was
shocked, and Tierney appalled, by the indiscretion of the incalculable
lawyer. Lord Liverpool declared that the speech was little short of
treason.[29] Many of the old Whigs left the House without voting, and
some of the independent country gentlemen who had recently sided
with the Opposition went into the lobby with the Ministers, who, to
their surprise, found themselves in a majority of twenty-nine. Some
of the Whigs were exasperated the more, since they believed that the
Government would have resigned had it been left in a minority once
more. "Poor Brougham is loaded with the reproaches of his friends,"
wrote Romilly, "and many of them who are most impatient to get
into office look upon him as the only cause that they are still destined

to labour on in an unprofitable Opposition."[30] Whishaw, a friend of
Lord Holland, wrote:

> This unfortunate mistake has been the general subject of
> conversation ever since. It has revived the drooping spirits
> of the *Courier*, has operated as a most important diversion
> in favour of the Ministers, and has perhaps laid the seeds
> of a new schism in the party of the Opposition.[31]

Vexed at the unlooked-for results of his oratory, Brougham tried
to get the Opposition Press to defend him. The very day after the
delivery of the speech, he wrote to Leigh Hunt in explanation of his
conduct, and in expectation, no doubt, of seeing an apologia in the
next number of the *Examiner*:

> In addition to my party labours I am far from being
> well, and have a pressure of private business upon me
> at this moment. The approach of Easter gives me the
> certainty of seeing you, and I should hardly have trou-
> bled you now but for the interesting state of affairs and
> the opportunity which it has given me of speaking out
> my mind at length upon the scandalous and unfeeling
> profligacy of *the Court*. I did so last night in a way to
> give much pain I verily believe to many persons—to
> the objects of attack certainly—but I find also great dis-
> content among many of the Opposition, who, though
> they received every word I said with a full chorus of
> cheering, and though the cheers continued in peals for
> some moments after I sat down, yet discovered in half an
> hour that a few timid and trimming Tories whose votes
> they had reckoned upon, took fright and went away, or
> at least *gave* my attack on the Court as *their reason* for
> going. The offence of lessening our minority was thus
> imputed to me, and to hear them talk you'd think that I

had kept them out of place. I care not even if I had done so—and as for a few votes—much better let wholesome truths be told to Parliament through the Press (our grand and guardian power) to the people than have a dozen more of our adversaries now and then vote with us. What I spoke I spoke deliberately, and with the design of its exciting a sensation throughout the country, whether it pleased the party or not.

I thought it right to give you this explanation in case the sort of clamour now raised reaches you, that the concluding sentences of my speech spoilt the division—for be assured they who are the loudest *now* in saying so were the loudest in cheering that peroration in their places.[32]

Much to Brougham's satisfaction, the *Examiner* of March 24 contained a vigorous defence of his ill-timed speech. Commenting on the numbers of the division, the article proceeded:

We understand, however, that this majority is attributed by some persons in the House to the very striking and very uncourtly conclusion of Mr. Brougham's speech on the subject—a conclusion every way worthy of that gentleman, whether as the supplier of Mr. Whitbread's place, as a patriot, as an orator, as a thorough observer of the signs of the times, as a man of taste and spirit, moral and political. We know not whether the rumour is gravely received by anybody, or who the principal persons are that complain; but if they are the trimmers, saintly or unsaintly, who are thus terrified at the abuse of bad works, and took advantage of it to side with the Ministers, we only say that we look upon them as having done a good work without knowing it; and if they are the ordinary expectants of office, who think that nations have nothing to do but to watch the ins and the outs, like a boy looking at the alternate figures of a weather-house, they are most egregiously mistaken in their impatience.[33]

Brougham's successes and failures during these critical days are amusingly portrayed in a clever pasquinade originally inserted in the *Courier* on March 29 and reprinted later in that most entertaining volume, the *New Whig Guide*. Written possibly by Croker, the Secretary of the Admiralty, it was entitled:

Failure of the Buccaneers and Loss of the Broom Fire-ship
It is with the liveliest satisfaction that we announce to the public the failure of the above enterprise, and the total destruction of the *Broom* fire-ship, in an action in St. Stephen's Bay, during the night of Wednesday the 20th inst. This buccaneer expedition was destined for a *coup de main* against the royal arsenals in Treasury Harbour, which they intended to plunder and burn, if they could not keep permanent possession of them.

Up to the above-mentioned day the fleet had proceeded with apparent success, under the command of the *Ponsonby* flag-ship, an old hulk fitted up for the occasion; it consisted principally of the *Tierney* hired trader, the *Wynn*, armed *en flute*, the *Monck*, a north-country collier, the *Milton*, a heavy lugger, the *Curwen* tender,[34] the *Broom* fire-ship, the *Gordon* bum-boat, accompanied by some other *Callcraft*.[35]

On Monday, the 18th, they had gained a considerable advantage over a squadron of revenue cutters, led by the *Vansittart*, which they defeated in Property Roads, by the assistance of a fleet of *country ships*, whom they decoyed to their aid by hoisting false colours. The *Vansittart*, however, we are happy to say, was not much damaged by the action, and, though driven to the *Straights* for the moment, will soon be refitted in the London docks. This partial success seems to have emboldened the buccaneers, and in some degree to have hastened their defeat, by relaxing the discipline of the squadron. They began to disregard the signals of the *Ponsonby,* and many quarrels arose about the future distribution of their captured booty. On the evening of the 20th, as they were standing-on under easy sail, the *Methuen,* an empty vessel leading the way, the *Broom* fireship insisted upon running in to blow up Fort Regent; the *Ponsonby* flagship remonstrated against the attempt, alleging that they should only lose time by it; that the defences of Fort Regent were strong, and they were sure of being repulsed; that it would create an alarm, and raise the country people against them; and that it would be better to wait till they had got possession of Treasury Harbour, and then they might demolish Fort Regent at their leisure. The *Broom,* however, relying upon her store of combustibles, and particularly the quantity of brim-stone she had taken on board, disobeyed orders, and, setting all sail, stood right in upon Fort Regent, blazing away on all sides. It was soon observed, however, that her fire was ill-directed, and that more of her shot hit her friends than the Fort; and the rest of the fleet therefore hauled off, and stood aloof from her, contenting themselves with cheering her as she bore down in her attack.

The mistake made by the *Broom* now became manifest: a tremendous cannonade was opened upon her; she tried to *manœuvre* to get out again, but failed; she missed stays, and mismanaged her *royals,* and she was soon so dreadfully cut up that she lay like a log upon the water. At this time a fresh fire was opened upon her flank by the Martello tower on the banks, supported by a detachment from the *Saintes,* and this completely silenced her.

The night was now so far advanced as to put an end to the engagement. The *Broom* was now seen *lying* in a pitiable condition. Her friends, however, determined to make an attempt to get her off, and about five in the afternoon, the *Ponsonby* sheer-hulk and the *Gordon* bumboat came down into St. Stephen's Bay, in order to try to tow her out. The *Broom,* however, would not answer the helm, was found quite unmanageable, and although she seemed to float for a moment, yet a well-directed fire, which was instantly poured into her from Castle-Ray, laid her upon her beam ends again.

What is now to become of her we have no means of guessing; whether they will attempt to get her under way with a *jury* rigging, or appropriate her to the *press*, we know not. It seems certain that all the captains of the other ships would object to her ever being again brought forward into the line of battle.

Brougham's onslaught did not find favour with the Whigs, but it delighted the Westminster Radicals. On March 23 Place wrote him an exhortatory letter of approval:

I can hold my tongue no longer, but must congratulate you on your manly English speech; my admiration alone would not however have caused me to trouble you with uncalled-for advice, but when you are in everybody's mouth, when all minds are employed upon you, I must tell you what passes, and advise you also.

My shop is in some degree a centre of communication, where all manner of persons bring all kinds of information, and where every one talks as he pleases. Those who really love their country expect to see you in the exalted station to which their hopes have raised you, and treat with scorn the insinuations and assertions of those whom the obsequious practice of late days and a hatred of liberty have caused them to utter. While some see your efforts producing symptoms of a return to the good old-fashioned language of better times, others would sacrifice you to their slavish fears and affect to wonder that you are not a prisoner in the Tower.

You, I hope, are not made for mediocrity—you have indeed stepped out, and taken the lead from those who cannot but envy and must soon hate you; you have placed yourself full in the front of the people; you have made yourself a distinguished and marked object to them. To you mediocrity cannot now belong; above it or below it you must be placed, either the great, the leading man, or nothing. You have in fact placed yourself in the most arduous of situations, assailed by friends and foes, by friends who hope for you, who fear for you—by enemies who dread you and hate you. . . . None but a strong-minded man, none but a man possessing vast powers could have possessed himself as you have done of the ear of the whole people of England; none but the best constituted mind can keep that possession, none but a man who is eminently useful can long retain it, none other deserves it.

Your enemies, the enemies of England, are calculating on your retrograding, as they call it, into the gentleman; do it, and they will be the first to bowl against you for having done it. Persevere, I beseech you, for this disgraced and too servile people, in whom, however, still resides the latent spirit and love of liberty which, in trying times and on many great emergencies, has brought them through with honour. Show them that if liberty sleeps she is not dead—and depend upon their assistance to awaken her. . . .[36]

Brougham replied the same day:

Many thanks for your kind and encouraging counsels. In some respects, I doubt not, the conduct of our parliamentary friends has been exaggerated to you. . . . Be assured of one thing. I shall hold my course firmly, happen what may, and all I expect or wish for is, that if I should be deserted in the House of Commons, I may be at all events supported in the country. This will rally our friends in the House, and at any rate will keep our enemies in check.[37]

The bitter reproaches levelled at Brougham by the Whigs were, indeed, largely undeserved. The Ministers were hardly more firmly seated on the Treasury bench after his outburst on March 20 than they were before. In spite of their majority of twenty-nine on that occasion, they found it expedient to give up the contemplated addition of £1000 to Croker's salary, as a sop to the country gentlemen, who were resenting Castlereagh's impertinent complaint of the people's "ignorant impatience of taxation". They also abandoned the war malt tax, thus sacrificing £2,700,000 of revenue. On the 21st the Prime Minister informed the Regent that the Government was hanging by a thread, and that every measure of conciliation had failed to strengthen his hands.[38] Two days later he wrote to the Earl of Lonsdale and the Duke of Rutland, complaining of the luke-warmness of their nominees' support. He spoke of the

impossibility of the present Government going on unless they are more steadily and cordially supported by their friends than appears to have been the case on some recent occasions. To myself personally I can assure you it is a matter of very little consequence whether I continue to hold the situation in which circumstances have placed me. But I feel that I have a duty to the Prince Regent, to the party to which on principle I have always been attached, and to the country in general, not to give up the Government without a struggle. I cannot, however, conceal from you the success of that struggle, and even the possibility of retaining the Government with any credit, depend in the present temper of the times upon the regular attendance and support of our friends in the House of Commons. . . . At a moment when we are exposed to the most acrimonious, systematic, and persevering Opposition that I ever recollect to have seen in Parliament, it is right that the consequences to which these proceedings may lead should not be withheld from you.[39]

Two days later (March 25) the Government again had to fight for its life. The Opposition had decided to throw out the navy estimates, and Tierney, having prepared a strong and apparently overwhelming case for their rejection, was confident of success. But the Ministers were saved by a brilliantly argued speech from Croker, and the Opposition spokesman was left utterly confounded.[40] The Tories went mad with joy at the total overthrow of the enemy. Commenting on this critical debate the *Courier* declared:

Defeat and dismay were immediately visible in the countenances of the party. They had actually intended to proceed to a division; they had made every effort to procure an attendance; all Sunday was passed in confident anticipations of triumph; St. James's Street, Pall Mall, and Brooks's were in an uproar. If any one met them and began either an indignant remark against Mr. Brougham for his atrocious attack on the Sovereign, or a condolence upon the body-blow which his intemperance had dealt to the hopes of the party, they immediately stopped him. "Wait till to-morrow—hear Mr. Tierney on the Navy estimates! He has been at it all night in his study, and at this moment he is walking up Highgate Hill to get himself in wind!"

The year 1816 closed with the Tory Government still in power, and with both of Brougham's aspirations unrealised. To neither the Whig chiefs nor to the rank and file had he proved acceptable as a possible party leader in the House of Commons; and his hopes, too, from the Westminster Radicals had been woefully disappointed. In attempting to satisfy two parties, he had failed to win the confidence of either.

From the very beginning the reformers had been divided on the question of a successor to Lord Cochrane. Whilst Place and most of the members of the Westminster Committee (which Cobbett denounced as the 'Rump') favoured Brougham, another section of the Radical movement distrusted him as a shuffling Whig lawyer out of place, an adventurer angling for office and popularity. Cobbett, who was now of this way of thinking, employed his *Weekly Register* to destroy the pretensions of the impostor, and to glorify old Major Cartwright, who if not brilliant was at any rate sound and trustworthy.

On several occasions during the session Brougham had disappointed his Radical friends. The Westminster Committee had arranged for him to speak on February 23 at a meeting in Palace Yard, convened to protest against the renewal of the income-tax. They regarded the occasion as important, presenting as it did an opportunity of bringing Brougham to the notice of the electors. But when 'Orator' Hunt began to interfere and made a blustering speech in the course of which he denounced the Whigs as anti-reformers and sinecurists, Brougham and his friends at once left the platform in high dudgeon, instead of staying to punish the swaggering and bullying demagogue.

No sooner had he retrieved his error in Palace Yard by his outspoken attack on the Prince Regent on March 20 than he again blundered most lamentably. Cobbett thought that the occasion of the ninth anniversary dinner of the Westminster electors, to be held to celebrate the election of Burdett in 1807, would serve admirably to destroy once and for all the 'Rump's' attempt to foist Brougham on the electors.

Upon being shown the list of toasts a few days before the event, he discovered that Brougham's name was placed immediately after those of the two members, whilst Cartwright's was nearly the last. Cobbett at once threatened to make a scene at the dinner unless the order was changed. Brougham had accepted the invitation, but had left instructions that he should be informed if Hunt put in an appearance. Hunt arrived; Brougham, who was at the House of Commons, was immediately informed, and half an hour later he sent his apologies to the chairman.

> I have been in constant expectation of getting away to the dinner [speciously explained in his note], but it has proved to be impracticable—from Romilly's motion in behalf of the persecuted Protestants in France. It is part coming on, and I am extremely anxious about it. I need not add how much I regret being thus detained from join-ing our friends in the celebration of a triumph which I really consider as the most important to the interests of the Constitution of any that has ever been gained under the present law of election.[41]

Nor were these his only blunders. The Radicals abused him for his support of the corn law, and for siding with the Tory 'Oligarchy' on the question of transporting Buonaparte to St. Helena, whereas the Whigs maintained its illegality.[42] The lynx-eyed Cobbett, too, pointed out that Brougham was ratting on the reform question; and, indeed, his statement on May 8, that "With one or two exceptions, our Constitution was never in a better state than now, except in one or two instances, in which it was best to try to remove its blemishes", was singularly out of harmony with his recent declaration in favour of annual parliaments and suffrage co-extensive with taxation.[43]

His popularity out of doors was even more seriously affected by his support of an annual allowance of £60,000 to the Prince Regent's daughter, the Princess Charlotte. Whilst Brougham declared that no man dissented from the grant, Place asserted that "Scarcely a man who was likely to have voted with him thought that a single shilling should either have been given to her, or added to her then enormous income. . . ."[44]

Sublimely unconscious of the tense feeling which his time-serving conduct had excited, Brougham was as sanguine at the close of the session as he had been at its beginning. The disillusionment was not long in coming. Place had at last discovered that Brougham would not do. The Whigs continued to think that they would soon be in office, and so long as Brougham could count on a high place in the Government he would never throw himself unreservedly into the arms of the Radicals.

At the end of September he wrote to his friend Bennet from Milan, requesting him to make inquiries as to the possibility of a dissolution of Parliament. Bennet at once wrote to Place and asked whether Brougham would be acceptable as a Radical candidate for Westminster in the event of a General Election. On October 12, Place replied to Bennet's letter of the 7th and informed him that Brougham's "absurd conduct in the last session" had totally disqualified him.

> I spoke of Burdett and Cochrane as I then thought, and as I still think, accurately and truly [wrote Place in his narrative history of Westminster politics]. I said, "Burdett must be one of the members for Westminster, and Cochrane must be the other". I showed how Brougham from his want of courage in some particulars lost ground in the House; I said, "I regretted that Cochrane should be the member for Westminster, and the more so as it is Brougham's own fault that has prevented his being returned free from all expense with Burdett. At the last general election in 1812 an offer was made to Mr. Fawkes, who declined it. It was then made to Mr. Roscoe, who also declined, and no choice being left, Cochrane was taken. Subsequently, circumstances made a fine opening for Brougham, and

it was both hoped and expected that he would prove he was the proper person. Advances were made to him, and some pains were taken to ascertain if he could be relied upon to maintain the right of the people to annual Parliaments and suffrage as extensive as direct taxation. This having been ascertained,[45] yet not in quite so open and satisfactory a manner as it was desirable it should have been, it became necessary that he should be made known to the electors, that they might have an opportunity to decide for themselves, without which no reasonable man can hope to be chosen by them. . . . It is . . . evident that to a body of people who do their own business the person to be elected must be made familiar, he must see and be seen by them on all proper occasions, he must speak to them, that they may judge him, and he must convince them, as well by his actions as his words, that he will maintain the principles they espouse, and that he has NO RESERVE. Brougham did none of these things; several good opportunities were offered him to mix in a proper manner with the electors; he availed himself of none of them; he stood in a doubtful point of view, on account of his being a lawyer. . . . The electors suppose his object is to obtain the Seals under the Princess if she should become Queen, and they say they will not be made a stepping-stone for him to mount. They say if Brougham is looking to the Court for preferment he has been consistent, but then he ought not to expect to be taken up by the people."[46]

1.   *Creevey Papers*, i. 192; Add. MS. 38108, fol. 137.

2.   *Ibid.*, i. 193.

3.   *Ibid.*, i. 248.

4. Add. MS. 38108, fol. 148.

5. Add. MS. 27809, fol. 26.

6. Add.MS. 35152, fol. 158.

7. *Ibid.* fol. 158.

8. *Ibid.* fol. 163.

9. *Creevey Papers*; i. 248.

10. The reference is to Place's disapproval of Brougham's views on the income tax.

11. Add. MS. 35152, fol. 166.

12. Informations for libel are of two kinds: (i) those filed partly at the suit of the Crown and partly at that of the subject; (ii) those filed only in the name of the Crown. These latter are also of two kinds: (a) those which are truly and properly the sovereign's own suits, and filed ex-officio by his own immediate officer, the Attorney-General; (b) those in which the prosecutor is really a private person, though nominally the Crown. (Blackstone's Commentaries, iv. 325, 1876 ed.)

13. *Parl. Deb.* xxxiv. 378.

14. *Ibid.* xxxii. 402.

15. *Ibid.* xxxii. 613.

16. *Ibid.* xxxii. 400.

17. *Ibid.* xxxii. 624.

18. *Ibid.* xxxii. 827.

19. *Ibid.* xxxii. 399.

20 *Ibid.* xxxiii. 451.

21. Romilly, *Memoirs*, iii. 236; *The 'Pope' of Holland House*, p. 146.

22. Add. MS. 30121, fol. 61.

23. Ward, *Letters*, p.136.

24. Add. MS. 27850, fol. 288.

25. *Ibid.*

26. Add. MS. 27809, fol. 27.

27. *Part. Deb.* xxxiii. 497.

28. Romilly, *Memoirs*, iii. 236.

29. Yonge, *Life of Lord Liverpool*, ii. 270.

30. Romilly, *Memoirs*, iii. 237.

31. *The 'Pope' of Holland House*, p.149.

32. Add. MS. 38108, fol. 161.

33. *The Examiner*, March 24, 1816. A week later Brougham's obliging friends returned to the subject in another editorial article.

34. An allusion to Curwen's importunate gallantry.

35. Author's note: This is a mistake of our correspondent; it should obviously be *small*-craft. Mr. Calcraft had now rejoined the Opposition.

36. Add. MS. 37949, fol. 37. By 1829 Place had changed his opinion of the merits of Brougham's speech: "It does by no means appear to deserve the praise I bestowed on it, nor scarcely any praise at all, so much do our feelings when excited and countenanced by those with whom we associate mislead our judgements and benumb our understandings. It now seems matter of surprise that I should have written such a letter, which had so totally escaped my recollection that if told I had done so I should have doubted it if not denied it until it had been shown to me. I still, however, think I did right in encouraging Brougham, but wrong in the description I gave of the value of the speech." (Add. MS. 27809, fol. 14.)

37. Add. MS. 37949, fol. 38.

38. Yonge, ii. 270.

39. Add. MS. 38262, fol. 323.

40. *Croker Papers*, i. 79; Hatherton MS., Diary, May 11, 1855.

41. Add. MS. 27540, fol. 277; Cobbett, *Register*, Jan. 3, 1818.

42. *Ibid.* 27809, fol. 30; Cobbett, *Register*, June 1, 1816.

43. *Parl. Deb.* xxxiv. 378; Cobbett, *Register*, June 1, 1816.

44. Add. MS. 27809, fol. 30.

45. In June 1814. See p.56, above.

46. Transcribing his letter to Bennet in later years, he wrote: "This letter contains what I then thought, or knew, was the opinion of the electors of Westminster, the true situation in which Mr. Brougham stood in respect to them, and my own opinions on the matters mentioned. I see no reason to conclude there was any mistake of any kind.—December 1829." (Add, MS. 27809, fol. 31.)

V

The Question of Leadership

THE CHOICE OF A LEADER

In conclave assembled, and patriots they,
All eager to rule and all loth to obey,
Yet doom'd to endeavour to settle together
On whom fails the choice of the Party's bell-wether.
. . . . . .

Sir G— T— arose in his elegant way,
And seem'd to be seeking for something to say,
When B—m, disregarding the Baronet's throes,
Presented to notice his elegant nose,
(We speak with respect of that *organum nobile*,
The happy approach to *perpetuum mobile*).
"I think," quoth the lawyer, "'tis needless to mention
What all of you know, my uncommon pretension.
Ye mark, that from first to the last of a session,
To talk is my trade—let us call it profession:
I'm loud and I'm long, and it need not he told
That I hammer the hot and I hammer the cold;

With great and with small that I equally deal,
And deem ev'ry topic a spoke for my wheel;
In *leading* besides I have ventur'd to dabble,
The London reformers, the Liverpool rabble,
The Palace-yard mob (though it was an affront
To be hiss'd and dismiss'd for a fellow like Hunt);
Make ME then your leader to thump and to thunder,
A pilot most excellent, bar a big blunder."—
Some grinn'd, shook their heads, while a spreading catarrh
O'erpower'd the lungs of the Man at the Bar.

The Morning Post, Feb. 6, 1818

AFTER the prorogation of Parliament in July 1816 Brougham set out for the continent to recruit his health, which his strenuous activities had somewhat impaired. Combining business with pleasure, he found time to take the waters of Aix, in Savoy, to study in Switzerland Pestalozzi's new educational system, and to enjoy the society of Italian savants. On August 24 he was at Geneva, writing to Lady Byron about her husband, who, he said, was living in the neighbourhood, avoided by his countrymen and associating with practically nobody at all.[1] In October Lord Lansdowne found him at Florence "very full of English politics, but apparently very indifferent to English law, for he spends his term at Rome, and only talks of returning after Christmas".[2]

Brougham was as firmly convinced as ever that the Government was shivering on the brink of dissolution. According to Place, he spent part of his time abroad in collecting information which, when disclosed in the House of Commons, would occasion the immediate resignation of the Ministers:

> I heard from several of his friends their, and his, notions at the display he was to make when the Parliament met again. The expectation, the exultation, was enormous; the contempt with which everything not in accordance with the notions of the clique at Brooks's was . . . perfectly ridiculous.[3]

This view of the state of Whig feeling is confirmed by their correspondence. Most of the politicians who frequented Holland House were eagerly anticipating a change; and Lady Holland herself told the Duke of Bedford that a Whig Cabinet ought to be prepared in advance. Sir Robert Wilson informed Grey that even Tierney, least optimistic of party leaders, was convinced that if there was a good attendance of the Opposition, the Ministers must be defeated. On January 7, Wilson, who, like Brougham, was somewhat apt to see things through rose-coloured spectacles, wrote to prepare his chief for a summons to form a Government:

> The quarterly deficit is a thunderbolt to the Ministers. They did not expect such a diminution, and I should not be surprised if they gave up before the meeting of Parliament. All their own friends anticipate their expulsion if they attempt to remain; and I assure you that the public attention and hope are fixed upon you.[4]

Brougham had not altered his opinion that the Whigs were on the point of coming in, but he had, before his return to England, effected another startling political gyration. In September 1816 he had written to James Mill that he was being received with open arms by the Italian *literati*, who believed that he had put himself at the head of the republican party in England.[5] In October he received the news of his being cast off by the Westminster reformers. The intelligence at once caused him to decide to eschew Radicalism for ever. He would strain every nerve to retrieve the errors of 1816 and ingratiate himself with the Whigs in order to secure the leadership of the party. Henceforward he should find political salvation within the fold of Whiggism. This metamorphosis was made easy because of the alarming aspect which the movement for radical reform had assumed in Great Britain.

Throughout the year 1816 economic distress amongst the wage-earning masses had been steadily increasing. The discontent bred by poverty and want found political expression in demands for a sweeping reform of a borough-mongering parliament that artificially kept up the price of the people's food, and whose sinecures maintained in comfort a small army of idlers. Radicalism, inspired by Horne Tooke, Bentham, and Burdett, had hitherto been a middle-class movement, but in 1816 it was seized upon by the working-classes, amongst whom the growth of a political consciousness marked the introduction of a new and important feature into English politics. Their leaders were 'demagogue' Hunt, the most daring and successful mob orator of the day, and Cobbett, whose vigorous and eloquent writing in his *Weekly Political Register* exerted an enormous influence throughout the country. The agitation was stimulated too by the venerable Major Cartwright, who went on another crusading tour through Great Britain, preaching the gospel of reform, delivering lectures, organising meetings, and preparing petitions to Parliament. The movement also contained extremists like Thistlewood, who were prepared to use physical force to attain their ends.

The Whigs, who still remained in theory the party of reform, looked with extreme disfavour upon this working-class agitation. During the war period they had tacitly abandoned their advocacy of reform, and had made no effort since to re-inscribe it on the party banner. They now professed to believe that the question was merely of secondary importance, and that the country's prosperity could be restored merely by a change of ministry, the cutting down of the army and navy estimates, and the abolition of some sinecures. They were not prepared to take up parliamentary reform until the 'people' loudly demanded it, and by the 'people' they meant, not the masses, but the middle-class and the property owners. Grey and Holland steadily resisted the importunity of the more progressive Whigs who vainly urged that reform, like Catholic emancipation, should be definitely made a party question. Tierney characteristically declared that, since the small shopkeepers had become reformers, the principle had better be recognised by the party, but that there was "no need for any development of plan".[6]

It was clear that the people could expect nothing from their rulers. The Tories could not even hold out hopes of a lasting peace, and were considering the possibility of their being once again involved in a continental war. Though Wellington had privately declared that the only means of preserving peace in Europe lay in universal disarmament,[7] Lord Liverpool, the Prime Minister, scouted the idea of reducing expenditure (a sore point with the Radicals) by recalling, in order to disband, the English army of occupation in France, his line of argument being that the safety of the French monarchy depended absolutely on the presence in Paris of British bayonets, and that a second overthrow of the restored Bourbons would bring about another European war. In his opinion retrenchment and economic reform were either futile or impossible. Smitten with the current Malthusianism, he believed that the Government could do little or nothing to diminish the crying evils of pauperism and unemployment, since they were occasioned by an excessive population, which emigration alone could reduce.[8] Thus, since Ministers were not responsible for the poverty and misery of the people, and could not lighten their burdens, he regarded criticism from the Opposition as not only factious but disloyal. In view of the danger of a great social upheaval, he relied on the patriotism and generosity of the Whigs to refrain from attacking the Ministry and forcing it to capitulate. And so 'the rally round the throne', and the closing up of Whig and Tory ranks against the anti-social demands of the Radicals were, as Wilson pointed out, "to be the watchword for the oblivion of the past and a new impulse to the Pitt policy".[9]

The Radical agitation in the country was for the time being ruined by the violence of the extremists. The aristocratic Radicals in Parliament discountenanced the movement, and Burdettites, Whigs, and Tories were almost unanimous in condemning the conduct of the agitators, though both sections of the Opposition denounced with equal vigour the Government's measures to suppress the Radical movement. Brougham informed Lansdowne, who in February 1817 was still in Italy, that the Opposition was united both against the Executive on the one hand and the mob on the other, and that the "mountains were becoming valleys".

> All differences among our friends are removed, and we are firmly united on almost every point (I mean even in the House of Commons), at once fighting against the Crown and putting down the pernicious and insane rabble, equally the enemies of us and of the people. Even Burdett has become moderate and reasonable, has met Lord Grey and gone to Lord Holland's in the evening. Lord Thanet brought this to bear ultimately, but I have had full explanations with Burdett and find him disposed to all fair and moderate conduct. Whether anything can come of this beyond the mere convenience of the present moment is another question, but it is very useful in weaning the people, or rather part of them, from those pernicious persons who have been misguiding them; and above all it is singularly useful in putting down the cry of alarm sounded by the Government for party purposes.[10]

The Radical agitation culminated in the Spa Fields riot (December 1816) and the 'Pop-gun plot' (February 1817), when the Regent was attacked in his coach after having opened Parliament. The Ministers, alarmed at the growing symptoms of unrest both in London and the provinces, appointed a secret committee in both Houses to examine the evidence upon which their fears were founded. The committees' reports were speedily followed by the introduction of Bills to suspend the Habeas Corpus Act and to restrict the freedom of public meetings.

This unlooked-for series of events played havoc with the Opposition's plans, and destroyed all their hopes of turning out the Government. "Nobody now . . . thinks of such a thing," Brougham was forced to confess on February 8.[11] The introduction into Parliament of the new coercion Bills had another far-reaching result: it finally wrecked the union of the Grenville and Foxite section of the Opposition, and split the Whig party in twain. The Grenvillites, true to their traditions, voted solidly for repression, whilst the main body of the party, under the leadership of Grey, strenuously opposed both the Suspension Bill and the Seditious Meetings Bill. Having now severed his connection with Radicalism and all its works, Brougham spoke of the Grenvillite secession with genuine regret:

> It would be a great pity if the Grenvilles left us, but it looks almost inevitable. . . . My notion is that we should avoid all separation to the very last moment, and even then let it be only temporary and on those points which can't be got over.[12]

The Whigs spoke strongly against the Government's repressive legislation, but at the same time let slip no opportunity of dissociating themselves from the reform movement out-of-doors, although they were prepared to turn it to their own advantage and to make party capital therefrom. Brougham wrote to Lansdowne (February 8):

> We intend to fight every point in detail, availing our-selves of the thousand petitions as if they were generally on grievance and distress, though they call for reform as well as retrenchment. For these operations the ground is laid, and we have begun with notices of all manner of good motions, papers, etc. etc. We are provided with a great artillery and ammunition for firing into their jobs, a number of which have come to our knowledge, and I purpose speedily to attack Castlereagh's whole foreign affairs, his absence the first night having prevented me.[13]

Since the beginning of the Radical agitation Brougham had not only assumed the unpretentious mantle of an extremely moderate reformer, but denounced, with all the violence and rancour of an apostate, those who advocated the very reforms which he had demanded only two and a half years before. His animosity was directed particularly against Cochrane, his old rival, who was now the only man in Parliament who dared to support the Radical programme and to meet the combined fire of Whigs and Tories. Place and the Radicals, furious at Brougham's unmeasured denunciations, determined that his conduct should not go unchallenged. They attacked him in their own press, and taunted him with having forsaken Radicalism because his expectations of being returned for Westminster had not been fulfilled. Brougham renewed his onslaught with redoubled vigour in a speech which won for him the plaudits of the Tory newspapers, the *Courier* in particular praising him up to the skies. Place replied by sending a copy of Brougham's Radical speech of June 1814 to Hone to be published in a special number of the *Register*, and by giving the original manuscript to Cochrane, who promised to read it in Parliament. Cochrane did so on February 17. Brougham made a shuffling reply, declared that they were much mistaken who imagined that "the mere production of a speech delivered by him at a tavern would make him swerve from the line of duty, merely from the foolish and childish desire of keeping up an appearance of consistency"; and he warmly repudiated the insinuation that he could prostitute himself at one time "to deliver opinions which were not the sentiments of his heart, for the purpose of being carried into the House on the shoulders of a rabble, and at another time to bend to prejudices he might have to contend with in the House".[14]

There can be no doubt that this exposure diminished enormously his popularity out-of-doors, though the stiffening of his attitude towards reform was calculated to find him favour with most of the Whigs. Curwen, a Whig and a personal friend, declared that Brougham had "destroyed himself", and that his conduct was "very bad". Place, who came into daily contact with a considerable number of politicians of various shades of opinion, reported "a general disgust against Brougham".[15] In his political narrative he wrote:

Should the [Whig] party ever succeed in ousting the administration and placing themselves in power, the reformers would be quite as obnoxious to them as they have been to their opponents, and it was therefore necessary to the Whigs in their view of the case wholly to disencumber themselves of all connection with the reformers, and this they did very effectually, without obtaining any one of their objects. Brougham, always short-sighted and ill-judging, always deciding himself and missing his points, yet never convinced, but continually blundering on, assumed to himself the bad pre-eminence of leading his equally ill-judging, unprincipled party to an extent which, being taken advantage of by Castlereagh and his colleagues, led to consequences in the passing of bad laws and the provocation of outrages by the people, and by Ministers against the people which, but for the infamous conduct of the Whigs, could not have taken place to the extent they did, nor have been carried on as this conduct of the Whigs caused them to be carried on.[16]

Thus were rudely shattered Place's hopeful anticipations of a useful change of system to be accomplished by a union of Radicals and Progressive Whigs with Brougham at their head. Reactionary Toryism remained in the ascendant because of the disunion, both in Parliament and in the country, of the two wings of the progressive movement.

The agitation for reform by the doctrinaires out-of-doors had resulted in the suspension of the laws of the land, in the unpopularity and impotence of the parliamentary Opposition, and in the triumph of the high Tories. With the whole question of parliamentary reform the Whigs were now completely out of humour. In the days of Pitt's ascendancy and of Whig tribulation, it had been one of the main planks in the platform of Fox and Grey. Since it had been abandoned, the party had felt badly in need of a new programme. The Whigs had always stood for Catholic emancipation, but in 1817 the times were very unpropitious for its successful canvass. Brougham, however, ever fertile in ideas, undertook on his own initiative to fill the gap. On March 13 he made a great speech on the subject of trade depression, which was intended as an attempt to convert his party to a moderate free trade policy. It met with the whole hearted approval of Lord Grey, who also felt the necessity of weaning the opinion of the country from reform, and of striking out boldly on lines hitherto neglected.

After producing a mass of statistics which showed the seriousness of the economic situation, Brougham proceeded to put the responsibility for the stagnation of trade on to the Government. The difficulties of the manufacturers, he argued, were increased by the heavy burden of taxation imposed to keep up our bloated military and civil establishments. And, he maintained, our foreign policy had not been conducted with a view to securing those commercial advantages which our influence abroad entitled us to expect. Our late allies, whom we had saved from destruction, had rewarded us by imposing fresh protective barriers against our traders.

His panacea for industrial stagnation was a revision of our commercial system on free trade lines. He advocated drastic reductions of duty upon imported goods. But whilst he urged the destruction of State interference in a "vast, complicated, and delicate commercial system"; whilst he demanded the repeal of the obsolete navigation laws, and the repeal of laws (passed in the interests of English iron-masters and English shipping companies) which imposed prohibitive duties upon imported Scandinavian ore and timber, Brougham, in deference to the Whig landed aristocracy, declined to extend his free trade principles to agriculture. He still supported the protective corn law of 1815:

> To the opinion which I originally entertained upon that law I still adhere. I feel now, as I did then, that its first effects are injurious, by cutting off a great article of foreign trade, but I look for an ample compensation of that injury in advantages of a higher nature; the ensuring a regular, a safe, and ultimately a cheap supply of the great necessary

of life, which no change of foreign policy, no caprice of
hostile governments can impede or disturb.

Brougham's impetuosity, however, got the better of his prudence,
and he could not resist the temptation of making a violent personal
attack on Castlereagh. The introduction into his speech of purely
party matters ruined all chance of effecting any change in our commercial system. Robinson (afterwards Lord Goderich), the President
of the Board of Trade, admitted the soundness of his arguments, but
Brougham's invectives had transformed the character of his motion,
which was defeated by a large majority. Embittered by his failure (for
which, indeed, he himself was responsible) he decided that he would
never again bring the subject forward.

At the beginning of July Ponsonby, the titular leader of the
Opposition, fell ill and died. The measure of his achievement is
to be gauged from the fact that the Tories genuinely regretted his
passing. There was not enough venom in him for the times, declared
Wilson, adding, "The devil himself is wanted to confront Castlereagh
and Co." Ponsonby's death afforded an opportunity of estimating
Brougham's success in winning the confidence of the Whigs. He had
begun the session well, and Whishaw, who spoke the sentiments of
Holland House, declared that he had risen much in the opinion of the
Commons.[17] But his intemperate conduct on several occasions during
the rest of the session completely effaced the favourable impressions
the Whigs had formed. On March 6 Whishaw wrote, somewhat
doubtfully: "Brougham, it is true, constantly attends and will become
by degrees the practical leader of the party. But this for some time will
be a great source of weakness, for many of them will not act cordially
under such a leader."

Brougham himself, realising that his own chances were nil, desired
that the Opposition should henceforth do without a leader altogether, unless, indeed, a man of straw like Lord George Cavendish
could be persuaded to act as a figure-head. He wrote to Lord Holland
(August 1):

You must have been shocked at poor Ponsonby's death, and of course you have heard all manner of stories and speculations as to a leader. Really to hear people talk, one would think first that it was a place in the gift of some body, and next, that it was a place of profit or at least pleasure; but at any rate you'd never doubt that there was some such thing as leader, whatever it might be. Yet nothing is more certain than that for some time past there has been no such thing and that for the present there can be none. And much better at once to have none than to have a nominal leader who was always committing us and who was just leader enough for that purpose. We shall now be a far more formidable Opposition, and on great questions where numbers signify, shall divide just as strong. The party will rally for the occasion round whoever brings forward a motion that deserves support. Romilly agrees entirely in this view with me, and those who talked so glibly of leaders never said a word to either of us. . . . But it is all settled now as it should be, unless some arrangement could be made with Lord George Cavendish, which would really be excellent if it began and ended in Burlington House; but I fear he won't agree to bestir himself and open his doors.[18]

Brougham alone was responsible for all the difficulties and embarrassment that attended the choice of a successor, for every one recognised that he would in any case continue to be the effective leader. At the very end of the session he had rashly thrown away the last of his chances, by his speech on the state of the nation. On that occasion (July 11) he surveyed in great detail the proceedings of Parliament during the year, and recapitulated all the Government's misdeeds. The House, he said, had answered the people's anxious expectations of redress and relief by taking away their liberties. "When at last we did inquire into their distresses," he complained bitterly, "and found that many means of relieving them were practicable; when Ministers themselves agreed that our system of commerce and trade required revision, we immediately passed to the other orders of the day." In the address to the Prince Regent with which he concluded, he set forth at full length the imbecility of the Government's financial, commercial, foreign, and social policy. The speech, which the *Examiner* characterised as "One of the most useful, proper, and constitutional speeches that has been heard in that House since the days of opposition to Sir Robert Walpole", contained another personal attack on Castlereagh, whose Irish administration was criticised in most bitter and unrestrained language. The Foreign Secretary repelled the insinuations in an equally inflammable outburst, which Brougham, much to the regret of some of his friends, allowed to pass unnoticed. Sir Robert Wilson wrote to Grey on July 18:

> There is a great attempt made by the Tory press to cry down Brougham as a Jacobin—a true *bonnet rouge*—and amongst his own party there are many who think him too patient of insult, so that he is likely to be damaged between both fires. I never mentioned before, the last feeling on the subject, because I am unwilling to circulate or extend such scandal, but I hear it so frequently noticed that I cannot help expressing regret Brougham displayed so much Stoic philosophy on the occasion, and permitted Castlereagh to carry away the trophies of a successful bully. I am sure Brougham restrained himself from deference to the interests or presumed policy of the Whig *modérés*, but he could have done himself and party more good by tossing back the outrage into the throat of the calumniator, and presenting muzzle to muzzle. An ungenerous enemy should never be allowed to profit by the slightest forbearance, and if he is permitted by the Speaker to leap into the arena as a gladiator, his accuser must not shrink from the grapple. I abhor the character of a duellist, but sometimes there are ruffians who must be encountered with their own system.[19]

The moderation of which Wilson complained availed Brougham nothing; his claims were passed over, and Tierney was temporarily adopted Leader in the Commons. Overwhelmed in mind by this new blasting of his dearly-cherished hopes, Brougham wrote bitterly to Lansdowne complaining of the shabby treatment he had received at the hands of the Whigs. His letter of July 21 throws so much light on his position in the party that we quote it *in extenso*:

> Where circumstances occur, out of which mis-understandings are likely to arise [he began], it is a better course to come at once to a frank explanation than to wait until the misunderstanding has actually arisen. Now, I greatly deceive myself, if such circumstances do not already exist among our friends, and I am sure it is better to talk the matter over immediately than to wait till the opening of next session.

The office-seeking politicians of the party strongly disapproved his policy of unsparing and unceasing attack on the ministry, and declared that he and a few other violent ones were alone responsible for keeping the Whigs in opposition:

> There are some amongst us who have, I believe, formed an opinion that the party, or rather a portion of it, might get into office were it not for some members of it whose conduct they think too offensive to the Court. I shall call the latter for shortness the ultras, among whom I do *not* reckon Burdett, etc. Their numbers are very much underrated by the Moderates, and their violence is extremely overrated. The great unfairness is indeed done them, of taking their character from the enemy's representations of it. I believe, with the exception of one insulated expression of Bennet's this session, respecting Castlereagh's conduct in Ireland, and one observation of mine last session respecting

the Prince, it would be extremely difficult to discover anything in either their measures or their language which went beyond the ordinary every day motions and words of a steady, consistent, and effective opposition. Nay, even those two expressions of which so much has been said, were far less extravagant than many familiar examples in better times—as Fox's refusal to be in a room with Lord North, Burke's tirade on the King's illness, Fox's, Grey's, etc., resistance a question of prudence, and many others. But I am not going into a defence of what it would be childish to attack in particular. Perhaps the objection to us is more general. I am sure it is taken from the opposite side. *They* never cease to rail at us, sparing on all occasions the Moderates. No abuse is too gross for the ultras, and the cry against them raised by the Treasury is their violence, their revolutionary principles. Once, this cry used to be raised against the whole party; now, it is found better generalship to raise it against a part, because some of our own friends are thus separated. They almost join in the clamour—at all events they listen eagerly to it, and they take good care to let the enemy know how his shot is telling. Indeed, he not only spares, he courts the Moderates, and they are unaccountably taken in with the notion that if "a few violent people" could be thrown overboard they could soon get into port.

From such members of the party he wished completely to dissociate himself:

I don't accuse any persons of the wish to get rid of men the moment their principles or the dislikes they may have occasioned, become cumbrous, or of beginning then to forget the services that have been rendered. But some there certainly are who have the notion in their heads whether they write it or not; and until the experiment is fairly tried I am sure they never will be undeceived. Well then, as far as I am in the way, I am most anxious to be considered as not belonging to the same party with those persons. I know that in a short time they will see their mistake, and then we shall all go on perfectly well together. But if I am wrong in this and they are right, so much the better. I shall heartily rejoice in seeing them obtain power, for I know they will exercise it nearly, if not entirely, as I could wish; and conceiving their administration to be substantially a Whig one, I should give it every support within my small means, unless indeed they again took fright at the dangers of being so supported. Either way a great good will be gained. I think I can venture to say that you will find Romilly of the same sentiments. I do not think we have ever differed upon any matter of the least importance.

For years Brougham had persistently denounced the vacillating and unenterprising policy of the regular leaders of the party. Rat-catching tactics, he said, were always ineffective and inexpedient:

To mention the general errors they are constantly committing would be endless. One principle they have is that an Opposition should do little or nothing, but be quiet and wait for blunders and await the event. Another is that we should seldom divide, and never but when we are strong—as if an Opposition could lose by being beaten in numbers. They really seem to confound the Opposition with the Ministry, to whom being beaten is of course very dangerous. To adopt feeble, milk-and-water measures and couch motions in unmeaning terms, for the sake of catching a stray vote or two, is another error. But the grand and general one is that of seeking popularity from the other side—addressing speeches as well as measures to the majority—conciliating the enemy—in short, playing his game. They make stout speeches enough, and many able ones now and then upon a set, regular party question, which no Ministry that is firmly seated cares much about. They shrink from—disapprove—shake their heads at the constant, galling opposition which alone does the business; which, for example, destroyed the Orders in Council and the income tax. Let me stop to mention a well-known fact, that the whole proceedings on both those occasions were loudly and decidedly condemned at first, nay for a considerable time, and more especially the very course which led to success; and the same course was condemned just as decidedly the second time, after its efficacy had been proved on the former occasion. Now, this affords an excellent instance of all I have been saying—for the Moderates cried out, or rather the Government cried out, against our violence, extravagance, indiscretion, and I know not what else; and our moderate friends agreed until they saw that a firm and marked line of conduct might succeed. In short, they did as usual—they took the enemy's word for it, and were alarmed at their own friends the moment the other side complained of them.

Brougham's speech of July 11 was only one cause of complaint, though it was the most serious, and had almost occasioned a breach with the moderate men of the party, who refused to vote for the address to the Prince Regent:

This motion too was brought forward, I may say, in concert with the Duke of Bedford, whose letter on the subject I showed several of my friends. But it was deemed expedient to show the distinction, and now you perceive the consequence, viz, a clamour raised by Government in a way I believe wholly without precedent—so much so, that some friends, who are the last I should have expected to give me that advice, have actually called upon me to proceed against the Treasury newspapers. When I mention Sefton as one, you will imagine the torrent of abuse must be setting in pretty strong. I don't mean to do anything, indeed, because my example would be gladly followed on the other side, and the liberty of discussing public men and measures would thus be abridged. But I assure you I abstain solely on this ground, for I feel convinced that I should otherwise feel it due to myself to interpose, so entirely have all fair bounds of political abuse been transgressed, and so plainly is personal and *private* malice at work. I own to you that I feel little one way or another from this systematic attack; but I am somewhat surprised to find that any of our own friends should be at all swayed by it. Is it not strange that they won't think and see for themselves, but must always allow themselves to be frightened at their own steadiest supporters, not because they see anything alarming in the conduct of these, but because the other side cry out "violent—rash—factious", etc.? Is it not more strange still to find them pleased with being spared by the other side, without ever thinking that the distinctions made are with the view of creating divisions amongst us? The conclusion they draw from seeing such attacks pointed at the ultras is that those ultras are bad allies. Perhaps the attacks rather show them to be good enemies.

Brougham finally appealed to Lansdowne to discuss the matter with those misguided members of the party, and to impress upon them the folly and futility of their policy; and he concluded by expressing a fervent hope that the future would bring "more united councils" and "more vigorous co-operation".[20] In his reply Lansdowne stated that the Opposition was so disunited that no man could hope to win the confidence of all its members; and declared that Brougham's real offence had been to introduce into his address to the Regent a great variety of topics which purported to represent the opinions of the whole party, although the leaders had not been consulted.[21]

Brougham replied to this criticism in another lengthy letter, in which he showed how little he was in sympathy with the narrow eighteenth-century conception of Party that was still dominant, and with the exclusiveness and snobbishness of the Whig and Tory aristocracy:

> I am extremely glad that I wrote to you, if it were only that it gives me confidence in one doctrine I have always held, and which the older and more regular party men certainly too much neglect, viz., the necessity in the present times of looking more than formerly may have been essential to the body of the people out-of-doors, meaning by people the well-informed and weighty parts of the community, to which I add—what is a plain inference and what some of our friends reject—the necessity of relaxing somewhat in what is called *party feeling*. Formerly it was only to be Pitt and Fox, and the Cavendishes, Russells, etc. Now, it is plain that those persons cannot settle the state by their agreements or differences. All this is as nothing *against* the principle of party, but is a modification and even an improvement of that corner-stone of free Government.
>
> As for my address, it was not the disinclination to vote for it that struck me—I saw plainly no division could be tried on so multifarious a statement—but the anxiety to show a *strangeness* to it, as if it was a motion for repealing the Act of Settlement or attainting the Queen or anything the most wild and wicked. But that is only one symptom. What I lament and what we ought to strive against is the heresy, no less absurd than pernicious, of letting our *adversaries choose for us* both our men and our measures. We do so the moment we listen to their praise or heed their

censure. Because Croker, Peel, Fitzgerald (from very much private personal feelings which I will one day explain to you, arising professionally in great part) rail at one and bepraise exactly what one does not do or propose—this is no reason for listening as if they were arbitrators between the different men or lines of conduct. This *'look-unto'* the other side, I speak of with much regret touching the past as well as dread of the future. Poor Whitbread almost began it. In old times it was unknown. Ponsonby gave wholly in to it, and we have a little sect among us whose vital creed it is. Yet can anything be more plain than that you are beaten if you follow such feelings? For what is it but doing all your adversary bids you?

When I mentioned my wish to disencumber the party of any impediments, I assure you I had no kind of merit of a *self-denying* sort, both because I think, with you, it is all for the present visionary, and because, were it real, I had much rather, I speak most sincerely, see you all in than have anything to do with it. I should indeed expect much good to the cause from even the most broad-bottomed and therefore timid and compromising arrangement, and it would be very difficult to make one that would not please me, provided I were a spectator and supporter only. [22]

The disunion of the Whigs, so faithfully described by Lansdowne in his letter to Brougham, overshadowed their prospects for the year 1818. On the one hand, the younger and more progressive members of the party, like Bennet, Wilson, and Althorp, were genuinely out of sympathy with the Conservative leadership of Grey, who persistently refused to steer a popular course and to face the now obvious fact that the reform question could no longer be shelved with safety to the country and with dignity to the Whig party. On the other hand, the Grenville Whigs had finally parted company with the followers of Grey. The *Buckingham Memoirs* are full of a project of the Marquis and his satellites to create a new party of their own, in order to facilitate and hasten their return to power. Their numbers were small, but they hoped to attract into their orbit all the independent members of both Houses. Grenville himself, worn out by thirty-six years of active political life, had withdrawn from the leadership in favour of his ambitious nephew, the Marquis of Buckingham. On the first day of the new session the Grenvillites, to the unbounded satisfaction of the 'Mountain' but to the disgust of the rest of the Whigs, abandoned their old position amongst the Foxites, and, headed by Charles Wynn and that time-serving politician Fremantle, took up their station on the front Opposition bench below the gangway.

Never since the dreary years that preceded Waterloo had the Whigs been so despondent as in the winter of 1817–18. Sir Robert Wilson's buoyant optimism had deserted him, and his letters to Grey breathed only a spirit of hopelessness at the triumph of reaction. Their last slender hope of office had failed them. The stability of the Tory Ministry depended in no little degree on the caprice or health of the Prince Regent. During the recess of 1817 he had been seriously ill. Rightly or wrongly, some of the Whigs thought that his death would be followed by the regency of his popular daughter, the Princess Charlotte, who could be counted on to dismiss the Liverpool Government and to bring in the Whigs. An extraordinary importance attached itself therefore to such incidental matters as the amount of blood letting to which the Regent was subjected, the number of grains of calomel he had to swallow, the number of leeches that were allowed to fasten on his belly, and his growing corpulency. Thus politicians speculated eagerly on the measurement of his waist, which was regarded as a kind of barometer that indicated either a lengthy or a brief enjoyment of the Ministers' offices and emoluments.[23]

But to the dismay of the Whigs the Regent recovered, whilst the Princess Charlotte died. With her death seemed to vanish the last hopes of Brooks's club. The dispiritedness of the Whigs was reflected in the languidness of their opposition during the early part of the session, and in the poor attendance of members. Grey and Lambton were informed that they need not go to the trouble of coming up to town to carry out their parliamentary duties.[24] Nor was Tierney in the Commons the man to infuse new life into the party. Every one agreed that the best plan would be to have no plan at all. Their best chance, said Brougham, would be to leave things alone and not to seem at all anxious about what their friends proposed to do. His own efforts, he said, had made his friends not only suspicious of his motives, but angry because he had been of more assistance in keeping in the Tories than in clearing them out. "They really treat you," he said naïvely, "for trying to serve them, as if you were serving yourself."[25]

Wilson's prophecy that the Whigs would never return to power until they put themselves at the head of the reform movement, was coming true. They were loud in their condemnation of Sidmouth, the Home Secretary, for the way he had exercised his new coercive powers; but they still strove to keep themselves, as a party, aloof from the popular agitation. Public meetings had become tainted with Radicalism, and the Whigs were no longer enthusiastic about employing the tactics which had defeated the income tax. Lord Holland and Brougham, indeed, had resolved to attend a county meeting to petition Parliament to repeal the Suspension Act; but the former, getting wind of a plan to bring forward the question of reform also, suddenly took fright and tried to prevent the meeting from taking place at all.[26]

Feeling keenly the reproaches of his friends, Brougham began the session with a most unusual moderation, and for some time he spoke extraordinarily little in debate. That, however, did not save him from further indiscretions. On March 3, when the question of the imprisonment of Radicals for selling political pamphlets arose, he took the opportunity of reprobating in most violent language the alleged blasphemous parodies of William Hone, in spite of the fact that Hone had been acquitted, and that Brougham's own religious convictions were notoriously unorthodox.[27] On May 15, when nearly all the Whigs voted against the proposed allowance of £6000 to the Duke of Kent, who was contemplating marriage, Brougham, much to his friends' disgust, went into the lobby with the Government.[28] And again, when Sir Robert Heron on May 19 brought a motion for the repeal of the Septennial Act, Brougham pronounced a quite unnecessary censure on his friends for denouncing as flagitious the conduct of those 'distinguished' eighteenth-century Whigs who had secured a monopoly of political power by keeping that Act on the statute book after all danger to the tranquillity of the country had subsided.[29] For these *faux pas* his own party took to calling him 'Blundering Brougham'. Bennet declared, "We [of Holland House] know that he is apt to take a crotchet into his head, and then he becomes quite silly".[30]

On June 2 Brougham made a lengthy speech in answer to Burdett's plea for annual parliaments and universal suffrage. He spoke with far greater moderation than at the time of his remarkable *volte-face* in the previous year. Far from condemning the views of the Radicals as wild, foolish, and disgusting, he now declared himself anxious to state that for those persons he felt no manner of disrespect. He thought them misled, but, he said, "Far be it from me to view with levity, or to treat with ridicule, opinions which are conscientiously held by a great body of people in this country". His speech gave umbrage out-of-doors, but it surprised and delighted the Tories, who were astounded to see all his reasoning powers and all the point of his satire directed against that system of Radical reform which his ambition had, only a short time before, prompted him to support. But whilst the Ministerial press congratulated him on his return to the true paths of political virtue and intellectual sanity, it expressed doubts whether the sincerity and duration of his conversion would not be conditioned solely by what he conceived to be his political interests.

Ricardo, whose views on reform were those of the Benthamites, was not at all impressed by this speech. He went on to say, with his usual insight and penetration:

> Brougham is a very clever man, but will never rank high as
> a politician, for there is no steadiness in his opinions, and

he appears to me to sacrifice too much to his immediate objects. Sometimes he wishes to conciliate the Whigs, and then the violent reformers receive no mercy at his hands; at other times one would conclude that he went so far in the cause of reform as even Burdett himself. A man who wishes to obtain a lasting name should not be a vacillating statesman, too eager for immediate applause.[31]

The reform debate was quickly followed by the dissolution of Parliament and a General Election. The Whigs made great efforts to diminish the overpowering majority of the Tories; and, by taking full advantage of the feeling that had been excited by the suspension of the Habeas Corpus Act and by the high-Tory methods of governing, they increased their numbers from about 140 to 170. Romilly triumphed over the Radicals at Westminster, and Sir Robert Wilson was returned for Southwark.

Great as was the interest excited by the Westminster contest, it was, if anything, exceeded by the unparalleled novelty of the Westmorland election, of which Brougham was the hero. He entered upon that fight with something of the spirit with which the crusader of old set out on a campaign against the heretic and the bigot. Since 1774 no one had ever dared to challenge Lord Lonsdale's right to elect two members for the county, the political destinies of which he controlled as absolutely as did any petty German tyrant those of his hereditary domain. Certainly no one but Brougham would have dreamed of breaking a lance with so powerful an adversary. The Earl regarded the representation of the county almost as much his hereditary right as he did his estates, and the interference of a hostile politician as a gross, unmannerly attack on his private property. That theory of representation was held too by the Whig aristocracy, and Brougham himself publicly admitted that the vast estates of the Lowthers fully entitled them to nominate one of the county members, and that his hostility was directed against only one of the sitting representatives, Colonel Lowther and Viscount Lowther, the Earl's two sons.

The extraordinarily lengthy accounts of the election given in the London newspapers (especially the *Morning Chronicle* and *The Times*) show how great was the interest aroused by the contest. No other election proceedings in the provinces were reported half so fully. Had Brougham succeeded in storming one of the strongest citadels of Toryism, the victory would have completely turned his head, and would have made the party, too, delirious with joy. Romilly's triumph at Westminster would have paled into insignificance. The excitement had risen to fever height by the end of June, when polling began, for to all intents and purposes the struggle had already been going on for six months with an intensity that alarmed the Tories and made Brougham confident of success.

The war of liberation began as early as January, and was carried on in London, in Parliament, and in the quiet and peaceful villages and townships of a county whose inhabitants were totally unaccustomed to political discussion, to the excitement and turmoil, the riots, the broken heads, the fractured limbs, and the drunken festivities that were the usual accompaniments of a popular election. For the first time for many long years the stirring scenes that occurred at regular intervals in Palace-yard and Covent Garden were transferred to a countryside whose unsophisticated inhabitants had never responded to the eloquence of a Burdett or to the vituperative oratory of a Hunt, and had never canvassed those questions of politics with which the electors of a great city like Westminster were knowingly familiar.

The forty-shilling freeholders who enjoyed the franchise numbered about 2500. All the parsons, justices, and attorneys were solidly with the Lowthers, but Brougham could count on the support of the Quakers, of a few Whig landowners like the Earl of Thanet, and also of the voters of the yeoman class whom the influence of Lowther Castle had failed to subjugate.

During his six months' canvass of the county, Brougham made great progress amongst the friends of liberty and independence, and delivered scores of rousing speeches in every village and hamlet to the astonished people. In London he formed a society of supporters, "The Friends of

the Independence of Westmorland"; and from his place in the House he
indignantly denounced a project of the Lowther electioneering agents
for manipulating in the Tory interest the register of freeholders. On the
other hand, the Lowthers, equally irritated by this impudent challenge
to their supremacy, made a great deal of capital out of a long-forgotten
incident. They resurrected from the family archives Wilberforce's letter
to Lord Lonsdale of 1806, in which Wilberforce had asked the Earl to
consider Brougham's claims to a seat. Full particulars of that episode
were sent to the newspapers, and the Lowthers threatened to publish
the whole correspondence. That gave a certain piquancy to Brougham's
situation, but it only made him redouble his efforts. Bennet declared
that the Whigs had promised to subscribe no less than £10,000 for the
contest, but, the very day he set off for Westmorland before the poll,
Brougham complained that he had been excessively ill-used by his party,
who had egged him on to fight the Lowthers and had then deserted him.
However, he added, he would have his revenge, and when he arrived
at Appleby he would give them a good dressing from the hustings.[32]
His letter to Lord Holland, written before the close of the election,
reveals the cause of his resentment. He believed that the Whigs had
conspired to keep him out of Parliament if he should fail to carry the
Westmorland seat:

> I don't now write to complain either on my own or on
> Romilly's account. I certainly do think that what has been
> done amounts to a complete dissolution of all party union.
> Every principle of a common interest or understanding
> has been grossly and childishly violated. In pursuit of the
> *newest*, the most untried man—the man who had the
> least claims on the party—Romilly, Scarlett, and myself
> have been wholly overlooked—Scarlett's great sacrifices in
> every way—two contests and a third pending—ten years'
> want of promotion in his profession—all overlooked—a
> lesson taught to all Whig lawyers that a man needs not be
> anything but new and untried, in order to be supported,

and the loss sustained by the party of the man who, in spite of party and court persecution, has worked his way to the head of his profession, and would have come into Parliament with all the weight of that high station.

Romilly had still higher claims to plead; and of my own—which are small enough, God knows—I say nothing—except that in 1812 I was more connected with the party and had gained (accidentally) a greater victory for it than I suppose the new favourite may win in several years to come—yet I was suffered to be three years out of Parliament without the offer of a seat on any terms. And now, when I had only this one chance of getting a seat should I be beat in Westmorland, I find the place occupied, and not only that, but the same sum that I was prepared to pay—raised in an instant for the new and untried supporter.

All this has quite made up my mind as to the futility of all party connection. It means only a dupery of sixty or seventy people who don't reflect—for the benefit of two or three sly characters who go about *earwigging* the powerful ones for their own purposes. But this I pass over. I say nothing of what is over. I only state to you a strong claim though not of an untried man—I mean Creevey.

. . . The authors of the intrigue I know not. I have never heard it mentioned without a loud and general roar of indignation. I purpose using it in every way and on all occasions to the utmost of my ability as an argument to prove my being wholly unconnected with party.[33]

A few days later, in a letter to Lady Holland, he flatly contradicted himself by declaring that when he wrote to Lord Holland he felt secure "in two places".[34]

Even whilst conducting an election campaign, he could not refrain from committing serious blunders which lost him the support of many

Whigs in the northern counties. A short time before his own election began, he went to Cockermouth for the Cumberland election to help Lord Morpeth against the Lowthers. But to all the Whigs' disgust he made a long speech in which he deprecated a contest, in order, he said, to save Morpeth the trouble and vexation of a ten days' poll. He wrote:

> I was drawn into Keswick, received at Cockermouth as if I had been the popular candidate for Cumberland and so everywhere else. My acting as a wet blanket has changed all this, and both in Cumberland and even Westmorland I am damaged inconceivably by it. I have also assisted the Lowthers incalculably. If I even had failed at Cockermouth to do any good by my long speech against a contest, I kept Curwen quiet, and what is more I kept down *all my party* among the country gentlemen who are almost the whole county
>
> . . . My thanks for all this I foresee. Morpeth will ascribe one-hundredth part of his seat to me (a seat which by the way he never can again expect to get), and our earwig friends will go on as before saying I am not to be trusted by the party—which Lord Lonsdale has got hold of and given in writing as his reason for resisting me here. New attempts will be made to exchange me for new men, and again I shall see *Cavendishes* subscribing their money to secure seats for others while Romilly and myself are unprovided for.
>
> These vile traits sour one at all party connection, and I trust next Parliament—if a total change of councils be not adopted, that the word party never again will be pronounced—for it is merely the cloak for earwigs getting their own way instead of allowing the cause to be served.[35]

The effects of his inconceivable blunder were deplorable. The Cumberland Whigs refused to come to help him, and Lord Morpeth would not propose his health at a dinner until he was forced by the whole company to do so.[36] Yet Brougham did not lose hope, and in London the betting was decidedly in his favour.[37] "He worked like a horse," wrote Lambton. "He was at once candidate, counsel, agent, canvasser, and orator, and changing his character every hour; and always cheerful and active. Really his energy of mind is beyond anything I could even have conceived."[38] Brougham's letter to Lambton (June 21) shows the Whig candidate in a most warlike and excitable temper:

> We are all in this county on the alert. I addressed the people last night in myriads, and a troop of horse under arms. I protested to the magistrates and made them answerable for the consequences. They denied having given orders, and the men were called off. No riot ensued. Troops are drawn round us everywhere. They are stationed in every direction leading to Appleby, etc. I mean to protest against them on every occasion. The men are all with us and speak very freely. Our people live well with them, and are assured they would not touch them. Indeed they generally wear my ribbons. The enemy are downcast to a great degree. I *have* the original of a letter from a captain in the navy offering £150 for four votes. It was received by his uncle on Monday, and I had possession of it on Thursday in a remote part of the county, so good is our intelligence. I have ordered instant proceedings, and Lord Lonsdale is, I hope, implicated. His name is certainly used. Other things of a similar nature are in store for them. . . .
>
> I have succeeded everywhere in organising my forces and marshalling them under leaders, to *march* in bodies with music and colours, the lame following in carts, etc., and those who have horses to ride. We have beds for them all in houses and barns, etc. The multitude, which is enormous, are to be camped. We have got the best arrangements for polling booths, on *sure and convenient ground,* and shall have

the entire command of them. The enemy are hiring a mob of miners chiefly from Aldstone [Alston] Moor, but we shall defeat them signally if they give battle.

So much for the movements in the field. I have added Scarlett, I hope, to my council.

I now must rely on *your friendship* for the only thing that remains. In elections I always consider myself as liable to go out any moment; indeed I am at any person's service who pleases—and especially I feel a presentiment of having a round with the Colonel. He has been heard to hint that it could hardly end otherwise, and I am much of his mind, for I do not spare him, and if he makes any way in the poll, I shall get particularly zealous respecting him and shall feel very desirous of an issue, should he open his lips. Indeed, already I have been near it with one of his partisans, who had actually written a letter and got a half-pay captain to carry it, probably reckoning on my despising it. Before sending it, however, the circumstance reached me through one to whom it had been communicated in confidence, and I said that I should be out with the fellow in five minutes after receiving his message, for that at election times I was not disposed to be very nice. This was on Friday morning and I have heard nothing since.

Now—I have no human being near me whom I can trust. Any of the gentlemen here would take fright, *for the effect on the contest*, and would inevitably *blab* so as to stop the proceeding by magistrates, etc., which I have always considered as the greatest evil in the world. I therefore entreat *you* to come over the day before, viz. Monday 29, *if you possibly can*, and stay with me three days. I was obliged to do this at Liverpool six years ago, when Strickland had to come out of Yorkshire to be with me, and on his going I was forced to have another friend from a distance—luckily enough—for the last day he went with a message. I

> can feel no comfort and security without such an arrange-
> ment. If *you* really cannot, and if Ossulston is with you,
> pray ask him, but of course to no other human being say
> a word of the matter, as I have to none.[39]

Until 1832 there was only one polling station for the whole county; an inconvenience which necessitated miles of walking from the distant villages to Appleby. From Kendal the procession of voters carrying blue streamers and with a band at their head, set out on a twenty-six mile tramp at eight in the morning of June 29, the day before polling began. Resembling a body of crusaders proceeding to the Holy Land rather than a riotous mob of electors, they arrived at Appleby in the afternoon. Brougham, who had gone out to meet them, created a storm of excitement amongst his enthusiastic supporters by one of his usual inflammatory and exhortatory addresses, in which he suggested that his bodyguard of stalwarts would not fail to do their duty by showing their enemies the bottom of the river if any violence were offered.[40] Brougham indeed had some justification for his complaints of the military display by which the Lowthers hoped to overawe and silence their adversaries. They had collected troops from all over the county, concentrating them in or near the town; they had brought from Liverpool four or five stage-coaches filled with stalwart sailors and carpenters enlisted for the duration of the election at five shillings per day, for the purpose of "keeping the peace"; and they had armed some two hundred special constables with unlawful weapons.

According to the correspondent of the *Morning Post,* Brougham had worked himself into a violent passion, and had nearly bawled himself hoarse with his half-hundred speeches, by the morning of Tuesday, June 30, when the contest formally began. His tactics were to bring as many voters to the poll at the outset of the fight as possible, with the idea of discouraging his opponents and coercing them into the belief that to prolong their opposition would be not only ruinously expensive but futile and imbecile. At first he met with success, but on the second day he fell behind and never after recovered the lead. On the

Friday he gave up hope and abandoned the field. His parting speech to his supporters was delivered in the same high key as all its predecessors, and he announced his intention of forming an Association to secure the political independence of the county, and of contesting every future election until this object had been accomplished.

His public declaration that the struggle was only beginning, and that his hostility would never cease until his enemies were humbled, alarmed and exasperated the Lowthers. In July De Quincey, the new editor of the *Westmorland Gazette*, the newspaper organ of the Tories, opened up a pointed attack on the "infamous levelling doctrines diffused by Mr. Brougham". "The snake is scotched, not killed; the spirit of error is not dead but sleeping, and sleeping only in respect to the ultimate object proposed, but active and alive for purposes of immediate annoyance," were his comments on Brougham's final harangue to his supporters.[41] But De Quincey's leading articles, however excellent as literary compositions, were hardly intelligible to the great majority of his humble readers; and he was, too, so little a man of the world that he was said to have narrated in his prospectus the whole details of his being hired by Lord Lonsdale against Brougham and the Whigs.[42]

The Lowthers could hardly have rejoiced more at Brougham's discomfiture than did the Radicals, who hated him as an apostate. They did not hesitate to avow their opinion that the only difference that existed between the Westmorland Tories and Brougham was, that the former were the friends of the persons *in* power, while the latter was one of the principal men in the faction which was *grasping* at power. Sydney Smith had good grounds for believing that Brougham's candidature was dictated largely by personal hostility to the Lowthers, whom he had never forgiven for the affront of 1806. The Radicals went one further in their imputation of motive, and roundly declared that Brougham had no other object in going down to Westmorland than to use the deluded electors of that county as so many asses, upon whose backs he might ride in triumph to the flesh-pots of Downing Street.

Flushed with their election successes, the Whigs decided in the summer of 1818 that the day of final victory was not far distant, and that a vigorous effort in the following spring would find them at last comfortably seated on the Treasury benches. At the beginning of August, Wilson was predicting with renewed confidence that, if they would take up a moderate measure of parliamentary reform, they would eat their Christmas dinner in Downing Street.[43] Brougham wrote to Lord Holland:

> ... The elections have done a world of good, both by beating the Government and destroying or nearly destroying our worse enemies, the Hunts and Co. It is our own fault if we don't make some play by this means. We have it once more in our hands and once more I fear we shall throw it all away. I have been endeavouring to improve it in various ways, and particularly by drawing up a dissertation on the state of parties and an argument in favour of party generally, for the *Edinburgh Review*, which you will soon see.[44]

Thus his diatribes against party and the selfishness of Whig politicians ceased as soon as he was assured that Lord Darlington's borough was still available, and that his Parliamentary career was not to be again interrupted. But he had failed to make himself *persona grata* with the Whigs, who, when they decided in July to elect a permanent leader in the Commons, chose Tierney. Littleton, a follower of Canning, had written in June:

> ... [Brougham] appears to wish to be moderate if he can; his present object is to place himself at the head of the old Whigs. But his temper will betray him at last, though he may succeed in gaining their confidence for a moment, which he has not yet done.[45]

Brougham's own letter to Lambton, written during the course of the 1818 session, fully bears out this testimony of a detached observer:

The debates have been successful generally speaking, but the session is flat and languid. Perhaps we should be more adventurous, and I am sure we should *divide* more. But the *earwigs* are in force—Macdonald and Co.—and I really can't tell what they would be at, for it is nothing but nods, and shakes, and wise looks, and hearing anything one suggests with all humility and then a shrug and walking away, as if one had the plague, or whatever worse disease some of us are supposed to labour under, and which is believed to keep us out of office. Yet I do nothing to offend any one. I keep in the background—never interfere with anybody, and do not even sit in my former place for fear of being thought to be putting myself forward. I can conscientiously act in this way, as Romilly having given up the Rolls is there regularly, and takes the most warm and effectual part, speaking better than ever, and with a weight and effect which no one even of the enemy can dispute. As long as his health and inclination enable him to do this, I feel no sort of qualm at pursuing the line I last summer promised the place-hunters I should.[46]

Brougham acquiesced in the party's choice, and determined to co-operate loyally with Tierney. He wrote to Lord Holland:

. . . I have had an hour's conversation with C. Long. . . . He said he had heard of our new leader, and that his answer was to everybody "that Brougham had not acceded and would blow it into the air". I said his information was peculiarly incorrect, for that I had been the first to accede, and was indeed one of the movers. He said a man must be credulous to expect me to act on such a plan, and that they were not afraid I should. I told him he was mistaken. . . .[47]

The spirit of the Whig party, revivified by election successes, was, however, destined to be temporarily overwhelmed by a great disaster, in the death of Romilly. As Grey said to his daughter, Lady Louisa Lambton, something had always occurred to blast their hopes just when things were taking a turn for the better.[48] The by-election in Westminster served only to intensify the hostility between Radicals and Whigs. Both Brougham and Bennet declined invitations to stand in the Whig interest.[49]

Only eighteen months previously, Tierney had expressed doubts as to the continued existence of the Whig party, but now he declared himself confident in the strength of his numbers and in the certainty of a speedy victory. Brougham, however, did not share Tierney's buoyancy of spirits, and had not recovered from his disappointment at not being given the leadership. His unhappy relations with his party offered a congenial theme to Tory wits, who poked fun at him in the columns of the *Courier*:

> The *Brougham steam-boat,* Darlington, captain, leaves her moorings at Billingsgate every day during the session, Saturdays and Sundays excepted; calls at Pepper-alley and Hungerford Stairs on her way, but no longer at the Temple stairs, and arrives at St. Stephen's Chapel at half-past three o'clock. She is true American built, her engine has been manufactured by Scotch and French philosophers, her boiler is heated by disappointed ambition, she emits an unexampled quantity of vapour, and for smoke and smell has no competitor. The accident which happened to her two or three years ago on the Regent's Canal, where she burst her boiler and scalded her friends, is not likely to occur again, as she has been taken into Opposition dock, and has safety valves manufactured by M'Kerrit of Liverpool, George Manners, Mr. Cawthorne, M.P., and Co.; so that she is now in a very promising condition. The proprietors, Messrs. Darlington, Thanet and Co., expect that by her present services she will be able hereafter to

make a voyage to the Dukedom of Cleveland and places equally desirable for them and their friends.

For further particulars apply to the Weathercock, Turn-again-lane; the Loaves and Fishes, Labour-in-vain-hill; the Magpie, Crooked-lane; and the Hope, Pudding Lane.

Tierney entrusted the statement of Whig policy at the opening of the session of 1819 to Macdonald, one of the 'Earwigs', whose anxiety to get into office was well known. The Opposition decided to take the offensive on the question of the resumption of cash payments by the Bank of England, a subject, said Lord Holland, which had recently become popular. Strenuous efforts were made by the Whips of both parties; but the Ministers fared better than they had anticipated, and the Whigs were defeated by a majority of 109.[50] The Tories, however, were not yet out of the wood. A motion to add Brougham to the Bank of England Committee (to inquire into the currency question) was defeated by only forty-two votes, and it was believed that had the question related to any one less unpopular than Brougham, the Opposition would have triumphed.[51] Things began to look black for the Government when Mackintosh's motion for a committee to inquire into the state of the criminal law was carried by 147 *versus* 128, and when Lord Archibald Hamilton's motion on the Scottish borough representation was carried by a majority of five.[52] Grattan's Catholic emancipation motion was lost by only two votes. The Ministers began to quake in their shoes. Lord Liverpool declared that he would resign if he were unable to carry the measures upon the necessity of which the Cabinet was agreed.[53] The most critical division took place on May 18 when Tierney brought forward a motion on the state of the nation, which was intended as a motion of censure on the Government. But the Whigs counted in vain on the support of the independent party in the House; and they were defeated by an overwhelming majority.

After his sorry failure to smash the Ministry, Tierney met with nothing but abuse from all his followers. All hopes of coming in had to be abandoned. The defeat was disastrous and demoralising. It gave a new lease of life to the Liverpool administration. The Whig party began to crumble and its members to disperse. The conduct of Opposition tended more and more to pass into the keener hands of the Radicals, whose ranks had just been strengthened by the addition of Ricardo, the greatest exponent of the economic doctrines of the Benthamites, and Joseph Hume, who, under the effective tutelage of Francis Place, became the most formidable critic of the Government's financial measures, and the most unwearied advocate of economy.

Other factors, too, contributed to increase the ineffectiveness of the Whigs. Tierney, who had completely lost the confidence of his troops, fell ill, and was unable to take part in the debates. It was seen that his day was at last over, and in September people understood that he had withdrawn from the leadership. A serious illness put Brougham also out of action for the greater part of the session, and the newspapers gave currency to the report that he was left with an incurable disease. Both Place and Mill, who in the heat of party passion had attacked him bitterly and violently, mourned his supposed impending fate. The former wrote:

> I care nothing about Tierney, who never deserved the respect of any honest man; but I grieve for Brougham. He had fine talents, good nature, and a strong desire to be useful, and had he but possessed a sound judgement to guide him, he would have been a man of vast importance; he was forgiving, liberal, and exceedingly industrious, but all these fine qualities have become useless if it he true that the greatest of all possible calamities has fallen upon him.[54]

But the time was not yet come for the writing of obituary notices, and by the beginning of the autumn session of Parliament Brougham was once more in high force.

Into the familiar story of the renewal of the Radical agitation and of the 'Six Acts' that were passed by the frightened Liverpool Ministry after the 'Manchester Massacre', it is unnecessary here to go. The

Whigs, who were powerless to prevent the new coercive measures from passing, had no constructive proposals of their own to suggest as an alternative to repression. Wilson anxiously desired his party to put itself at the head of the reform movement in the country, and himself set the example by speaking at meetings in his own constituency. He was the only Whig who in September attended a great gathering of reformers in Westminster.[55] Brougham, too, urged the importance of holding county meetings as a means of organising public opinion against the threatened attack on the people's liberties; but his opinions on reform were much more moderate and diluted than those of his zealous and impulsive friends; and he was so anxious to avoid giving offence to the Whig leaders that he declined to commit himself to the support of projected meetings in Cumberland and Westmorland until he had ascertained the views of Lord Grey.[56] The Whigs, he said, ought to announce their complete separation from the Radicals; and at Kendal he made an important speech which, betraying as it did his repugnance to large popular meetings, delighted the Tories.[57] On that occasion he was reported to have avowed that

> *he* was no friend to the plan of moving great bodies of the people from their homes to attend meetings at a distance; nor could *he* see why the good men of such consider-able places as Bolton should not meet at home, and leave the Manchester folks to meet at Manchester. . . . Such assemblies as were not necessary might be fairly deemed inconvenient, and though there was nothing unlawful in them, they had better be avoided.

But the main cause of the indisposition of the Whigs to encourage county meetings was not their detestation of the Radicals so much as their unwillingness to pledge themselves to that reform for which the people were clamouring. Lambton admitted the truth of the *Courier's* gibe, that the only reform favoured by the Whigs was the displacement of the Tory Ministers:

Let the Whigs ruminate upon this accusation—let them deny the truth of it if they can; and then let them no longer rely upon *their* powers of delusion, but try some honester expedient to prove themselves the friends of the principles they profess, and to deserve the respect and confidence of the country.[58]

This wavering, half-hearted attempt on the part of the Opposition to rally public opinion proved a lamentable failure. The Duke of Devonshire and other prominent Whigs refused to have anything to do with county meetings, in spite of earnest remonstrances from Grey, Lord Fitzwilliam, and Brougham.[59] Grey made no movement in favour of reform because he feared to break up his party; but in spite of his caution and forbearance he doubted whether he would be able to keep the Opposition united:

> . . . A crisis is approaching in which it appears to me that the union and steadiness of the Whig party in taking and supporting a line of their own will be of vital importance to the interests of the country. If this cannot be done there will be nothing left for me but to disband the party, or at least to relinquish for ever the share which I have had in conducting it.[60]

Everybody agreed that a great crisis was fast approaching. Even Brougham, who was far from being an alarmist, was dismayed at the threatening aspect of affairs, and at the prospect of military rule:

> I have been met by the extraordinary news of the Ministers having removed Lord Fitzwilliam for expressing his honest opinion and attending a county meeting, to which is added the further determination of increasing the army above 20,000 men. I am not apt to be alarmed, but I confess these things do fill me with dismay. There is a character of violence

and military vigour about them quite foreign to the nature of Lord Liverpool, who must have been duped by stories of plots and pikes. I see Wellington distinctly in the measure, and I can hardly doubt that a design is formed of making the Government of this country less free—and permanently so—and all to avoid the nuisance (which I admit to be a great one, but one we have been in all times exposed to) of Hunt and his crew. To what extremities the country may be driven by such desperate councils no man can foresee, but I fear very unquiet times are at hand—and Wellington and Castlereagh are woefully mistaken if they think that such plans ever can succeed in England without a civil war. I trust in God that none of us are so vile as to lay our account with anything else should Parliament agree to support an absolute Government—for absolute it would in reality be, if all freedom of speech and of writing were confined to the two Houses and the Government agents.[61]

In a letter to Allen (of Holland House) on the crisis, Brougham made the interesting suggestion that the situation should be discussed at a party meeting to which not merely the Whig members of both Houses should be invited, but also outside men of note, who could be taken as representing Liberal opinion in the country:

> . . . In these things I see Wellington and a new reign of terror. Indeed I question much if the old trick of an alarm and green bag is to be played off for the sole and *comparatively legitimate* purpose of keeping their places and getting out of a present scrape. It seems but too probable that attempts are going to be made to change the Government permanently, that is, to make it less free. The infatuation of many persons is such that, from disgust at Hunt and the Press (in which I join with them), they would be secretly well pleased at the change, not aware

that it could not in the nature of things rest there. For what chance is there of Parliament (which of course will be left quite untouched) long holding either any respect in the country or controlling the Crown, if it is the only place where men can speak their sentiments? What chance is there of free opinions being long permitted to get at the public through reports of debates if all other discussion is stopped?

. . . Surely the Whigs must *now* see the necessity of rallying. I mean those who lately were doubting and even averse to meetings. If the Cavendishes wish for a civil war, they have only to encourage Government by holding back from us. My belief is that but for this division among us we never should have seen Lord Fitzwilliam's removal, and if I were the Duke of Devonshire I should be ashamed of keeping a Lord-Lieutenancy on such terms.

. . . I consider Wellington as playing the most execrable game that a man can—and I hope to God he may be either torn to pieces, or what would be a longer torment, utterly disgraced in the country.

. . . The party ought plainly to assemble a week before Parliament meets, and there should be a meeting of both Lords and Commons and resolutions entered into. I would suggest also the propriety of a general meeting of Lords, Commons, *and others*, but with such selection that none but persons of some importance could attend—which might be contrived by each member of either House bringing whom he pleased. . . . One thing is clear—something extraordinary should be done to mark that we will not allow the Constitution to be changed at the mere cost of a *short and hard-fought session*.[62]

The only hope of salvation for the country, declared Wilson, lay in a change of government. That which the strenuous and even frantic exertions of the Whig party had, after five sessions of incessant parliamentary warfare, been unable to bring about, the death of George III. on January 29, 1820, brought within the range of sober possibility.

1. *Rylands Library* MS.
2. Add. MS. 34459, fol. 179; 35152, fol. 219.
3. Add. MS. 27809, fol. 32; 35153, fol. 1.
4. Add. MS. 30121, fol. 259.
5. Add. MS. 35152, fol. 219.
6. Add. MS. 30121, fol. 256.
7. *Ibid.* fol. 202.
8. *Ibid.* fol. 206.
9. *Ibid.* fol. 207.
10. Lansdowne MS.: Brougham to Lansdowne, Feb. 8, 1817.
11. *Ibid.*
12. Lansdowne MS.
13. *Ibid.*
14. *Parl. Deb.* xxxv. 370-74.
15. Add. MS. 36627, fol. 34.205. Holland House MS.
16. Add. MS. 27809, fol. 32.
17. *The 'Pope' of Holland House*, p.165.
18. Holland House MS.
19. Add. MS. 30121, fol. 308.
20. Lansdowne MS.
21. *Life and Times*, ii. 320.
22. Lansdowne MS.: Brougham to Lansdowne, Sunday (probably Aug. 3, 1817).
23. Add. MS. 30122, fol. 7.
24. Lambton MS.: Wilson to Lambton, Aug. 24, 1817; Jan. 17, 1818.
25. *Life and Times*, ii. 331.

26. Add. MS. 36627, fol. 36.
27. *Parl. Deb.* xxxvii. 749.
28. *Ibid.* xxxviii. 734.
29. *Ibid.* xxxviii. 809.
30. Add. MS. 36627, fol. 47.
31. *Letters to Trower*, p.55.
32. Add. MS. 36627, fol. 38.
33. Holland House MS.: Brougham to Lord Holland, Thursday.
34. *Ibid.*: Brougham to Lady Holland, Friday.
35. *Ibid.*: Brougham to Lord Holland, Sunday (June 28, 1818).
36. Holland House MS.: Brougham to Lord Holland, Monday (June 29, 1818).
37. Lambton MS.: Wilson to Lambton, n.d.
38. Add. MS. 30108, fol. 18.
39. Lambton MS.
40. *The Times*, July 3, 1818.
41. Pollitt, *De Quincey's Editorship of the Westmorland Gazette* p.9.
42. Monypenny, *Life of Beaconsfield*, i. 39.
43. Add. MS. 30122, fol. 230.
44. Holland House MS., n.d.
45. Hatherton MS., Diary, June 2, 1818.
46. Lambton MS.
47. Holland House MS.
48. Lambton MS.: Grey to Lady Louisa Lambton, Nov. 8, 1818.
49. Add. MS. 27842, fol. 37.
50. *Parl. Deb.* xxxix. 275.
51. *Memoirs of the Regency*, ii. 302.
52. *Parl. Deb.* xl. 197.
53. Yonge, ii. 400.
54. Add. MS. 35153, fol. 72.
55. Add. MS. 30123, fol. 80.
56. *Life and Times*, ii. 346.
57. *The Black Dwarf*, iii. 697; Add. MS. 38280, fol 146.
58. Add. MS. 30109, fol. 59.

59. Chatsworth MS.: Grey to the Duke of Devonshire, Sept. 23 and Oct. 23, 1819; letters of Brougham, Tuesday (Sept.) and Sunday (Oct. 31, 1819).

60   Chatsworth MS.

61. Chatsworth MS.

62. Holland House MS.: Brougham to Allen, Monday (probably Nov. 1, 1819).

VI

Brougham, Queen Caroline, and the Canningites

There is he whom they call
Squire Brougham of Brougham Hall,
    Who would pass for a man of condition;
In blood, to be sure,
He may match Peter Moore,
    But the Hall is a mere imposition;
The fellow's a hack politician,
A tailor in all but ambition,
    Who offer'd to bilk
    For a gown of black silk
    The Queen—and her whole Opposition.
                    —Theodore Hook

THE Napoleonic wars had rudely shattered the solidarity of the Tory party which the statesmanship of Pitt had evolved from the ruins of 1783. The death of its renovator in 1806 had completed its dissolution into a series of groups and connections each of which was dominated by one outstanding personality. The Whig party, too, had succumbed to the disintegrating and disruptive forces in English political life after 1792, and its elements came to be controlled by separatist leaders like Grenville, Fox, and Whitbread, as were those of their opponents by Canning, Wellesley, and Perceval. This effacement of the old landmarks had had the inevitable result of lowering the standards of political morality and public virtue, and of introducing into politics a series of coalitions and counter-coalitions which gave full play to the rivalries and ambitions of unscrupulous politicians who were more than ordinarily willing to sacrifice their political principles for personal ends. With the coming of peace, the accession to the premiership of the Earl of Liverpool, whose leadership, though otherwise colourless and undistinguished, was marked by the success with which he reconciled conflicting personal animosities and rivalries, and with the return of Canning in the spring of 1816 came the temporary restoration of the old two-party system, to the exclusion of that of government by *bloc*. Within ten years, however, that system was once more on the verge of collapse. The failure of the Tories of the old school, like Liverpool, Castlereagh, Eldon, and Sidmouth, to find a remedy for the post-war distress and to solve the problems of poverty and unemployment, paved the way for the rise to power of a new school of abler, more enlightened and more progressive men like Canning, Peel, and Huskisson. But the high Tories were still in the saddle; and only the creation of a new party composed of Liberal Tories and Conservative Whigs, with a new progressive programme with which to appeal to the country, could hasten the defeat and rout of the reactionaries.

If during the years after Waterloo Canning was the main disintegrating force in the Tory ranks, the corresponding disruptive tendency in the Whig camp was represented far more strongly by the amazing personality of Brougham. For five sessions he had striven incessantly, with the old Opposition as his instrument, to destroy the Tory Government, but without the least success. By 1820 it had become tolerably clear that reactionary Toryism was far too strongly entrenched to succumb to attacks organised on traditional party lines, and that Brougham's eloquence, noisy and even thunderous though it was, was, in itself and unaided, unable to lay low the walls of Jericho. But the open rupture, which the death of the old king made inevitable, between the Prince Regent (now George IV.) and his wife gave Brougham, her chief professional adviser, a new weapon of attack against the now doubly unpopular Ministers; and the secession of Canning from their ranks in December seemed so much like the desertion of a doomed vessel that it made the creation of a new centre party of progressive Tories and moderate Whigs an obviously feasible project of statesmanship. As will be seen in the following pages, that conception was not destined to be realised as speedily as its chief exponents could have wished; but the delay was not of long duration, and the political history of the next six years is a record of the gradual break-up of both the great historic parties, and of the *rapprochement* between the new Tories and the Broughamite Whigs.

The Prince Regent, who succeeded his father as George IV., was a liar, a drunkard, and a profligate. In 1785 he had contravened the Royal Marriage Act by going through a form of marriage with Mrs. Fitzherbert, a Roman Catholic lady; and ten years later, whilst she was still alive, he espoused the Princess Caroline of Brunswick-Wolfenbüttel. Soon after the birth of his only child, the Princess Charlotte, he deserted his wife and openly violated his marriage vows. In 1806 he coerced his Whig Ministers into making an official inquiry into her conduct; but, though she was acquitted of the serious charges brought against her by her profligate husband, her reputation was damaged, and the King was obliged to censure her for her levity and indiscretion. The Tory Opposition, which persecuted her fourteen years later, now eagerly espoused her cause as that of an injured and much-maligned woman, and inveighed against the Whigs for countenancing so dastardly an attack on her honour. Perceval, her legal representative, published a defence of her conduct; but when in 1809 he was called upon to form a Government by the Prince Regent, whom it thus became necessary to conciliate, he made frantic efforts to buy up every copy in circulation, and was said to have spent £10,000 of secret service money in the attempt.

So long as the Whig Opposition after 1807 had anything to hope from the Regent, who had professed Whig principles, they were careful to steer clear of his matrimonial embarrassments. But in 1811 he grievously disappointed their hopes of office, and by 1812 he had finally broken with his old allies. The men of the 'Mountain', wildly indignant at his treachery, now warmly took up his wife's cause, regarding it as a splendid weapon with which to harass an ungrateful prince. In 1809 Brougham himself had been introduced to her, and soon became her confidential adviser. From the very beginning of his long connection with her he cared little or nothing about her wrongs. His correspondence with Creevey and others shows that his sole object was to make personal and party capital out of her quarrel with her husband. In 1811 he became her recognised legal adviser, a position which obviously had great advertising possibilities—and no one perceived more clearly than he did the value and importance of advertisement. Her daughter, too, was an extraordinarily useful pawn in the game. The aged and hopelessly insane king might reasonably be expected to die at any moment, and the health of his son, the Regent, was so wretched that he too might at any time go off without a warning. In that event he would be succeeded by the Princess Charlotte ('Little P.', as Brougham called her); and, according to Bentham, who was likely to know, Brougham was looking forward to her calling upon him to form a Whig Ministry. But even if his hopes of being Prime Minister were a little extravagant, it was at any rate certain that he would be given high office with a seat in the Cabinet, whilst Romilly would be Lord Chancellor.[1] The stakes for which he was playing were thus desperately high, and the energy and imprudence with which he carried on his warfare against Carlton House alarmed Lord Grey and all sober-minded Whigs, who were inclined to be squeamish about provoking a complete rupture with the Prince Regent.

In June 1814 Brougham brought off a brilliant *coup* by persuading 'Little P.' to break off her contemplated marriage with the Prince of Orange. She was not at all enamoured of the prospect of living abroad, but had it not been for Brougham's skilful and timely intervention she would have given way to her father's wishes. The position as Brougham saw it was this. If she married the Prince of Orange, she would have to live in Holland. For some time her mother had seriously been thinking of going abroad in order to escape from the petty annoyances to which she was constantly subjected in England. Nothing but her attachment to her daughter prevented her departure; and if the marriage were to take place she would certainly leave the country. From Brougham's standpoint that would be little short of a disaster. He would lose his hold on her, and her political importance would be immeasurably diminished. His line of argument was chosen with extraordinary skill. He persuaded 'Little P.' that her marriage would be swiftly followed by her mother's departure, that the Prince Regent would at once institute divorce proceedings, get his decree, marry again, and thereby imperil her succession to the throne. As Creevey admiringly observed, it was one of Brougham's most brilliant moves in the game. His arguments had an almost miraculous effect on the young Princess, who at once announced her determination not to proceed further with the marriage.[2]

A few weeks later, however, 'Mrs. P.', to Brougham's intense disgust, left the country. That step seemed to take the game completely out of his hands. "She deserves death," he wrote; "yet," he added, "we must not abandon her in case P. gets the victory."

Misfortune seemed to dog Brougham's every effort to damage the Regent and his Government, for in the autumn of 1817 the Princess Charlotte died. He regarded that event as little short of a calamity. It put an end to the pleasing prospect of being called upon to form a Ministry, for, in the event of the death of both George III. and the Prince Regent, the crown would pass into the hands of the Tory Duke of York.

'Mrs. P.', however, was still found fit for service, and in 1819 Brougham began another long and bafflingly-complicated series of intrigues with her on the one hand, and the Government on the other. The tortuousness of his conduct gave rise to what was probably a well-founded suspicion in the minds both of friends and foes, that he was willing to betray the cause of the injured Princess for his own personal advancement. In June of that year he made a proposal to the Prime Minister that she should renounce the title of Queen and undertake never to return to England; and in return for those concessions her allowance of £35,000 a year should be increased to £50,000, and should be secured to her for life, instead of terminating with the demise of the Crown. Not only did he make this proposition without the knowledge of his client, but he did not even inform her of his having done so, although he continued frequently to correspond with her. That extraordinary conduct bore every appearance of being dictated by a desire to throw her over and to extort some personal advantage from the Ministry. But in any case it was taken to mean that her chief legal adviser felt a want of confidence in her innocence. In 1814 he had argued that the acceptance of Castlereagh's offer of an allowance would look like an abandonment of her just rights and a tacit confession of her guilt. The same objections were equally applicable in 1819. Why, then, did he in that year make a proposal almost identical with the one the acceptance of which he had so strongly deprecated?

Lord Liverpool replied that the overture would be considered after he had received a personal communication from the Princess. But since Brougham failed to apprise her of his proceeding, the whole matter necessarily fell into abeyance. On August 5, however, Brougham, much to his professed annoyance, heard that she intended to return to England. He wrote:

> I am confident from her letter of to-day that she now intends to come, and I am still more clear that her coming would be pregnant with every sort of mischief (not to mention the infernal personal annoyance of having such a devil to plague me for six months). I think it exposes things to the risk of clamour and violence, which no one can hope to estimate, far less to direct, or, in case of necessity, disarm. In short, the question, both before being brought on, and after, would not be considered with even tolerable coolness and fairness, were she here. I therefore am disposed to prevent her coming by every means in my power.[3]

With that object in mind, he informed her that he would meet her at Lyons, in the south of France; and on August 17 she wrote saying that she was about to set out from Pesaro. He then committed another serious indiscretion by failure to keep his appointment. "He could not go—he was busy," was his only excuse.[4]

The death of George III. on January 29 brought the crisis to a head. The Queen promptly made up her mind to return to England to assert her rights. Brougham, meanwhile, was anxiously deliberating how he could best turn the situation to his own advantage. Would he gain more from the Tories by making a private settlement of the Queen's affairs whilst she was still abroad, than from the Whigs by bringing them into office as the uncompromising champion of her rights? It would seem that he had great difficulty in making up his mind whether the Queen ought to be kept out of the country, or whether it would be better to precipitate a great conflict with the Government (in which case it would surely be overthrown) by urging her to come over and throw herself on the country. In the summer of 1819, as we have seen, he had been apparently working for a settlement, and had been anxious to keep his client out of the way. But on February 5—precisely a week after the accession of George IV.—Brougham told Creevey that he had already requested her to set out with the utmost speed, and to be on the shores of northern France in immediate readiness for the Channel crossing. His only fear at that moment was that the death of the new king, who had been desperately ill and who was still not out of danger, would *ipso facto* effect a settlement of the Queen's business without giving any advantage to Brougham himself; and that it would give the Tory Government a new lease of life under the sovereignty of the Duke of York, "I never prayed so heartily for a prince before," he wrote.[5]

Whilst the King was still in so precarious a state that his recovery was doubtful, he began to press his Ministers to institute immediate divorce proceedings against his wife, having already decided that her name should be excluded from the Liturgy. On February 10 they replied in a long and closely-reasoned minute, and begged to be excused from entering upon so perilous an undertaking. They urged that the course suggested by His Majesty—that the proceedings should take the form of an Act of Parliament—was highly irregular, and that the decision of an ecclesiastical court was an indispensable preliminary to a legislative Act. They expressed a doubt whether the evidence which the Milan commission of inquiry had been gathering since 1818 was sufficient to secure a verdict before any tribunal and they delicately suggested that it would be highly inexpedient to enter upon a course which would allow the defence to bring forward recriminatory evidence which would completely ruin his own reputation and shake the monarchy to its very foundations. They recommended him to content himself with an Act of Parliament that should stipulate for the Queen's permanent residence abroad, whilst giving her an ample allowance.

On February 17 the King expressed his readiness to sacrifice his personal views and to abide by the decision of the Cabinet not to initiate divorce proceedings.[6] Brougham, however, was warned that if his client attempted to set foot in England, a Bill of Pains and Penalties would instantly be introduced into Parliament. The matter now rested, therefore, with the Queen. Would she accept a settlement on the lines suggested in June 1819 and in the Cabinet's minute of February 10, or would she brave everything, return to England, and demand her rights as Queen? And would Brougham advise her to take the moderate line, or would his personal interests demand her presence in London, the downfall of the Government, with the prospect of high office for himself?

His urgent summons to the Queen at the beginning of February seemed to make the Ministers' places not worth three months' purchase, and seemed to imply that he was inexorably bent on the Government's destruction. There were no signs of that accommodating spirit which he had so manifestly exhibited only six months before. But he was now to alter his plan of campaign with the lightning rapidity of a consummate quick-change artist. Sometime in March, if not earlier, he made it known in ministerial circles that he was willing to come to terms with the Government; and he hinted that the

Queen's arrival might yet be prevented in time to avert the conflagration that every one was expecting. A rascally paragraph that appeared in a notorious newspaper a little later was equally applicable at this somewhat thrilling juncture:

> Through the kindness of my landlord, wrote 'Jonathon Thackston' to the editor of *John Bull,* I have been favoured with a sight of your excellent journal, which, were it not for your gibes and jokes (undeservedly, I assure you) on his brother, Henry Brougham, I should like very well. Mr. Henry Brougham, I can assure you, is a patriot, at *heart,* whatever blarney he may puff off with the mob. I have heard his brother, on rent days, or 'saturnalibus', as Mr. James facetiously termed them, declare, that Henry only waits for an opportunity to display his love to his Prince and his country—that in order to do this, he would have no objection whatever, to serve with any man, or *set* of men, Whigs or Tories (the latter for choice, on account of indignities received from one Turney, or Tierney, who wishes, it seems, to keep Mr. Henry in leading-strings). I think, sir, between you and me—I wish not the matter to go farther—that Ministers might do worse than tip Mr. Harry the siller.[7]

Brougham at this time seemed to hold the fate of the Government in his hands. The Ministers themselves were fully aware that they would be unable to survive the storm that would break over their heads if the Queen were to arrive. Was her legal adviser willing to come to terms with them; and, if so, would his terms be sufficiently moderate for the Government to accept? He now let it be known that all difficulties would be swept away if he were given a silk gown—which, giving him precedence at the Bar, would ensure his permanent success as a circuit lawyer, and would add many thousands to his yearly income. That proposition had been considered at Carlton House, but difficulties had cropped up, and, what was worse, the fact that

such difficulties existed had leaked out and had become known to
Brougham himself. Becoming impatient at the delay, he wrote on
March 30 to Lord Hutchinson, hinting that he might not be able
much longer to keep his impatient client in check, and that if the
Ministers desired to make an amicable arrangement, they had better
waste no more time.

That letter was shown to Canning, and it occasioned great alarm.
He pointed out to Lord Liverpool on April 2 that Brougham had taken
the significant step of dispatching a messenger to Italy the previous
night. "The danger is most portentous," he declared. "At least it should
appear so, in all reason, to those who care very much about the existence of the Government."[8]

Canning was seriously concerned to hear that George IV. was
putting difficulties in the way of a peaceful settlement. It was most
obvious, he said, that the change that had taken place in Brougham's
language and conduct during the last few days had been occasioned by
the rumours he had heard of the indisposition on the part of Carlton
House to comply at all. "Every motive and every consideration of
policy, whether relating to the particular question or to Brougham's
situation in respect to it and to us, dictated (as it appears to me) an
immediate and graceful compliance with his wishes about the s[ilk]
g[own]," Canning wrote to the Prime Minister in a second letter on
April 2. Then he proceeded:

> The delay, and still more the rumours which he *must* have
> heard—even if he have not the *certainty*—of an indisposition
> to comply at all—have naturally and necessarily given time
> to the Opposition to work upon him, and have led him
> to doubt whether he has not a better game before him in
> fighting the Queen's battle than in conspiring with us to keep
> the peace. The silk gown given (or promised) at once, and
> handsomely, would have fixed him. We have already missed
> that advantage, and I should not be at all surprised if he were
> now to decline the offer, if made to him on any other ground

than that of his *claim* to the thing. He would have accepted it originally on the express condition of keeping that claim dormant. I am perfectly convinced that the only chance of avoiding the extremity of mischief, is that you should be enabled to see him immediately and make the tender. If it goes over till the beginning of term, there is an end of the matter. He will then take a course of defiance, and he will take it with great advantage after all that has passed—after his speech in the House of Commons—and after his professed willingness (which he may boldly avow *when* he no longer professes it) to have taken the silk gown quietly as a favour. I am the more apprehensive that this will be his course, because in my judgement it appears to be the course which his interests point out—supposing (that is) his interests to be connected, as I presume he thinks them, with the overthrow of the Government. I have not the slightest doubt but the hostile discussion of this question will overthrow it: get into that discussion how we may; and I confess I do not see how we can get into it much more awkwardly than through a squabble on a miserable point of etiquette; for it is—it will turn out to be—no more. As to the silk gown Brougham will have it. He will have it upon his own terms, and without any service to render for it, if he does not get it (or if it is now too late to offer it) on ours; and he will have it from the same hands that now withhold it. But in the meantime we shall have lost all the advantage to be derived from it, and (if that were worth considering, when all is at stake) shall have brought him and Tierney together again on a question upon which, with a little management and temper, they might have been kept asunder.[9]

Lord Liverpool, thoroughly impressed with such cogent reasoning, sent a reply entirely to Canning's satisfaction. It was plain, said the latter, that no irreparable mischief had yet been done. But it was doubtful whether Eldon, who hated Brougham, would consent to his being given a silk gown even though the circumstances were so exceptional. Canning now urged that if the Chancellor was at all inclined to be obdurate, the importance of the occasion warranted the matter being brought before the whole Cabinet.

> Did any case ever arise before, in which the giving or withholding a silk gown might be the risk or safety of the Government? And when such a case arrives, does it not entirely change the nature of the discretion to be exercised, and make that which before was matter of department, matter of state?[10]

On the following day Lord Liverpool wrote to Eldon, and impressed on him the importance of the occasion. The letter to which he referred was that written by Brougham on March 30.

> Sir Benjamin Bloomfield brought me the enclosed letter yesterday by the King's commands from Brougham to Lord Hutchinson. He showed me at the same time a memorandum of Lord Hutchinson of what had since passed between him and Brougham. The latter has fixed the 27th of this month to meet the Princess at Aix-la-Chapelle or Lille; he wishes Lord Hutchinson to go with him. Lord Hutchinson is willing to go if the King and his Government approve of it. I trust they will succeed if they are in earnest in the business, but I really do feel the question of the silk gown to Brougham (together with any others to whom it might be proper to give it at the same time) as a matter of the very utmost importance. I am persuaded the character of the monarchy, and the reputation of a large part of the Royal Family, depend upon keeping this question out of *hostile discussion* in Parliament. The possibility of doing this must in a great degree rest with the Princess's advisers.

I am satisfied that Brougham for his own interest will be sincere in this business if he does not consider himself as ill-used, but I should really deplore the unfortunate determination of such a question upon a mere matter of *etiquette*. I am likewise persuaded that if the question does really come into hostile discussion in Parliament, it must end in the destruction of the present Administration. I cannot therefore refrain from urging you in the strongest terms to consider this point, and to feel that if it must be done, the sooner it is done the better.[11]

Whether the silk gown was actually offered or not is uncertain, but the probabilities are that it was. The *John Bull* newspaper, whose political intelligence was often more than semi-official, positively asserted on December 24 that the offer had actually been made; and Campbell, who had joined the Whigs and had become intimately acquainted with Brougham, declared that Lord Liverpool and the Chancellor had indeed promised it.[12]

Brougham's conduct during the next few weeks seems to point to the conclusion that his ambition had now taken a higher flight, and that he could no longer be satisfied merely with a silk gown. On April 11 he presented his appointment as Queen's Attorney-General in open court, where it was accepted, Lord Eldon declaring that "he would consult no views and regard no considerations in the matter, except such as were purely professional".[13] The appointment, indeed, could only be of a temporary nature, and would depend on the issue of the trial. If Caroline was divorced or compelled to abandon her rights, Brougham would have to revert to his stuff gown. It was known that he had delayed presenting his appointment, on the pretext that he was anxious to refrain from taking any step that would precipitate a crisis; but it is clear that his delay was occasioned solely by his negotiations with the Government. But he could no longer be bought off with a silk gown, and it seems clear that he was now bent on compassing the destruction of the Liverpool Ministry. What is not so evident, however, is whether he meant to bring in a Whig or a Coalition Ministry of Whigs and moderate Tories. It is more than probable that he had not himself made up his mind. About this time he was boasting to his friend Creevey that he was more likely than any one else to be the next Prime Minister,[14] an opinion he must have confided to other individuals, for on February 25, 1821, Campbell wrote:

> His plan certainly was (in Lord Castlereagh's phrase) to keep the King and Queen both open. He thought he should be able to make a tolerable bargain for the Queen, and to acquire such favour with the King as to be placed at the head of a new Administration. As a politician he is looked upon with distrust by all parties.[15]

Lord Liverpool, feverishly alarmed by the proceedings in the Court of Chancery, made one more desperate effort to push back the tide that was sweeping onwards to his ruin. Four days later, he made an offer identical in its financial terms with the proposal which Brougham himself had put forward in June 1819. Brougham was desired to communicate the substance of the proposal to the Queen, but he failed to do so. This extraordinary conduct is intelligible if we assume that at that moment he did not desire a peaceful settlement. He declined, too, to go to Geneva to consult with her, but, significantly enough, requested her to come within a day's journey, or, at most, a day and a half's, of Calais; and he showed himself especially anxious to keep the game all in his hands. It was of the utmost consequence, he told her impressively, that no one should know where the rendezvous was to be.

The Queen left Pesaro on the very day of Lord Liverpool's communication with her legal adviser, but it was not until the end of May that she arrived at St. Omer, an illness ("a dreadful spasms in my estomac which I got upon the Mont Cenis from the horrible cold I found there") detaining her for some time at Geneva. At St. Omer on June 3 she met Brougham and Lord Hutchinson, whom the Prime Minister had deputed to see her, in the hope that an eleventh-hour arrangement might yet be made. Not until then did Brougham inform her that Hutchinson was bringing the proposals of April 15 for her consideration. Acting under Brougham's advice, she instantly rejected them; but, in departing immediately afterwards from St. Omer and taking ship for England, she accepted the counsels of Alderman Wood, who had also come to see her, and whose meddling interference Brougham greatly resented.

There is abundant evidence of the Queen's dislike and distrust of her chief legal adviser, whose sincerity she doubted, but with whose assistance it was difficult to dispense. "If my head is on Temple Bar, it will be Brougham's doing," she exclaimed.[16] Others, too, openly avowed their suspicions. The Duke of Wellington declared that the Government had committed but one blunder—and that was in trusting Brougham to work for a settlement. He had betrayed everybody—king, queen, ministers, and Lord Hutchinson, added the Duke.[17] Canning wrote to Huskisson on October 2:

> Brougham has had his game too, and from a much earlier period, I suspect, than we apprehended. He dreaded compromise. He thought he saw how it might be effected. He barred that course by offering his own mediation. He thus got the thing into his own hands; and having got it there, he let it languish till success was hopeless. He *could not* go to Geneva, but he could go the circuit; and all this time, marvellous to think again! Liverpool thought Brougham in earnest and plain dealing![18]

On June 6 the Queen, accompanied by Alderman Wood, arrived in London. The commencement of proceedings against her raised her to the height of a national heroine, and she at once became the idol of the London mob.

With the course of the proceedings in the House of Lords, and with Brougham's conduct of the defence, we are not here concerned. The main interest lies in the political crisis which the Bill of Pains and Penalties occasioned.

Whilst, on the one hand, Brougham was manifestly striving to reap as much personal advantage as possible out of the question of the royal divorce, the leader of his party, on the other hand, was insisting that the Whigs should preserve a strict neutrality, and that their sole object should be to see that justice was done. As early as August 1819 Grey had warned Brougham that he must not expect to receive any help from the Whigs in promoting fanciful and dangerous schemes to damage the Government. Grey's cautious and disinterested action was fully shared by most of his friends; and even Sir Robert Wilson, who was later to become so violent on the subject, had, before the Queen's arrival, decided to give her a wide berth.[19]

But as the months of 1820 slipped by and the weakness of the Government became apparent, many of the bolder spirits, falling victims to temptation, could not refrain from lending a hand in speeding up the work of destruction. Lord John Russell, for instance, who in January had agreed with Mackintosh that the party should remain strictly neutral, in August was reviling the 'Big-wigs' for their indifference; and, as is clear from the Creevey correspondence, the Holland House politicians also came in for a good deal of sharp criticism. Lord Holland, indeed, regarded the whole affair as tiresome and vulgarising. He wrote to Lambton:

> The Queen's arrival supersedes all other considerations in the closet, the Cabinet, Parliament, or the public. Such is the happy effect of that beautiful institution called monarchy, and such the disposition of that enlightened nation called England. A man of consummate wisdom and exquisite genius who has served his country and adorned the Senate for near half a century dies in the morning, and an ugly mad woman, *pour ne pas dire autre chose*, lands in the afternoon—not ten people in the metropolis think twice of the first melancholy event, and the whole world from the Prime

Minister to the scavenger in the streets are occupied and agitated at the second. For the life of me I can feel no interest and little curiosity about these royal squabbles, degrading no doubt to all concerned, and disgusting and tiresome I think to the bystanders.[20]

That a change of Government was bound to come, nearly every one was convinced. Canning and the Prime Minister had quite made up their minds on the point. On the Whig side Lord Grey was one of the few who believed that his friends' hopes were illusory. A change of Ministers, he told Wilson, was merely the dream of a Bedlamite.[21] By the end of February, Wilson, on his part, had not only abandoned all idea of neutrality, but was confident that the Queen would consent to be a compliant tool in Whig hands. On the 28th he wrote to Lambton:

If she comes Ministers will be expelled, or the King will give up the ghost. Her coming is more than ever necessary, but with an understanding that to assist change she would withdraw after a certain time and not prevent coronation. This is my counsel, and I am certain it would be effectual if ably conducted. B[rougham] concurs in the opinion, if the premises be as authentic as I am confident they are.[22]

But even Wilson, in spite of his confidence in a speedy victory, had not made up his mind on the question from what elements the next Government was to be formed; and he acknowledged that there was some difficulty on that point.[23] The King hated his Tory advisers, but he detested the Whigs much more, and it was certain that he would apply to them only in the last resort. In May it was generally believed that he had sought the advice of Lord Grenville, but that statesman prudently declined to commit himself. A Ministry formed under the auspices of the Buckingham faction could not have endured a week.

On or about June 25, Canning, who disapproved of the proceedings that were about to be instituted in the House of Lords, put his office at the King's disposal. On the following day, however, George IV. desired him to remain in office, and permitted him to take his own course with respect to the Queen's 'business'.

The first tentative suggestion of a coalition of Whigs and discontented Tories came from Brougham himself. On May 12 he created an extraordinary sensation in the House by declaring (without the previous knowledge of the front Opposition bench) that at that juncture no single party could form a Government that could win the confidence of the nation. On the following day Wilson wrote to Grey:

> You will hear much of what fell from Brougham last night about a Ministry composed of all parties. My opinion is, notwithstanding Lambton's explanation to you, that this was a designed and deliberate proposition. Certain it is that the *House* and the *Treasury bench* assented to the principle, and that it will be acted upon by some means or other *I have not the slightest doubt*. . . . Whether any arrangement is practicable is another question, but I am sure that the offer should not be rejected, if made, without very serious consideration, for such reflection is due to the country, and a different course of proceeding would incur a heavy responsibility. It must, however, be done with a most disinterested feeling, so that no suspicion may be attached to the parties. I wish Lambton and some others would hold more statesmanlike *silence* at all events on the subject. . . .[24]

Wilson's hopes of a coalition seemed to be justified by the remarkable division that took place in the Commons three days later; and, according to Charles Wynn, who was in touch with both parties, it encouraged a further discussion of Brougham's suggestion. Several prominent Tories either stayed away or went into the lobby with the Opposition. One Minister (Vesey Fitzgerald) and one ex-Minister

(Peel) abstained, whilst another Minister (Bagwell, Master-General of the Ordnance in Ireland) voted with the Whigs.

But Wilson's confidence was not justified by the event, and his letter to Grey on May 19 (a week after the debate) was an acknowledgement of the prematureness of his hopes:

> Things remain *in statu quo*, Parliament unwilling to act, and *party* on all sides adverse to take the initiative. My own belief is however that a strong independent body is forming which will be eventually the commanding force.[25]

The truth would seem to be that Canning was not yet prepared to join forces with the Whigs—otherwise he would have insisted upon the acceptance of his resignation in June. And, further, his objections to the Government's policy were doubly reinforced by the Cabinet's decision, reached before the introduction of the Bill of Pains and Penalties into the Lords, to insert a divorce clause. Yet even then he did not resign. And in his letter to Lord Liverpool on July 30, declining to exchange his office of President of the Board of Control for that of Home Secretary, he seemed willing to allow himself to be involved in the impending ruin of the Government (which, since April, he had never doubted would follow from their policy), rather than to expose himself to the misrepresentations that, in the event of his going out, would be freely indulged in.[26]

Until the beginning of October, when Brougham opened the case for the defence in a brilliantly successful speech, many of the Whigs, among them Lord Grey, believed in the Queen's guilt. Their attitude greatly encouraged the Government, but exasperated their own friends, whose sole object was to turn the Ministry's embarrassments to political account. Wilson in particular was overcome with vexation:

> I am quite mad with many of our friends. They are doing all they can to lose this only opportunity to discomfit a wicked Administration. They are holding language quite

at variance with justice as well as common sense, for why should they make themselves pillars on which the Ministers may prop their falling cause? They exaggerate everything against the Queen, and diminish the value of everything in her favour. They are quite madmen, and deserve to be out of office for life. I would do all I could to keep them out if it were not for a few others and the public.[27]

A day or two later, Wilson informed Tierney that he should withdraw from the Opposition in consequence of Tierney's and Grey's hostility towards the Queen. The Whigs, however, were not in the least disturbed by his threat, and took no notice of his inflammability. Few shared his views on the subject, and Duncannon, who, as Party Whip, was likely to know the feelings of the rank and file, declared that everybody was highly pleased with the moderate course which Lord Grey had consistently followed.[28]

On November 10 the Lords divided on the third reading of the Bill, which was carried by so small a majority that Lord Liverpool, foreseeing that it would never get through the Commons, announced that it would be abandoned. Whigs who before had been sceptical, were now confident of victory. Even the cautious Tierney offered to stake anything that the Tories would be out.[29] Even before the division Lord Grey's friends had half-convinced him that he would shortly be sent for, and he had already begun to plan out a Ministry.[30] Brougham was to be Solicitor-General, but on November 10 he told his brother James that it was his fixed intention not to take office. The bait had not been made sufficiently attractive.

My course is clear. I will not lose my influence in the country, so capable of being turned to the best purposes. This I should lose by taking such a place as Solicitor-General, and I can make as much money as I have occasion for, without place. If they come in, I shall be a far better support to them if I am out of office.[31]

Whilst Sir Robert Wilson was betraying his optimism by going to Brandenburgh House to obtain an assurance that the Queen would be most reasonable and accommodating when the new Ministry should be actually formed, the more level-headed men in the party still retained their doubts.[32] Lord Holland, for example, had decided that there would be no change, and that the Opposition's game was to play for the support of the higher orders, and to commit itself to as little as possible. No amicable arrangement, he thought, could be expected from the King, and the only hope for the party lay in the possibility of winning over public opinion. To effect this, the Whigs must become parliamentary reformers.[33]

Reform was occupying the attention of Lord Grey also, and on December 5 he wrote a curious letter to Wilson asking for the views of the rank and file. It is remarkable that the leader of the Whig party should in the year 1820, after the reform question had agitated the country for four years, be ignorant of the opinions of the party as a whole. After expressing a hope that Wilson had been cured of his credulity with respect to a change of government, Grey proceeded:

> If, contrary to my confident expectations, the King should ultimately be reduced to the necessity of sending for me, it is a good thing if he shall previously have shown so strong a determination not to do so, till every other resource had failed him. If there still is in our ranks a single individual who has a weak side towards the Court, even such a man must be convinced that a Whig Administration can have no strength or security but in the confidence of the people. But how is that confidence to be obtained or possessed amidst such difficulties as any Administration which can now be formed must have to encounter? Would the repeal of the Bills,[34] the Alien Bill, reduction of establishments, and Catholic emancipation, command and retain it? Is Parliamentary reform a *sine quâ non*? What degree of reform would satisfy those who insist on it? And

is it right or honest to sacrifice for that object, under any
modification the attainable good which I have stated, if
such connections should be offered? If you can satisfy me
by a rational answer to these questions, you will save me
many a sleepless night.[35]

Grey addressed similar letters to other important members of the
party. His letter to Lord Holland shows that though his mind was
moving in the direction of Schedule A of the Reform Bill, he was not
yet prepared to make an efficient measure of reform a *sine quâ non*,
because such a pronouncement of policy would be likely to break up
the party.[36]

The fate of the Government seemed again to be sealed when, on
December 12, a month after the withdrawal of the Bill of Pains and
Penalties, Canning threw up his office. Was it, as people hinted, a
master stroke of policy dictated by a desire to avoid being involved in
the impending collapse of the Ministry? That this seemingly opportunist conduct would indeed occasion the dissolution of the Government
was widely believed. The dream of a coalition seemed no longer to be
the dream of a Bedlamite. The resignation, wrote Wilson exultingly
to Grey on the 21st, would prove "That I had some good foundation
for my credulity, and I have reason to believe his resignation will produce immediately all the consequences I anticipated". "The Signet," he
added, "must go to you, and you will, rely on it, have to charge yourself
with the serious responsibility."[37] One of his letters to Lambton points
distinctly to a Government formed out of a new centre party:

If *amiable adjustment* could be accomplished between the
parties *complaining* and *offending*, succession would not be
difficult; but otherwise difficulties would augment from
the nature of the cause which produced the change.[38]

Another letter suggests the possibility that the arch-conspirator
Brougham was again intriguing to be taken in by the Tories:

Hutchinson sees Bloomfield every day and has access to Liverpool, or perhaps I am more correct in saying correspondence with him, but I do not know the subject of communication, but as he also sees Brougham frequently, I can guess the object. Many circumstances combine to make me think attempts will be made to strengthen Government, but I cannot imagine the proposal will ever embrace a person about whom we are most interested, unless he consents to foreign employment.[39]

Croker, too, thought it possible that Lord Liverpool might make an offer to Brougham, especially in view of the fact that the Government had lost in Canning its greatest orator.[40]

Canning's motives are purely a matter of conjecture. The reason he publicly put forward was that, having been a confidential adviser, and still being a personal friend of the Queen, he could not with any show of decency continue to act as a confidential adviser of the King, who was bent on compassing her ruin and degradation. But the proceedings against Her Majesty had been abandoned. Why then, it might be asked, should he resign? In his explanation to the King he declared:

The discussions respecting the Queen which may now be expected in the House of Commons, will be so much intermixed with the general business of the session, that a Minister could not absent himself from them without appearing virtually to abandon the parliamentary duties of his station. On the other hand, to be present as a Minister taking no part in the discussions must produce not only the most painful embarrassment to himself, but the greatest perplexity of his colleagues, and the utmost disadvantage to the conduct of your Majesty's affairs.[41]

E.J. Stapleton, who edited Canning's official correspondence, considered this explanation to be inadequate, on the ground that his office of President of the Board of Control did not necessitate daily attendance in the House and constant participation in debate. "To mix up India with the Queen's trial," declared Stapleton, "really required an ingenuity which it was unnecessary to anticipate."[42]

However that may be, it is clear from Canning's unpublished correspondence that he strongly disapproved of the Government's proposed settlement of the Queen's affairs. She was to have an allowance of £50,000 a year, but, said Goulburn, the Ministers,

> can take no steps which can have the effect of upholding her as a person free from all taint or reproach. They must . . . consider the Queen's guilt as established by the majority in the House of Lords and by many of those Peers also who voted in the minority on the ground of expediency or from other motives; and considering her guilty they must consider the insertion of her name in the Liturgy or the providing her with a royal residence as altogether out of the question.[43]

Canning detailed his objections to the Cabinet's policy in a long letter to Lord Liverpool:

> . . . You are driven . . . as it appears to me, inevitably to admit that the continued omission *is* stigma . . . and you are driven to justify the infliction of that stigma, by reference to what has passed in the House of Lords. . . . You assume to the House of Lords a complete and conclusive jurisdiction upon a question over which the Constitution assigned to them only a divided authority. You advise the King to act not upon the final decision, but upon the preliminary opinions of the House of Lords. And you expect the House of Commons to sanction the act of the King, and to adopt the opinions of the House of Lords, implicitly, without examination, after having been defrauded by the House of

Lords, at the instigation of the King's servants, of their due share in the proceeding on which that act was founded. . . . What should one think of a proposal to the House of Commons, to approve of the imprisonment of a man, taken up under a Bill for suspending the Habeas Corpus originating in the House of Lords, which had been read a third time there, but not passed? . . . And is not the Bill of Pains and Penalties equally a Bill, equally requiring the sanction of both Houses, and the consent of the Crown to pass it into a law? . . . If the two Bills differ in anything, it is in this that the Bill of Pains and Penalties partakes of the nature of a judicial process. Be it so. And is not that a reason *the more* for not relying on anything short of its final issue? Who ever heard of a process in any court of judicature, in which the prosecutor might desist, at his own pleasure or connivance, from his suit, and yet claim the effect of a verdict? . . . A legal process must have a legal issue. . . . If not condemnation . . . acquittal . . . with all its benefits.[44]

These extracts from this important letter provide a conclusive answer to Stapleton's argument that, after the abandonment of the proceedings in the Lords, there was no obvious motive for resigning. Stapleton's other contention, that Canning's main object was really to free himself from the necessity of sanctioning Castlereagh's repressive policy both at home and abroad, carries equally little weight. Less than twelve months before, Canning had supported the Six Acts; and, further, had he wished to resign on account of his supposed differences with Castlereagh, he might have insisted on the acceptance of his resignation in June, when the situation of the Government, too, was as perilous as it was in December.

But if Wilson and Brougham were expecting that Canning's resignation would synchronise with the formation of a centre party of Whigs and Canningites, they were disappointed. For Canning went out into the wilderness alone, and all his friends kept their places. All the

Canningites in the Upper House—the Duke of Portland, the Marquis of Stafford, and Lords Morley, Granville, Amherst, and Bagot—had voted against the Government in the division on the third reading of the Bill of Pains and Penalties; but they were not asked, and they did not offer, to resign their posts.

Throughout this exciting year, the only signs of a desire to form a centre party had come from Wilson, Brougham, and the Whigs themselves. There is no evidence that Canning and his friends were as yet contemplating such a coalition. Nothing is more clear than that Canning went out of office in December 1820 without the slightest expectation of returning in Whig company. Not only did none of his friends follow his example, but they made it clear that their sympathies were not with the Whigs. Sir George Warrender, for instance, wrote on December 24:

> Had I resigned at the same time (and if I do not, I can assure you it is from no strong attachment to my office) I should have acted most unfairly by Mr. Canning in giving to his retirement a character which does not belong to it, and which would have been the less warranted, as I should certainly feel no difficulty out of office in decidedly supporting the course proposed to be followed by Ministers, supposing that course to be as I understand it—namely, that the Queen retaining the full and unquestioned possession of all her rights and privileges, shall have an establishment without any condition annexed to it, and suitable to her rank and station as Queen Consort living in a state of separation from her husband, but that nothing shall be done voluntarily to honour and exalt her.[45]

Lord Binning wrote to Huskisson on November 13:

> Every man has his speculation now, and mine is, that the Government will not be changed. . . . The Whigs have as

usual overshot the mark, and have rendered themselves more unacceptable than ever to the King—and I have not the least doubt that they and their friends the Radicals will now display so much indecent acrimony and violence that all men who dread a change on a revolutionary spirit will be desirous of supporting the Government. . . . I think it an unfortunate circumstance that Granville, Morley, Amherst, and the Duke of Portland all happened to vote against the Bill. It will create endless speculations and insinuations. Of course there was no help for it, as their honest opinions must have governed their votes.[46]

One factor, however, seems to be of considerable importance with regard to Canning's motives; and that is, he was as sure on December 12 as he had been in April, that the Government's days were numbered. It is then at least conceivable that he regarded himself as an alternative Prime Minister, notwithstanding the King's hostility towards him. However that may be, we find him writing to Huskisson, who was then (December 17) in Paris, warning him to return home before the following Easter, since important developments would then be taking place:

I still continue to think that in some way or other they will break down, or be broken down before Easter. I think so notwithstanding all the reliance that may be placed on the blunders, the intemperance, and the dissensions of their opponents, and on the alarms and fears of the *squirearchy*. We may possibly struggle through the Liturgy and the Palace, but we shall be left weak and lingering to meet other questions and impressions and prepossessions, such, for instance, as those growing out of the Milan Commission (not always perhaps over-scrupulous in its proceedings) with all its collateral circumstances of Hanoverian connection and singular expense—such again as the final yielding to the King upon the divorce—such as the £100,000 at least to be voted for the Milan Commission. . . . Are these matters that will be gulped by our country gentlemen? Or will they not attempt something like a censure upon those, by way of a set-off for other unpalatable votes? . . . This is only one of the many possible combinations of circumstances, by some or all of which I retain my opinion that a change will be brought about before the question of the Queen is finally set at rest.[47]

Canning's confident expectations, however, were shattered within a few days after the meeting of Parliament; and to the surprise and dismay of the Whigs, they found themselves in a painfully small minority on every question concerning the Queen. On January 30, only a week after the opening, Huskisson informed his chief that the battle was over and the enemy routed:

The newspapers will inform you of the course of our proceedings since the opening of the campaign, and of our marked success against the first great attack from the Opposition. A majority of 310 refusing to entertain the proposition that it was ill-advised and inexpedient to omit the Queen's name in the Liturgy is, I own, more than I expected. I did not accurately calculate how far the dread of the Whigs would operate to induce the country gentle-men to shrink from the avowal of those sentiments which they have most loudly proclaimed out of doors. However, it must be remarked that their alarm has been much increased by the recent conduct of Lord Grey and others at county meetings, whilst on the other hand the tone of the speech, and the declaration of Government that noth-ing further was, is, or had been in contemplation against the Queen, and that, after making a liberal provision for her maintenance, the question would be for ever at rest, as far as they were concerned, has greatly reconciled them to the Government. On this principle, many of our friends (Littleton for one) who had come down to vote for Lord A. turned against him, and the same feeling caught Portman and one or two other county members, who are generally more inclined to Opposition.

The original plan of the Opposition was to begin with Lord T.'s motion of censure which now stands for Monday next; but Lord A. would not yield; and upon this as upon some other points there have been dissensions among them. After their defeat on Saturday morning, the more violent, including all the Mountain and not a few of the Whigs (the Duke of Bedford among others) were for a course more decidedly factious—to make their way out of doors is their advice, but I believe this course is not to be attempted, except as far as it can be pursued by the old course of making speeches in the House.

Tierney is adverse to any other system, but they are all at variance, and equally out of temper and out of spirits.[48]

Popular enthusiasm for the Queen died down as rapidly as it had been stimulated; all the more so, in fact, when the reformers in the country came to understand that the Whigs had taken up her cause merely in order to make political capital therefrom. In February the 'Big-wigs' proposed to set on foot a voluntary subscription on her behalf, by which it was hoped to raise two or three hundred thousand pounds. Falling in with their views, Brougham advised her to decline the provision offered her by Parliament. His advice was accepted, but deep was his mortification when he learnt that the subscription meeting was a miserable failure, and that things were looking, as Creevey said, "damned ill and black". His chagrin deepened when he heard that the Queen was abusing him for his advice, and that she had decided after all to accept the provision which, only a week or two before, she had refused.

Castlereagh could now enjoy his triumph over the Whigs. Brougham, he wrote on March 13, had left town for the circuit, apparently broken down both in body and mind, as well as in reputation. The Opposition, he said, was thoroughly demoralised and disorganised. The 'Mountain' was in rebellion, with Hume and Bennet offering battle against the old Whigs.[49]

By this time Brougham had come to the conclusion that a change of government would not take place until the Tory phalanx had been broken up. For, now that the Queen had accepted the Ministry's terms, nothing more could be hoped from her; and her death in August released him from a situation that had for some time tended only to embarrass him. Many years later he wrote to Althorp:

> . . . I owed her no gratitude. She had always behaved as selfishly and as treacherously as possible—but I did not like to abandon her to her fate, knowing that she was sure to be ruined in twenty-four hours, though about every other day things happened that gave me a full right to throw up the case. I am speaking of the *early parts* of the affair and of the *last part*—of the parts before the trial began (if we can call it a trial) and of the parts near her death.[50]

But the Minister's triumph at the total discomfiture of the enemy was destined to be of short duration, and by the end of April 1821 the whole political situation was once more in a state of flux, as a result of the quarrels between the King and the Cabinet on questions of patronage. Two factors dominated the situation: George IV.'s hatred of his Prime Minister, and Lady Conyngham's political flirtation with the Whig chiefs. Brougham and other members of the Opposition were quite willing to use her, as they had attempted to use the Queen, as a tool; and they were prepared to justify their accession to office by such discreditable means, on the ground that it would destroy the solidarity of the Tory party and undermine the power of Lord Liverpool. Lord Lansdowne was to be the head of a new Government, which would probably receive Canningite support.

The intrigue began at the Pavilion, the royal residence at Brighton, in April, when Lord and Lady Lansdowne, together with other leading members of the party, were entertained to dinner and treated with marked favour. The King, too, seemed willing to forget his animosity against Lord Grey, whom he consented to include in the projected Ministry.[51] A new squabble with the Ministers in July over the question of admitting the Queen to the coronation ceremony increased the expectancy of the 'Outs'; and Wellesley's going to Carlton House in a tremendous hurry and being admitted by the back door, seemed to Brougham and other anxious observers of events a sure and certain portent of a coalition Government.[52]

But once more the Whigs were cruelly hoaxed and disappointed, and by the middle of September the King had made his peace with his Tory advisers. Every year seemed to add to the truth of the lines:

> Naught's constant in the human race,
> Except the Whigs not getting into place.

The whole project of an *entente* between Brougham and Canning as yet hung fire. It is clear from Canning's unpublished correspondence with Huskisson that he was still relying on the Tories, not on the Whigs. During the year 1821 no less than four series of negotiations took place between Canning and the Prime Minister, and nothing but the King's hostility to his late Minister prevented a junction. Canning's willingness to accept the Governor-Generalship of India, rather than cause the downfall of the Liverpool Ministry by holding out for high office at home, is a decisive proof that in 1821 he was not meditating an alliance with the Whigs as a means of countering the King's hostility. He wrote to Huskisson:

> I preferred India, opening to me in a certain way—that is, though an undoubted voluntary vacancy, and by the unsuggested solicitation of the Court of Directors—to—not office—but a struggle for office, liable to end

either in a second rejection—*or*, in the breaking-up of
the Government.[53]

Thus until the spring of 1822, when Canning, disheartened by
his long spell of unemployment and impotence, accepted the
Governor-Generalship after Lord Hastings' resignation had been
properly received, things remained in *statu quo*. Whig opposition
in Parliament languished, and after an unfortunate speech on
agricultural distress on February 11, which was mercilessly cut
up by Huskisson and Ricardo from opposite sides of the House,
Brougham himself remained much in the background for the
rest of the session. The fighting was done by the 'Mountain',
but no impression was made on the Government. A few years
later, Hobhouse had occasion to recall the activities of Hume
and his other friends during the course of this year; and he
observed:

> It almost destroyed us; we divided on every item of every
> estimate; we were glued to these seats. The evening sun
> went down upon us in this hostile array; and when he
> arose in the morning, he shone upon our undiminished
> ranks. If ever Opposition despised hunger and thirst and
> watchfulness for conscience sake, it was the Opposition
> that was led by my honourable friend during those
> neverending sessions. [274]

Tory ballad-makers told the story of the campaign in characteristic
fashion:

A pack of hounds of Whiggish breed, who sought to get their name up,
And all throw off in gallant style whene'er they put the game up,
At Brooks's met to form their plans—In *vulgum voces spargere*
Not Brooks's club, as heretofore, but Brooks' great menagerie.

When 'loaves and fishes' formed the only object of the chase, Sir,
No dogs had better noses, or could go a better pace, Sir;
And all excell'd in 'giving tongue' whene'er they took their station,
To growl about the grievances of this *unhappy* nation.

Small Bennet, Lushington and Wood, engaged to raise the ghost of
A certain royal funeral, already made the most of;
While Wilson, in his grief at being laid upon the shelf, Sir,
Thought the most important subject for discussion was—*Himself*, Sir.

Says Joseph Hume, "Though Croker's cuts have made an alter'd mon o' me
I'll still be foremost in the throng for preaching up economy;
I'll hunt down all the charges in our armies and our navies";
"And *I* will be your whipper-in," cries gallant Colonel Davies.

Then Curwen would repeal the tax on tallow, cheese, or leather.
Says Calcraft, "I've a better plan, and let us pull together;
Vansittart means to ease the malt, so let *us* work the salt tax—
If salt should be the word with *him*—why, *then*, we'll try the malt tax."

Says Creevey, "I must needs confess, when I was at the India Board,
I ne'er did much but read the news, or loll upon the window-board;
But since my hopes of lolling there again are all demolish'd,
I'll prove the whole concern so bad, it ought to be abolish'd."

"I care not who," says Lawyer Brougham, "from place or pension budges;
What salaries ye lower, so ye leave alone the Judges;
Who knows but I, by chance, may be hereafter for the Bench meant,
Then that is surely not a proper object for retrenchment."

"'Tis wisely said," George Tierney cries, who to the last had tarried;
"Too far by patriotic feelings some of ye are carried;
Economy 'tis very well at times to snarl and bite for,
But have a care, lest bye and bye there's *nothing left to fight for.*"

Brougham vents a loud complaint, that royal influence increases,
And holds that members of the House should give up all their places;
But, shifting Master Harry, pray which way would int'rest turn you,
If George the Fourth forthwith was pleased to make you his Attorney?

Then Johnny Russell made a speech, and some of it was pointed too,
About "Reform in Parliament", and "*state of things in ninety-two*";
But though 'twas called a sharp harangue, and he had clearly read for't,
He never spoke of throwing open Tavistock or Bedford.

But the hopes of the Opposition suddenly revived on August 12, when Castlereagh committed suicide. His dramatic withdrawal from the scene necessitated a reshuffle of the cards. Would the change be partial or complete? was a question that agitated all minds. All kinds of rumours were speedily circulated. It was variously conjectured that Lord Wellesley, the Duke of Wellington, Sir Charles Stewart, Peel, and Canning were to be offered the seals of the Foreign Office; and it was rumoured that Landsowne and other moderate Whigs were to be approached with a view to coming in to strengthen the existing Ministry. Others, again, were positive that Lord Liverpool was meditating a timely retreat, and that the Whigs were to be called upon to form a Government.[55]

Few Whigs believed in total change. Grey was convinced that the old Ministry would be patched up; and even Wilson saw no reason for delaying a hasty journey to Paris.[56] Brougham affected complete indifference. He wrote to Creevey:

> Who cares one farthing about it? We know the enemy is incalculably damaged anyhow. . . . He has left behind him the choice between the Merry Andrew and the Spinning Jenny [*i.e.* Canning and Peel]; and the Court—the vile, stupid, absurd, superannuated Court, may make its election and welcome. The damaged prig or the damaged joker signifies very little. I rather agree with Taylor that they will take Wellington for the Secretary of State, and that Canning

will still go to India. . . . I rather think I should prefer the
very vulnerable Canning remaining at home.[57]

Brougham was now expecting to find political salvation in a junction
with the Canningite party; and there is no reason to doubt his statement
in his autobiography that, for many years before 1827, he had been
convinced that the best if not the only hope of carrying Catholic emancipation lay in a coalition between Canning and the moderate Whigs. His
conduct at this critical moment leaves one with the impression that he
had hopes of coming to terms with Canning either immediately or in the
near future. For on August 19, a week after Lord Londonderry's death, he
met Canning at a dinner party at Storrs, Colonel Bolton's country seat
on the shores of Lake Windermere. John Bolton was a Liverpool slave-
dealer, and a Tory well known both in Lancashire and Westmorland. For
many years it had been his custom to entertain to dinner the leading
counsel on the Northern Circuit on their way down from the Appleby
to the Lancaster Assizes. But he was also a violent Lowtherite; it had
been one of his under-strappers who had engaged the services of some
two-score professional bruisers for the Westmorland election of 1818; and
on this account Brougham had for some time refrained from attending. Now, however, when he was asked whether he would care to meet
Canning at Storrs previous to his departure for India, Brougham jumped
at the opportunity, and eagerly accepted the invitation.

The news of the Windermere dinner occasioned much excitement
and gossip amongst both Whigs and Tories. The Opposition positively
asserted that terms were proposed, and Grey became alarmed about
Brougham's continued loyalty to the party. Sir Walter Scott's honest
simplicity was rudely shocked at the apparent disingenuousness of
his friend's conduct.

> [The *rencontre* at Storrs, he declared], gives rise to strange
> conjectures, and though I think no man's general principles
> are sounder than Canning's, yet in his minor movements I
> could never entirely acquit him of something like finesse. It

was owing to this that the manly plainness of Castlereagh (poor fellow) baffled his extraordinary talents in the race of ambition. If this meeting with Brougham was meant to intimate a hint of a possible coalition just in order to quicken movements elsewhere, it was singular bad taste.[58]

Brougham wrote both to Grey and Holland to explain the suspicious circumstance of the meeting. To Lord Holland he said (August 26):

> . . . It is very true that I met Canning at dinner. It was at Bolton's, where a part of the circuit dine every year, but I had not been there of late, he being a violent Lowtherite. However, when it was put to me whether I had any objection to go this time on account of Canning being there, I said, as the fact was, that I had all the rather go on that account, and should be very glad to see him again before he went to India.
>
> He talked very properly about Castlereagh's death. I mean with right feeling of course, but without the least canting, which one hears so much of in many quarters. I can't believe him so foolish as to come into office. If he does it is only to be accounted for by the importunities of his friends, for he must see that the miserable creatures in office will be eternally intriguing against him, and make his life uncomfortable, and then turn him out to have some low dunce of their own choosing. Indeed, if he has any *ambition*, India is more power than Prime Minister here (which he never can be). A Minister in England has no real power—he has some patronage, but he governs by compromises with the Court and with the country or Parliament, that is, by intrigue and talk, and after all, he divides his power, not merely with his colleagues, but with the Opposition.
>
> However, I don't expect him to take any such wise views. His going depends on the King and the Chancellor, and as

the latter has *not* spoken of retiring for some time and has been weeping bitterly of late, there seems a chance of his retiring. Canning at his Liverpool dinner talked with an 'if' about the King sending for him, from which I conclude that Lord Liverpool has given him hopes. I don't think he had any some days ago. Whether his being among them will do them *on the whole* any good is to me doubtful. He is very unpopular in the country, and not at all liked in the House, and cannot long agree with the dunces. Perhaps we shall have as fine a sight with him in office as if even the consummation were granted to us of the spinning jenny trying it alone. . . .[59]

The King, who was in Scotland, was in no hurry to come to a decision, and three weeks elapsed before an arrangement was attempted. Canning, on his part, seemed to care little about his ultimate destination. On August 26 he wrote to Huskisson: "It is not possible that curiosity should not be alive, but I have not been asked any questions, and I go on taking leave, just as if there were no risk of any impediment to my going. Indeed, there may very likely be none in the end; and I am sure there is but one consideration which in any degree qualifies my sincere wish that there should be none".[60] And on September 8 he wrote: "I have heard nothing. I know nothing. And I care nothing except that, if possible, there should be nothing for me to hear."[61] Eight days later, Lord Liverpool's pertinacity having extorted the King's reluctant consent to accept Canning as Londonderry's successor, the ex-President of the Board of Control had installed himself at the Foreign Office.

The crisis of August 1822 had an interesting and significant sequel. Lord Grey, alarmed at the political coquetry at Colonel Bolton's, and fearing for Brougham's allegiance, attempted to wean him from a possible alliance with the Liberal Tories, by offering him the lead of the House of Commons upon the formation of a Whig Ministry. Grey had not the slightest expectation of being called upon to form a Government, and his overture to Brougham was obviously dictated merely by a desire to make sure of so unsteady an ally. He wrote:

On you must depend, in the first degree, the efficiency of
any Administration that can be formed, in whatever situation you might be placed; and it is upon this that I hope
you will not be unwilling to state to me confidentially
and explicitly what your views and wishes are, under the
assurance that they cannot be deposited more safely, or
stated to any person whose disposition would lead him
more cordially, as far as he had power, to assist and to
promote them.[62]

The difficulties which Grey had to encounter in November 1830
are already foreshadowed in Brougham's reply. For he positively
declined office, and urged, as he had done in 1820, that Scarlett and
Denman could be given the Attorney and Solicitor-Generalship. On
no account, he said, would he abandon his profession. That was an
intimation that nothing less than the Mastership of the Rolls could
satisfy his ambition. Such an office (a life appointment) could be held,
too, with a seat in the Commons, which Brougham had determined
never to leave. In a second letter, Grey urged that the sacrifice was
unnecessary, and pointed out that all the great eighteenth-century
lawyers, like Mansfield, Thurlow, and Wedderburn, had begun their
official careers either as Attorney or as Solicitor-General, and had risen
either to the Woolsack or the Chief Justiceship.

The correspondence on that subject went no further, but it must
have caused Lord Grey a good deal of uneasiness. He was already
beginning to regard Brougham with mistrust, as a supporter whose
assistance was too powerful lightly to be dispensed with, but who
could not be tolerated in an independent position either in or out
of office. "In office," said Grey insistently, "you must be, or the
Government, I am persuaded, could not go on . . . and your saying
you will take no office is, in my mind, tantamount to saying no Whig
Administration can be formed." That language was to be echoed and
re-echoed in November 1830, and the truth of the proposition amply
to be demonstrated.

1.   Bentham, *Works*, x. 472.

2.   *Creevey Papers*, i. 198; Dudley, *Letters to Ivy*, p.249.

3.   *Canning and his Times*, p.266.

4.   *Creevey Papers*, ii. 23.

5.   *Ibid.* i. 297.

6.   *Canning and his Times*, p.286.

7.   *John Bull*, Jan. 14, 1821.

8.   Add. MS. 38193, fol. 112.

9.   *Ibid.* fol. 114.

10. *Ibid.* fol. 118.

11. Add. MS. 38284, fol. 26.

12. *Life of Campbell*, i. 379.

13. *Canning and his Times*, p.289.

14. *Creevey Papers*, ii. 23.

15. *Life of Campbell*, i. 394.

16. *Life of Denman*, i. 163.

17. Hatherton MS., Diary, June 22, 1820.

18. *Canning and his Times*, p.300.

19. Lambton MS.: Wilson to Lambton, n.d.

20. *Ibid.*: Lord Holland to Lambton. The allusion in Lord Holland's letter is to Henry Gratton, who died on June 4, and whose parliamentary career had begun in 1775.

21. Lambton MS.: Wilson to Lambton, n.d. (c. February).

22. *Ibid.*: Wilson to Lambton, February 28, 1820.

23. Add. MS. 30123, fol. 167.

24. *Ibid.* fol. 155.

25. *Ibid.* fol. 159.

26. *Canning and his Times*, p.295.

27. Lambton MS.: Wilson to Lambton, Aug. 26, 1820.

28. Lambton MS.: Duncannon to Lambton, n.d. (Sept. 1, 1820).

29. *Memoirs of R.P. Ward*, ii. 93.

30. *Life and Times*, ii. 450.

31. *Ibid.* ii. 402.

32. Lambton MS.: Wilson to Lambton, Nov. 30, 1820.

33. Add. MS. 30123, fol. 206.
34. The Six Acts.
35. Add, MS. 30109, fol. 142.
36. G.M. Trevelyan, *Lord Grey*, p.372.
37. Add. MS. 30123, fol. 227.
38. Lambton MS.
39. *Ibid.*
40. *Croker Papers*, i. 184.
41. *Official Corr. of Canning*, i. 6.
42. *Ibid.* i. 7.
43. Hatherton MS.: Goulburn to Littleton, Dec. 19, 1820.
44. Add. MS. 38193, fol. 144.
45. Add. MS. 38742, fol. 159.
46. *Ibid.* fol. 132.
47. *Ibid.* fol. 156.
48. *Ibid.* fol. 171. 'Lord A.' was Lord Archibald Hamilton; 'Lord T.' was Lord Tavistock.
49. Alison, iii. 222.
50. Althorp MS.: Brougham to Althorp, Thursday (January 5, 1832).
51. *Croker Papers*, i. 190.
52. *Creevey Papers*, ii. 16.
53. Add. MS. 38743, fol. 90.
54. *Parl. Deb.*, N.S., xv. 692.
55. *The Times*, Aug. 14-22, 1822.
56. Lambton MS.; Wilson to Lambton, Aug. 17, 1822.
57. *Creevey Papers*, ii. 44.
58. Scott, *Familiar Letters*, ii. 150.
59. Holland House MS.
60. Add, MS. 38743, fol. 201.
61. *Ibid.* fol. 207.
62. *Life and Times*, ii. 444.

VII

The Last Years of the Liverpool Ministry

The accession of Mr. Canning to the Cabinet, in a position too of surpassing influence, soon led to a further weeding of the mediocrities, and among other introductions to the memorable entrance of Mr. Huskisson. In this wise did that Cabinet, once notable only for the absence of all those qualities which authorise the possession of power, come to be generally esteemed as a body of men who for parliamentary eloquence, official practice, political information, sagacity in council, and a due understanding of their epoch, were inferior to none that had directed the policy of the empire since the Revolution.

Coningsby, Book II. Chapter I.

IN 1822 the country entered upon a new and happier phase in its history. Under the guidance of the new school of Tories led by Peel, Canning, and Huskisson, the Government set its face once more in a reforming direction, and the work which Pitt had abandoned in 1792 was resumed. With the passing of Londonderry and the relegation of Sidmouth into that inconspicuous place for which his mediocre abilities alone fitted him, passed also the period of stupid and unintelligent reaction engendered by the fears of the French Revolution. Close observers had long ago noticed that the younger men in the Tory ranks were being steadily alienated by the obscurantist tendencies in the policy and principles of the party leaders, and by the indifference with which their claims to high office were regarded. But their opportunity had now arrived. Canning was back at the Foreign Office, Peel succeeded Sidmouth in the Home Department, and Huskisson in 1823 was given the Board of Trade and a seat in the Cabinet. Whilst Canning in the sphere of foreign affairs henceforward sought to dissociate the Government from the policy of the continental despots and to put himself at the head of the Liberal Movement in Europe, Peel at the Home Office swept away the worst abuses of the spy system, initiated a drastic reform of the penal code, and in 1829 provided London for the first time with an efficient police force. And on Huskisson descended the mantle of Pitt as an economic reformer. With the assistance of an able subordinate, James Deacon Hume, he reconstructed the whole commercial system of the country on moderate free-trade lines, modifying the obsolete Navigation Laws, codifying and simplifying the Tariff Laws, amending the Corn Laws on a sliding-scale principle, and repealing the Combination Laws which pressed so heavily on the working classes.

But this attempt to create a new progressive Conservative party out of the superannuated eighteenth-century Toryism did not go unchallenged. Some of the representatives of the old order—Eldon, Westmorland, Bathurst, etc.—still remained in the saddle; and Lord Liverpool had all his work cut out in attempting to preserve harmony between the two contending wings of the party. Thus, if the next four years ushered in a new period of constructive social and economic reform, they also witnessed the beginnings of the break-up of the Tory phalanx into a party of progressives led by Canning, and a party of hide-bound reactionaries who swore by Eldon and Wellington. Immediately the moderating and restraining influence of the Premier was removed, the whole structure fell with a crash.

But the Whig party too was being steadily broken up. The Lansdowne group, inspired largely by Brougham, and bent on the rout of the ultra-Tories from power, gave the reforming Ministers their hearty support, and looked forward to the speedy formation of a new Coalition Ministry with Canning at its head. But Grey, who had not formally abandoned the leadership of the Whig party, and who still commanded a considerable following, had never succeeded in overcoming his dislike and deep distrust of Canning, and could never be induced to countenance an alliance between the Opposition and the Liberal Tories.

The new progressive policy of the Liverpool Administration had another important result. It put the Whigs, as an Opposition, under a total eclipse. Its success seemed to give colour to Canning's view that what the country needed was not a revolutionary change in the representative system, but able and enlightened administration, and a sounder economic policy. The Tories had begun to steal the Whig thunder. Their claim to be more progressive than the Whigs had some foundation in fact, for many of the Whigs (Grey included) were protectionists in principle, and were hardly more zealous supporters of reform than were the Tories. Radicals like Place could look with deep complacency on the progress that was being made, and had no desire to see the Opposition supplanting the Government:

> The present Ministers have been more liberal than the Whigs were. This is seen by the people, who are, therefore quiescent under their control. They are pleased with the removal of restrictions on trade and commerce, with the amendments and consolidation of some of the laws, as for instance, the modification of the Navigation Laws, the exportation of wool, the repeal of all laws against combination of workmen to regulate their wages, repeal of the laws against emigration of artisans, repeal of the laws against extensive partnerships in ship insurances, the annihilation of the Levant Company, the consolidation of the Bankrupt Laws, the proposed consolidation as well

as the useful alterations of the Customs and Excise Laws, more particularly those of the Customs as suggested by a gentleman in the Custom House named *Hume*, into whose arrangements no lawyer has been permitted to stick his cloven foot. These and similar proceedings, with others contemplated and avowed, lead the people to conclude that, notwithstanding the ultra-Toryism of the Administration, it is less exceptionable than any former Administration, and, upon the whole, one which does not make a change in favour of the Whigs desirable. The people know that the present Ministers cannot live for ever, that they cannot as they die off be replaced with even such men as themselves, that the more the present Ministers do, the more must be done by any set of men who may succeed them, and that it is therefore better to encourage them to go on with the amendments they are disposed to make, on the persuasion they entertain that the Whigs would not even do so much.[1]

Brougham's excessive desire for a coalition of Moderate Whigs and Liberal Tories was clearly revealed in his violently objurgatory language upon hearing that Canning had accepted the Foreign Office and the lead of the House of Commons. All his reliance had been placed on Eldon's bitter hostility to Canning, and Brougham had been confident that Canning would never commit the blunder of accepting office, involving as it did the risk of his being again thrown out in a few months' time, when there would be no Governor-Generalship upon which to fall back. He wrote:

His coin is now about cried down—at least hardly current. He is stamped as a joker, and therefore dares not joke. . . . All these things, and his gout and irritability, I try to console myself withal, but still I own I am somewhat low.[2]

Several months elapsed before Brougham recovered from his disappointment. At the end of the year, however, the Whigs again appear to have gained the impression that the Tories were out of favour at Carlton House, and that the King was agreeable to a change of Ministers. Even Lord Grey seems to have been deceived, and, much to Creevey's amusement, a design was set on foot to cajole Brougham into accepting the Attorney-Generalship, and to gain his consent to the elevation of his rival, Scarlett, to the Woolsack. But it soon became clear that George IV. was content to go on as before, and that nothing more could be hoped from Lady Conyngham, for with some astuteness Canning had won her over by giving her son, Lord Francis Conyngham, a place in the Foreign Office.

At the beginning of the session of 1823 Canning was already being lionised at Brooks's, and the Opposition press readily took up the cue.[3] The Whigs declared that he was the most popular man in the country, and on February 24 Wilson in the Commons congratulated him on his liberal foreign policy.[4] Brougham told Lansdowne that the course the Whigs ought to steer was

> . . . to increase [Canning's] differences with his colleagues, and not to commit ourselves on our points of difference with him. My solution is 'abstinence' from needless attack for a while—and as all the lawyers will be away from the time of his election till Easter, this course will be the easier to follow.[5]

Thus it is obvious that the Whigs were still hoping much from Canning, and were bent on precipitating a Cabinet crisis.[6] They were confident that he and the high Tories would soon come to an open rupture. Creevey declared:

> I never saw a fellow look more uncomfortable than Canning. . . . People in office are in loud and undisguised hostility to him: it may be heard at all corners of the

> streets. I never saw such a contrast as between the man-
> ners of ministerial men even to him and what it used to
> be to Castlereagh.[7]

During the first two months of the session Brougham endeavoured to bring the Opposition into line with the new policy. He himself gave the lead not only by refraining from pressing the Government in the division lobby, but by pronouncing extravagant eulogies of Canning's foreign policy.[8] These startlingly novel tactics astonished outside observers who had not been initiated into the mysteries of the new strategy. "Why does he make such love to Canning?" bewildered people were demanding.[9] Those who could remember Brougham's furious onslaughts on the extravagantly expensive military estab-lishments of 1816 fairly gasped when they heard him regret that the Ministers, who were proposing to add 4000 seamen to the navy, did not mean to increase the number still further.[10] But when, on April 17, Canning pointedly declared in the Commons that

> he thought it hopeless in the then state of the country
> and the Parliament to form an Administration which
> would agree on emancipation, and upon all other general
> measures, so as to be able to carry on the general business
> of the nation,

Brougham's temper once more got the better of his prudence, and his angry reply betrayed his mortification at the disappointment of his hopes.[11] He declared himself to be in a state "almost bordering on despair" with regard to the Catholic question, and, proceeding to stigmatise Canning's conduct in accepting office in a disunited Cabinet as "the most incredible specimen of monstrous truckling, for the purpose of obtaining office, that the whole history of political tergiversation could furnish", he created that stormy scene which, but for the timely and effective intervention of Sir Robert Wilson, who suggested that Brougham was referring to Canning's political, not personal, character, would have ended in the arrest of the two leading members of the House.

The possibility of a junction had for the time being to be abandoned, and on the 30th Brougham made a violent attack on Canning's foreign policy. But a month later (May 22), by which time his anger had spent itself, we find him congratulating the Canningites on their liberal economic policy.[12]

His speech on July 16, when he audaciously attacked Lord Chancellor Eldon,[13] shows that he was still bent on driving a wedge between the two wings of the Tory party. Significantly enough, too, Canning and his colleagues on the Treasury bench in the Commons received the attack in silence.[14]

In 1824 Brougham was still attempting to use the Catholic question for party purposes. Hobhouse declared that Canning was being supported much better by the Opposition than by his friends on the Government side of the House.[15] At the beginning of May, nearly every one believed that the Ministry was breaking up. The Whigs, it was said, were crying up Canning to the greatest degree, and were confidently anticipating a coalition with him.[16] Lord Liverpool was expected to retire, and Canning to form a Ministry with Lansdowne and Holland.[17] Croker dwelt significantly on the compliments bandied backwards and forwards between Canning and the Whigs, and on the fact that the Foreign Secretary was the only Minister who went to Lord Mayor Waithman's dinner, Waithman being a strong Opposition man. Croker added:

> To these circumstances are to be added Canning's uncalled-for eulogy on Sir Robert Wilson in his speech on the Spanish question, and several other panegyrics pronounced by him on individuals of the Opposition which were repaid by the Opposition in the same coin—all this is indicative of anything but cordiality amongst the Ministers, and their union is, in my opinion, precarious. Canning has never been averse to coalitions of

this nature—he has twice or thrice been on the point of junctions with the Opposition.[18]

But these fears of a dissolution of the Government were again temporarily dissipated on May 11, when an important debate on the state of Ireland took place in the House of Commons. Canning reiterated his reasons for taking office without the assurance of being able to carry emancipation, a question, he said, which could not be made a *sine quâ non*. And he went further in declaring that it had a better chance of success under a divided Government than under a Government all the members of which were pledged to carry it. He believed, too (and no doubt he was right) that the House of Commons was in advance of public opinion on the subject. He repeated his declaration of April 17, 1823, that no Ministry could be formed that could at once carry a measure of relief to the Catholics and conduct the general business of the country. He also reminded the Whigs that he and they differed *toto caelo* on the subject of reform, to some measure of which the Opposition, he said, was pledged.

> But whether [the Opposition were pledged or not], it was impossible for him to find a united Government, had he joined them, since they must have been divided, either among themselves, or with respect to him, upon the question of parliamentary reform.[19]

It was said that Tierney was loudly cheered by a large body of Whigs when he denied that they were anxious to coalesce with Canning.[20] He protested, too, that his party was not pledged on the reform question:

> A bond of party it never could be. Indeed, how should it be? Some of his friends were agreed upon it, others were opposed to it. And, among these who concurred, there were a thousand shades of opinion as to the specific degree

of reform. Not so with the other question. . . . All that he and his friends wanted was, to make the right honourable gentleman the most powerful part of the Cabinet, on condition that he would uphold the principles which he had avowed. The right honourable gentleman, then, ought not to represent them as an unworthy set, with whom he cautiously sought to remain at a distance.[21]

"I was not sorry, I own, to hear Canning properly chastised," wrote Fremantle, who was now in office; "first, because I think his assumption and individual lust of popularity most odious, but also because I thought the whole tenour of his speech dirty and intriguing."[22] But the whole debate went to show quite clearly that though the formation of a centre party was for the moment out of the question, an ultimate junction was almost inevitable.

It was in this year, too, that Lord Grey, to all intents and purposes, abandoned the leadership of the Whig party. His health, it is true, was failing, but it is significant that he decided to make his bow precisely at the time when it was generally believed that the Liverpool Government was to be succeeded by a Coalition Ministry.[23] Ever since 1807 he had felt a cordial dislike of Canning, and, now that there was a real possibility that they would both find themselves in the same Administration, Grey refused to entertain the idea of taking office. "*In* office," he said, "it would be quite impossible for me to support the fatigue and anxiety which must attend any leading situation in the Government."[24] Again in 1826 he informed Lord Lansdowne that he had come to a "final and fixed determination" never to take office "under any circumstances". Whilst he did not abandon his parliamentary duties altogether, he now left the management of party affairs to Lansdowne and Holland, neither of whom was averse to a junction with Canning. Thus the significance of Grey's retirement from the leadership is that it facilitated the formation of the much talked-of Liberal-Tory alliance.

By the year 1825 agitation in Ireland had grown to such proportions that the Government, becoming seriously alarmed, introduced a Bill to suppress the Catholic Association, which had been formed in Dublin in 1823 by O'Connell to work for the emancipation of the Catholics. The Ministers spoke of this organisation, which rapidly assumed national dimensions, as being, on account of its vast ramifications, "calculated, by exciting alarm and by exasperating animosities, to endanger the peace of society, and to retard the course of national improvement".

At the very beginning of the session (February 3) Canning made it clear that his views on the Catholic question had undergone no change. Replying to Brougham, he declared roundly that he

> must reserve to himself the right of judging how, when, at what period, and in what manner, to give up either his office or his life in support of that or any other cause; he would not consent to have the opportunity chosen for him, especially by one who might happen to have some collateral interest in the event.[25]

The most important debate on the Unlawful Societies in Ireland Bill took place on February 15, and not only did Canning speak warmly in its favour, but he disappointed Brougham and the Whigs still more by his elaborate re-statement of views on the whole question of emancipation. His speech affords a decisive proof that at this time he had no thoughts of throwing up his office and combining with the Opposition to pass a Relief Bill. Replying to an imputation that the success or failure of the question rested entirely on the choice he was about to make, he said:

> If it is meant that by resigning my office I could then, unshackled, and acting as an individual member of this House, bring the question unreservedly before you, I answer that whilst in the Government as well as out of it I retain the power of taking such a part. But if it is meant that, after going on so long with my colleagues in

the Cabinet upon the principle of free action respecting this question, I ought now to demand the formation of a new compact—that is a course, sir, which I should disdain to take: I would ten thousand times rather quit office than turn round upon the Administration of which I am a member and insist upon changing the footing upon which I entered it. But again, sir, I declare that in office as well as out I am at perfect liberty to moot this question whenever a sense of duty impels me to do so. Whether I shall do so while in office—whether I should do so if out of office . . . are points which I reserve for the decision of my own unfettered judgement. I hold it to be a question in which the vote and speech of no man ought to be irrevocably promised beforehand for any specific time.[26]

Canning did not content himself merely with reaffirming his determination to remain unpledged. He warned Brougham that in opposing the Unlawful Societies Bill, he (Brougham) was doing incalculable harm to the Catholic cause, since he was alienating some of its best supporters:

I do not undervalue the services of such an advocate in any cause which he thinks fit to espouse. I acknowledge freely his great talents and acquirements, his accumulated knowledge, and the prodigious power with which he brings all these qualities into action. . . . But, valuable as these qualifications must at all times render him as an advocate to those whose cause he undertakes, he may still experience disappointment in the quarter where he expects to find his chief reward; and may discover that he has mistaken the road, not only to the general approbation of the country, but even to the good graces of those whom he most immediately aims at pleasing.[27]

To this outspoken accusation Brougham angrily replied with a *tu quoque*, asserting that Canning himself had offended most deeply by raising the 'No Popery' cry against the Catholics. That Brougham could make such a charge shows how deep was his resentment with Canning for not throwing up his office and joining forces with the Whigs to oust the Tory bigots. Canning rightly judged, however, that the time was not yet ripe for the passing of a Relief Bill. There was, he said, a great inert mass of opposition in the country to the Catholic cause, and only by slow degrees could that opposition be overcome. He went further in declaring that an Administration formed for the specific purpose of carrying emancipation would not only fail to do so, but would "light up a flame throughout the country which it would be most difficult indeed to quench".[28]

"I am *persuaded*," wrote Sir Robert Wilson emphatically on February 16, "Canning will quit the Government before the session is over, or carry some measure in favour of the Catholics."[29] Stapleton, Canning's private secretary, revealed no secret in 1831 when he declared that in 1825 Canning seriously deliberated the expediency of resignation as a means of furthering the cause of religious equality.[30] But he believed that resignation would merely throw the Government into the hands of the ultra-Tories, and would mean the destruction of the Liberal policy at home and abroad which he and his friends had inaugurated since 1822. So that even when Burdett's Relief Bill passed through all its stages in the Commons, Canning, as he definitely declared on May 26, had no intention of abandoning the Ministry in order to form a Government with the Whigs and to appeal to the country against the old Tories. That Bill had been brought in on March 23, had passed its second reading on April 21 by a majority of 27, and the third reading on May 10 by a majority of 21; but it was rejected by the Lords a week later.[31] The smallness of the majority in the Lower House fully confirmed Canning in his considered belief that for emancipation the nation was not yet ready, and that an appeal to the country for a mandate would be not only futile but disastrous. As he told Brougham on May 26, the Catholic question was not everything, and the adoption of his advice would be "fraught with calamity to the country".[32]

The efforts of 1825 to relieve the Catholics had another important result. Burdett, as we know, had nearly succeeded in breaking up the Government; but he had divided the Whig as well as the Tory party. It was the first occasion on which that section of the Opposition which was taking its stand on the question of a substantial reform of Parliament, and which refused to compromise its opinions in order to facilitate the passing even of a Catholic Relief Bill, came openly into conflict with the other wing headed by Lansdowne and Brougham, which was willing to join forces with the Liberal-Tories to destroy the power of the ultras. The split came on the Elective Franchise of Ireland Bill, which aimed at the disfranchisement of the Irish forty-shilling free-holders, and which had been introduced by Littleton in the expectation of making the Relief Bill more palatable to the delicate tastes of the Tory peers. Whilst the moderate Whigs, whose opinions were loudly and lengthily proclaimed by Brougham, were prepared to accept emancipation though coupled with such an odious measure, staunch reformers like Lambton and Hume announced that they would vote against the Relief Bill if the other were identified with it. And when Brougham attempted to persuade them not to endanger so great a reform by voting against it, Lambton angrily declared that he would be browbeaten by no one. He did not, indeed, carry out his threat, but abstained altogether from the division, as did several of his friends.[33]

Wellington himself declared that the Catholic question had all but broken up the Ministry.[34] The only hope of salvation, said Eldon, lay in an immediate dissolution of Parliament, for the 'No Popery' cry that could be raised in the country would discomfit the 'Catholics', as it did in 1807. In August we find Brougham on the *qui vive* for a General Election, making frantic efforts on behalf of friends of emancipation, and urging the Duke of Norfolk to bring in Jeffrey for a short period "to give us a thundering speech on the Catholic question".

> He has extreme fame in the country; is an enthusiast with
> us on that subject, as you see by his *Review* (many of
> the best Catholic articles being *his*); and such prodigious
> expectation would be raised as to give us *some novelty* on
> a hacknied topic, and would do us a world of good, the
> more so as Jeffrey is not a committed party man, and
> would only consent to come in for the occasion and then
> retire.[35]

The dissolution, however, was deferred until the following year; and in any case Jeffrey's assistance was not needed, since the Catholic question did not arise in 1826, Parliament's time being taken up mainly with financial and currency matters. The Whigs continued to give Canning their support, especially in the debates on the Bill to abolish the use of one- and two-pound notes. "Their conduct," Canning handsomely acknowledged, "and particularly that of Mr. Brougham, has been in the highest degree honourable and praiseworthy."[36]

But nevertheless, Brougham was getting more and more disconsolate on account of his continued exclusion from power. In April 1826 Campbell declared that he was "left like a fish on dry land when the sea suddenly retires. You can hardly imagine the degree to which he droops. He has lost his spirits altogether, and is quite flat both in business and in society."[37] The chief cause of concern to the Opposition was that Canning remained the uncompromising opponent of parliamentary reform. On the Ministerial side the Cambridge election did much to alienate the Secretary at War from the high Tories, and to drive him, first into the camp of Canning, and finally into that of the Whigs. He was justly annoyed with Lord Liverpool for permitting three anti-Catholics, two of whom were actually colleagues in office, to oppose him, and he intimated that his defeat would be immediately followed by resignation. "I am strong in the University itself," he wrote to Littleton, whom he asked to canvass the voters in Staffordshire, "and among the lawyers in London, but the great majority of the electors are rural reverends, and if they come up in mass against me, their charge will be as formidable as that of the Black Hussars." But he added, "all the Whigs are with me"; and, indeed, it was to them that he chiefly owed his victory.[38]

As Palmerston said, the General Election of 1826 left the balance of power between the Government and the Opposition practically unchanged. The real dividing line was now, not between those in and those out of office, but between the Liberals and the Illiberals. In a memorable letter Palmerston observed:

> The real Opposition of the present day sit behind the Treasury bench; and it is by the stupid old Tory party, who bawl out the memory and praises of Pitt while they are opposing all the measures and principles which he held most important; and it is by these that the progress of the Government in every improvement which they are attempting is thwarted and impeded. On the Catholic question; on the principles of commerce; on the corn laws; on the settlement of the currency; on the laws regulating the trade in money; on colonial slavery; on the game laws, which are intimately connected with the moral habits of the people—on all these questions and everything like them, the Government find support from the Whigs and resistance from their self-denominated friends.[39]

Thus the old party divisions had almost ceased to exist, and the old names of Whig and Tory had again become as meaningless as they had been during the war years that had ushered in the nineteenth century. Nothing but the continuance in office of a neutral Prime Minister kept the old Ministerial vessel afloat, and delayed the advent of a new Government formed on Liberal principles. On February 17 Lord Liverpool was found unconscious in his house.[40] That fit of apoplexy occasioned the crisis which brought his Ministry to an end.

Contemporaries marvelled at the long continuance in power of an Administration which its enemies had characterised as "beyond all comparison the most contemptible in pretensions of any that have ever governed a great nation". But the Cabinet that had come into being in 1812 was not the Cabinet which collapsed fifteen years later. The mediocrities had been gradually weeded out, and highly-gifted men had from time to time been introduced to fill the gaps. Canning's opposition had been withdrawn in 1814, and in 1816 he had entered the Cabinet as the successor of the incompetent Earl of Buckinghamshire. In 1818 it had been strengthened still more by the adhesion of Wellington, in 1822 by the appointment of Peel to the Home Office, and in 1823 by the exclusion of Vansittart and the inclusion of Huskisson and Robinson. And finally, the personal gifts of Lord Liverpool, the 'Arch-mediocrity', his prudence, his temper, his moderation, and his ability to smooth away jealousies and difficulties, remained strangely underestimated or unrecognised.

1.   Add. MS. 35144, fol. 109.

2.   *Creevey Papers*, ii. 50.

3.   *Memoirs of the Court of George IV.*, i. 418.

4.   *Political Life of Canning*, i. 298.

5.   Lansdowne MS.: Brougham to Lansdowne, Dec. 18, 1822.

6.   Broughton, *Recollections*, iii. 11.

7.   *Creevey Papers*, ii. 63.

8.   Temperley, *Foreign Policy of Canning*, p.87.

9.   *Creevey Papers*, ii. 65.

10.   *Parl. Deb.*, N.S., viii 192.

11.   *Ibid.* viii. 1079.

12.   *Ibid.* ix. 439.

13.   During its course he said: "As to Lord Liverpool being Prime Minister, he is no more Prime Minister than I am. I reckon Lord

Liverpool a sort of member of Opposition, and after what has recently passed, if I were required, I should designate him as 'a noble lord in another place with whom I have the honour to act'. Lord Liverpool may have collateral influence, but Lord Eldon has all the direct influence of the Prime Minister. He is Prime Minister to all intents and purposes . . . "

14. *Memoirs of the Court of George IV.*, i. 480.

15. Murray, *Corr. of Byron*, ii. 297.

16. *Memoirs of the Court of George IV.,* ii. 68.

17. *Ibid.* ii. 70.

18. *Croker Papers*, i. 267.

19. *Parl. Deb.* N.S., xi. 723.

20. *Memoirs of the Court of George IV.*, ii. 75.

21. *Parl. Deb.*, N.S. xi. 722.

22. *Memoirs of the Court of George IV.*, ii. 76.

23. *Life and Opinions of Earl Grey*, p.425.

24. Lansdowne MS.: Brougham to Lansdowne, Sept. 12, 1826.

25. *Parl. Deb.*, N.S., xii. 75.

26. *Ibid.* xii. 495.

27. *Ibid.* xii 496.

28. *Ibid.* xii. 496.

29. Add. MS. 30124, fol. 137.

30. *Political Life of Canning*, ii 172.

31. *Parl. Deb.*, N.S., xii. 1149; xiii. pp.123, 558, 766.

32. *Ibid.* xiii. 890.

33. *Ibid.* xiii. 558; Memoirs at the Court of George IV., ii. 247.

34. *Desp. and Corr.*, ii. 483.

35. *Hist. MSS. Comm.*, vol. 63; MS. of the Duke of Norfolk, p.346.

36. *Political Life of Canning*, iii. 44.

37. *Life of Lord Campbell*, i. 430; *Peel Papers*, iii. 117.

38. Hatherton MS.: Palmerston to Littleton, Jan. 2 and Jan. 9, 1826.

39. Bulwer's *Palmerston*, i. 172.

40. A short time before, he had intimated to Arbuthnot that his shattered health would necessitate his retirement at the end

of the session of 1827. He was, too, unwilling that Catholic emancipation, which he knew must soon be conceded, should be carried during his Premiership. (Parker, Peel Papers, iii. 358.)

VIII

The Coalition Ministries of 1827

ANNUS MIRABILIS

Come, lay your jarring discords by,
And hail this happy day,
And mingle in sweet harmony,
All ye that mingle may—

The sun and moon no more shall move
In useless opposition,
But soon shall form in peace and love
A heavenly coalition.

Ye wandering comets! cease your flight!
Why should ye keep asunder?
In one mysterious blaze unite
And fill the world with wonder.

. . . . . .

Buxton shall scribble for the *Age,*
And Brougham write squibs for *Bull*—

> Bishops shall caper on the stage
> And lawyers cease to gull.
> Canning calls Brougham his *learned friend*
> "My honours—come and share 'em";
> Reformers their assistance lend
> To countenance Old Sarum.
>
> THEODORE HOOK

IT was quickly discovered that the stroke which left Lord Liverpool a helpless paralytic had also terminated his political life; yet eight weeks elapsed before the King commissioned Canning to reconstruct the Government. The Cabinet agreed to treat the Prime Minister's illness as a temporary indisposition, a decision which was largely due to a desire on the part of both wings of the Tory Party to await the issues of the corn and Catholic questions that were about to come up for discussion in the House of Commons. No division took place during the debate on the Corn Bill, but Burdett's motion on the Catholic question was defeated by four votes. That indecisive result made it necessary for the King himself to choose between Canning and Peel, or between Canning and Wellington. Could he have made an unfettered choice, George IV. would have appointed a Peer holding Lord Liverpool's opinions on the Catholic question. Canning held out for the substantive power of Prime Minister, and declined to serve under either Peel or the Duke, who, on their part, realised the impossibility of forming a Government without Canning's assistance. Perceiving at last that no Protestant Ministry could be made, the King on April 10 requested Canning, from whose opinions he differed only on the Catholic question, to remodel the Government on the same principles as those on which Lord Liverpool's had been based. By accepting that commission, and by endeavouring to retain the services of the six anti-Catholic members of the late Cabinet, the new Prime Minister showed his willingness to conduct a Ministry half the members of which would hold views on the question of catholic emancipation fundamentally different from his own. He was as certain in 1827 as he had been in

1825 that "An attempt to force the question upon *this* country by a Government united on this point, and for the purpose, would be the prelude to another catastrophe like that of the India Bill of 1784".[1]

But the immediate resignation of all the old Tories in office caused Canning to seek aid elsewhere. All along he had expected that Eldon and Peel would resign, but the precipitate action of the rest took him completely by surprise. Wellington's resignation was dictated much more by personal jealousy and dislike than by political differences, and he defended his conduct on the ground of Canning's incivility towards him.[2]

The voluntary retirement of the old Tories had two important results. It completed the disruption of the Tory party, and it threw Canning into the outstretched arms of the Whigs. Huskisson declared truly enough

> that if the King is driven to look for counsel in new quarters, the step was not taken till every expedient had been exhausted to retain in his service those who had hitherto been in his Cabinet, or to procure the assistance of others who had concurred in the general policy of the late Administration.[3]

Canning saw the hopelessness of forming a stable Government without assistance from the Opposition; but the first overtures for an alliance came from the Whigs themselves. Wellington firmly believed that negotiations began even before Lord Liverpool's seizure, but he was almost certainly mistaken. Canning knew, indeed, that Liverpool was meditating resignation at the beginning of the year, and in January rumours were being circulated that Canning and the Whigs were forming a compact. But there is no trace in Brougham's autobiography, and none in Stapleton's life of Canning, or in the official correspondence of Canning, of negotiations before February 17. If, as Wellington asserted, Huskisson conducted the negotiations on behalf of the Tories, we might reasonably expect to find traces in his correspondence. But not only do his papers contain not the slightest evidence of such intrigues, but they show clearly that Canning approached the Whigs only in the last resort. Nor is it clear why, as the Duke believed, Brougham should have deputed Sir Robert Wilson to act for the Whigs. Brougham did not leave London for the circuit until March, so that he must have been in town whilst the alleged intrigues were on foot; and we may be sure that his vanity would never have permitted him voluntarily to hand over such supremely important business even to a friend, so long as he himself remained on the spot.[4]

On the contrary, Brougham aspired to take the leading role in the exciting drama that was gradually unfolding itself. He had determined that he himself should be the architect of the new political structure that was to arise over the ruins of the Liverpool Ministry. He started off with two important advantages. He had Lord Lansdowne, the leading exponent of coalition in the House of Lords, almost completely under his thumb; and he had the Whig press on his side. His influence over *The Times*, the most powerful newspaper in the country, was at this period very great, and whenever he went down into the country to make a big speech that journal sent special representatives to report him—an expense which few papers could then afford.[5] Probably inspired by Brougham, *The Times*, on February 20 (only three days after the beginning of the crisis) suggested in its leader columns that the most acceptable way out of the *impasse* would be a union of Whigs and Canningites. Lansdowne should not insist on the Catholic question being made a Cabinet question, nor should he make the appointment to office of many of his friends a *sine quâ non*. "Let but the cause succeed, and we are willing to place ourselves out of the account", was the self-abnegating principle upon which the Whigs ought to act.

As early as February 19 or 20 the Opposition met to discuss the situation, and after much deliberation decided to support without reservation a Government of which Canning might be the head. They promised their aid no matter whether Canning might be able or not to further the Catholic question. The meeting was of members of the Commons only, Russell (who a month later was opposed to a junction), Abercromby and Fazakerley being amongst the speakers who favoured coalition. Brougham himself was unable to attend, being engaged in the law courts at the time, but he had previously let it be known that he was strongly in favour of whole-hearted co-operation with Canning. On the 22nd the latter was informed of the proceedings at the meeting; and thus within a week of the commencement of the interregnum, and actually more than a month before Canning was authorised to form a Ministry, a compact between him and the moderate Whigs was already in the making.[6]

Had Brougham not perceived that a considerable time would elapse before the King could be coerced into making a decision, he would probably never have attempted the circuit at this season. Before he left London for the north on March 9 or 10, he had already determined in his own mind that Canning would succeed to Liverpool's inheritance, that Canning would need Whig help, and that he himself would not cause any embarrassment either at Windsor or in Downing Street by demanding office. Before his departure he authorised Wilson, who remained in town to look after his interests, to make this declaration respecting office, either to Canning or to any one else whom it might be necessary to enlighten.[7]

Whilst on circuit at Lancaster, however, Brougham became sadly perturbed by rumours that Canning might possibly form an exclusively Tory Ministry without making any stipulation regarding the Catholic question. He had worked himself into a perfect frenzy when on March 18 he wrote a hurried note to Wilson requesting him to send more positive news than was available at such a distance from town, and reaffirming his willingness to give all possible assistance to Canning in order to keep out the ultra-Tories.

> For my own part I will only say that I am ready to back him in whatever way he himself would deem the most effectual. It is our duty, and we should all be found at our posts. But so should we if he were to give in and throw his good principles over.[8]

Sir Robert Wilson, fearing that Canning might shrink from the task of forming a Government unless he were sure of Whig support if deserted by the Protestant Tories, thought it advisable that Canning should be again informed that the Opposition, and Brougham in particular, would rejoice at the opportunity of assisting a Liberal Ministry. At Wilson's suggestion, therefore, Brougham wrote from York, on March 26, a more carefully-written letter that could be shown to Canning without giving offence. In it he reaffirmed his own "disinterestedness", and his unwillingness to thwart "unworthy womanish prejudices in certain quarters".

> I have, I know full well, he continued, a very consider-
> able influence in the country, which would be injured by
> taking place; and like to use it for purposes which your
> men in office rather laugh at than assist. Besides, with an
> ample income, professional and private, I have no tempta-
> tions to change my course of life.[9]

But the most important and significant points in this amended letter are those in which he vouches for the support of *all* the Opposition members whom Canning "needs to care about"— for some 'corn prejudices' amongst Whig protectionists must soon be dispersed before the light of reason; and, second, in which Brougham says that the inclusion of Peel, the leader of the anti-Catholic party in the Commons, in a Liberal Cabinet, will be no obstacle to Whig co-operation. "We may think him an ordinary man, and far inferior to Canning; yet we respect him, and value the victories he has gained over his prejudices."

On Sunday, April 1,[10] Brougham wrote a third letter to Wilson, from York. Its tone shows that he was becoming impatient at the postponement for what seemed to him an almost interminable period, of the day of settlement. And his old fears were returning that a patchwork Ministry exclusively Tory in character, and formed on Lord Liverpool's principle of leaving the Catholic question an open question, would yet be made. In that event, he declared, the Whigs ought to offer a strenuous opposition. Referring to his earlier letter of March 26, he said:

> As I fear I omitted to state my views with sufficient full-ness as to the course I think we are bound to hold, if all our firm and most disinterested efforts should fail towards forming an united Government on the great Irish ques-tion, and in case, by the place-seeking disposition of some, and peace-keeping views of others, the country should still be cursed with the continuance of the present scandalous and ludicrous plan of 'No Government', I add a few lines to prevent misapprehension and disappointment, and in this I believe Lord Lansdowne entirely concurs with me. I think, in the above event, we owe it not more to the country than to ourselves, on views of principle as well as of honour, without a day's delay, to form a powerful and vigorous Opposition *as a party* acting together. We shall have abundant materials for this. We shall have no con-nection with either Hume and Co. or the Benthamites. We shall, however, be sure to have their votes nine times in ten; but we shall pursue our own course, and act with firmness and union against the wretched policy of a divided Government.
>
> I care not whether we muster 80 or 180—indeed I had as lief the lesser as the greater number. I know the country will be with us; and I believe many of the Tories will join when it may be required. No man can say we have been too hasty in forming this resolution after all our fair and disinterested conduct, while we hoped others had right principles.[11]

Brougham enlarged on this topic in an interesting letter to Lord Lansdowne of the same date. The Whigs, he said, had "ceased to act as a party, and the country has naturally enough given over talking about what has no existence owing to ourselves".

> Our business is to reorganise or to form a steady Opposition on liberal but steady and intelligible grounds, and rather to limit our numbers than sacrifice union and vigour to numerical force. For such a party we have sufficient materials. But I do trust we shall no longer hear of such a measure being unnecessary, and I shall expect to find our excellent friend Abercromby prepared with better reasons than heretofore against it. He says, "the country has decided against party". It is easy to say so as an excuse for dropping the labour, and the very thankless labour, of public life. The country have not decided any such thing, unless you mean by the country, Dr. Black and Cobbett and Place the tailor.

With the Radicals, he said, the Whigs ought not to hold the least fellowship; they were

> a set of drivellers who call themselves a kind of *doctrinaires*, and hold opinions subversive of all liberty, as that the minister is never to be blamed, but only the system, and that you are bound to exact impossibilities from men out of place, and be thankful for mere nothing from men who have the power to give you all you have a right to or wish for. These men have much of the press in their hands, which makes them look bigger than they are. They are in their religion intolerable atheists, in the politics bloody-minded republicans, and in morals somewhat gross, and most selfish latitudinarians.

Brougham hoped that all the leading members of the party would cordially accept his view of the necessity of re-organising the Opposition:

No doubt the new state of things makes some modification necessary in our party union, both with reference to the divisions of the Government, and to the ultras on our own flank. Therefore we should direct our attacks mainly against one branch of the Ministry and certainly give our support to whatever good measures they, or any of them, bring forward. But this, while it saves us from the old and vulgar cry *against faction and factious opposition*, will not weaken, but rather strengthen our party union and our operations in Parliament and the country. A plain, explicit and distinct understanding must, however, be come to as soon as possible with all our leading men. I hope the Duke of Devonshire will have no difficulties. I am sure the Duke of Bedford and Tavistock will have none, and I think we may rely on Lord Fitzwilliam. I think for Lord Darlington I can answer. The vulgar charges of seeking office can hardly be revived against us after all our refusals of place, and candid and liberal support of our antagonists. But if it is revived we need care but little for it.[12]

Meanwhile Canning had seen the King on March 28, and the *aut Caesar aut nullus* attitude he had adopted had been made possible solely by the fact that from February 22 onwards he had been sure of Whig support. But Brougham's fears that a divided Ministry would be formed on the model of the Liverpool Cabinet, were not altogether unfounded; and nothing but the wholesale resignations that fell down on Canning like an avalanche prevented these fears from being realised.

The Cabinet, as Canning temporarily arranged it, was to consist of nine Catholics and three Protestants. Brougham's hopes of a Ministry united on the question of emancipation were thus dashed at the outset:

The fact is [wrote a Canningite] that more discordant opinions upon all points were never tumbled together in a

Cabinet. My most *decided opinion* is, that unless Canning
can form his Government upon the principle of slowly,
decently, and securely *pushing* on the Catholic question,
it will never stand. As a really neutral Government upon
that question it will *not* receive the steady support of the
ex-Tories, and it will meet sooner or later with the opposition of the Whigs.[13]

These misgivings soon began to be shared by Brougham himself.
Upon his return to London on April 15 he received the disturbing news of the appointment of the anti-Catholic Copley as Lord
Chancellor. "He was sure it could never be." There was good reason
for his alarm, for on the 20th the negotiations between Canning and
the Whigs broke down. Lansdowne had reluctantly agreed to shelve
the questions of parliamentary reform and the repeal of the Test and
Corporation Acts, but stood out for a Catholic Lord Lieutenant and
Chief Secretary of Ireland, as an earnest of the Government's intentions. George IV. insisted on the appointment of Protestants to these
offices, and Canning was unable to meet Lansdowne's demands.

Lansdowne at once left London, having declined to accede to
Canning's terms. Furious at the disappointment of his fondest hopes,
Brougham broke out into open rebellion against his chief, whom he
virtually deposed from the leadership. Described as being in a state
bordering on insanity, he went to Brooks's Club, called a meeting of
all available members who favoured Coalition, and harangued them
with such effect on the necessity of accepting Canning's proposals
as the only alternative to the return of the die-hard Tories that the
seditious spirit spread like wild-fire amongst his exasperated audience. It was agreed to send a deputation under Lord Auckland to
remonstrate with Lansdowne and to urge him to re-open negotiations.
Their importunity triumphed over his reluctance, and the views of
the Coalitionists prevailed. But for Brougham's rebelliousness, the
Coalition would certainly never have been formed. He wrote on the
21st: "The negotiation is on again to-day, with a fair prospect of suc-

cess. These difficulties come from some of our friends being still in the year 1780. . . . My principle is—anything to lock the door for ever on Eldon and Co."[14] He had already declared that he would go into violent and factious opposition if the Whigs refused office; and on the 23rd he warned the Duke of Devonshire, who was in favour of a junction, that a second breakdown of the negotiations would probably cause the disintegration of the Whig party:

> Though I don't like to intrude upon you at this moment, I think it my indispensable duty to inform you of the state of the opinions and feelings at present *universal* among our friends in town, both Lords and Commons, with a very few exceptions indeed, because, if you were not aware of it, you might be the means of shutting the doors to negotiation with the rest of us upon Lord Lansdowne's refusal to join Mr. Canning.
>
> They all feel one desire and one only—to form such a union upon fair and honourable grounds as may secure the grand object alike essential to the interest of the country at large and to our own views as a great and powerful party—the exclusion of the ultra Tories. The Irish members feel this most strongly, and Catholics not in Parliament have spoken and written to me on the subject. To attain so necessary an object they desire to see a sacrifice of all lesser matters, and I am anxious that this should be known to you. If the negotiation now breaks off it will probably tot be renewed, and our friends will take their own course. It may lead to the breaking up of the party, but it is more likely to produce a very violent opposition, from the sense men will have of being overlooked and undervalued in the estimate of political and parliamentary importance. Either result I should regard as most fatal to the best interests of the country.[15]

If, however, Brougham believed that the Duke of Devonshire could be induced to take Lord Lansdowne's place as leader of the Coalition Whigs, in the event of Lansdowne's refusal to join the Government, he was mistaken, for the Duke intimated that he would not take office without his chief.[16] The latter returned to town on the 25th, after having again refused Canning's terms; but by the evening of the following day a provisional settlement was arranged, and the influence of Brougham, weightily exerted through the Duke of Devonshire, brought about the desired Coalition. Thus Brougham, who, only three or four weeks previously had emphatically declared that the party ought to continue in Opposition unless the new Government was definitely united on the Irish question and was determined to carry it, was now the most imperious advocate of the Coalition which was about to continue that "scandalous and ludicrous system of No-Government, and to pursue that wretched policy" of a divided Ministry.[17] For the Catholic question was to remain an open question; and although it appears that there is no truth in the oft-repeated story that Canning actually promised the King never to bring that question forward, but, on the contrary, to see that it was permanently shelved, the chances that a relief Bill would be passed seemed to be as remote as ever.[18] Brougham's passionate demand for a junction with Canning caused him to lay himself open to a still more glaring inconsistency of conduct when he told Lansdowne that Canning's alleged pledge to the King mattered nothing:

> What signify the vague words said to be used by him, and repeated (perhaps exaggerated) by the King—"I promise not to force the King's conscience"—"I won't cram it down his throat" nay, "I form a Government on the principle of Lord Liverpool's". Does not any one who has sense look to things? Liverpool's Government was a bare majority, and that *against* the Catholics. His will be three to one for them. Liverpool himself was against, and Canning is for. Liverpool had none of us—he will have the best of us.[19]

It was arranged that the Whigs should have three seats in the Cabinet (Lansdowne to have the Home Office, Tierney the Mint, and Lord Carlisle the Privy Seal), but that they should not take office until near the close of the session. Several Whigs were to take secondary posts at once. The Duke of Devonshire reluctantly undertook the duties of Lord Chamberlain, Scarlett became Attorney-General, and Abercromby eventually became Judge-Advocate. It was not until July 16 that Lansdowne, Carlisle, and Tierney took office; and in less than a month Canning was dead.

If the junction rent the Tory party in twain, on the Whig party, too, it had the same disastrous effects. For Lansdowne and Brougham failed to bring over to their side the followers of Lord Grey. As we have seen, he had in 1824 abandoned for all practical purposes the leadership of the Opposition. In 1826 he had told Lansdowne that he had come to a final and fixed determination never again to take office under any circumstances.[20] In 1827 he again declared that he had given up politics, but, as Brougham observed, such a declaration had become almost an 'annual' with Grey. "He always thinks exactly as he says at the time, but he takes different views when his spirits get up."[21] He took no part in the negotiation between Canning and the Whigs, and he ceased to correspond with Lansdowne, Holland, and Brougham. Under no circumstances would he have taken office in a Ministry of which Canning was the head, so deep and incurable was his distrust of that statesman; but his objections to the Coalition were more than personal.[22] He admitted, indeed, that Canning's hostility to parliamentary reform was no bar to the Whigs taking office, and that reform should not be made a *sine quâ non* in forming any Government, since public opinion was not sufficiently strong in its favour.[23] But he denounced the Coalition as unprincipled, because the Catholic question was still to remain on the shelf. And he firmly believed that government by the old Tories, with all its obvious evils, was infinitely to be preferred to the sacrifice of the unity of the Whig party, in destroying which Lansdowne and Brougham had committed an unpardonable sin. He complained, too, that the

Coalition was a very one-sided affair. The Whigs ought not to have accepted office except on equal terms with the Tories; and they had been given only three out of twelve Cabinet places.[24]

The larger part of the Opposition sided with Lansdowne and Brougham rather than with Grey, who found himself almost alone in the House of Lords, declaring that he was almost without political connections of any kind. In the Commons the Coalition was supported whole-heartedly by Brougham, Tierney, Macdonald, Abercromby, and Scarlett, and, at the outset, was opposed by Duncannon, Althorp, Russell, Milton, Hobhouse, Folkestone, Tavistock, and Nugent. But when Parliament reassembled after the Easter vacation, during which interval the Ministry was being formed, most of the 'Malignants' deserted the Opposition benches and joined forces with Canning and Brougham on the Government side of the House.

Whilst the Whigs were thus hopelessly divided upon the merits of the new Ministry, the Radicals looked upon it with an indifference not unmingled with contempt. The spectacle of the Whigs taking office with Tories seemed only to give colour to their favourite assertion that between Whig and Tory there neither was nor could be any essential difference. Hume excited the wrath of such fervent preachers of the new order as Brougham by bringing forward in the Commons, at Place's instigation, such inconvenient and ill-timed questions as economy and the freedom of the press.[25]

The new Ministry's life was destined to be neither a long nor a merry one. Harassed by 'friends of liberty' like Hume, on the one hand, and, on the other, by the vexatious and factious opposition of the old Tories now deprived of their places and emoluments, Canning's spirit almost broke down, and his health was undermined by the fatigues of an exhausting parliamentary attendance. Nor would the Whigs work harmoniously with their Tory colleagues. They maintained intact their own organisation; they would not consent to receive 'treasury notes' from the Tory Whip, and never would attend, it was said, unless summoned by their own Whip, Lord Duncannon.[26]

Brougham too, as Canning found to his cost, was from the very first a disturbing and disruptive influence; and he almost plagued the Prime Minister to death. His thirst for power had not been satisfied by the conspicuous success he had achieved in bringing about the Coalition. His only reward was a patent of precedence, which he obtained on May 31 when he appeared in silk before the Privy Council. At the very outset he knew that he had no chance of being given office, on account of the King's undying hatred of him since 1820. Lord Bath had been given a blue riband in 1823, although he had declared that if he had seen Bergami and the Queen sharing the same bed, he would still have voted against the monstrous Bill of Pains and Penalties. But for Brougham there was no forgiveness, and there could be none for the man who (so the King believed) had alluded so offensively to his legs, and who had even threatened publicly to prove His Majesty a bigamist. Hence we get the reference in Brougham's letter of March 26 to the "womanish prejudices in certain quarters"; and in his speech in Parliament on May 1 he said truly enough:

> I never dreamed of taking office under the present arrange-
> ment. I am much more certainly and inevitably out of
> office, and out of office am more likely to continue, than
> even the right-honourable gentleman himself.[27]

Brougham himself declared that he had been offered and had refused the office of Attorney-General, but the falsehood was too palpable to deceive anyone. For once he spoke the truth when he told Creevey that he was to be sacrificed to the King's personal feelings. As Wilson observed, Brougham's disinterested professions were confined to words:

> He was not indeed actuated by any *sordid* motives, but
> his vanity could not brook exclusion; and he accused Mr.
> Canning of having taken advantage of his expressions in the
> note which I transcribed, and in the autograph which I sent,

to keep him out of office when, by the intimation of a wish, he might have prevailed over the King's objections.[28]

Wilson's statement is borne out by Brougham's own letter to Althorp of April 20:

> . . . God knows I speak a disinterested language if ever man did. I am at all events to have no office; political is out of the question, professional equally so because certain objections continue in a high quarter, and I having positively desired that I should on no account stand in the way of so great and good a work as a junction to keep out Eldon and Co., my *waiver* was used *rather hastily* before any objection had been taken! But I speak the more freely for the measure, because I cannot possibly be biased by selfish views.[29]

Brougham told Creevey that the leaders of the Coalition Whigs took office strongly protesting against his exclusion, and swearing that they would submit to his proscription only so long as he himself did. His letter of April 27 to the Duke of Devonshire confirms that statement:

> I forgot last night to say (while you were receiving your lecture and were *under sentence*)[30] how much I wished that, *now all difficulties are got over*, you should just say a word or two to Canning by way of *protest* (upon taking office). I told you what Lord Lansdowne was to do this evening, in order to save *my honour* in the transaction, namely, to protest against my exclusion and to say he only consented to it on the ground of *my* allowing it myself.
>
> This is right on constitutional principles, and I feel awkward in being as it were left by the party, unless they make some such protest. I am sure you will see the reasons

of this feeling. Of course it cannot be helped as far as
regards the public, etc.—but I should wish to have it
known in the Party where I have so long held a peculiar
situation that I have not been deserted.[31]

Brougham's suspicion and jealousy of Canning, whom he soon came
to regard as a rival, and his mortification at being passed over, made
him so dangerous and uncertain a supporter of the new Government,
that his friends were kept in a continual fever and alarm. All their
ingenuity and persuasiveness were needed to calm his wrath at hearing
that the Chancellor (Lyndhurst) had offered him a silk gown at the
King's request, on condition that he should not go to Court to kiss
hands. And when he heard a report that his old enemy Lord Lowther
was to be given office, he became frantic with rage, sent off a letter
to the Foreign Secretary threatening *bellum ad internecionem,* and
behaved like a madman at Brooks's. Wilson angrily remonstrated with
his impulsive friend:

> Why will you so impetuously credit the inventions of the
> enemy? London streets are ringing with your threats, and
> the malignants are chiming the bells in ecstasy. Is discre-
> tion incompatible with genius, and to "hear before you
> strike" the very maxim to be forgotten in your universal
> magazine of memory? Such suspicious propensity must be
> as fatal in party as in friendship and in love.[32]

So frequently did his friends press his claims to office, in the hope
of soothing his feelings, that Canning, thoroughly exasperated with
their importunity, one day burst out with "Damn him, he shall have
my place!"[33] Both Croker and Herries believed that Canning was on
the verge of an explosion with Brougham.[34] In July the Prime Minister
tried to get rid of him altogether by offering him the judicial post of
Chief Baron of the Exchequer, with an income of £7000 a year for
life.[35] But Brougham declined to be shelved whilst still in his prime

and with all the world before him, and he refused to take the bribe. When it was suggested that the Chief Barony was only one stage from the Woolsack, he observed, "That is true; but, out of parliament, where am I to get post-horses to take me that stage?"[36]

The general belief was that the Coalition could not last. "We cannot go on; the coach must all be unpacked and re-packed again",[37] Tierney was reported to have declared. But whatever might have happened had Canning been spared, his death (August 8), brought about by the incessant toil and worry of official life, made a reshuffle inevitable.

George IV. was still so embittered against the old Tories for having deserted him and for having attempted to take out of his hands the choice of a new premier,[38] that he never once thought of sending for Wellington or Peel, but authorised Goderich, Canning's chief lieutenant in the Lords, to remodel the Ministry. Lansdowne consented to waive his own pretensions and loyally agreed to serve under another Tory chief. But the Coalition was all but broken up by the King's refusal to allow Lord Holland to be brought into the Cabinet with the seals of the Foreign Office, and by the Whigs' refusal to allow the King to give the Exchequer to Herries, an ultra-Tory and an anti-Catholic, whose moral character was widely impugned. Herries was suspected of having used official information during the Napoleonic war to create a large fortune. Both these difficulties would have been easily overcome but for Goderich's nerveless incompetence, and utter inability to manage the King. On September 1, however, Lansdowne, though he had placed his resignation in the King's hands, finally decided to remain in office, submitting both to Holland's exclusion and to Herries' appointment to the Exchequer. His decision was doubtless influenced by the important fact that his party was seriously divided on the two outstanding questions at issue.[39] Many, like Lord Holland himself, thought that Lansdowne had blundered when he demanded an additional infusion of Whiggism into the Ministry;[40] and Lord Duncannon was by no means alone in urging the impolicy of breaking up the Government on account of Herries, whom he considered a fitter Chancellor of the Exchequer than Palmerston, whom Goderich had originally selected for the post. "I cannot think the appointment of a man without weight in Parliament or political connections in the country was a good reason for retiring", added Duncannon.[41]

At the time of Canning's death, Brougham was busily engaged on the northern circuit, although the newspapers magnified a slight cold with which he was attacked at York into a serious and even dangerous illness. He not only heard the news without dismay, but felt that a personal rival was removed from the scene; and he could scarcely conceal his satisfaction at the prospect of having everything his own way in the next session of Parliament. The first letter he wrote after hearing the news from London, was addressed to Lansdowne (August 9). After expressing his willingness to continue to support the Government out of office, he went on:

> I can answer for myself *now* not only because I have tried the experiment of supporting Government without any official connection with them, and found myself quite comfortable in what had appeared an anomalous and difficult situation, but furthermore, because I am sure any little difficulty which there might be before exists no longer, for I never could for a moment feel annoyed by giving all kinds of aid to Huskisson or Sturges Bourne, or whoever might be made leader. I can answer for myself serving *under* them with perfect docility and submissiveness for years, and never feeling the least degree of uneasiness or awkwardness in my position. I am not sure that it would always have been so under Canning, but unhappily that is now gone and nothing remains but that those who remain should draw closer than ever the bands which unite them, for the sake of our principles.
>
> I hope due advantage will be taken of the *only benefit* this lamentable calamity has brought with it, namely, removing the objection to Lord Grey joining, and to Wellington being Commander-in-Chief.[42]

The Coalition Ministry had been none too strong even when Canning was alive and at its head; its main prop had now been taken away, and Huskisson and his friends entertained grave doubts of their being able to keep the Ministry afloat, for any considerable period of time. Brougham, however, scouted the idea of abandoning the struggle, and in his letters to Lord Holland and Wilson (August 11) he threatened to sever his connection with the Whigs if his 'chicken-hearted' friends talked of submission to the ultras.[43] He wrote to Lord Holland:

> . . . I write this to remind you that these are times for men to act like men, and that you must by main force keep Tierney from his wonted course of twaddle. I see him shaking his head and looking wise and saying we can't carry on the Government in the House of Commons now Canning is dead. Let him speak for himself. I say we can. I say he himself is more than a match for all Peel can bring against him. But I say whether he is or not, I am, and I say it without the least vanity, but because there are always some Tierneys and Abercrombys who distress themselves, choose also to be so kind as to distress all their friends and to be faint-hearted for others. I have had the agreeable lot of making all manner of sacrifices for twenty years to the Party and to be rewarded for it by constantly hearing Tierney saying, "Well, we can do nothing—we are nobody—we have no debaters," or, as Tierney calls it, *no staff*, and he would say so if he and I sat on one side and Lethbridge[44] alone on the other.
>
> Now I wish all concerned to take notice that if any one advantage is lost at this crisis by any of our men doubting our perfect ability to beat Peel and Lethbridge, they and I no longer belong to the same Party, and I'd rather coalesce with the devil than be so insulted by one's own friends. In fact, what do we lose by Canning?

Much no doubt in debate, but I mean, what that we could not well spare? In the Commons we are strong enough to try the blindfold and tying up one hand. In the Lords Canning made us enemies and did us no good.

I need not add that all idea of office being out of the question for me, I speak more for the good of others and the Party, or rather, my principles— than from any motive of interest.

As for Peel, mark well, he never once *has been fought*— he knows not what it is—owing to silly Benthamites and Irish blarney—he never yet has been put to his strength, except you say those two battles I fought him in, and I suppose he did not gain much by either. Indeed nothing but the incurable folly and love of *stultifying themselves* which rages in some of us could ever make him think of trying to face our united forces.

I think he had even a better chance when the personal hatred of poor Canning gave him allies.[45]

Canning had died on the Wednesday; and on the Thursday Brougham had already made up his mind that what was needed was a broad-bottom administration that should include both Grey and Wellington. If, however, an extended Coalition should prove an impossibility, all 'malignants' both Whig and Tory, he declared, should be set at defiance. On the 13th he communicated these views to Grey in a remarkable letter. "Such a tissue of personal vanity, selfishness, and ostentatious display of independence and liberality, with so much arrogance, it has never fallen to my lot to observe in the correspondence of any public man, high or low", declared Sir Willoughby Gordon, who was informed of its contents.[46] Though civil in form, Grey's reply revealed the bitterness of his feelings against the man who had been more responsible than anyone else for the cleavage in the Whig party. His letter was not at all reassuring; he could see no more reason for supporting Goderich than Canning, since the principle upon which both Ministries were founded was the same; and Brougham feared that next session the Coalition Whigs would be marshalled "in open hostility with him".[47]

Whilst he boasted of his having acted purely from disinterested motives, instancing his refusal of the Chief Barony with its salary of £7000 a year, other letters revealed his mortification at having been again sacrificed to the King's resentment. He told the Duke of Devonshire that he was "really the only man among our party who has a right to complain of the King, being the only one excluded";[48] and to Wilson he wrote:

> I think it right to let you know one circumstance, because it may open your eyes, if they are still closed, to the degree of the King's violence against *all the heroes* of 1820. You will hardly believe that even at this moment, when there is hardly anybody but myself left to take the labour of the fight in the House of Commons, the King's objections to me are said to be as strong as ever. Whether the Government ought not to have put all these down with a strong hand is another question. I own I am glad no such attempt was made, for had it led to a rupture with the King and a bringing in of the malignants, I should have been in despair. I need not say that I mean to fight for them as hard as ever, and as formerly I shall have all the magnanimity to myself.[49]

He alluded to the subject in a second letter (August 15) to Lord Holland, who had sent him reassuring news of the readiness of the Whigs to continue the struggle against the ultra-Tories:

> I am very glad you can give so good an account of Tierney, and hope he will continue so, and that while the grand object is to keep out the old leaven, we shall not find any *ferments* among the new. One thing is ever to be kept

in mind by all. Canning was the great and indeed only obstacle to the *Outs* coming in again. Therefore we must hold the door faster than ever against them. . . .

As for my not taking office—you misunderstand me if you think I make or affect to make any self-denying ordinance. But the fact is so. I can't afford to give up a large and certain income for a small and precarious one; and the only places I can take (the professional ones) there *are objections* to my having. I therefore am quite willing to back the Government as before—from the *Hill Fort.*[50]

Lord Holland had succeeded in assuaging his fears regarding his chicken-hearted Whig friends, but a few days later Brougham received the alarming intelligence that the Ministry was likely to be broken up on the question of the appointment of Herries as Chancellor of the Exchequer. Brougham detested Herries on account of his politics, and, upon first hearing of the appointment, he expressed his disgust in several letters to friends in London. "I fear such appointments as that violent ultra and concealed malignant, Herries, augur no great good to the Godly", he told Wilson.[51] Not unnaturally, Brougham's marked disapproval encouraged Lansdowne and his colleagues who were conducting the negotiations with Goderich in London, to make a firm stand on the question of the Exchequer. Their annoyance and dismay upon hearing a few days afterwards that Brougham was demanding the immediate withdrawal of their opposition to Herries, on the ground that their persistence would bring about the collapse of the Ministry and the return of the ultras, may readily be imagined. As in April, Brougham was now perfectly prepared to abandon both principles and personalities and to give way in anything and everything, rather than cause the old Tories to regain the upper hand. He wrote to the Duke of Devonshire on August 26:

I really am put in a bit of an alarm by these silly rumours, but I fear from what I hear that *some great big* folks have not been doing quite so prettily as we could wish. Now, we cannot certainly have this *stockjobber* crammed down our throats, if he does not fully and frankly and immediately clear himself by disclosing how he got his wealth, whether by marriage, lottery ticket, highway robbery, cheating at cards, horse-racing at Doncaster, or any other legitimate mode of amassing wealth. But if he does deny most thoroughly that he ever made a farthing directly or indirectly in any manner of way, if he denies this satisfactorily then our objection ceases and we may safely take the dose, for as to the manner of giving it to us, by the King, I care little for that, our honour and character being quite secure and above all suspicion, especially as the ultras are crying out for Herries and as he belongs to them. We should, for the present, be very forbearing as to the little irregularities of the King. Our Party has always ruined itself and hurt the public by standing too high on its stirrups with kings. Had they, in 1784, been more quiet, and in 1809 and '11 and '12, the public had gained immensely. Only think and how greatly our power will be augmented after another year's co-operation together—why, the King won't try such things then. Is not there a strong inducement to pocket as much as we can and to shut our eyes as hard as possible? I hope you will excuse my earnestness on this matter.[52]

He wrote at greater length on the subject to Lansdowne, the same day:

I hasten to answer yours just received. Abercromby's letters had prepared me for mischief, and for a week my thoughts have unceasingly been upon the point, and I have, I own, come to a very clear opinion, which I shall frankly and fully state to you.

If Herries cannot answer upon his honour the following question in the negative and in a *manner* to leave us no doubts, anything is better than even an hour's hesitation. "Have you ever, while in office, including private secretary to any minister, directly or indirectly, in any manner of way derived any gain or endeavoured to derive any gain from, or by means of, or in any relation to the funds or other securities, or any loan, gift, favour or accommodation from any man connected with the stock exchange or the moneyed interest?" This is a searching question. If he boggles he should be thrust out of his present office as well—if he fairly and satisfactorily answers—and still more, if he explains how he came by his fortune, there is an end of the difficulty, and I, for one, would be clear against making any further objections, and this for two reasons. The man ought to be held up after being suspected—this is just—and then, though he is an odious brute and of bad principles, it is far better not to quarrel with the King on any punctilio, at least till we and our new allies have acted a year or two together. My opinion is decidedly against ever being very nice and punctilious with a King, I mean about points of honour and ways of doing things—about essentials is another matter, but I reckon it no essential that he should make a fuss about a man, not positively bad and rather, on the whole, eligible for the particular place, though objectionable generally. Neither do I hold the *balance* in the Cabinet of Whig and moderate Tory, to be at all an object of jealousy, always to be watched and trimmed. I had rather forget the distinction, for this year at least, and shut my eyes to the King's doings. Next year we shall be ten times stronger. Don't ever trust to the impossibility of making a Government. A King who don't mind throwing everything else into confusion and Ireland into rebellion, could easily manufacture a Government.

But our game should be—bearing and forbearing for the present. . . . The Whigs have always erred on *personal punctilio* with the King and the enemy. In 1784 they did so about your father and preferred the abominable Coalition which lost them nine-tenths of their influence and all their character. Soon after they put the seal on this act of folly by indulging in another punctilio about *Pitt* going out and then coming in again, because he had taken office "unconstitutionally" (this is akin to the present case in one point, though but in one). In 1809–11 and '12 they rained all influence they retained by showing that they *never would come in*, and also on a ground of mere punctilio. Since that time by individual services and really useful acts to the country, and by the progress of liberal opinions at home and abroad, we have regained our popularity and much weight, but all would be lost by a recurrence to our old errors. God forbid we should so act. I regard this as a crisis, and that everything depends on our avoiding a premature quarrel either with the King or each other.

As for the office, surely Palmerston (a most excellent person in all respects) is our man, and let Herries go to the War Office. But still rather than quarrel let him in God's name have the Exchequer if he be but clear of the funds. In a year all will go well and we shall never repent acting prudently now.[53]

From this reasoning Lansdowne differed *in toto*. He expressed the grounds of his objection to the proposals in a brief note to the Duke of Devonshire (August 28):

I had a long letter from Brougham this morning to the same effect as yours. Upon the first part of it, I should say that no man was fit to sit in a Cabinet or even take any office in a Government to whom such a question as he suggests

could be put. On the second part, that though he might
be willing to see a Government go on very much degraded
in opinion, those who are actually in it must be governed
by different feelings.[54]

In his letters to Lansdowne and the Duke of Devonshire, Brougham
really ignored the main grounds of their objection to Herries. He himself was perfectly prepared to accept Herries as Chancellor, provided
he could clear himself of the charges brought against him. Lansdowne
and the Duke of Devonshire's objections were of a political nature,
and these Brougham entirely disregarded. They urged that Herries
belonged to the ultra-Tories and was known to be extremely hostile
to the Whigs; that the second lead in the House of Commons would
devolve upon him, and not upon either a Whig or a Canningite;
and that even if they were disposed to acquiesce in his appointment,
they would be unable to carry their party along with them. These
were weighty objections, which Brougham, in his anxiety to keep the
Coalition in power, totally ignored.

Lansdowne, who had not forgotten the rebellion at Brooks's, felt
himself aggrieved at Brougham's meddling and embarrassing interference from a distance with the delicate negotiations that had been
going on since August 8. On September 6 he wrote complainingly:

I have as sincere a deference for your judgement as that of
any man, but I think it right you should know that in the
last discussions respecting an appointment which I had
first been led to consider as *most* objectionable, by a statement of yours which had been communicated to me, I
was met by the observation I could not deny, that *you* were
well known to be quite ready to acquiesce in it; precisely
as in the first negotiation with Canning, in attempting
to obtain some security not for personal objects of my
own, but for the public, as far as Ireland was concerned,
I was met by the statement, pretty well founded, that

my Whig friends in St. James's Street were ready to join Government on any terms.[55]

Meanwhile (September 4) Brougham had written to Spring Rice, Under-Secretary at the Home Office, a letter which must be interpreted as an early warning that, in view of his exclusion from office, he should go his own way without paying too much regard to the entreaties of his friends:

> . . . I rejoice in the prospect before us for the next session. I shall have some half-dozen reforms in our law and policy well matured, for I must avail myself of the influence my singular position gives me in the House to do permanent good; viz., all the weight of being out of place (both weight with the King and country) and the favour of the old Tory Opposition, who I do not think will quarrel with me rashly.[56]

His singular position ("My peculiar and I may say unprecedented situation," he described it in another letter),[57] was giving much concern to other people. Within a short time of the settlement of the difficulties attending the formation of the new Ministry, Huskisson, as Leader of the Commons, was being pressed to bring Brougham into office as the only means of ensuring his allegiance. "The position of a powerful unplaced friend in the House of Commons must necessarily be a ground of discomfort to any Government," wrote Lord Morley warningly on September 17.[58] But Edward Ellice, who was in communication with Brougham, informed Morley a few days later that Brougham, far from intending merely to take "the embarrassing attitude of an unplaced supporter and protector", as Huskisson himself thought would be the case, was even prepared to go into opposition unless he was bribed to remain on the Treasury benches. Conveying this startling and disconcerting piece of intelligence to his friend at the Colonial Office, Morley again urged that something should be done to placate such a dangerous supporter.[59] Further news only confirmed Ellice in his opinion, and on October 19 he wrote to Hobhouse:

> What is to become of our learned and unaccountable friend of Brougham Hall? He will either be in office, or opposition, and is trying all in his power to smooth his way to place at headquarters, and writing his complaints of ill-treatment in the most querulous terms to some of his old allies! They ought to make him King of regenerated Greece, as they wished to send Lord Grey to India![60]

Rumours that Brougham was likely to mutiny had evidently reached Paris by December, for on the 21st Lord Granville, our ambassador there, wrote home suggesting that one of the Law offices should be offered as a sop to the unruly and unmanageable lawyer:

> Why not make Brougham Solicitor-General, if some law arrangements can be made which will remove Tindal from that situation? The position of Brougham in the House of Commons out of office and professing to support the Government, is too powerful, too commanding; ministers are too much at his mercy, and he is so crotchety and so irritable that you can never be sure of him for two days, if you have him not in harness.[61]

Whilst every one was thus convinced of the danger of allowing Brougham to remain a free lance, the general anxiety to gratify his ambition was in itself a remarkable tribute to his extraordinary power. The fate of the Government seemed to lie in his hands. He could make or mar the fortunes of ministries. His friends referred to him as the "Earl of Warwick, or the Kingmaker".

The King's personal objections to him were by no means the only difficulty in the way of his elevation to office. There were probably good grounds for believing that even some of the Whigs, such as

Althorp and Tavistock, who were inclined to give the Government a trial, would never put up with Brougham in high political office.[62] Croker, who remained faithful to Canning and Goderich, had warned the latter that all the Tory element in the Ministry would mutiny if he gave Brougham the leadership of the Commons. And Goderich had had the sense to see that Brougham would never do.[63]

The new Ministry's existence was to prove even more fretful and uncertain than Canning's. Hardly had the difficulties attending its formation been overcome, than the disturbing news of the battle of Navarino reached England (November 20), creating consternation amongst both Whigs and Tories. "This precipitate act of Codrington's", wrote Huskisson, "almost makes me despair". He feared that it would be for the Government "*Le commencement de la fin*".[64]

Brougham, however, was overjoyed at the news of the destruction of the Turkish fleet; and, sharing the enthusiasm of all Liberals at the discomfiture of the Turks who were striving to crush the Greek revolt, he was correspondingly exasperated with his Whig friends who lamented that 'untoward event':

> I am in a rage beyond speech, he wrote to Wilson, at the cold-blankets who are going about damping the pubic joy at this great event, the most important these twenty years. Really they don't deserve the divine favour shown them. They are playing the game of the malignants. If it had not been for the good courage and sense of the Lord High Admiral, we should have been still more in the mire and slough of despond, merely for gaining a victory. I am for seeing the Turk out of Europe even if Russia is to have Turkey (the Greeks the Morea of course). It brings them only more within the power of England and France.[65]

Another letter on the same subject contains an interesting reference to Lord Grey, who, he said, "will never be quiet till he is resisted—no face of tears will mitigate him".[66] On October 22 he declared that he no longer felt anxious about the line Grey proposed to take.[67] Yet a few weeks later we find him expressing a wish to see Grey forming a union of the respectable men of all parties.[68]

By the beginning of December the Government, thanks to Goderich's hopeless incompetence, was already tottering to its fall. Huskisson wrote on the 11th, ". . . Poor Goderich is quite unnerved, and in a most pitiful state. . . . His health has been suffering, his spirits are worn out, and his fitness for business, and power of deciding upon any questions that come before him, are very much impaired".[69] The Whigs too were becoming thoroughly dissatisfied with their own situation, and, upon the King's refusal still to allow Lord Holland to have the Foreign Office, Lansdowne decided to resign. Abercromby wrote on December 3:

> I receive daily such letters of complaint from alien-
> ated friends and sulky adherents, both in London and
> Edinburgh, that I hardly know in which capital the storm

Brougham as a Frenchman, from Punch, *1848*

is rising most rapidly. . . . To he defeated in fair battle, to be turned out by Court intrigue, is what ought to disturb no man; but to turn themselves out from want of concert, courage, and capacity, and to be despised withal, is no pleasing predicament. I am really ashamed, humbled, and heart-broken.[70]

After weeks of painful indecision the end came on January 7, when Goderich received his dismissal. The long and complicated story of the final deadlock between Herries and Huskisson over the question of the chairmanship of the proposed Finance Committee of the House of Commons, is fully told in Huskisson's voluminous correspondence, and it need not detain us here. On January 9, 1828, Lyndhurst advised the King to send for the Duke of Wellington, and with the latter's acceptance of the royal commission to form a Ministry, the ill-starred Coalition of Whigs and Canningites came to its inglorious end.

1. Add. MS. 38749, fol. 135.

2. *Ibid.* 38749, fol. 199.

3. *Ibid.* fol. 213.

4. See Add. MS. 30124, fol. 232, 249; *Letters of Lady Louisa Stuart*, pp.41, 48; Bagot, *Canning and his Friends*, ii. 361-66; *Official Corr. of Canning*, ii. 267; *Peel Papers*, i. 453; *Desp. and Corr.*, iii. 462; *Greville Memoirs*, ii. 173; Temperley, *The Foreign Policy of Canning*, pp.524-530.

5. Mr. A.I. Dasent states, in his *Life of Delane*, that Brougham was "in his younger days a leader-writer for *The Times* at a salary, it is said, of £100 a month" (i. 64). His statement, however, is based on a misreading of a passage in Moore's Diary. (17 July 1822).

6. Hatherton MS.: Littleton to Canning. Feb. 22, 1827.

7. Add. MS. 30111. fol. 285.

8. Add. MS. 30115, fol. 122.

9. *Official Corr. of Canning*, ii. 300.

10. Professor Davis, in his article in the English Historical Review
    (October 1923), entitled "Brougham, Lord Grey, and Canning,
    1815-30", dates this letter August 12. The following considerations
    lead me to reject this date in favour of April 1.

    The letter is inadequately dated 'Sunday', and written from
    York. If it was written in August, Sunday, August 12, is indeed
    the only possible date, in view of its contents. But on August 12
    Brougham was not at York, but at Durham. On the 11th he was
    at Brougham Hall, and, writing to Wilson that day, he asked him
    when replying, to "direct to Durham, where I go to-morrow"
    (Add. MS. 30115, fol. 118). That he did go is certain, for on the 13th
    he wrote to Grey from Durham (*Life and Times*, ii. 485). Therefore
    the letter cannot have been written on August 12.

    The evidence for April 1 is decisive. He told Wilson that it was
    a continuation of his earlier letter, in which he had not given his
    sentiments sufficiently fully. That earlier letter was the one written
    on March 26. In his narrative, written soon after the events took
    place, Wilson declared that he received the letter in question before
    the coalition had been formed, adding, "I did not give this letter for
    Mr. Canning's perusal". The letter, a continuation of that of March
    26, must, then, have been written on either the first or the second
    Sunday after March 26 (*i.e.* either on April 1 or 8), for on the third
    Sunday, April 15, Brougham was in London again. Brougham is
    much more likely to have "added a few lines" to meet the deficien-
    cies of his letter of March 26, six instead of thirteen days later. And
    this additional fact is conclusive. He wrote to Lansdowne another
    inadequately dated letter ('York, Sunday') which, however, fortu-
    nately bears the postmark April 1, 1827. In this letter Brougham uses
    the same arguments as in his letter to Wilson, and the actual phras-
    ing is similar. To Wilson he speaks of "the place-seeking disposition
    of some"; to Lansdowne he writes: "We may conclude that Canning
    is playing the unworthy game of place-seeking". He tells Wilson

that the Whigs must "form a powerful and vigorous opposition *as a party*, acting together. We shall have abundant materials for this." He writes to Lansdowne: "Our business is to reorganise or to form a steady opposition on Liberal but steady and intelligible grounds". "For such a party we have sufficient materials." And he adds, "to hold the least fellowship" with the Radicals "is wholly impossible"; whilst in his letter to Wilson he phrases it "we shall have no connection with either Hume and Co. or the Benthamites".

These facts are conclusive for the date April 1.

11. Add. MS. 30115, fol. 120.

12. Lansdowne MS.

13. Hatherton MS.: Wilmot Horton to Littleton, April 15, 1827.

14. *Creevey Papers*, ii. 114.

15. Chatsworth MS.

16. *Ibid.*: The Duke of Devonshire to Lansdowne, April 24. 1827.

17. Tavistock wrote to Althorp on April 25: "Brougham has written constantly, but is so determined to go all lengths with Canning, and is so wild on the subject, that I cannot go entirely with him"—(Althorp MS.).

18. Canning told Lansdowne that he was quite free as regards the Catholic question—(Althorp MS.: Abercromby to Althorp, n.d.).

19. Lansdowne MS.: Brougham to Lansdowne, Monday.

20. *Ibid.*: Brougham to Lansdowne, Sept. 12, 1861.

21. Landsdowne MS.: Brougham to Lansdowne, n.d.

22. Abercromby wrote to Althorp in April: ". . . It is a precious moment, and the Whigs will incur serious responsibility if they throw the country back into the hands of those whom we have so long but so unsuccessfully opposed. Lord Grey as usual is violent, ill-tempered and influenced wholly by personal feelings and not at all by public principle. The means by which he seeks to run down Canning are such as I should expect from a more prejudiced and less gentlemanlike Tory than Westmorland. I am no defender of the life and character of Canning, but I should scorn to depreciate him or any other man by vilifying his parentage and reproaching him

with the frailties of his mother. To the honour of Opposition I have found no one person who does not express their total disapprobation of such vulgar abuse. Lord Grey says he wishes to go to India, and I am so shocked with the vulgarity of his tone that I am almost disposed to wish him a prosperous voyage in the terms which Eldon applied to Canning on a similar occasion"—(Althorp MS.).

23. Parl. Deb., N.S., xvii. 731.

24. Lambton MS.: Ellice to Lambton (April) 1827.

25. Add. MS. 36628, fol. 41.

26. *Peel Papers* i. 491.

27. Parl. Deb., N.S., xvii. 422. He referred to Dawson, late Under-Secretary for the Home Department.

28. Wilson, *Narrative*, p. 26.

29. Althorp MS.

30. "At Lady Jersey's, ha! ha!" the Duke of Devonshire wrote on the letter at this point.

31. Chatsworth MS.

32. Wilson, *Narrative*, p.28.

33. Broughton, *Recollections*, iii. 239.

34. *Desp. and Corr.*, iv. 80.

35. *Life and Times*, ii. 489.

36. *Desp. and Corr.*, iv. 182.

37. Colchester, *Diary*, iii. 520.

38. Add. MS. 38749, fol. 187: Huskisson to Croker, April 12, 1827.

39. Chatsworth MS.: Abercromby to the Duke of Devonshire, August 29, 1827.

40. Althorp MS.: Lord Holland to Althorp, Aug. 28, 1827.

41. *Ibid.*: Duncannon to Althorp, Sept. 16, 1827.

42. Lansdowne MS.

43. Add. MS. 30115, fol. 118.

44. Since the formation of the Coalition Ministry in April, Lethbridge had brought himself into prominence as a leader of the ultra-Tories.

45. Holland House MS.

46. *Desp. and Corr.*, iv. 126.

47. *Life and Times*, ii. 487. Brougham's interpretation of Grey's letter was very different from its real meaning and tone. He wrote to Lansdowne: ". . . I wrote to reason with and soothe him. I gave him the offcome of Canning's death and his own declarations as to 'the poles asunder'. He is very kind and friendly in his answer—wishes me much to go to see him, but adds 'that he hopes our differences on polities will not make us dry in meeting'! Really, I don't comprehend this, nor can I see what he would be at, or what except personalities we differ in at all. Next session must show, and we shall be marshalled I fear in open hostility with him."—(Lansdowne MS.).

48. Chatsworth MS.

49. Add. MS. 30115, fol. 82.

50. Holland House MS.

51. Add. MS. 30115, fol. 82.

52. Chatsworth MS.

53. Lansdowne MS.

54. Chatsworth MS.

55. *Life and Times*, ii. 489.

56. Torrens, *Melbourne*, i. 235.

57. Chatsworth MS.; Brougham to the Duke of Devonshire, Sept. 5, 1827.

358. Add. MS. 38751, fol. 5.

59. Add. MS. 38751. fol. 76.

60. Add. MS. 36464, fol. 71.

61. *Ibid.*, 38753, fol. 38.

62. Colchester, *Diary*, iii. 528.

63. *Croker Papers*, i. 387.

64. Add. MS. 38752, fol. 69.

65. *Ibid.* 30115, fol. 126.

66. *Ibid.* 30115, fol. 128.

67. Lansdowne MS.: Brougham to Lansdowne, Oct. 22, 1827.

68. *Creevey Papers*, ii. 140.

69. Add. MS. 38752, fol. 204.

70. Chatsworth MS.: Abercromby to the Duke of Devonshire.

IX

Brougham's Last Years
in the Commons

GAFFAR GREY

A Parody on the well-known ditty, "Alice Grey"
By Lord Faux of Crow's Nest.

He's all my fancy painted,
Ye Gods, he is a trump;
To coalesce his quondam friends
Along with Canning's rump.
O few have sighed as I have sigh'd
For office or for pay,
And I feel my heart is breaking
For the love of Gaffar Grey.

'Tis true I said on Friday week
I'd ne'er a placeman be;
But what I said on Friday week
Was fudge and flummery.
I'm Chancellor named and Baron Vaux,
With fees and ample pay;

Oh, my heart, my heart is breaking,
For the love of Gaffar Grey.

For him I'll sit upon the Bench,
For him I'll hear appeals;
Reform the House, retrench expense,
And carry purse and seals.
By night I'll haunt his parties,
And tend his steps by day,
And all the while my heart will beat
For the love of Gaffar Grey.

I've sunk beneath ambition's sun,
And am a Peer at last,
So now my wheedling course is done
The weary conflict's past.
When laid within my peaceful grave
May Whigg'ry haply say,
Oh, his heart, his heart was broken
For the love of Gaffar Grey.

John Bull, Dec. 5, 1830.

"THERE are now no Whigs, no Tories", wrote Francis Place in January 1828. "All are mixed up in one mess, and the contention is who shall be in place. Happily the country takes no part in their squabbles. . . . Swift's prayer need hardly be repeated now, for it is all but accomplished—

Thus I said whilst looking round them
May their God, the Devil confound them."[1]

Wellington, who on May 2 had told the House of Lords that he would have been worse than mad if he had ever thought of aspiring to the premiership—a situation for which he admitted he was not qualified, now kissed hands as First Lord of the Treasury. The King instructed him to form a Ministry on broad lines, and expressed a wish to retain Lansdowne and Carlisle in his service. But Lansdowne had already decided to resign, and, in any case, no offer was made to him. His letter to the Duke of Devonshire, written probably on the 19th, shows that he fully approved the Prime Minister's decision:

> Many thanks for the report of your conversation with the Duke of Wellington. I quite agree with him that consider-ing his and Peel's opinions on the Catholic question, it would be as little advisable for them to apply to me as it would to me to form a connection with them.[2]

Though Wellington's Ministry was therefore composed of none but Tories, his success in reuniting his party was only nominal. He bit-terly offended the high Tories by excluding their sturdiest champions, Eldon and Londonderry, and by giving office to the Canningites whom they had furiously opposed since the previous April, and from whom they differed in opinion on almost every question of importance. The Duke's initial failure marked the beginning of a long concatenation of events which profoundly influenced the history of his party and of the country. It led inevitably to the separation of the Canningites from the high Tories five months after their amalgamation; the dismissal of Huskisson and the resignation of his friends was followed by the appointment of another President of the Board of Trade and the defeat of Vesey Fitzgerald at the Clare election; the triumph of O'Connell threatened the destruction of the Protestant ascendancy in Ireland and forced the Duke to concede Catholic emancipation; the Relief Bill brought about the disruption of the Tory party; and the alienation of the Protestant Tories occasioned the fall of Wellington's Ministry and ushered in the Reform Bill.

To Brougham and to the Whigs generally, the inglorious collapse of Goderich and the Coalition came neither as a shock nor as a disappointment. Althorp, who had justly complained that the late

Government had used its patronage in such a way as to retard the Catholic question, would certainly have opposed it, had it survived.[3] Several days before the crash, Brougham was abusing the Ministers and plotting their overthrow. He desired a new Coalition on a broader basis, that would include the Canningites, Wellington, Peel, and Lord Grey.[4] But the mandate to the Duke upset all his calculations, and his vexation knew no bounds when he heard that the Canningites had joined the Government, for he had hoped that they would strengthen the Whig Opposition against the high Tories. Sir George Warrender wrote to Huskisson on January 15:

> It is as well that you should know what is passing and is said at the clubs. The Whigs behave perfectly well towards you, and all say they have no claim whatever and that you are perfectly free. At the same time they say and feel that all depends on you, and they were in the greatest dismay at Brooks's last night at the general belief that all was arranged with the Duke. Lord Sefton came to White's, obviously for the purpose of contradicting your accession to the new arrangement, and he read to me a letter dated 8th last evening which I feel certain was from Brougham—entreating and desiring Sefton everywhere to deny and contradict the sinister reports about you as most ingeniously tending to weaken and dishearten their party (*i.e.* the Whigs). Of course I said nothing one way or the other.[5]

In spite of his disappointment at the accession of the Huskisson party to office, Brougham affected to make light of the Duke's strength:

> The Parliament is likely to open in a very 'unsatisfactory' state, as our friend Castlereagh (God rest his soul) was wont to say. The chief 'feature'—I mean Peel—will find it quite impossible to calculate on a majority on any one question, except perhaps a motion for turning them out

or reforming the Parliament; and how he is even to get through the forms of a debate, if he is opposed by all the parties not in office, seems inconceivable.[6]

To both friends and foes Brougham's conduct at this time was tantalisingly inexplicable. It was rumoured that Wellington, realising that the versatile Whig lawyer was one of the principal obstacles in the way of a peaceful and easy session, contemplated giving Lord Darlington, now Marquis of Cleveland, the Garter, in the hope that the recipient might be willing to manage his unruly nominee. Said Edward Ellice humorously: "I have no doubt the Duke will bribe any person to kill a knight, if the vacancy would ensure Brougham's silence and neutrality for the session".[7]

In Whig society, too, the main anxiety appeared to be respecting the course Brougham intended to steer at the beginning of the Parliamentary campaign. Tavistock demanded of Hobhouse, "How are we to act with the lawyer? There's the rub. Do what you will, in the way of party, he will be the stumbling block. I am more and more for acting alone, at least till we can find a leader in whom we can place confidence".[8]

Heedless of the anxiety he was causing his friends, Brougham was meanwhile concerting his plan of operations. On January 18 he had a long talk with Francis Place, with whom he had always kept in touch notwithstanding their political differences. Place wrote of him:

> He has several good projects in hand, one, a parliamentary commission to inquire into the state of the law preparatory to a reform with a view to the formation of a code, for which I am to furnish him some cases as proofs of the operation of the law on trade. Brougham says his prime object is totally to abolish *common law*, and for this purpose he may command my time to any extent, and employ it in any way not dishonourable to me.[9]

Place received the impression that Brougham was bent on pressing the Ministers hard. Some, however, were at the moment fighting bye-elections, and Brougham agreed that it would be indecorous to attack absent opponents. But Place, with an eye to the furtherance of the cause to which he had so long devoted himself, urged that Brougham might, nevertheless, make a speech which could not fail to be of use, and which would become the text-book for all the reformers in the kingdom. The burden of this suggested speech (to be delivered during the debate on the Address) might be that the Ministers had failed either to point out the causes of the people's distress, or to find a positive remedy for the ills from which they were suffering. A beginning might be made by a reference to the national debt, the existence of which was one of the chief causes of bad trade and unemployment. Having fully described the seriousness of the burden, Brougham should then go on to complain that no scheme for its liquidation had been suggested. Then he might refer to the weight of the taxes under which the people groaned; to the oppressive game laws—a potent source of crime; to the excise duties—and their tendency to encourage smuggling; to the huge standing army; to the state of the laws and the magistracy, "and so on to the end of the chapter". All that would be excellent, said Brougham. But he soon recovered from his momentary lapse into enthusiasm, and, recollecting that his chief object was to secure recognition for his claims to the leadership of the Opposition, he at once raised the very considerable objection that, to deliver such a comprehensive speech without previously consulting his parliamentary friends (and he knew that if he did consult them they would be unanimous in voicing their disapprobation)—a speech, too, that everyone would consider an *ex cathedra* pronouncement by a Whig leader—would be a gross breach of decorum. "This I knew very well, and did not therefore press him to do it," said Place.[10]

Brougham's speech on the Address was thus a somewhat colourless effort, but observers noted the important fact that he spoke and acted as leader of the Opposition. But the measure of his success in getting his claims recognised may be judged from the circumstance that, though he boasted that he was at the head of two hundred members of the House of Commons, an official dinner which he gave on Sunday, February 24, to his friends in both Houses, was attended only by Lord Durham, Lord Sefton, the Duke of Leinster, Lord Stuart, Lord Essex, and four Scots barristers.[11]

Even a man of Brougham's energy and capacity could not unite and lead a party which had not yet recovered from the body-blow given by Canning the previous April, although Canning's death had removed the chief cause of the cleavage in the Whig ranks. The followers of Grey and Lansdowne still retained their own identity, and could not forget their past differences. The Coalition Whigs had treated Grey with studied neglect; and, indeed, he might not have been very unwilling to take office in the Wellington Ministry, if the King's objections could have been overcome. Ellice wrote to Lambton on January 5:

> There is not one individual connected with the Whig party in whom the country has the slightest confidence, except Lord Grey, and yet by some strange and truly Whig blunder Lord Grey is the only person of the party who is treated by them with contumely and indifference.[12]

After the fall of the Goderich Ministry he wrote:

> Lord Grey is the only popular Whig of parliamentary power in the country. Lord Lansdowne has passed into the same order as Lord Goderich. Lord Wellesley is an old woman, and there can be no strong Liberal Administration unless Grey takes the lead in it.[13]

It was in this year that the alarming state of Ireland brought the Catholic question to a head. Goulburn's Act (1825) had failed to suppress the Catholic Association, which, under O'Connell's skilful leadership, worked up popular agitation to such a pitch that the ascendency of the Protestant interest and the peace of the country were seriously endangered. In May the Canningites seceded from the Ministry on the question of the disfranchisement of the corrupt constituency of East Retford. Vesey Fitzgerald, a supporter of emancipation, and an Irish landowner, was appointed to the vacant Presidency of the Board of Trade, and sought re-election for the County Clare. To the consternation of the Tories, he was defeated by O'Connell himself, as a result of the revolt of the Catholic forty-shilling freeholders against the Protestant landlords.

At the beginning of August Wellington, realising that emancipation could no longer with safety to the empire be delayed, began to prepare the King for the worst. Peel, too, saw that the time had come for him to haul down his colours, and, yielding to the Duke's wishes, refrained from throwing up his office. Dawson, Peel's brother-in-law and a Protestant member of the Government, declared in a speech at Derry that the Catholic Association must now be conciliated since it could not be suppressed. Throughout the year the Ministers succeeded in keeping secret their intention to concede the Catholic demands, and it was therefore not known whether Dawson spoke with authority. Brougham wrote to Wilson:

> I see a talk of old Eldon coming in again. But *is* the Catholic question really to be carried in any way? Or is Dawson to hark back and say he meant nothing? We must come *aux prises* with these fellows at last. Nor can there be a doubt that the moment we have a right understanding among ourselves, especially with Lord Grey, there is an end of them.[14]

As Brougham thus admitted, the Whigs were still disunited, and he and Grey were still at loggerheads; but his confidence in the power of the Opposition to destroy the Ministry was not altogether unjustified. Wellington himself was fully aware of the insecurity of his position. His Government had been seriously weakened by the defection of the Canningite squad, by the repeal of the Test and Corporation Acts, and by O'Connell's triumph at the Clare election. He was now about to antagonise a powerful section of his remaining supporters by conceding Catholic emancipation. During the last years of the Liverpool Ministry, the real Opposition had sat on the Treasury benches. That situation was now about to recur. In October 1828 Grey was half expecting an offer from the Duke, but he had decided not to take office.[15] If Wellington, said Ellice, would only bring in Grey and Brougham (and Ellice was confident that they would come in if asked) the Prime Minister could well afford to laugh in the faces of both high Tories and Canningites, and could easily pass a Relief Bill.[16]

In December Brougham was as much in the dark as to the Duke's intentions as he had been in January, and he told Althorp that they ought to bring the whole strength of their forces into the field for the meeting of Parliament in the following February. He meant to turn out the Ministry if no Catholic Bill were forthcoming. Lord Holland was of the same mind, and wrote to Althorp on January 6, 1829:

> Anglesey's . . . recall . . . will facilitate matters at the commencement of [the] session, and unite all persons, I trust, in a vigorous effort to accomplish that great measure by divesting the enemies of it of power, place, and consideration. I hope, however, the attack will not be confined to Ireland and Catholics, but that some of you will condescend to cast away a thought on foreign politics. Never was there such baseness and mismanagement. In one short year we have contrived to lower the character of the country in a manner unparalleled in history. We have broken off all diplomatic relations with two countries in Europe (one *unquestionably* our oldest ally). We have estranged Prussia, lost our ascendency in Portugal, and aggrandised France. . . . Our boasted love of peace has left the East more embroiled in war than ever. In short, there is no end to our blunders.[17]

All doubts and fears respecting the Catholics were, however, at once removed by the statement in the King's speech (February 5, 1829) that an attempt would be made to settle that vexed question. Not only did Brougham refrain from taunting Peel and the Duke with having abandoned their principles whilst retaining their offices, but he eulogised them during the debate on the Address for having profited by experience and for having conquered their inveterate prejudices.[18]

Wellington succeeded with the aid of the Whigs in carrying Catholic emancipation, but he broke up his party in doing so. One result of the defection of a considerable body of ultra-Tories under the Dukes of Cumberland and Newcastle was that Brougham began seriously to entertain the idea of a junction with Wellington. As early as April 1829, when the rebellion of the Tory irreconcilables was only in its incipient stage, he wrote to Wilson:

> The ultras seem completely beaten for the present, and I expect to see them almost all take the first opportunity of making a rally and showing the Government that they have forgotten all that's past. You see the alarm some of them and all the shabby ones in and lounging about Government are in—for fear of any co-operation between Wellington and us. This is particularly remarkable in everything that Lord Londonderry says. To be sure it will be a strange spectacle to see Lord Grey still excluded from office for the sake of such as Lord Aberdeen, etc.[19]

After the passing of the Relief Bill, the political situation remained for some time in an extraordinarily fluid state. The Tory party was hopelessly divided into three groups, the high-fliers under Cumberland, the Wellingtonians, and the Canningites under Huskisson. The Whig party, too, was disunited and leaderless. In October the Prime Minister sounded the Whigs as to their willingness to support the Government, but he declined to bring them in *en bloc*. In his reply Althorp made it clear that the Duke must strengthen the Cabinet from the Whig ranks, or the Opposition would attempt its destruction.

Towards the end of October Wellington and Huskisson met at Sudbourne as the guests of Lord Hertford,[20] but the Duke made no effort to secure Canningite support. Huskisson and his friends, indeed, were not at all desirous of re-entering a Ministry which had treated them inconsiderately, and with whose policy they disagreed. He wrote to Littleton on November 12:

> . . . The meeting was fixed for the 18th. I postponed going till the 21st, that I might not be considered one of the Duke's *reunion*, and, for the same reason, I stayed on four days after he and his tail were gone. . . . The usual courtesies and habits of private society have long been restored between the Duke and myself; and this is all that I ever expect or wish from him. To say the truth, they are the best part of him, since he has ceased to dazzle me as a hero, and attempted to shine as a minister. I can scarcely recollect any one measure of the latter which I envy him, the Catholic question excepted. For that settlement he would deserve every praise; but his conduct to Canning and to Anglesey and, not less than this, the mean considerations by which this great measure was justified, giving it the character rather of an apology for doing wrong, than of grace in doing right, will be no inconsiderable drawbacks in history, even to this chapter of his political fame. What will it say of his foreign policy up to the present moment? . . . Three years ago England stood pre-eminent in the estimation of all Europe; now the whole Continent, from one end to the other, Absolutists as well as Liberals, rejoice in our humiliation. We shall never gain the goodwill of the former, so long as we have a free press and freedom of speech in Parliament; and yet to them have we sacrificed Greece (as far as England could sacrifice it), Portugal, and

the confidence, the kind feeling of the civilised world, and the ascendency we held over it—an ascendency which, national pride apart, was mainly useful, in our hands, to prevent the triumph of either of the two extreme parties which the French Revolution had engendered, and the loss of which ascendency threatens at no distant period again to bring them into collision. [21]

In the winter of 1829–30 the Whigs were still as disunited as they had been in 1827. Lord Durham's hopes that his father-in-law would emerge from his obscurity at Howick to re-create the party were not realised. Grey informed Russell on December 13:

My position remains as it was—which I cannot perhaps describe better than by calling it a friendly neutrality. Nothing could give me greater pain than to find myself placed in opposition to the Duke's Government; but unconnected with it as I am, I must judge and act upon their measures as they arise.[22]

The Duke of Devonshire complained that the party would never be worth much so long as its individual members insisted on following their own devices and going their own way. Ever since the fall of Goderich, indeed, Brougham had been striving hard for the leadership of a united party, and his letter to Wilson of (probably) April 11, 1829, shows that, in his own opinion, he had been entirely successful in outstripping all competitors:

My doctrine is this, and as long as I am a leader of the Opposition I shall above everything pursue it. I expect the party to be treated with proper respect and gratitude, and I shall never fail to resent whatever lowers it. We have been going on too long doing all for others, and letting those we did all for treat us like a worn-out garment, laying us aside and even disowning us when we no longer served their turn. The consequence is, though we are very useful, we are extremely despised. The enemy whom we have driven into all the good they do, get all the credit of our measures, and O'Connell and such like fall a-kissing their worst enemies and forget us the moment after we have been fighting their battles. This must no longer be. . . . I detest Tierney's doctrine of self-distrust and stultification—*on ne vaut jamais que ce qu'on veut valoir*. We have taken a low tone so long ourselves, that all others—friends and foes—treat us as we treat ourselves. Henceforth I warn you a new line must be taken. The party, as such and by name, must be made respected or it must cease to exist. I regard this as the first object and as comprehending all others.[23]

In January 1830 his patron, the Marquis of Cleveland, abandoned the Whig for the Tory party. Brougham felt scruples about continuing to sit in the House of Commons as the nominee of a Tory peer. He felt his situation painfully embarrassing. What was he to do? If he resigned his seat, might he not again find himself in the same unhappy predicament as that in which he had been from 1812 to 1816? Resignation might easily mean political extinction. There remained only one alternative—to turn Tory himself. It is highly probable that he would have followed his patron's lead had not the Duke of Devonshire made a timely offer to bring him in for Knaresborough, where Tierney's death on the 26th had just created a vacancy. After two days' delay, Brougham gratefully accepted the invitation. How real was the danger of his secession from the Whig party, may be judged from Abercromby's and Lord Holland's letters to the Duke of Devonshire. Abercromby wrote on February 2:

All I see and hear makes me more glad *even than I was before* that you have taken this course. It will do much good, and I really believe to be the means of saving the political reputation of the greatest man in the House of Commons.[24]

Lord Holland wrote on January 30, hardly less emphatically:

I must write a line to express if I can my satisfaction at your prompt and handsome offer to Brougham. . . . If I had not thought that the suggestion rested on public grounds chiefly, I should never have made it at all, and I really did not feel myself warranted on such a subject to write to you in the direct way you kindly say that I ought to have done, from a fear of appearing over-meddling or over-inquisitive. I preferred conveying my notions in a way that, if you did not agree with them, would not in any way call upon you to communicate your own.

I have not seen Brougham nor do I know whether his situation is such as to incline him to accept your offer by immediately vacating his present seat. But of this I am sure, that the offer and the promptitude of it must, in all cases, relieve him from many embarrassing and delicate scruples, and that it is the greatest possible service that could have been rendered to what yet remains of party or, indeed, to the public cause. I am sure I shall always feel it so, and so will many, many others when they hear of it.[25]

Brougham was now decidedly of the opinion that the Ministers could not remain in office without strengthening themselves from the ranks of the Opposition. He saw that so long as George IV. lived a strong and permanent Whig Government was out of the question, and that to Wellington's there was no real alternative. To press the Government hard would therefore be futile and disastrous. It was his policy to give them all the support in his power; it was his hope that they would recognise his services and bring him in to high office. No man, he said, exposed himself to more misrepresentation and vilification than he did during this session by trying to keep open the door to a good understanding with Peel; and he even went so far as to declare that if the state of party politics should ever occasion personal or party conflict between himself and Peel he should feel like abandoning Parliament altogether.[26]

Month after month he continued to support the Government and to refrain from even the slightest show of opposition. But, to his growing astonishment and dismay, there came no sign, no overture, no communication of any sort from the Duke. With surpassing dexterity Peel kept the prospect of office dangling before the eyes of the deluded lawyer, and fooled him to the top of his bent. It was obvious, indeed, that this could not go on for ever; that, sooner or later, the scales would fall from his eyes, and that there would be a violent explosion. Croker admitted that the Ministers were incapable of carrying on the government of the country, but both he and Peel were unwilling to acknowledge their inadequacy by making overtures to the Opposition. But, declared Croker, directly Brougham should have lost all hope and Huskisson all patience, Peel would find that he would be unable to stand alone.

On June 5 George IV. died, and was succeeded by his more popular brother, the Duke of Clarence, as William IV. But the weeks continued to slip by, and still there was no sign. Brougham's impatience became manifest on June 28 when, said Croker, he read the King and the public a short but pithy lecture on the text that without a certain and zealous majority in the Commons, no Ministry could hope to stand; and that no acquisition of strength in the Lords would supply the defect of support in the Lower House.[27] He thus darkly hinted that not even Lord Grey could bolster up a tottering Ministry; that his own active co-operation in office was indispensable, and that if they did not make haste to come to terms he would go into violent opposition and accomplish their sure and certain destruction.

A few days later he was said to be in a state of excitement bordering on insanity. On June 30 he created a scene in Parliament, and narrowly escaped receiving invitations to meet the victims of his withering sarcasm with loaded revolvers in Battersea Fields or on Wimbledon Common, after referring to the occupants of the front ministerial bench as the "mean, fawning parasites of the Duke".[28] A week later (July 6) he launched a second attack, giving Peel "more that night than I had ever done this session before—having exerted myself considerably—by way of getting into wind for the October session, when I would advise Peel and Co. to be on their guard from morning to night".[29]

This warning was emphasised a few days later by the writer of an anonymous pamphlet, which was generally attributed to Brougham himself—a supposition which is not at all ruled out of court by the fact that the author spoke of Brougham in most glowing and complimentary terms. Hitherto, it was said, the Whigs had refrained from attacking the Government with their heaviest artillery. But if

> Mr. Stanley, if Sir James Graham, if Lord Althorp and, above all, if Mr. Brougham, *in himself a mighty host,* were to unmask the battery which may now *at length* be supposed to be ready charged . . . if *they* were to hold up the Government and their measures to the wonder of the country, how could so baseless a fabric continue to exist even for a short period?[30]

Wellington must replace the row of cyphers on the front Treasury bench by men in whom the country had confidence. He must either cease to govern, or must consent to share his power with new colleagues recruited from the ranks of his opponents.

Brougham himself reviewed this pamphlet in the July number of the *Edinburgh Review.* The burden of his complaint against the Ministry was that the Duke would not give office to the leading Whigs. The Opposition, declared Brougham, could no longer show any forbearance. He denied that the approaching general election would appreciably strengthen the Government:

> We therefore regard a junction of the men of sound
> principles in all parties, to give the country an efficient
> Government, as the certain result of the Duke's blind
> obstinacy, and his resolution to meet a new Parliament
> with the same incapable Ministry by which he so greatly
> lowered his reputation in the old.

On July 24 Parliament was dissolved, and a general election followed. On three previous occasions (1818, 1820 and 1826) Brougham had vainly contested the county of Westmorland, and in January 1830 he had, as we have seen, been brought in for Knaresborough after severing a fifteen years' connection with the Marquis of Cleveland. But he had always disliked the idea of sitting for a close borough, and had long desired to represent a great popular constituency. At the beginning of July the *Carlisle Journal* announced that he was to stand again for Westmorland. The intelligence, however, was false, as his letter of July 12 to the Duke of Devonshire shows:

> I am glad to inform you I believe all will be quiet in
> the north. I shall escape the annoyance of a contest for
> Westmorland. The terms on which they are willing to
> settle are very advantageous, and my brother (James)
> has conducted the treaty in a very successful and capital
> manner. He will be brought in himself for a close seat, and
> we shall have one for Carlisle (I believe young Howard of
> Corby). This will be a clear gain of two to the party, and
> if other parts of the country do as well, Mr. Duke Arthur
> will have but little to brag of in his dissolution.[31]

Five days later the *Leeds Mercury* printed a lengthy article on the subject of the Yorkshire election, and suggested that the electors could not do better than reward Brougham's magnificent services to the cause of social reform by bringing him in free of personal expense, as one of their four members:

> The honourable and learned member for Knaresborough
> stands without a rival among the public men of the
> present day in their claims upon the gratitude of their
> country and of mankind. He has no competitor in the
> House of Commons, either in eloquence, in statesmanlike
> talent and information, or in the good he has effected for
> his country and for the human race. . . .There is no great
> cause involving the public interests, the rights of man, the
> reform of abuses, the redress of wrongs, the improvement
> of the law and of the Government in all its departments,
> which has not found a ready and effective support in the
> mighty eloquence of Mr. Brougham. . . .

The *Leeds Mercury's* suggestion was taken up with enthusiasm, and on July 23 he and Lord Morpeth were proposed as Whig candidates. He was, indeed, opposed by almost all the country gentlemen ("the silly, impotent, superannuated landed dons," he called them[32]), on the ground that he was not a Yorkshireman and held no property in the county. But he was immensely popular with the manufacturers and business men of the West Riding, who still remembered with gratitude his services to commerce in 1812. If we are to believe Grenville, Brougham had, several years before, been chosen as parliamentary leader of the 'Saints' after Wilberforce's retirement, and on July 13, just before the close of the session and on the very eve of the election, Brougham had made a very splendid speech, advocating the emancipation of the slaves. The Yorkshire Quakers, Methodists, and Nonconformists in general, and all anti-slavery enthusiasts, regarding him as the champion of freedom of conscience and of the slaves, determined to spare no efforts to secure his election for the county for which their great hero and leader, Wilberforce, had himself sat.

His chances of success were very considerable, but he did not seem at all elated at the glorious prospects before him. On July 24 he wrote:

> There was a time, when I was younger and more ambitious, when this extraordinary event would have given me great pleasure. I *now* look upon it more as a bystander, and only like it because it bears a strong testimony to our opinions and principles, and because it gives me (whether I accept or refuse) a great weight and power to promote those principles in Parliament and the country.[33]

To be chosen a representative of the largest and wealthiest county in England would be the highest honour that a grateful people could bestow upon him; but, foreseeing as he did the trend of the political situation during the next few months, he realised that his position as member for Yorkshire would have its disadvantages as well as its glories. He was convinced that the Wellington Ministry must fall before the end of the year, and give place to a Whig Government. He himself would then be called upon to take office. Acceptance of place would force him to resign his seat and seek re-election. How could he, "a pauper," he asked, stand the expense of another contest for Yorkshire? The thing was impossible. He would find himself once more out of Parliament, "which would not do at all". Nothing could make him easy, he said, but the knowledge that a seat would be reserved for him, upon which he could fall back upon taking office. He could then allow his candidature for Yorkshire to go forward "without a pang". On July 24 he wrote to the Duke of Devonshire and explained the position as it appeared to him. He had a remarkable proposal to make. He asked the Duke to return his brother William, "a stout Whig and a very clever lawyer," for Knaresborough. As soon as Brougham took office, his brother could resign in his favour, and return, if necessary, to private life. But the Duke might be unwilling to provide for two brothers. In that case, said Brougham, his "old friend," Zachary Macaulay, the philanthropist and father of the great Macaulay, would be quite willing to take William's place, and vacate when required.[34] Brougham had already made the same proposal to Lord Fitzwilliam, but the latter had just given Scarlett, the Whig lawyer, the only seat he had had at his disposal.

It does not appear how the Duke of Devonshire replied to this remarkable letter, but at all events Brougham allowed himself to be nominated for Yorkshire; and on the 27th he began his canvass in earnest. The York Assizes had begun only a few days earlier, but during the following week he found time to make a thorough tour through the industrial parts of the county, where his influence was strongest. Thousands of people, thrilled by his overpowering eloquence, received him with extraordinary enthusiasm. Nothing quite like that triumphal progress was again to be witnessed in Great Britain until Gladstone went on his famous Midlothian campaigns.

During his canvass of the county Brougham put forward four grand Reform proposals. He declared himself for a drastic revision of the Corn Law, which, he said, in spite of the sliding scale, made dear the people's bread without conferring a real advantage on the farmer. He advocated the abolition of the remainder of the East India Company's trade privileges, and a speedy extinction of Colonial slavery. He urged a moderate measure of parliamentary reform—the enfranchisement of all inhabitant householders—and of the great unrepresented towns, and a Triennial Act.

His election on August 6 placed him on the pinnacle of his fame. It was, he said, a "grand triumph", giving him "a great influence and power".[35] He himself, writing in extreme old age, declared that when, as Knight of the shire, he was begirt with the sword, it was the proudest moment of his life.[36] His popularity in the country, and especially with the middle-class, was now at its height. What Macaulay wrote of him in the following year applied with as much force in the summer of 1830. "He is, next to the King, the most popular man in England. There is no other man whose entrance into any town in the kingdom would be so certain to be with huzzaing and taking off of horses."[37]

At the time of his election, the July number of the *Edinburgh Review* had not appeared; and Brougham, intoxicated with his triumph, hurriedly dashed off an announcement of his victory to Macvey Napier, who obligingly inserted it as a footnote to Brougham's article on the state of parties:

Of all the portentous signs for the present Ministry, he
wrote, the most appalling is the nearly unanimous choice
of Mr. Brougham to be member for Yorkshire. This is
assuredly the most extraordinary event in the history of
party politics.[38]

The General Election went against the Ministry, and the Opposition
gained some thirty seats. The beginning of the year had seen a remarkable revival of the demand for Parliamentary Reform, as a result of economic distress and of the activities of the newly-founded Birmingham
Political Union and the Metropolitan Association for Radical Reform.
The French Revolution, which came at the end of July in the very
midst of the elections, strengthened the popular demand for change.
Brougham hailed the downfall of Charles X. and his despotic minister
Polignac with undisguised satisfaction, and addressed a remarkable
congratulatory letter to the Duc de Broglie, the popular premier who
formed a Government under Louis Philippe. For three days Paris
had been the scene of terrible street-fighting between the soldiers and
the mob, and some six hundred lives had been lost. But Brougham,
who was alleged to have declared in a moment of excitement whilst
electioneering in Yorkshire that he hoped to see the day when the
heads of kings should be made footballs for little boys to kick along
the streets, told De Broglie that they in England would follow the
glorious example of the Parisians whenever the necessity arose:

Their promptitude in resisting, their sagacity in feeling, as
if by instinct, that it was a case for arms and not for courts
of law; but, more than all, their signal temperance and
even humanity in victory, are the finest lessons to other
countries that any people ever offered in any age.[39]

So much importance did he attach to the events in Paris, that he
insisted on writing on the subject, in the next number of the *Edinburgh
Review*, in spite of Macaulay's complaint that he had already prepared

an article. Over Napier, who had succeeded Jeffrey as editor in 1829, Brougham exercised a merciless tyranny, and made the *Review* entirely subservient to his own interests. Macaulay, wrathful at Brougham's "intolerable dictation", summed up the situation in an angry and piquant letter to Napier:

> The present constitution of the *Edinburgh Review* is this, that at whatever time Brougham may be pleased to notify his intention of writing on any subject all previous engagements are to be considered as annulled by that notification. His language, translated into plain English, is this: "I must write about this French Revolution, and I will write about it. If you have told Macaulay to do it, you may tell him to let it alone. If he has written an article, he may throw it behind the grate. He would not himself have the assurance to compare his own claims with mine. I am a man who acts a prominent part in the world; he is nobody. If he must be reviewing, there is my speech about the West Indies. Set him to write a puff on that. What have people like him to do, except to eulogise people like me?"[40]

The October number of the *Edinburgh* contained another important article from his pen, entitled, "The General Election and the Ministry". Nothing is more remarkable than the contrast between the tone of that article and that of the earlier one written in July. Brougham now spoke of the Ministry as "imbecile" and of Peel with contempt. All the Ministers, with the single exception of the Duke, he pronounced to be

> men of no account, destitute of all will of their own, blindly submissive to the dictates of an imperious colleague, and that colleague profoundly ignorant of any civil lesson which can befit a statesman's vocation. It is of no moment that they should *almost* all be persons devoted to

the worst principles of policy, foreign and domestic—the well-wishers of arbitrary power in every form, the enemies of improvement at home as of liberty abroad.[41]

Whereas in February Brougham had professed to think so highly of Peel that he could not bear to consider even the possibility of their being in opposition to each other, in October, referring to the repeal of the Test Act, he declared:

> It must be confessed that if the man who plays the part Sir Robert Peel here played be not unprincipled, he is at least a politician whose principles hang somewhat loose about him. The safety of the Established Church required him one day to oppose the motion; what, then, became of the Church and its safety, when he volunteered to pass the self-same Bill the next day, merely because forty members had decided against him more than for him? Did that change his opinion of the measure? Did that remove the dangers from the Church? The truth must be told. He was determined at any rate to secure his own and his family's establishment in office.

This startling change of tone was occasioned by the disappointment of his hopes. A whole session had gone by, and Wellington had made no offer of place. The General Election had followed. The glorious victory in Yorkshire, the Government's numerous reverses elsewhere, and the Duke's unwillingness to share his power with the Whigs, convinced Brougham that it was his interest swiftly to compass the Ministry's destruction, and that it was in his power to do so.

The tide of public opinion was now rising strongly in favour of Reform and against the Ministry. Would Wellington attempt to defy that public opinion, as Charles X. and Polignac had attempted to do in France, was a question that began to agitate the country after the elections. Brougham wrote on August 17:

I think the [Duke of Wellington] has no right to complain of any one who supposes him capable of trying some
coup d'état; for his whole conduct looks like a man who
is not trusting for support to the ordinary means of legal
majorities and debates. But one thing I am ready enough
to believe, namely, that his Grace will not try any such
coup d'état NOW, after his dear friend and ally Jules has
been so beaten.[42]

Writing a few days later, he said:

What the Duke and Peel *can* mean exceeds my fancy to
guess. Legitimate means they have none after they have
in vain, like Jules, dissolved the chambers. Will they try a
coup d'état? I hardly think their nerves are up to that, but
I am sure the failure of Jules will make such senseless creatures as Aberdeen and Co. shrink from what I doubt not
THEY were asses enough to think of a few weeks ago.[43]

Meanwhile Wellington had been making some half-hearted efforts
to bring the Canningites back into the fold. In July he invited Lord
Melbourne to take office, but the future Whig Prime Minister replied
that he would come in only in company with Huskisson and Lord
Grey. The Duke refused to make an offer to Grey, and the negotiations
were broken off.[44]

The Canningites themselves were divided on the question whether
they should join the Government or throw in their lot with the Whigs.
Huskisson and Granville still regarded Wellington as a political enemy,
and regretted that they were engaged to meet him on September 15
at Liverpool, for the opening of the new Manchester and Liverpool
Railway. Brougham regarded that occasion as presenting so splendid
an opportunity of effecting an alliance between the Whigs and the
Canningites that he decided to make the journey to Liverpool himself.
He had now definitely determined to turn out the Ministry.[45] But his

appointment with Huskisson was never kept, for in the afternoon of that very day Huskisson met his death on the new railway near Eccles. The tragedy had important political effects, which Palmerston admirably described in a letter to Littleton (September 25):

> . . . As to [the Ministers] making any serious attempt to strengthen themselves, in any way at least in which it would be practicable to do so, I greatly doubt it; and they must now be less inclined to do so than before, since it cannot be concealed, that our recent loss has relieved them from one of their most formidable opponents. The difficulties also, of any junction between the friends of Canning and the Duke's Cabinet, are increased instead of being diminished by the loss of Huskisson, even if the Duke were to be desirous of such an union; because they would enter his Cabinet more completely destitute of means or influence to carry their opinions into action, and would be more decidedly considered by the public, as submitting to be instruments, instead of being admitted to be colleagues.

Palmerston continued:

> Have you read Brougham's last pamphlet[46] about the new Parliament and the Government? It is uncommonly able and powerful, but too violent and bitter and personal; and it savours more of resentment for neglect than of public zeal. I am told he is in a state of wonderful excitement, what with fury at having been so long and successfully practised upon by the Duke, and exaltation at his Yorkshire triumph. But if he launches out, sets all his canvass as he probably will, it will puzzle our friend Peel to keep up with him. After all, however, one should not be much surprised if the Government were to turn out stronger than people suppose. There is no answering for

the absurdity of mankind, and it is not impossible that all these convulsions on the Continent, which have been the direct and immediate consequences of the Duke's system of foreign policy, may be, with many well-meaning men, a reason for giving him their support. As to home affairs, do not you suppose that they will give members to some of the great towns? Can Tennyson's admonitory eloquence at Birmingham have been wholly thrown away? Lord John Russell's motion will probably be announced by Peel in the first week of the session amidst cheers from all sides of the House, and Goulburn will maintain that when he declaimed against first steps he meant election by ballot!

I suspect the Whigs would be very glad if our little squad would join their ranks, but do you not think that our maxim should be co-operation whenever practicable, but no incorporation?[47]

Brougham, too, was aware that Huskisson's death had considerably lowered the value of Canningite stock, but nevertheless he was extremely anxious that the remnant should join openly with the Whigs. Grey, Althorp, Stanley, Lambton, and others were of the same opinion.[48] On September 17 Brougham wrote to the Duke of Devonshire:

The Huskisson party have lost more than half their value, but there are among them men of most valuable talents, as Palmerston and Grant, and of excellent sense and dispositions as Lord Granville, and of excellent talents and dispositions and temper too, as William Lamb. Also their LATE conduct has been perfect—above all praise for sense as well as honour. My notion, therefore, is to draw closer the ties that unite us, for the doubt is now unhappily ended which prevailed against avowed junction, viz., the offence it would give the ultras and some few of our own older stagers.[49]

But the Canningites might make a mistake. If they allied themselves with the wrong party, said Brougham, they should have no peace. He felt, however, that he could rely on their judgement and good sense:

> If they do join [Wellington], by all the Gods and Goddesses, and by the river Styx, let them look sharp. They are ruined if they do. What made R. Grant get me to propose him for Norwich? I it was who sent to him the two deputations that came to beg me to name a man—and R. Grant called on me repeatedly and consulted confidentially on the subject. Again, was not I asked by Huskisson, who sent his secretary to me about it, to subscribe and get our Whig friends to subscribe for R. Grant, he, Huskisson, putting down £100? I offered £50 and to get others to do the same, but it went off, on finding a doubt of R. Grant standing. But surely, to join the man who so vilely used Huskisson as soon as the breath is out of his body, would be as bad as they did by Canning's memory, or indeed, worse—for they refused the junction till three or four months after Canning's death. I cannot and will not believe it, but if it prove true, Palmerston will return to insignificance with a ruined character, and no real good will ensue to the dictator. I shall deeply regret it on account of a man whom I really like, and because it will hurt the character of public men generally. But I have not any fear of the results.[50]

A few days later Wellington began another negotiation with the Canningites. Palmerston's answer was in all essentials identical with Melbourne's in July. His friends must come in as a party, and in company with Grey and Lansdowne.[51] For such sweeping changes in the Cabinet the Duke was no more prepared in September than he had been before the General Election. To avoid a useless protraction of the negotiations, Palmerston left London on October 12 for Paris.

A few hours before his departure he wrote an interesting account, of what had passed between him and Wellington:

> I have had a proposal from the Duke to join his Government, and saying that if I was disposed to do so, he had it in his power to offer me a high office which would probably be agreeable to me if I did not object to my colleagues. This was made through a common friend.[52] My answer of course was that taking into view a great variety of circumstances, which, as they must naturally suggest themselves, I felt it unnecessary to detail, I could not singly join the Government constituted as it now is. The office meant was, I believe, Murray's.[53] I did not say that it was like asking me whether I was disposed to jump off Westminster Bridge. I take it that the Duke is told from all quarters that he must strengthen himself, but does not himself feel the necessity as strongly as Peel does, and is reluctant therefore to take the steps by which alone he would acquire the strength he wants. But the fact is, that it is not the accession of one or two, or even three individuals that would strengthen the Government. Such accessions would exterminate the men who became his new instruments without adding materially to the force of the Government. He must either go on as he is, or make up his mind to a reconstruction of his Government upon an extended principle. This was poor Huskisson's decided opinion, and one on which he had made up his mind to act, had any proposal been made to him; and his loss cannot weaken, with respect to those he has left behind him, the force of those reasons which were held to be conclusive when he was still with us. Do not mention what I have now told you, as I think that there ought always to be a sort of understanding on these matters that if an offer is not accepted it is not to be talked about. I rather believe the plan was, to propose to Melbourne, Grant, and myself, to

come in with Goderich, but I do not know why, instead of
such a proposal, the Duke made the one to me alone, which
he himself could scarcely, I think, have supposed it possible
for me to accept. But *could* the other have been closed with,
if made? Goderich is an excellent fellow, and an able head of
a department, and would be a most agreeable colleague, but
would the public have seen in him any security for us three,
against a repetition of *May* 1828, whenever we might be less
necessary, and not properly acquiescent; or would they have
considered his accession with us any pledge that we should
have weight enough in the Cabinet to be able to give effect
to our opinions, and should not soon be reduced to the
alternative of going out again, or being parties to a system
of which we disapproved? Every public motive which led
us to go out in 1828 would equally have operated against
going in now, and there are many new reasons, springing
from subsequent events.[54]

After Palmerston's return to London on October 26, the day of the
meeting of Parliament, Wellington reopened negotiations, but immediately broke them off upon hearing that the Canningites regarded a large
accession of Whigs to office as a *sine quâ non* of their own adhesion. Then
followed those exciting days which decided the fate of the Government,
and the future of the Whig and Canningite parties. Littleton, on behalf
of the Canningites, made a last endeavour to bring the Ministers and his
friends to an agreement, but he was just twenty-four hours too late. On
the previous evening the King's speech had been put into its final form
at a Cabinet dinner, and Wellington had decided to oppose all reform.[55]
His famous declaration in the House of Lords on November 2 was the
last straw which caused the Canningite party to go over to the Whigs and
to accept the principle of Parliamentary Reform. Wellington, who cared
little for party, and who was never an ordinary party leader, for once made
the mistake of attaching too much importance to party. His declaration
of hostility to all reform was mainly dictated by a desire to reunite the

shattered Tory party; instead of attempting to win over the Moderate Liberals in both wings of the Opposition, he strove to regain the favour of the High Tories whom he had hopelessly alienated eighteen months before. Their reply to his efforts at conciliation was to combine with their enemies, the Whigs and the Canningites, to defeat the Ministry on the Civil List question (November 15). Wellington at once resigned; the ultra-Tories were at last revenged.

After a period of twenty-three years there was again to be a Whig Ministry. The Whigs went mad with joy. Durham wrote to Lady Durham the day after the division:

> I went to Berkeley Square to tea. About ten o'clock arrived Henry and Wood, shouting and hurra-ing. "We've beat 'em", "They're done for", etc., etc., to the great horror of Lord A. and Lady G. Hervey who were there. After hearing the particulars I went to Brooks's, which I found in the greatest commotion and delight. A Mr. Cholmeley, the member for Grantham, overheard Holmes, the whipper-in, telling Sir Charles Forbes that he had been to the Duke to announce the event: that the Duke had said, "Ah—well—much obliged to you—the game's up—the foreign ministers are upstairs, I may as well be the first to tell them".[56]

Brougham had done more than any other man to turn out the Tories. He was the most powerful and popular politician in the country, but he was no longer recognised as leader of the Whigs. Grey had, in March, warned his son, Lord Howick, that Brougham must not be put in command; and Grey had his way, for a short time later took place that famous meeting at the Albany when Lord Althorp was chosen to lead a reunited party. But in spite of the definite selection of a new chief, Brougham was still bent on arrogating that position to himself. His latest contribution to the *Edinburgh Review* had disgusted as many Whigs as Tories, and the wild speeches he had been delivering since his triumph in Yorkshire, filled many members of the Opposition with dread and alarm. "I see on all sides great jealousy of Brougham's assumption of the office of leader, great distrust of his prudence and intentions", Ellice informed Grey.[57]

Brougham had deeply committed himself at York on the question of reform; and during the interval between the elections and the meeting of Parliament he found it necessary to prepare an outline of a plan to reform the representative system. His proposals bore not the slightest resemblance to those which were soon to be embodied in the Reform Bill. He intended to do nothing more than disfranchise some five or six close boroughs and to deprive a few others of one member; to give members to the few great unrepresented towns; to disfranchise non-resident voters and to enfranchise all householders in the boroughs.

Brougham's motion was fixed for November 16, but when that day arrived the Tories were out—a Whig Government was on the point of being formed, and the whole political situation was in a moment transformed. To the utmost alarm of the Whigs, however, Brougham emphatically declared, not only that he had the greatest repugnance to putting off his motion, but that no change that might take place in the Administration could by any possibility affect him. Twenty-four hours before, he had been in favour of postponement.[58] "I will not let my motion be made the stepping stone of a party", he now threateningly declared. On the 17th the Duke of Bedford wrote:

> I found him at Holland House last night under great excitement. Angry at having been persuaded to put off his motion—too absurd! Lord Holland thinks he ought to resign his reform measures into the hands of the new Ministers. The lawyer thinks differently.[59]

Brougham's threatening attitude was occasioned by the almost insulting offer of the Attorney-Generalship which Grey had made to him that morning. It was a post infinitely beneath his pretensions, and he rejected the offer with scorn and contempt. The office he had long coveted was the Mastership of the Rolls, a permanent judicial office which might be held with a seat in the House of Commons, which he was determined never to leave. But it was clear that with him in an irremovable office, and exercising an unbounded dominion in the Lower House, no Government could be safe, for none could count on his unfailing support. Althorp for one, who was to have the Exchequer and the lead of the House, flatly declined to belong to a Ministry which gave Brougham the Rolls; and without Althorp's assistance Grey himself was not prepared to form a Government.[60] Althorp's objections might not, after all, have been insuperable, but the King himself had made up his mind that Brougham could not be allowed to wield such over-whelming and irresponsible power over the new Ministry. In his book on the Reform Bill, Roebuck stated that the objection was suggested to the King by the Whigs themselves, who wished to get him out of the House of Commons. Brougham saw the work for the first time in 1861, and, after reading that statement, wrote: "I feel quite confident that Roebuck is entirely wrong in his suspicion of the Whigs—that is, in reality, of my colleagues having suggested it. Grey, I am quite certain, did all in his power towards my having the Rolls."[61] Brougham chose to declare in 1861 that he had not coveted the Rolls in 1830. "Roebuck", he wrote in the same letter, "is also wrong in saying I very much desired the office. I was willing to take it and should have been pleased to have it, but I also felt the objection which Grey stated—that it would involve me in a Yorkshire contest, to retrieve my seat in Parliament, and that another contest I could not afford to risk. This was one of his reasons urged in favour of my taking the Great Seal when I refused it."[62]

Brougham himself believed that the objection came either from the King himself or from the Tory leaders. [63] In the letter quoted above, he declared: "I have often discussed it with Wellington, and he denied ever having spoken a word to the King or to any one else on the subject".[64] Brougham, in truth, was probably right. Croker asserted that the outgoing Ministers warned William IV. against giving Brougham the Rolls.[65] Lord Grey stated that the King had given him "*Carte blanche* as to all offices both in Government and the

Household but Brougham", and that "Brougham is the difficulty, and it really is the only one with the King".[66] Lord Durham, writing on the 17th declared, "The great difficulty, I foresee, will be with Brougham. He has frightened so many people (*the King among the rest*) by his wild speeches, that it is hard to place him in a situation which would please him and at the same time not offend others."[67]

In the morning of the 17th, Brougham took occasion to declare in the Court of King's Bench that "The representation of Yorkshire was the only place he would have".[68] It was an intimation that the difficulty had not been surmounted. Freely translated, his angry declaration read, "Give me the Rolls unless you want me in Opposition". Boiling over with indignation at his situation, he made that afternoon in the House of Commons what Palmerston eloquently described as a second "fly out". When the question of the postponement of election committees was being discussed, Brougham angrily protested against delay:

> What do *we* want with the presence of the Ministers on election petitions? We can do as well (I speak it with all possible respect of any future Ministry); but I say we can do as well without them as with them. I have nothing to do with them except in the respect I bear them, and except as a member of this House. I state this for the information of those who may feel any interest in the matter.

The following day brought a solution of the problem no nearer. Lord Sefton wrote of Brougham:

> He is really in a state of insanity, complains to everybody that he is neglected, and threatens to put an extinguisher on the new Government in a month. In the meantime he keeps swearing he will not take anything—that he ought to be offered the Seals, though he would kick them out of the window rather than desert his Yorkshire friends by taking a peerage.[69]

Brougham himself wrote to the Duke of Devonshire on the 18th:

> . . . Morpeth on account of Yorkshire won't take office.
> I shall take none either. I have refused Attorney-General
> as a matter of course, and there are (*though certainly there
> ought not to be*) difficulties about other offices. But I am
> well pleased to have none, for I cannot think of giving
> up Yorkshire after the kind way it behaved to me, and no
> other place than Chancellor is any temptation to me. I am
> delighted to stand in my high position *out of office*, and
> essential to the stability of those in office. I am a useful
> check on them, and being a disinterested, I am therefore
> a more effectual supporter.[70]

In the evening of the 18th, Lord Grey, then in a "dreadful state of anxiety and annoyance", and declaring that Brougham stood between him and rest,[71] wrote to his equally exasperated follower, to request his attendance in Downing Street the following morning. Brougham called; but upon being offered the Great Seal, he at once declined to take an office which would deprive him of the representation of Yorkshire and of his seat in the Commons. Later in the morning, Grey having failed to induce him to give way, Althorp, Sefton, Duncannon, and other Whigs saw him at the House of Lords; and, after representing that his refusal of the Great Seal would mean the break-up of the Government, the return to power of the Tories, and the exclusion of the Whigs for another period of twenty-five years, they at last extorted his acceptance.[72]

Brougham made his appearance in Parliament as member for Yorkshire for the last time in the evening of that day. His appointment was not generally known, but the fact that he did not make another 'fly out' was regarded as significant. "His countenance was tolerably complacent this evening in the House, and the physiognomists thought he was caught", said Littleton.[73] On the following Monday Brougham took his seat on the Woolsack.

"SAMSON AND DELILAH". Lady Holland is cutting off Brougham's hair. He is lying asleep in her lap. Lord Grey whispers to her, "Hush. How astonished he'll be when he wakes." Lord Durham is coming in with the Lord Chancellor's wig.

1. Add. MS. 35146, fol. 94.
2. Chatsworth MS.
3. Althorp MS.: A letter of Althorp's, Jan. 25, 1828.
4. Broughton, *Recollections*, iii. 232.
5. Add. MS. 38754, fol. 115.
6. *Creevey Papers*, ii. 146.
7. Lambton MS.; Ellice to Lambton, Jan. 26 (1828).
8. Add. MS. 36464, fol. 182.
9. Add. MS. 35146, fol. 95. Brougham made his famous speech on the state of the courts of common law on February 7, 1828.
10. Add. MS. 35146, fol. 96.
11. *Creevey Papers*, ii. 154.
12. Lambton MS.
13. *Ibid.*

14. Add. MS. 30115, fol. 95.

15. *Corr. of Princess Lieven and Earl Grey*, i. 158.

16. Lambton MS. n.d. (c. Aug. 1828).

17. Althorp MS.

18. *Parl. Deb*. N.S. xx. 89.

19. Add. MS. 30115, fol. 89.

20. In his British History in the Nineteenth Century (p.222), Mr. G.M. Trevelyan wrongly states that Wellington and Huskisson never met between their quarrel in May 1828 and their last meeting in September 1830, on the occasion of the opening of the Manchester and Liverpool Railway.

21. Hatherton MS.

22. Add. MS. 38080, fol. 46.

23. *Ibid.* 30115, fol. 103.

24. Chatsworth MS.

25. *Ibid.*

26. *Desp. and Corr.*, vii 457.

27. *Croker Papers*, ii. 68.

28. *Parl. Deb.*, N.S. xxv. 825; Ellenborough, Diary, ii. 295.

29. Chatsworth MS.: Brougham to the Duke of Devonshire, July 12, 1830.

30. *The Country without a Government*, p.9.

31. Chatsworth MS.

32. Chatsworth MS.: Brougham to the Duke of Devonshire, July 28, 1830.

33. Chatsworth MS.

34. *Ibid.*

35. Chatsworth MS.: Brougham to the Duke of Devonshire, Aug. 28, 1830.

36. *Life and Times*, iii. 42.

37. *Life of Macaulay*, i. 186.

38. *Edin. Review*, July 1830.

39. *Desp. and Corr.,* vii. 172.

40. Napier, *Corr.*, p.90.

41. *Edin. Review*, Oct. 1830, p.262.

42. Chatsworth MS.: Brougham to the Duke of Devonshire, Tuesday (August 17, 1830).

43. *Ibid.*: Brougham to the Duke of Devonshire, Friday.

44. Hatherton MS.: Littleton to R. Wellesley, Dec. 20, 1830.

45. Grenville, ii. 48-49; Robinson, *Letters of Princess Lieven*, p.241; *Letters of Princess Lieven to Earl Grey*, ii. 83.

46. *What has the Duke of Wellington gained by the Dissolution?* published anonymously, but attributed to Brougham.

47. Hatherton MS.

48. Chatsworth MS.: Brougham to the Duke of Devonshire, Sept. 21, 1830.

49. *Ibid.*

50. Chatsworth MS.

51. *Life of Palmerston*, i. 382.

52. Lord Clive.

53. The Secretaryship of State for War and Colonies.

54. Hatherton MS.

55. *Ibid.*, Littleton to R. Wellesley, Dec. 20, 1830.

56. Lambton MS.

57. G.M. Trevelyan, Lord Grey, p.221.

58. Broughton, *Recollections*, iv. 68.

59. Russell, *Early Correspondence*, i. 314.

60. *Life of Althorp*, p.261.

61. Lansdowne MS.: Brougham to Lansdowne, Sept. 24, 1861.

62. Lansdowne MS.

63. *Ibid.*

64. *Ibid.*

65. *Croker Papers*, ii. 80.

66. Trevelyan, *Lord Grey*, p.241.

67. Lambton MS.

68. Add. MS. 27789, fol. 200.

69. *Creevey Papers*, ii. 214

70. Chatsworth MS.

71. Walpole, *Russell*, i. 160.

72. Strong rumours had been circulated that Lyndhurst, the Lord
    Chancellor in the Wellington Ministry, was to be invited to remain
    in office. Brougham had used his influence against the proposal.
    On the 17th he wrote to the Duke of Devonshire, "Lord Grey
    was most graciously received by William IV. who spoke most
    kindly and cried. . . . He then gave Grey *carte blanche* to form a
    Government. . . . A shameful idea prevailed of keeping Copley,
    whose wife was indecently joyful on the defeat! But I have very
    strongly protested in right quarters"—(Chatsworth MS.)

73. Hatherton MS.

X

In High Office

Brougham's name will be on every patriot lip
While England shall be England. He foresaw
Reform must come, or vengeance would let slip—
For they were half unchain'd—the dogs of war;
And did not slack his step e'er 'twas too late
To stand between his country and its fate.

The Patriot Ministry (1831)

THE promotion of Brougham to the highest judicial office in the kingdom, to the seat that had been occupied by a long succession of great statesmen and eminent lawyers—by Bacon, Clarendon, Somers, Cowper, and Hardwicke, created a profound sensation throughout the country. Such had been the terror and aversion that his name had inspired amongst the Tory country gentlemen and the clergy, declared one of his friends, that, had the appointment been made a few years earlier, it would have been regarded as the precursor of a revolution.

His regret at having to quit the political arena where for fifteen years he had fought and struggled with the hardihood and courage of a prize-fighter was so profound that until 1853—nearly a quarter of a century later, he never had the heart to revisit the House of Commons.[1] Within a few months of his taking leave of the representative chamber, he was panting to return, and vowing that he would devise some means of getting rid of his peerage the moment the fall of the Whig Government should relieve him of the Seals. With pardonable vanity he continued to sign himself "H. Brougham", thus intimating to the world that a peerage could not enhance the splendour and dignity of the position he had occupied as the representative of the great county of York, and as the most popular parliamentarian in the country.

Realising how impossible it was that he could ever again become a commoner, he speedily came to the conclusion that the next best thing to strive for was a long spell of office. He genuinely regretted Wellington's suicidal refusal to share his power with the Whigs in the summer of 1830. A Coalition Government would have had this incalculable advantage over the Reform Ministry—the opposition to it would have been negligible, and it would probably have lasted for many years. Brougham truly declared that no man was "less exclusive in his political propensities" than he.[2] The administration of which he had just become a member, had, he said, two cardinal defects. Many of the Ministers were without administrative experience; and some of them cared too little for office to take the trouble to maintain themselves in power. He recalled to mind the abortive negotiations of 1812, the reluctance of his Whig friends to take office in April 1827, and their almost indecent haste to quit in January 1828. "Of this folly . . . of this worse than childish folly there must be an end." He for one would feel it no reproach to regulate the destinies of a great nation; he for one would put up with the vexations, the dull routine, the harassing duties of office, and would leave no stone unturned, no step untaken, to secure a long continuance of power. These were the motives that guided his conduct after 1830. They were not exclusively personal and selfish. He professed a genuine alarm at the progress of a spirit in the country hostile to aristocratic government. He thought that the exigencies of the time needed a strong Government, and he for one was prepared to do his utmost to give strength and permanence to the Reform Ministry.

The story of the passing of the Reform Bill has been so fully and authoritatively told that we need not linger over it here. When, more than a quarter of a century later, Brougham wrote his own account of the history of the years 1830–1832, his vanity caused him to arrogate to himself all the glory of the struggle for the Bill. He represented himself as being the real driving force in the movement for Reform, but the truth is that the part that he played in the drama of these eventful years was comparatively small. The aristocratic Whigs who had tried to keep him out of the Cabinet, were careful to exclude him from the Cabinet Committee of four which was appointed to prepare the Bill. To his intense annoyance he found that Graham's claims to a seat on the Committee were preferred to his own. He discovered, too, that his opinions on the subject of Reform carried little or no weight in the Cabinet, and that his suggestions were invariably disregarded. He wrote to Althorp on March 1, 1831:

> I feel averse to give any advice, for I know that all I ever have given has been rejected by all of my colleagues—without the least consideration. One says I am a lawyer—another I am a judge—a third has a third reason—and all join in rejecting the counsel tendered—none so regularly, I grieve to say, as yourself.[3]

It is indeed hardly matter of wonder that his views were systematically scouted, especially when he began to express a tender regard for the 'pocket' boroughs. His objections to wholesale disfranchisements, and his opposition to other features of the Bill and to methods of procedure, gave much anxiety to his harassed colleagues. Finding himself however in a minority in the Cabinet, he agreed to swallow his objections to Schedules A and B, and in the *Edinburgh Review* he gave the Bill his blessing. Parliamentary Reform had never been a subject in which he had been particularly interested, and he had thought no more of changing his opinions than of changing his clothes. "Were I left to my own wishes," he now declared, "and to follow my own

Reform doctrines, I certainly should be a very moderate and very gradual Reformer." He protested that the Ministry ought not to stake its existence on the success or failure of the Bill.[4]

Brougham himself is mainly responsible for the halo of romance that has long surrounded his activities during the struggle for the Bill. There is, however, a grain of truth in the story he told to Roebuck of the dissolution of Parliament in April 1831 after the Bill had passed its second reading by a majority of one. It is certainly true that the Chancellor took upon himself the responsibility of ordering the Horse Guards (which he had no authority to do) to attend the King to the House of Lords. Brougham recounted some of the circumstances of that celebrated affair in a letter to Althorp written at the beginning of 1836. There is no reason to suppose that his recollection of such a recent and memorable occurrence was faulty, and he would not wilfully have perverted the facts to Lord Spencer, who must have known them himself. Grey and Brougham went to see the King after the Cabinet had put the King's dissolution speech into its final form. But, said Brougham, Grey

> took fright on the dissolution, 1831, in the ante-chamber, when I sent to the Horse Guards and the Earl Marshal, and altered the speech, and had it copied by a man I had stationed on purpose in the ante-room, all before we went to the King, who, however, forgave and even commended what I had done; but I don't believe Grey's family ever forgave it, because I have no doubt he told them the words I used (about a council of war when a charge had been ordered) and also that I had said, "I shall go to the King immediately, whatever you do," on which he went with me.[5]

On the other hand, Campbell's story of Brougham's famous speech in support of the Bill, delivered on October 8, 1831, in the House of Lords, when he was alleged to have concluded by falling down on the Woolsack in an attitude of prayer, was a malicious fabrication.

Littleton was present throughout the speech, which took over three hours to deliver, and described it both in his diary and in a letter to his wife; but in neither account is there any mention of the play-acting which Campbell mentioned with such glee.[6]

The crisis of the struggle for the Bill came in May 1832 when William IV. refused to create enough peers to enable the Ministry to carry their measure. Grey at once resigned. In his Memoirs, Brougham declared that the King requested him to form a Government. Of that story there is no independent confirmation, but it is perhaps true that the King urged him not to give up the Great Seal. In his speech on October 8 Brougham had imprudently acknowledged that the Bill was not altogether to his liking, a declaration which caused Reformers out of doors to fear that he would endeavour to retain office in the event of his colleagues' resignation, and that he would support a much smaller measure of Reform. And now, in May, his younger brother, William, went to the trouble of explaining to a meeting of London Reformers that their fears of the Chancellor's faithlessness were unfounded. Asserting his brother's unwavering loyalty to the Bill, he said, "A report has been very prevalent that the Lord Chancellor is to continue in office and form part of a Government, but not Earl Grey's Government. This report I have authority to contradict." The Tories seemed to have looked forward with some confidence to his joining their ranks; but when the King urged him to remain in office, he was reported to have replied that there was not "A shadow of a shade of a vestige of a possibility of his so disgracing himself ".[7]

But Wellington's desperate attempt to form a Government in order to pass a Reform Bill almost identical with that which his party had opposed tooth and nail, met with the failure it deserved. The Whigs returned to power, and on May 18 took place that famous interview between Grey, Brougham, and the King, at which William IV. wrote the authorisation to his Prime Minister for the creation of a sufficient number of peers to ensure the passing of the Bill. It has long been known that the letter quoted by Roebuck (who received it from Brougham) in which the royal permission appeared to be given to

"Earl Grey and his Chancellor, Lord Brougham", is spurious, but with whom it originated is still a mystery, as is also the precise purpose for which it was written.[8]

With the passing of the First Reform Bill Lord Grey's work was accomplished. He was over seventy years old, but in October he decided to remain at his post a little longer. His retirement, he explained to Althorp, would destroy the Whig party for ever, would bring about the return of the Tories to power, and the subversion of Government itself.[9] "With such a prospect before me I will bear much." In October 1833 he again decided that his services were indispensable, and that he must remain at the helm for at least another session.[10]

Grey's extreme anxiety to spend his remaining years in retirement at Howick, was, of course, well known to his colleagues. Brougham hoped that he himself might succeed to the Premiership, and accordingly he began to strive for the succession. With that object in view, he worked out a plan whereby he might separate the judicial from the political functions of his office, rid himself of the Great Seal, and become a politician pure and simple. One day in 1832 he was indiscreet enough to ask Lord John Russell whether the party would accept him as the next Prime Minister. Russell coolly replied, "Not at all!" In spite of this rebuff, Brougham set himself to work upon the feelings of the Whig members of the House of Commons, and attempted to enlist a band of followers who would support his claims. His activities excited general remark. "Night and day", said Littleton, "is he engaged in inventing civilities to members. Mr. Le Marchant, his secretary, is seldom absent from his post in the Lobby, ostensibly for the purpose of sending the Chancellor intelligence of what is happening, but really for the purpose of keeping up a constant intercourse with members."[11] In May 1831 Brougham wrote to Althorp, requesting him to get his brother into Parliament,

> I feel most anxious to keep him in Parliament, I don't say
> merely because while he is there I am daily kept up to the
> full knowledge of all that goes on in House of Commons

and can act upon it often so as to do much good and prevent much mischief. But I put it on a different ground. My brother has great claims on me. He has devoted himself to me for years, and spent a great deal of money in electioneering on my behalf. I have had opportunities of rewarding him since I came in. *He* has always refused office both in 1827 and now. It would have been no great thing for one, in my station in the Government to have got him a place—he most generously relieved me from all such exertions by declining office.[12]

The first Reformed Parliament met at the beginning of 1833 after a General Election which gave the Whigs and their allies a majority of three hundred over the Tories. Ere two sessions of the new Parliament had gone by, the Whig Ministry, in possession of such overwhelming strength, had fallen to pieces. Within its ranks were Radicals like Lord Durham, who, by 1833 had quarrelled with nearly all his colleagues; and Conservatives like the Duke of Richmond, Stanley, and Graham. It had to rely on the support of the Radical party headed by Grote, and of the Irish party which, commanded by O'Connell, singularly fulfilled, in the opinion of many contemporaries, a prophecy made by Henry Grattan to Tierney immediately after the Union of 1800. "My country", he had declared, "owes yours a large debt, for centuries of misrule and tyranny. She is about to repay you. Pass a few years and she will pour into the bosom of your legislature a hundred of the damnedest rascals that ever crossed the Channel".[13]

The year 1833 saw the beginning of a new period of political and social reconstruction. The first effective Factory Act was passed. Slavery was abolished throughout the British Empire. The Bank Charter was revised so as to stimulate the growth of joint-stock banks. The first attempt to reform the Irish Church was made. The first parliamentary grant for Education was made in 1833. The Poor Law Reform Act was passed in 1834. The Scottish boroughs were reformed in 1833 by the Scottish Burgh Act, as were the English boroughs in 1835 by the

English Municipal Corporations Act. The India Act of 1833 remodelled the Government of British India and abolished the trading privileges of the East India Company.

"I wish from the bottom of my heart that the Ministers would move quicker in the work of reforming abuses. But after all, we are moving in the right direction, though not, I think, at the right pace", wrote Macaulay in 1833.[14] Much greater progress might have been made in the work of reconstruction, but for the disunion of the Government and the continual Cabinet crises that periodically threatened to dissolve the Ministry. The first came in October 1832 on the question of the Irish Church, Althorp being unable to agree to Stanley's very moderate measure of reform. Two months later, Brougham caused a deal of trouble by threatening to resign on account of Grey's unwillingness to remove Durham from the Cabinet, in order to facilitate changes in the constitution of the Irish Government. At the beginning of 1833 Hobhouse wished to throw up his office because he disagreed with the Army estimates. In July the Irish Church Bill again shook the Ministry to its very foundations. Six months later, Lord Grey was with the greatest difficulty dissuaded by Brougham and others from resigning, after he had failed to induce a majority of his colleagues to agree to armed intervention in the Portuguese revolution. In May 1834 the Conservatives in the Government parted company with the Whigs on the question of the appropriation of the surplus revenues of the Irish Church to secular purposes. Brougham distinguished himself on that occasion by his extraordinary endeavours to keep the Ministry together. "I for one," he said, "will never abandon the public service and leave all in remediless confusion as long as I can find any six men to stand with me—that is certain."[15] Much to Grey's annoyance, no doubt, Brougham went so far as to usurp the functions of the Prime Minister by going to see the King to acquaint him with the state of affairs, and to assure him that the difficulties occasioned by the resignation of the Stanleyites could easily be surmounted. "My views of all things and all men were laid before him both verbally and in writing very fully," he declared. The Chancellor, indeed, was so anxious for the Government to continue, and so put out of humour by the occurrence of anything that was calculated to disturb its tranquility, that, after hearing of Lord John Russell's famous speech which occasioned Stanley's withdrawal, he wrote the offending statesman a letter beginning, "Henceforward the name of Whig and driveller are synonymous".[16]

Six weeks later the Reform Ministry broke up as a result of the famous O'Connell affair. The Catholic Relief Act of 1829 had done nothing to pacify the people of Ireland, whose grievances—an alien Church ministering to a small minority of the population and deriving its revenues from the mass of the Catholic peasantry; and a monstrously unjust land system (which, unlike their political disabilities, deeply affected their lives)—the English Parliament had done nothing to remedy. To meet the terrible outrages committed by an infuriated populace, who defied the efforts of the military to collect arrears of tithes, the Government had in 1833 passed the strongest measure of coercion that that unhappy country had ever had to endure. Introducing it into the House of Lords, Grey explained that its virtue lay in the combination in its provisions, of "The Proclamation Act, the Insurrection Act, the partial application of martial law, and the partial suspension of the Habeas Corpus Act". The Coercion Act had been passed for one year only, and in 1834 the Ministry had to decide whether the state of Ireland necessitated a renewal of the whole Act, or whether the most stringent provisions of the Act—the courts-martial and public meetings clauses—might be omitted.

On April 18 Wellesley, the Lord Lieutenant, informed the Government that he desired a renewal of the Act for a period not exceeding five years, and he did not suggest the omission of any clause.[17] He wrote an official despatch to Melbourne, the Home Secretary, on May 20, and it met with Grey's entire approval.[18]

Meanwhile Littleton, who had succeeded Hobhouse as Irish Secretary, was piloting his Irish Church Bill through the Commons, where it was being opposed both by the Tories, who thought that it went too far, and by the O'Connellites, who complained that it did not go far enough. Littleton came to the conclusion that his Bill could not be carried without the support of the Irish party, and that he could not gain their support except by modifying the Coercion Bill.

On May 23 Wellesley wrote to Littleton, his son-in-law, and urged him to consult Brougham, "whom I most sincerely esteem, love, and admire", who, he knew, was willing to go to all lengths to prop up the tottering Ministry. Littleton and the Chancellor met the following Sunday, and agreed that concessions ought to be made. On June 11 the Lord Lieutenant sent what he intended should be his final despatch on the subject; and he declared that "None of the extraordinary powers can be omitted without material injury to the efficacy of the law".

But the whole situation was suddenly transformed on June 19 by a letter which Brougham sent off to Wellesley, urging him to give up the meetings clauses. Neither the Prime Minister nor the Home Secretary was aware of the step taken by the Chancellor, who, however, had communicated his sentiments to Althorp the previous day, though he did not state that he intended to write to Wellesley:

> The insurrection part of the Act is the real substance, he told Althorp. The sunset and sunrise part—all the rest is fringe and mere personal spleen against O'Connell and his agitations. If we strike out the part about meetings, and keep, and if necessary, improve, the rest, O. is appeased, and will give us the Act ten years, if we choose. I am very clear of all this. Do you well consider it. It is really the thing.

Brougham advised Littleton to write to Wellesley to the same effect. The Chief Secretary did so the same evening, his and Brougham's letters reaching Dublin on the 21st. The Lord Lieutenant at once wrote to Grey and informed him that the obnoxious clauses could be dispensed with, although, only ten days previously, he had, after mature reflection, and on the advice of his expert assistants, declared that these same clauses were necessary for the maintenance of peace in Ireland.

The Prime Minister had already made up his mind to resign if he could not induce the Cabinet to accept the meetings clauses. On the other hand, Althorp, the Leader of the Commons, told Littleton on the 23rd that *he* would resign if the clauses were retained. Melbourne, too, though very angry with Wellesley for suddenly changing front and for not communicating in the official channel, acknowledged that the clauses could not be carried against the advice of the Lord Lieutenant, and that the Cabinet would have to yield.

It was on the 23rd that Althorp suggested to Littleton that he should speak to O'Connell and try to induce him to keep quiet. The Chief Secretary saw the Irish leader that very morning, and, relying on Althorp's positive assurance that the inclusion of the disputed clauses would occasion his own resignation and the fall of the Ministry, Littleton spoke with the greatest freedom. Two things are very remarkable. Littleton informed neither the Prime Minister nor the Home Secretary, the Cabinet minister responsible for Ireland, that he intended to give O'Connell his confidence, but relied solely on Althorp's authorisation. And, both Duncannon and Edward Ellice, who were in the Cabinet, had had interviews with O'Connell before the 23rd, and had given him hints as to their opinions on the Coercion Bill. These conversations too were unknown to the Prime Minister.

O'Connell pledged his word that Littleton's strictly confidential information should not be repeated; but that very day, or at the latest, the day following, he transmitted the substance of this communication to Ireland, for insertion in the *Dublin Register* and the *Pilot* newspapers, of both of which he was the private correspondent.

The Cabinet meeting at which the decision was finally taken, was held at Holland House in the evening of Sunday, June 29. A majority of the Ministers favoured the omission of the meetings clauses, but when Grey refused to give way, and threatened to resign, the majority reluctantly agreed to accept the clauses. Althorp failed to keep his promise to resign. Wellesley's object in making a complete change of front, had been merely to facilitate the passing of the Tithe Bill; but when informed of the Cabinet's decision, he cheerfully turned round again, and wrote another official despatch (July 2) strongly urging the retention of the clauses. On the following day O'Connell caused the famous flare-up in the Commons by disclosing the substance of his conversation with Littleton. "There—now the pig's killed", whispered Althorp to Russell, who was seated next to him. Littleton, aware that a full explanation of all the facts must produce the immediate dissolution of the Ministry, showed a desperate fidelity to Althorp and Brougham by refraining to state that his authorisation to speak to O'Connell came from the former, and that his letter to Wellesley would never have been written but for the latter, with whom the idea originated. On the 7th the Opposition pressed for the production of the Lord Lieutenant's private correspondence, but instead of resisting the motion, as was afterwards done in the Lords, Althorp resigned office, and occasioned by that act the dissolution of Grey's Ministry.[19]

Both Lord Grey and his family seriously believed that Brougham had been intriguing against him and plotting his overthrow. The Chancellor, they said, had long been bent on ousting the Prime Minister and on usurping his place. But, upon cooler reflection, even Lady Grey, who detested Brougham, was forced to admit that her imputation of baseness was undeserved, and that he had been actuated solely by a strong desire to facilitate the business of the session, and, in particular, to smooth the way for the passage of the Tithe Bill. Nor, indeed, was it his interest to destroy the Government of which he was Chancellor. "Of his anxiety to uphold the fabric of Lord Grey's administration," wrote Littleton, "there was as little doubt in the minds of all who knew him as there was of his affection and regard for Lord Grey personally".

Brougham's extraordinary attempt to keep the Whigs in office after Grey's resignation, proved conclusively that his and their interests were identical. But for his exertions, indeed, it is certain that the Melbourne Ministry could not have been formed.[20]

On July 9, the King, having received the resignations of Grey and Althorp the previous day, sent for Melbourne, and desired him to enter into communications with the Duke of Wellington, Peel, and Stanley, with a view to the formation of a Coalition Ministry.[21] Melbourne declared that the project was impracticable, but it was really Brougham who defeated it. In the Lords that night he spoke, said Greville, like a man possessed, and made the amazing declaration that the Government was still in existence, although its head had disappeared. His sense of duty, he proceeded, would not permit him to abandon his country and forsake the King. But he did not content himself merely with contradicting Althorp's positive announcement in the Commons that the Ministry was at an end. He took an even more audacious step. He wrote to Wellesley:

> I have in writing stated to the King that I *would not resign*, because I *knew* full well that there is no kind of difficulty in reforming the Government without Lord Grey. I have, however, repeated this, and I think it will end so. The King is very kind and gracious and must now see that Coalition at present is hopeless.[22]

On the 11th he wrote to Landsowne:

> The state of things is not smiling for the country, but very much so for myself individually—for I *now* see the prospect [of] a little rest which I have not had these thirty-five years, and an end of a Cabinet which has been trying for three years to destroy itself, and has at length done so by the most *unintelligible* action yet done by man.
>
> I enclose a copy of my letter to the King, which pray return. The answer was most gracious, and only said that though all but impossible, yet a Coalition Government was such a public good that His Majesty thought it his duty not to throw away any chance of it. I agreed in this and in Melbourne's letter or minute declining to form one.
>
> My communications with the Commons show that unless Althorp will take a part, they are resolved to have

a Tory Government *for the avowed purpose of destroying the Tories and getting a strong Government* with weight in the House of Lords! This is like revolution, but it is the doing of such men as Abercromby who have discovered that we cannot debate (that is his ground literally!) and therefore cannot govern!

Of all curses save me from men who, wanting firmness, want the plain sense to avow it, and cloak it under refinements and crotchets. I rejoice to say that Rice, Melbourne, Palmerston, and I hope Grant, and I know Ellice, don't see it in this light. Nothing will induce Stanley to join any Government but Lord Grey's! So Graham's intrigue has failed.[23]

Brougham's bitterest reproaches fell therefore on the head of the unhappy leader of the House of Commons, whose action, he was reminded, had "sealed the fate of the country":

Rather than be plagued by two or three speeches addressed to a House of Commons which has more confidence in you than ever, you have done your best to dissolve the only Government the country will bear, and I hear that Abercromby and Rice are afraid to remain. I regard them, next to you, as the cause of all the mischief which may ensue: they, too, are resolved to fly from their posts, and deliver us over to the Tories and the mob in succession, because they don't like being badgered. I shall do all I can to ward off the calamity; but how can I if every one in the House of Commons is afraid to keep his ground? . . . I really must say I look upon all of you as answerable, and most deeply answerable, for the event. One thing, of course, you must make up your minds to. As you and your companions in desertion will most probably prevent a Liberal Government from being made, you are, of course,

FALL OF THE VAUX HALL PERFORMER.

"FALL OF THE VAUX HALL PERFORMER". Brougham is here balancing himself on the tight-rope between Toryism and Whiggism

prepared to give your cordial support to a Tory one. Surely you don't mean we should have no Government?[24]

The accusation was obviously unjust, and in his reply (July 10) Althorp rightly reminded Brougham that his own behaviour had not been altogether blameless, and had indeed materially contributed to the crisis:

I admit that I am answerable as the proximate cause of the dissolution of the Administration; but the situation in which I was placed was not by any act of my own. I wish you would look a little at the share you have taken in the business. Without communicating with one of your colleagues, with the view I know of facilitating business in Parliament, you desired Littleton to write to Lord Wellesley, and you wrote to him yourself to press him to express an opinion that the three first clauses of the Bill might be omitted. He did express that opinion; and I

thought, and still think, that when the Lord Lieutenant of
Ireland said that any circumstances of expediency would
induce him to carry on the Government of that country by the ordinary law to whatever extent he made that
admission, it was the duty of the Government here to
agree with him. He had said he did not want the court-
martial clauses—we properly omitted them. He then said
he could go on without these three clauses, and I think
we ought to have omitted them also. But you, having
originally produced the difficulty by writing to Lord
Wellesley, gave your decision directly against what you
had advised Lord Wellesley to do. The consequence of all
this was, that I got placed in a position which rendered it
impossible for me to go on. This impossibility, I admit,
was mainly produced by Littleton's communication to
O'Connell, but even without this the difficulty was likely
to be enormous.

I am aware that the man who, by his resignation,
produces the dissolution of an Administration, takes a
great load upon his shoulders; and more especially when
there is so much difficulty in forming another; this load
is increased greatly when he cannot explain the causes
which compelled him to take such a step without involving others whom, for every reason, he is determined not
to involve. That load I must bear. But it never can compel
me to support measures of which I disapprove, though if
no other than a Tory Government can be found, it may
render it incumbent upon me not to give them a factious
opposition[25]

Brougham succeeded in convincing the King that neither a
Coalition nor a Tory Government would be acceptable to a House
of Commons overwhelmingly Whig and Radical in character; and
William IV. commissioned Melbourne to form a Ministry. Althorp

was persuaded not to retire into private life, and the only serious difficulty that cropped up was occasioned by Littleton's threat to resign, in order, as he thought, to facilitate arrangements. Althorp, declaring that the O'Connell affair had placed him in the same boat as Littleton, avowed that nothing should induce him to accept office if Littleton remained out. In a state of great excitement at the prospect of no Whig Government, Brougham sent for Littleton to see him at the House of Lords, and succeeded in persuading him not to commit that "act of insanity". "I had him *privately whipped*", the Chancellor informed Wellesley, "and convinced him that by *facility* he would be giving us *difficulty*".[26] After "a devil of an upset" the Ministerial coach was, to the delight even of the Radicals, at last set on its wheels again. Francis Place declared that while Brougham had "laid himself open to severe censure by his carelessness, his disregard of truth, his contradictions and absurdities", he was, after all, "not a bit more of a rogue than any other man in the Cabinet"; that he was "more useful than the whole of them put together". "I hope and believe that he is now our master, and that he will be the King's master . . . I wish Brougham to lead".[27]

Thus the crisis of July 1834 had resulted in nothing more than a change of Premier. The next number of *Blackwood's Magazine* contained an amusing squib which purported to tell how "Allsop and Buckram decoyed Gray out of the house and then slapped the door in his face", and how Buckram, conspiring to "send old Foozle about his business", wrote a letter to Old Marcus O'Well-sly, John's steward on the estate:

> He's been often talking about it, poor noddy, declared
> Buckram to Allsop, so 'tis doing him a charity after all.
> You shall write him a letter, telling him that after this row
> with Dan you can't think of keeping your place longer,
> and as Gaffar has a notion that you know his ways, and
> that he can't well keep the books without you, ten to one
> but he gives up his place too. Then you and he shall walk

> gravely out at the front door, and make as if you had bid
> goodbye to us, for good and all; but as soon as the door
> is shut, trip up his heels, as if by accident, and run round
> by the back of the house. Sheepface and I will hold the
> back door open for you till you can get upstairs again
> into your office—and then to with the door in his face,
> and all's snug.

Brougham was overjoyed at the retirement of Lord Grey and the succession of Melbourne, whom he thought he could more easily "manage". He declared, indeed, that he might have had the Premiership himself had he wanted it, but that he had come to the conclusion that things would be better "with Lamb at the Treasury".[28] "All is firm and goes on well", he informed Wellesley. "Melbourne rises with every difficulty, and I think will have fewer to struggle with than his inimitable predecessor". But neither Brougham nor any one else was prepared for the King's sudden dismissal of his new Government on November 14, just five months after its formation.

The new political crisis was occasioned by the death of Earl Spencer (November 10), which removed Althorp from the Exchequer and the leadership of the Commons, to the Lords. On the 13th Brougham wrote to Althorp and implored him not to abandon public life, but to accept a less arduous office. The King, he thought, was incapable of harbouring a design to take advantage of the situation and to dismiss the Whigs:

> . . . Your removal from the House of Commons, and as
> soon as a convenient arrangement is effected, also from
> the Exchequer—is an event of great moment now. The
> House of Commons, and the country, are not at all pre-
> pared either for a change of Ministry *on this account* or for
> your going into retirement. The latter may tempt you, I
> admit, and that you should take some department suited
> to your own taste and which will not tie you too much

to office hours, or keep you too much in town, is all very fair and very well.

But your leaving us is deserting the cause and the country, and is, in fact, bringing in the Tories and bringing on a convulsion—for that must ensue—that on public grounds you never can dream of, this is clear. . . . For the public the prospect would be frightful. It is no statable ground for dismissing a Ministry that an event has happened to weaken them in Parliament. "Wait till you see", is the irresistible answer to that. They may resign if they think they are too weak. But no King has ever yet turned a Government out on such a ground, there being no other difference. Indeed, the whole would look like a *trick*, and like taking advantage of the Parliament not being sitting—and that never *would be forgiven.*

It would look exactly like the old King George III., and, to say the truth, it would be exactly like one of his crafty movements.

The King himself is utterly incapable of harbouring any such design, but there are others who plague his life out, and who are, of course, hard at work with him on this score. They are blind enough to think February never will come, and that before Parliament meets, something may turn up in their favour.

The loss, moreover, in the Commons, though I admit it to be irreparable, is clearly greater or less accordingly as the *House of Commons itself* chooses—for they may transfer as much or as little of their love and confidence to John Russell, and I am clear they will give him quite enough to carry on the Government. The truth is, that now the Commons and country are determined to have a Ministry to their mind, and will feel it a positive insult to be told they cannot have that merely because by the event of a death they lose one leader. The Government to replace this (if some people are bad and others are mad enough to let us go) *must be Tory*. Stanley will not, and Graham dare not, join them; if they did it would exasperate our people still more. The country (I have it from every quarter, but especially Scotland and Ireland) will not bear an election. They may not like us desperately now, but they detest our adversaries, and would be in love with us the instant we were out, nay, would at once become in love with *all we had done* in office.

A new change of Government would soon be necessary, and *then* nothing but huge and rapid reforms in Church and State could stay the tide, let who would stand at the helm.

If I only cared for personal gratification I should, I could, desire no better a position; but my opinion is very decidedly that this could only be enjoyed by danger if not ruin to the country, and I therefore heartily deprecate it.[29]

On the following day the King informed the Prime Minister that his Government was at an end. The Ministry, said William IV. (so Melbourne informed Wellesley) "was so weak in the House of Lords, that he was sure that with the diminution of strength it must suffer in the House of Commons from Lord Althorp's removal, it could not go on, and he therefore thought it right not to trouble him to make new arrangements, and he had resolved to place the Government in the hands of the Duke of Wellington".[30]

Late that evening, Melbourne returned to Downing Street. The only Ministers he saw before retiring for the night were Palmerston and Brougham, who called on his way from Holland House, where he had been dining. Melbourne informed them that the Ministry was at an end, and obtained their promise not to divulge the news until after the Cabinet had met in the morning. The next day's *Times,* however, contained a short paragraph announcing Melbourne's dismissal, with the comment, "The Queen has done it all". It has always been supposed that Brougham betrayed the secret, calling at Printing House Square after leaving Downing Street.[31]

Brougham's indignation knew no bounds. In a wild state of excitement he wrote to his friend Wellesley:

> The court intrigue has succeeded, and His Majesty, solely because Althorp was removed from the House of Commons, has made the Duke of Wellington Minister and summoned the three Secretaries of State to give up their respective seals to-morrow, when he holds a council to receive them. No difference of opinion—no disapprobation of our measures—no disagreement among ourselves is pretended. But we are said by His Majesty not to have the House of Commons now that Althorp is gone from it, and this *sequitur* (worthy of all the powers of reasoning which distinguish the eminent logician now at the head of His Majesty's council) is "therefore let me have a Ministry whom neither this nor the next House of Commons can endure!". Observe, the reason given about loss of confidence makes it extremely difficult to dissolve said House, for if he dissolves his Ministers because the Parliament confide too *little* in them, he cannot very consistently dissolve his Parliament for confiding too much, but still less could he do so after meeting them, and their passing a vote in our favour, so that I expect a dissolution.
>
> I wrote to His Majesty a letter of which I enclose a copy. The thing is strong, for it tells His Majesty "You choose to ruin the country. I wash my hands of your proceeding and hold you answerable for the consequences". Above all I warned His Majesty against dissolving, as that would make another dissolution necessary afterwards. Nevertheless, his answer is extremely gracious, the most so I ever received. I think this has a view to my new position as an Opposition chief. His Majesty says he well

> knows "the ability and indefatigable zeal which I put in
> all I undertake". Aye, but His Majesty's royal father and
> brother could have told him correctly of the zeal I have
> when in *opposition*, and which his new Government will
> soon see.[32]

The King's precipitate and premature action startled the Tories as much as the Whigs. Peel, whom Wellington suggested to William IV. as Prime Minister, was away in Italy, and his return could not be expected for many days. The Duke accordingly decided to retain the seals of all the chief offices in his own possession, until the absent Premier could dispose of them himself. A good story is told of Brougham's resignation of the Great Seal. Wellington sent a message requesting him to deliver up the Great Seal to him personally on the following Friday morning, although Brougham had arranged to keep it until the Saturday, in order to dispose of all the outstanding business in the Court of Chancery. Upon receiving this communication, the Chancellor wrote to Lord Lyndhurst saying that the Duke, besides being Home Secretary, Foreign Secretary, Colonial Secretary, Lord President of the Council, and First Lord of the Treasury, would also be Lord Chancellor, and that he (Brougham) should therefore give notice to the Bar that Wellington would give judgements in the Court of Chancery on the Friday afternoon, and would sit and hear appeals on the Saturday morning. Lyndhurst, it was said, was dull and literal enough to beg Brougham to do no such thing, since the Duke had no such intention![33]

On the 17th in the Court of Chancery, Brougham informed the Bar that "no power on earth should induce him to remain in office longer under the present circumstances". But when he continued to sit in court for another week, people began to apply the lines of Prior to him:

> He fitted the halter and travers'd the cart,
> And often took leave, yet seem'd loth to depart.

But the conduct that laid himself open to the most damaging imputations, and that which, perhaps more than any other of his strange pranks, fatally destroyed his prospects of returning to office in a Whig Administration, was his extraordinary offer to Lyndhurst, who was to succeed him as Chancellor, to take the office of Chief Baron of the Exchequer, in order that the country might be saved the sum of £5000 a year. The letter in which he made the offer, has not hitherto been printed. It was written on November 22:

> Having resigned the Great Seal, I am by law entitled to my pension, which was granted to me under the Act of Parliament as a compensation for the large professional income which I sacrificed, as well as for the expense which I incurred by the burden of the peerage. Upon your Lordship resolving to keep the office of Chancellor, that of Chief Baron of the Exchequer will become vacant, and I beg leave to state that I am willing to take upon me the duties of that office, whereby the country will be saved the charge of my pension.
>
> Although this would throw upon me great labour and effect a considerable saving—with a very small addition to my income not exceeding £1000 a year—yet as I well know all men's motives are liable to be misrepresented, and as I am resolved that no man shall have the possibility of misrepresenting mine—I shall positively refuse to take the salary belonging to the office, beyond the expense, whatever it may amount to, of the circuits and any expense of chambers and court—but the whole of which cannot exceed £800 or £1000, and I shall take less if the actual charges are less.
>
> By this arrangement the country will be saved about £6000 a year, and if there be (which I understand there is not) any patronage attached to the office, I shall decline also to exercise that. . . .[34]

The offer to Lyndhurst was a blunder which none of Brougham's friends defended, and which his enemies ridiculed with all the powers of sarcasm and irony which they were capable of wielding. The *Times*, which had recently turned against him, sneered at his willingness to work "under price"; insinuated that his real motive was to put the Tories in the wrong if they rejected such a plausible proposal to economise, and to prevent his rival, Scarlett, from securing the appointment; and it brutally declared that "it would be much cheaper, and infinitely more prudent, to pay Lord Brougham an additional £5000 a year for doing nothing, than to allow him to attempt the discharge of the functions of Lord Chief Baron".[35] The *Courier's* attack was equally galling. "How would this learned person have sneered and scoffed had Mr. Croker offered to continue to discharge the duties of secretary to the Admiralty to Lord Grey, that the public might save his retiring pension, or had Lord Eldon offered to undertake the duty of Chief Justice when Lord Denman was appointed. If Lord Brougham really wishes to save the public money, he has only to do as Sir James Graham has done—refuse to take it."[36]

Lyndhurst and the Tories were relieved of an awkward situation by Brougham himself, who, on the 29th, withdrew his offer on the ground that his acceptance of judicial duties would interfere with his parliamentary work. Lord Holland observed:

> . . . He has placed himself by his multifarious pranks in such a condition that whatever he does or leaves undone will be construed in the way most disadvantageous to him. The offer in the meanwhile is somewhat perplexing to Peel and the Tories, tempting them on one hand to spike through for a season such great and yet such flying artillery, and not without advantages, to begin by saving £6000 per annum and lowering, if not removing, the most vexatious of their opponents. *Per contra*, they silence their own small shot, for they cannot go on peppering the character and disparaging the attainments of one they make a judge—they

offend all the high fliers of their party generally and they disappoint Scarlett and Wetherell exceedingly, they affront *I fear a large party*, Brougham's personal enemies at the Bar—and though they may appear for a time to disarm him, it is not improbable that his restlessness may break through the restraints of judicial decorum, and that if censured or in any way reprimanded for such proceedings, that he should throw up his seat on the bench and, seizing a popular opportunity, assume, if not what Strangford calls his "pristine purity", his old faculty and practice of indefatigably harassing his enemy.[37]

Melbourne had long been aware of Brougham's patronising attitude towards him, and had become increasingly disgusted at the Chancellor's strange antics, his want of discretion, his meddling with things with which he had absolutely no concern, and his incurable egoism. Thus Brougham's latest and most glaring indiscretion profoundly irritated the late Prime Minister, who wrote to Lansdowne on December 7:

Brougham never mentioned to me his proposition to Lyndhurst until after he had made it. I was perfectly astonished. I think it a step which proves a greater want of judgement, a grosser ignorance of his own situation, than any which he has yet taken. The original error is, in fact, only made more glaring by the subsequent retractation; but I am not sure that this will be the general impression. I very much doubt whether the King would have been persuaded to have made him a common-law judge, and I am quite sure that he would have been right in resisting it.[38]

It was the general belief that Brougham's conduct during the summer had contributed towards the fall of the Whig Ministry. His meddling interference with the King's wishes, combined with his gross exhibitions of bad temper in the Lords, had lost him the royal favour; whilst his grotesque behaviour in Scotland during the parliamentary recess changed the King's dislike into positive detestation.

The O'Connell affair had seriously diminished the popularity and influence of the Whig Government, and Brougham, with his customary resourcefulness, conceived the idea of touring Scotland in the hope of winning back the ground that had been lost. He was the first modern politician to go on a political campaign in the country of this kind; but the aristocratic Whigs looked upon such a novelty with extreme disfavour. It was not until a much later day that the value of such campaigning was at all appreciated, and that Brougham's example was widely followed. His plan was soundly conceived, but badly executed, and he returned to London with his political stock seriously depreciated.

At no period of his life had he previously displayed such political infidelity as was now revealed to his startled and apprehensive colleagues. They dreaded to open the morning papers lest they should read of some new prank or bizarre proceedings of the Chancellor that would bring him, and indirectly the Whig party, into further discredit and contempt. During those weeks in the north he steered to every point of the political compass, and took advantage of every wind that blew. At one moment he spoke like a Radical, at another, in familiar Whig accents. When he found himself amongst full-blooded Reformers, he denounced the corruptions in Church and State, fulminated against the law of libel and the taxes on knowledge, and descanted eloquently on the "march of mind". In Whig company he enlarged on the virtues of "moderation" and "compromise" and "gradual" improvement, praised Earl Grey, and spoke sharply of Lord Durham, Hume, and O'Connell. The eccentricity of his manners astounded even those who were well accustomed to his strange antics. Hobhouse wrote of him:

> At Ayr he behaved so strangely that no one knew what to
> make of him. At Dumfries he got extremely intoxicated,

sat up all night, and was carried to the race-course next morning in a sedan-chair, dressed in his wig and gown. No wonder that, when he returned to Edinburgh, his friends shut him up for six weeks.[39]

The culminating feature of that "vagrant and grotesque apocalypse", as Disraeli aptly described the Chancellor's Scottish progress, was the speech at Inverness, where he received the freedom of the borough, and made himself ridiculous by his absurd references to the King. He declared that

> he had enjoyed the honour of serving that prince for nearly four years. To find that he lived in the hearts of his loyal subjects in the ancient and important capital of the Highlands, as it had afforded him (Brougham) only pure and unmixed satisfaction, would, he was confident, be so received by His Majesty when he (Brougham) told him, as he would by that night's post, of the gratifying circumstance.

That extraordinary speech was seized upon with delight by the *Examiner*, which printed a highly entertaining

LETTER FROM A GENTLEMAN WHO TRAVELS FOR A LARGE
ESTABLISHMENT, TO ONE OF HIS EMPLOYERS, MR. WILLIAM KING

> Dear Sir, the account here forwarded,
> Of favours since the 4th
> Presents a very handsome stroke
> Of business in the north.
> Our firm's new style don't take at all,
> So thought the prudent thing
> Would be to cultivate the old
> Establish'd name of King.

Believe me, Sir, so great a zeal
In this behalf I've shown,
Credit's been turn'd to your account
Which strictly was my own.
Does any one admire my nag
Or think my gig's the thing,
This horse and shay, I always say,
Belong to Mr. King.

If any friend attention shows,
And asks me out to dine,
When company my health propose,
In toddy or in wine,
My heart's eternal gratitude
About their ears I ding
With, "Be assur'd I'll mention this
Next post to Mr. King"!

I met with Grey the other day,
Who, since he left the firm,
Has travell'd on his own account,
And done, I fear, some harm
So thought it right, where'er he went,
To whisper round the ring,
"Perhaps you don't know *how* he lost
The confidence of King."

With what I still propose to do,
And what's been done already,
I trust the firm will henceforth go
On prosperous and steady
Should any chance the senior clerk
Into discredit bring,
I hope, Sir, you'll remember who
Has serv'd the House of King.

Brougham's political campaigning was of too sensational a kind—it smacked too much of the itinerant demagogue and of the methods of the men of the school of Cobbett and Hunt—not to shock profoundly the taste, and outrage the feelings, of sober politicians of the old Whig type. The King, too, was deeply vexed at the Chancellor's patronising attitude. "He can't bear these exhibitions in Scotland", said Melbourne.

Before the end of the year Brougham had succeeded in alienating, not merely the King and the leader of the Whig party, but also his most powerful supporter in the press:

> *The Times* for fifteen years, the editor declared, praised, supported, or, if you will, patronised his Lordship. So long as we supposed Lord Brougham to be actuated by honourable and elevated motives—guided by fixed and enlightened principles—aspiring to power through none but direct and manly means—disposed to use it virtuously, and capable of using it wisely, we did by every possible exertion, through evil report and good, zealously, boldly, indefatigably, nay, if we had said affectionately it would be no more than the fact, strive to maintain and extend the influence of Lord Brougham throughout all classes of society.[40]

The Times turned against him in the summer of this year. Brougham himself attributed the change to a variety of causes—to his success in preventing the formation of a Tory Government in July; to his advocacy of the abolition of "taxes on knowledge"; to his formation of a *Society for Diffusing Political Knowledge*, to "end the violent and slanderous press"; and to his warm support of the Poor Law Act of 1834. It accused him—most unjustly—of basely conspiring to drive Lord Grey from the Premiership; it charged him with having taken the principal part in altercations in the House of Lords such as would have disgraced the penny-club of an ale-house; it called in question his legal learning; it denounced him as a "mountebank who has not only disgraced the Cabinet of which he formed part, but has dragged the Great Seal through the kennel, and degraded, by his unnumbered antics and meannesses, the highest office of the Law and State in England". Commenting on the fact that he was still supported by the *Caledonian Mercury*, the *Liverpool Mercury*, and the *Leeds Mercury*, it declared:

> The reputation of Mercury, as a god, was not very respect-
> able, and the subjects he took under his protection were
> not those whom men delight to honour. The Caduceus,
> with its twisted serpents, may symbol the tongue and
> venomed sting of some of those gentry whom Mercury
> loves. Mercury, as every schoolboy knows, was the purse-
> bearer and jack-of-all-trades of the gods; and if he looked
> down among the sons of men for one with occupations
> as varied and a nature as flighty as his own, there cannot
> be a doubt upon whom his choice would fix. Can we,
> then, wonder that our man of all work is a favourite with
> the *Mercuries*?

The Times, in its vendetta against a former ally, went so far as to hint that Brougham's mind was giving way. "For some months", it declared, "Lord Brougham has been under a morbid excitement, seldom evinced by those of His Majesty's subjects who are suffered to remain masters of their own actions". Other papers and journals took up the cue. The Chancellor, said one, "is rapidly falling into a condition, perhaps the most pitiable and humiliating that a human being can by possibility be brought into".[41]

A day or two after the dismissal of the Whig Government, Brougham, thoroughly disgusted with the aspect of affairs, left London for Paris, "Perhaps", said Lord Holland facetiously, "to get chosen deputy there and sign himself *Henri Brougham*".[42]

Even amidst the gaiety of the French capital, however, Brougham's restless mind would not allow him to forget politics, and he again took up his pamphleteering pen whilst still abroad. On November

21, Edward Lytton Bulwer (afterwards Lord Lytton), then a Radical member of Parliament, published a pamphlet addressed to Lord Mulgrave, the late Privy Seal. *A letter to a late Cabinet minister on the present crisis* was an enormous success. Twenty-one editions were exhausted in six weeks, and it elicited no less than ten replies. The references to the late Lord Chancellor as a backslider on Reform stung him to write a lengthy reply on December 3, and Bulwer caused it to be printed in the later editions. He privately described it to Lord Durham as a "long-winded affair, strong in declarations for Reform, and wonderfully barbarous as a specimen of English. The school master was indeed *abroad* when it was written".[43] In a private letter to Bulwer, Brougham declared himself anxious to be reconciled to Lord Durham, with whom he had quarrelled in the summer; and he hinted too that he desired to be received once more among the Radical reformers. Bulwer wrote to Durham:

> I felt it necessary markedly to hint that he could only thoroughly clear himself in our eyes, by vindicating himself from all disunion with you. . . . As to the policy of any temporary union with Lord Brougham, you are the best judge, and of this I say nothing more than that while I believe that he would have silently and quickly crumbled away *in* office, I venture to predict that *out* of office he is likely to get himself up again in public opinion. . . . Three or four seasonable and eloquent speeches will go far towards redeeming him, though my own private opinion is that he will be always more dangerous than useful as a member of the Government. As to my remarks generally, my whole object was to receive the man on his own request and professions among the ranks of Reformers, and, without vindicating detailed errors, or expressing any opinion of his conduct as a *minister*, to extend to him, as one of those ranks, the benefit of a general amnesty.[44]

The tone throughout the printed letter to Bulwer is one of pained surprise that the motives governing his actions during the past four years should have been so flagrantly and systematically misrepresented. He protested that he had never ceased to be a genuine reformer of abuses both in Church and State; that he had never differed from even the most thorough-going advocates of political and social change, apart from his hostility to annual parliaments, universal suffrage, and the ballot. He protested that he had never sought the long succession of public meetings and speeches in Scotland with which he had been so unjustly reproached. That he had been rewarded with nothing but abuse for his generous offer to work for nothing and to save the country £12,000 a year was, he said, only a proof that at a moment of excitement no party man could ever expect even the semblance of justice.

> My life, excepting four years, was a continued sacrifice of interest to my principles as a Reformer and friend to liberty; and even in taking office four years ago, I made a sacrifice both of feeling and of interests which some alive, and some, alas! no more, well know the cost of. But all the time I was in Opposition, did I ever show the least slackness to do my duty in the cause of free opinion and of opposition to the Court? What abuse did I ever spare? What bad measure did I ever leave alone? What minister did I ever suffer to rest while the country was to be served by opposing him? With whom did I ever compromise, or treat, or do otherwise than absolutely refuse all parley? Surely, even where Reformers differ, these are facts which, as they give the best pledge of sincerity on the one part, ought to receive the most favourable construction as to motive on the other.

1. Ross, *Reminiscences*, p.32.

2. *Desp. and Corr.*, vii. 457.

3. Althorp MS.: Brougham to Althorp, March 1, 1831.

4. *Ibid.*

5. Althorp MS.

6. Hatherton MS.

7. *Ibid.*

8. *The Times*, Feb. 22, 1924.

9. Althorp MS.

10. Hatherton MS.: Ellice to Littleton, Oct. 21, 1833.

11. Hatherton MS., Diary, April 6, 1833.

12. Althorp MS.

13. Hatherton MS., Diary, Jan. 28, 1833.

14. Rylands Library MSS. No. 133: Letter of Macaulay, May 6, 1833.

15. Add. MS. 37311, fol. 143.

16. *Ibid.* 37307, fol. 47.

17. Add. MS. 37307, fol. 100.

18. *Ibid.* fol. 101.

19. Authorities for the O'Connell episode: Lord Hatherton's *Memoir*; Add. MS. (Wellesley Papers); Hatherton MS.; Althorp MS.

20. *Life of Campbell*, ii. 63.

21. Torrens, *Melbourne*, ii. 5.

22. Add. MS. 37311, fol. 250.

23. Lansdowne MS.

24. Althorp MS.

25. *Ibid.*

26. Add. MS. 37297, fol. 399.

27. *Ibid.*, 35149, fol. 308-311.

28. Torrens, *Melbourne*, ii. 13.

29. Althorp MS.

30. Hatherton MS.

31. Croker believed that it was Ellice who divulged the secret.

32. Hatherton MS.

33. Hatherton MS.: T. H. Lister to Littleton, Nov. 27, 1834.

34. Althorp MS.

35. *The Times*, Nov. 28, 1834.

36. The *Courier*, Nov. 28, 1834.

37. Althorp MS.: Holland to Lord Spencer, Nov. 20, 1834.

38. Torrens, *Melbourne*, ii. 51.

39. Broughton, *Recollections*, v. 19.

40. *The Times*, Aug. 23, 1834.

41. *Ibid*. Aug. 19, 1834.

42. Althorp MS.: Lord Holland to Althorp, November 20, 1834.

43. Lambton MS.

44. *Ibid*.

In Opposition Once More

I must be a stock or a stone not to be sensible that my treatment affords an instance, almost unparalleled, of gross injustice.

DAMAGED almost irretrievably by his imprudent and reckless conduct during the summer of 1834, Brougham returned to England the following February to find himself shunned by almost all his old colleagues. Stung to the quick by their coolness, he in turn avoided their company, attended hardly any of their dinner parties, and almost abandoned Brooks's Club. Lord Wellesley was one of the few who stood by him and defended him, but even he felt it necessary to lecture him on the impropriety of his late proceedings, and to advise him to take a moderate and prudent course during the session that was approaching.[1]

Fighting shy of the Whig connection, Brougham began to associate more and more with the Radical party, and again began to desire to come to an understanding with its members. Roebuck, one of its leading lights, became his constant companion and worshipper. Brougham declared that household suffrage was the grand point that they ought to attempt to gain.[2] What was even more symptomatic of another veer in the direction of Radicalism was that he began to contribute to the *British and Foreign Review*, the new Radical periodical which had been recently founded, said Brougham, chiefly in order to 'propagate sound opinions on foreign subjects.'[3]

After his arrival in England, Peel, the new Prime Minister, dissolved Parliament and appealed to the country for the new Conservative programme of progressive Reform, laid down in the famous Tamworth manifesto. The General Election deprived the Reformers of nearly the whole of their vast majority, but the Tories still remained in a minority in the Commons. Peel's bid for power failed, not because, as Disraeli declared, he tried to construct a party without principles, but because the tide of Reform still ran strongly through the country. With a minority in the Lower House, his overthrow could only be a matter of time; and, in fact, his Ministry survived only until April.

The session opened on February 19, when the Whigs asserted their supremacy by carrying Abercromby's election as Speaker, in opposition to Manners Sutton, the Government candidate. The debate on the Address took place, in the Lords, on the 24th, and Brougham, still smarting under a sense of personal injury and indignity at the King's dismissal of the late Ministry, threw all prudence to the winds, forgot his friend Wellesley's wise injunction, and launched as powerful, biting, and withering attack on the Government as had ever before come from his mouth. Extracting his sharpest rapier from his intellectual armoury, he used it with a vigour and incisiveness that reminded the victims of his sword-play of his most tremendous onslaughts on the mediocrities in the Liverpool Administration in his best House of Common days.

The question of Ireland has been fatal to many English Ministries. It had already caused the fall of three Governments since the beginning of the century. It had broken the Tory party in 1829, as it was to break the Liberal party more than half a century later. It proved fatal to Sir Robert Peel, who, after being defeated on the Irish Church question, announced, on April 8, his resignation. Lord Grey, who was sent for, was asked only for advice. He recommended the King to summon Melbourne, and it was Melbourne who was requested to form a Whig Ministry.[4] A week, however, elapsed before any arrangement could be made. Not until the 16th would William IV. consent to the measure of Irish Church Reform which Melbourne made a question *sine quâ non*. To the great delight of Ellice and the Radical elements of the Whig party, Grey declined an invitation signed by Melbourne, Lansdowne, Holland, Palmerston, and Spring Rice to take the Premiership, although he was strongly pressed by his family to do so. Melbourne had privately urged him not to take the Treasury, intimating, indeed, that he would willingly serve under him. Grey also declined the Foreign Office: he would, he said, be satisfied if his son, Lord Howick, were given office.

Althorp too was urged in vain to re-enter the political field and to take the Privy Seal. He had resolved that he would never again join a Government in which Lord Grey had a considerable influence; but the fact that the ex-Premier was to have no share in the Ministry did not cause Lord Spencer to alter his decision. Drummond,[5] whom Melbourne sent to Althorp to offer him a post, declared that Althorp had the highest personal regard for Grey, but that "Lord Grey's anger at the name of O'Connell, or the mention of any of his doings, deprives him almost of reason, and warps completely his judgement on Irish affairs".

Spring Rice, Palmerston, and O'Connell, as well as Brougham himself, occasioned serious difficulties. Rice at first determined not to take office in a Government which, he said, would be wholly dependent on Radical support. Palmerston, who had always been unpopular at the Foreign Office, narrowly missed losing his place, which had been intended, first for Grey, then for Russell. A large section of the party wished the Irish Attorney-Generalship or the Irish Mastership of the Rolls to be given to O'Connell, but the minority (some sixty or seventy) had their way.

Much to Duncannon's vexation, Russell was given the Home Office. Neither Littleton nor Wellesley was asked to go back to Ireland. The former, who informed Melbourne that he would accept nothing less than Cabinet Office, was raised to the peerage as Lord Hatherton. Wellesley was offered a Household appointment. His indignation against Melbourne, who had never forgiven him for writing that unfortunate letter to Grey the previous June, was terrible and uncontrollable. Even his son-in-law did not dare to approach him for several days after the appointment of Mulgrave as Lord Lieutenant:

> When he saw me, wrote Lord Hatherton, the storm that burst from him against Lord Melbourne was terrific. It lasted at the full stretch of his voice for exactly an hour by the clock on his mantel-piece, during which time I found it in vain to attempt to speak or to withdraw. "Am I a man to be treated with disrespect? I who have spent a long life in the service of the country, who for my services have received high rank—I, who have added millions to the empire? Am I to be treated with contumely or indifference by this puppy, this damned scoundrel? Sir, the offence can only be expiated by blood! I'll send instantly for my respected and gallant friend, Lord Howden. He shall arrange a meeting between us to-morrow morning!" He repeated this threat continually. As his strength expended itself, his reason returned, and he contented himself with saying he would suppress his feelings, but, depend on it, he would have his revenge.

Wellesley never forgave Melbourne. Years after, he added a strange codicil to his will, by which he gave his books and manuscripts to Alfred Montgomery, his private secretary, whom he directed to "publish my papers as shall tend to illustrate my two administrations in Ireland, and to protect my honour against the slanders of Melbourne and his pillar of state, O'Connell".

Very soon after the curt dismissal of the Whig Ministry in November 1834, Melbourne decided that never again should Brougham sit in the same Cabinet as himself, and he early communicated this decision to the rest of his colleagues, who, reluctantly in one or two cases, agreed with him. On February 1, however, Lord Grey, who had long since recognised the injustice of the charge of treachery he had hastily brought against Brougham, warned Melbourne against his proposed permanent proscription of a man who, in spite of his inexcusable conduct, had rendered, and was still capable of rendering, great services to the party:

> I do not wonder at your positive exclusions, nor am I much disposed to dissent from them, except that positive exclusions, with a view to future events, of which one cannot beforehand calculate the exigencies, are never prudent, and seldom possible to be adhered to. . . . In concerting the measures to be taken, how can you reject, from merely personal reasons, which it is difficult to assign, the co-operation of a person like Brougham, who was intimately connected with you in office, who professes the same principles, and who, whatever may be the justice of the censure which he has so generally incurred, will, immediately after the opening of Parliament, by his extraordinary activity and talents, again attract the attention, and not improbably conciliate the favour of a great part of the public?[6]

"If left out he would be dangerous; but if taken in he would simply be destructive. We may have little chance of being able to go on without him, but to go on with him would be impossible", was Melbourne's decided opinion.

In his *Life of Melbourne*, Torrens declared that up to the very moment of the Prime Minister's fatal communication on April 13, Brougham had no suspicion that, in Disraeli's phrase, he was "destined to be the scapegoat of Whiggism, and to be hurried into the wilderness with all the curses of the nation and all the sins of his companions".[7] But on February 14—more than six weeks before the fall of the Tory Ministry—Melbourne wrote him a stinging letter which must have prepared him for the worst. A more scathing indictment of one Minister by another has rarely been made in personal correspondence. It reads like the summing up of a hanging judge:

> You must be perfectly aware that your character and conduct have since November last formed the principal and general topic of debate and discussion. I believe myself to have said little or nothing anywhere upon the subject. I have written little or nothing, except to one or two persons, and that in the strictest confidence. At Lord Holland's, where politics are talked every day and all day long, it is of course to be expected that more observations have been made; but if you believe that any hostility or malignity towards you has prevailed there, so far as I have been witness to what has passed, I can assure you that you are misinformed.
>
> It is a very disagreeable task to have to say to a statesman that his character is injured in the public estimation; it is still more unpleasant to have to add that you consider this his own fault; and it is idle to expect to be able to convince almost any man, and more particularly a man of very superior abilities and of unbounded confidence in those abilities, that this is the truth. I must, however, state plainly that your conduct was one of the principal causes of the dismissal of the late Ministry, and that it forms the most popular justification of that step.[8]

Brougham demanded to know what crimes he had committed.

> You domineered too much, you interfered too much with other departments; you encroached upon the province of the Prime Minister, you worked, as I believe, with the press in a manner unbecoming the dignity of your station, and you formed political views of your own and pursued them by means which were unfair towards your colleagues,

Melbourne replied, and went on significantly:

> We stand at a new point of departure, and it is now right
> and expedient that I should determine for myself upon
> what principles and with whom I will again engage in
> public affairs. You seem to consider my letter as putting
> an end to the political connection which has subsisted
> between us. You will observe, however, that it does not
> express such a determination; and I beg to repeat and
> press upon your attention that it is my letter only, and
> does not express the sentiments of any other individual.
> If you suppose that my conduct has been influenced by
> any notion that you are so lowered and weakened as to be
> powerless, I can assure you that you are much mistaken.
> Nobody knows and appreciates your natural vigour better
> than I do. I know also that those who are weak for good are
> strong for mischief. You are strong for both, and I should
> both dread and lament to see those gigantic powers, which
> should be directed to the support of the State, exerted in
> a contrary and opposite direction.[9]

Thus prepared for the smashing blow that was impending, Brougham had recourse to the old expedient of declaring that he meditated a voluntary retirement from politics. On April 3, he wrote to Macvey Napier:

> What you say of any *alienation* between us here is almost all
> groundless. The underlings of the party had been persuaded
> by such lies as the papers circulate, that the King and Court
> turned them out of their places because I was too strong a
> Reformer, and I believe those underlings would throw their
> own fathers and mothers overboard to get back to their
> mess of pottage. If they had known my extreme aversion
> to office, and my all but irrevocable determination never
> again to hamper myself with it, and thereby and by party

connection to tie up my right arm and prevent me from doing my own appointed work, these gentlefolks might have saved themselves the trouble of wishing to get rid of me as an obstacle to their restoration. But Lord Althorp's fixed and immovable resolution to remain out, shakes mine; for, in truth, I hardly see how a Government (a Liberal one) can show itself with nobody in it whom the people care or even know anything about.[10]

He wrote another remarkable letter on the following day to Althorp, in which he poured out torrents of indignation against the Whig hierarchy. He felt sick of business, he said. "I feel it . . . hourly, and more now than last January, when a sense of duty brought me home to my hateful vomit." He went on to speak of his colleagues in "that odious House" to which he was "doomed":

All of them abhor me. I don't know which side would give most to hear I was dead. I know the Whigs have repaid thirty years' devotion and the loss (for the cause) of my seat, where I had power, by not only throwing me overboard the instant my back was turned, but by conspiring to assas- sinate my character in every foul way men could devise, when *not one of them had the manliness to tell me up to this hour* what I had done to displease them. All this I know. I know that I have been treated as no man since the Athenian Republic ever yet was used; and that the poor creatures I allude to, not having courage to murder me outright, have been trying (weakly and in vain, I admit) to destroy my power and influence in the country, which has grown under these bitter attacks. Now all this would have given me a good ground of declaring off, and remaining at peace among my books, where I could have been happy, and also done service to mankind in my favourite pursuits. Yet I did not think I was at liberty to do so; so I reflected long. I resolved opposite ways. I at last felt convinced that I had no right to consult my wishes, my tastes—nay, my pride and my personal honour, which I could only consult by destroying the Whig party, and installing the Tories for life in place. I therefore said not one word to any human being. I came back to Parliament. I took and still take the foremost part alone and without any communication with any one, for I am shunned by my late colleagues as if I had the plague, merely because the Court are afraid of me. The Tory and turncoat newspapers abuse me, and I am declaimed against on account of the Poor Law Bill! Except that I won't go to Holland House (where I ascertained the focus of spite against me to be situated), and that I live a good deal to myself—naturally in such unparalleled circumstances—I wish to know what one thing I have done to show the world that there is the schism which exists and which can never be healed? I was occupied all the while these creatures were plotting and working my political destruction, employed night and day in writing volumes to serve them. I actually wrote seven pamphlets for the party and against the enemy, when all the world knew by every post what was going on, and that *Abercromby alone* kept aloof from the plot, while not one human being had ever told me (or *could*, or till this hour *can* tell me) what the cause of complaint was.[11]

Thus Melbourne sprang no surprise upon the bitterly aggrieved ex-Chancellor, when, on the night of April 13 he went to Brougham's house in town to acquaint him that the Great Seal was to be put in commission. He was told that not only his colleagues, but the King, mistrusted him. "You must be conscious", Melbourne was reported to have said, "You must be conscious that last year you committed many, many indiscretions". "Am I mad?" Brougham shouted repeatedly. "Am I mad, do you think?" Melbourne gave him time to calm himself, and then said soothingly, "Come now, I want to consult you about all the legal arrangements".[12] The Prime Minister left him with the impression that it was the King who was mainly responsible for his ostracism; with the hope that the royal anger would evaporate after a season, and that he would be reinstated at the end of the session.

His partisans attributed his exclusion from office to the spiteful jealousy of his late colleagues, who hated him on account of his manifest superiority of talents and achievements. Was he thinking of the intrigue against himself—had he at the back of his mind a recollection of the treatment he himself received at the hands of the Whigs in 1835, when, in his *Historical Sketches* (1838) he wrote of Chatham and the intrigue that removed him from office after the accession of George III.:

> There can be little doubt that this scheme was only rendered practicable by the hostility which the great minister's unbending habits, his contempt of ordinary men, and his neglect of everyday matters, had raised against him among all the creatures both of Downing Street and St. James's. In fact, his colleagues, who necessarily felt humbled by his superiority, were needlessly mortified by the constant display of it; and it would have betokened a still higher reach of understanding, as well as a purer fabric of patriotism, if he, whose great capacity threw those subordinates into the shade, had united a little suavity in his demeanour with his extraordinary powers, nor made it always necessary for them to acknowledge as well as to feel their inferiority.

The main reasons which prompted Melbourne to withhold the Great Seal have already been succinctly given in his letter of February 17. In an undated letter to Althorp (probably written on February 18) Brougham substantially acknowledged the justice of the accusation:

> Certainly, before I went abroad, I never was charged by any of my colleagues—at least to my face and to my knowl-

edge—with *domineering*—interfering in other people's
departments, etc., etc. Perhaps, however, the charge is well
founded. How could it be otherwise than that I should
interfere, when these very people insisted on my doing
their business for them? Who ever heard of a Chancellor,
say they, doing so and so? Aye, but who ever heard of a
Chancellor being called on to bring forward all the bills of
the Home Office, from the Scotch Reform and Borough
Reform down to the Poor Law Bill? Never was there a subject that Grey did not say the Government was gone if I
did not speak, and generally if I did not undertake it. All
this, you see, necessarily led to my *interfering,* and naturally
led to my even going beyond what was necessary, because
nobody likes to be set up as defender of measures he had
no voice in framing. However, I daresay I was quite wrong.
As to *domineering*, it is possibly true. I am of a hasty and
violent, at least vehement, nature, and not bred in courts
or offices, and never was a subaltern, therefore I am a bad
courtier. However, I meant no harm, and never grudged
work; and always, both in and out of Parliament, was working as hard as a horse for the party, and never once for
myself, or to thwart them. But the thing I marvel at is no
one even whispering a word of this before. So of the going
to meetings—especially in Scotland—a thing not of my
seeking—God knows. If either King or any one else had
said a word, I should have been too glad of excuse to Miss
Spalding, whom I had promised a tour on the Rhine, and
Scotland was the substitute. But nobody ever expected any
meetings, though now all say it was inevitable. Why was it?
I had gone year after year to Westmorland, and never seen
one, and never expected one there.

However, as I said before, I am a bad courtier, and
as I won't leave the people, so the Court leaves me, as
it has good right to do; only it is the first time a Whig

> Government ever abused a colleague because the Court hated him.
>
> How Melbourne plans to do I cannot tell. His real friends will do well to warn him against trusting to Fred or Lady Cowper[13] who, of course, be for Conservative declarations, and this with a view to coalitions. After what I have seen and heard these five days, I can believe anything. But coalition with Stanley and Graham, till church is settled, seems impossible—with Peel madness.
>
> I am glad to be out of it, and so are you. I also am glad to find the people as grateful and as sensible as some others are the contrary.[14]

Nearly everyone believed that Brougham's sun had at last sunk beneath the horizon, never to rise again. Even Greville, who disliked him, was moved at the contemplation of the eclipse of a man who had just missed greatness.

> When one thinks, he wrote, of the greatness of his genius and the depth of his fall, from the loftiest summit of influence, power, and fame, to the lowest abyss of political degradation, in spite of the faults and the follies of his character and conduct, one cannot help feeling regret and compassion at the sight of such a noble wreck and of so much glory obscured.[15]

Believing that his was a tale that would need no more telling, the *Times* at once set to work on an obituary notice. But more than thirty years were to pass before Delane brought that necrology from the pigeon hole to which Barnes had consigned it; and not only was it left standing in type for thirty years, but the man who wrote it (William Stowe) preceded his victim to the grave by no less than thirteen years, for he died of fever at Balaclava whilst acting as war correspondent in the Crimea.[16]

Brougham soon made the discovery that his political downfall had effected a material alteration in his position, not only in Parliament, but as a contributor to the *Edinburgh Review*. He found he could no longer dominate it as he had done in the palmy days of 1830; and Macaulay was at last revenged. Brougham complained that Napier, like Melbourne, was putting him on the shelf.

> This is the common lot of those who, in any concern, outlive their contemporaries. . . . But at the same time I really do feel that I ought not to be merely made a hack of—'offered' such and such books—that is, whatever nobody else likes to do. Yet it does so happen that of late years this is my position. . . . My resolution now is, that I shall review such things as suit my taste and my views on subjects and on public affairs, and if there is any kind of objection *in any quarter* (which I am well aware in these times of intrigue and jobbery is very possible), I cannot help it and shall interpose no obstacle to the conductors or contributors of the journal, and should be very sorry to stand in the way of any other arrangements or connections. Ex-ministers are always in the wrong, I know full well. However, if the base and truly jobbing plan of some *would-be ministers* and their adherents (in London) had taken effect, and you had '*for fear of giving offence*' kept all politics out of the last as you had done out of the number before, my belief is that the *Review* would have died in the course of the spring.[17]

In subsequent letters, however, he declared that he would maintain his connection with the *Edinburgh* so long as it did not discredit itself by degenerating into a ministerial journal, and "while it supports its old honest principles and does not let itself be made a tool of Holland House or any other class of place-loving politicians".

Throughout the session of 1835 Brougham acted on the assumption that he would be reinstated in his old office not later than the beginning of the following year. He would not, he said, hold even the slightest personal intercourse with any of the members of the Ministry, but he would not allow his private quarrel with Melbourne to interfere with his duty to the public.[18] But the ministers inflicted fresh torture on him by making not the slightest acknowledgement, either public or private, of his services in the House of Lords. He wrote bitterly to Lord Spencer:

> I go on day after day defending them, their only speaker. I never even have had *one civil word* from one of them—not only not one acknowledgement in speeches, while they loudly praise any man who even makes a decent speech on the enemy's side—but I don't value their praise—not only *not one cheer* (there they sit dumb while I am doing their work which they can't do themselves) except from Holland, who cheers everybody: but what really is inconvenient and hurts them as much as me, they never beforehand have even given me one hint of what they meant to do, though every clerk in office knew it, and though they could only do it through me and my friends. . . . Yet all this I have borne, and gone on doing *their* business. It required some face, indeed, to leave me alone for days to fight it [the Corporation Reform Bill] and *they* not even to give up their dinner parties to come to the House. . . .[19]

In June he heard that Campbell, the Attorney-General, was destined to have the Great Seal. The rumour was premature, but it filled Brougham with despair. "I am again to be flung out!" he cried. Public duty prevented him from going immediately into Opposition, but he saw that nothing more was to be gained by continuing to support an ungrateful Ministry:

> . . . I believe, he wrote to Althorp in September, a short time only will now elapse before men see that I have no

longer any views of ambition connected with this country. I have maturely reflected on the false and unnatural position in which others have placed me. I cannot go into Opposition because I am by my principles and strong opinions bound to support the Government, and to do so very strongly, in proportion as they require support (for example, I have been defending them and calling for support to them in many a long page which I have just sent to the *Edinburgh Review*, but this is between ourselves). But I really feel my pride so much hurt at having to be the constant advocate of men whom I despise and even dislike, that I don't think I am bound to submit to it longer. I can do them no good in the House of Lords. Their constant attacks upon me, and the infamous lies which they and their newspapers propagate of me daily and weekly, prevent me from being of any use to them in the country. Therefore, I proceed a little upon *your* principle, and ask myself why I am obliged to remain in this country? I can be of just as much service in Provence as in England. I have worked hard of late: for instance, since I came here I have written three elaborate lectures, and written as many articles which, I believe, will do good to the cause I have at heart. But I could have done the same at Cannes. The lectures are to be delivered as anonymously as the articles are to be printed. There can be in *Parliament* only two parties, and I must be either for a Government or against it. I don't see, then, why I should not go where I please.[20]

Brougham never once attended the House of Lords during the year 1836. He had previously ordered a chateau to be built for him at Cannes, and it was to Cannes that he went to reside. He was the first distinguished Englishman to take up his residence in the Riviera, and it was due mainly to the force of his example that Cannes became a popular winter resort for the wealthy and leisured class of this country.

On January 16 the Great Seal was put into the hands of Sir Charles Pepys, who became Chancellor as Lord Cottenham. To Brougham the blow was the more severe because Melbourne allowed him to learn the news from the press. It was that day, rather than April 13, 1835, that was the real climax of his career.

> I must be a stock or a stone [he wrote, in a letter the bitterness and poignancy of which have seldom been exceeded] not to be sensible that my treatment affords an instance almost unparalleled, of gross injustice. Whether the ministers have acted from fear of one or two newspapers, or of a set of jobbing members of Brooks's calling themselves the Whig party, or from all these fears combined, is quite immaterial. They have done or submitted to such an act as never yet, I verily believe, was known among men bound together, even by the tie of party, but still more of Cabinet connection. As for the party, my sacrifices to it have been constant, long, and ungrudging, down to the last, when I gave up affluence and power, to enable them to come into office, and embraced (with my eyes open to the consequences) the course of ending my days under the pressure of all kinds of difficulty. My eyes were not, indeed, open to that other consequence which has ensued—namely, that I was connected with a set of men who would take advantage of my leaving the House of Commons and the power I then had, and would further take a still more base advantage—namely, of treating me as they durst not treat any one whose principles they were secured by, I mean that advantage has been taken of the perfect knowledge they had that no personal injustice, be it ever so aggravated, would ever drive me to act contrary to my principles and attack them. This, they and the

party were sure of, and on this they have basely reckoned throughout.[21]

Over the remaining years of his life we need not linger. He never succeeded in regaining the confidence of the Whigs, but it is pleasant to think that before Melbourne died he and the man whom he had condemned to political extinction were reconciled, and even became friends again. Brougham continued to coquet alternatively with the Tories and the Radicals, but both parties were wise enough to keep him at arm's length, Lord Derby, in 1849, grievously disappointing his hopes of returning to the Woolsack. In 1839 there occurred one of the most famous episodes in his life. He was one day involved in a carriage accident in Westmorland, near his home. The news spread to London that he had been killed, although he had in fact sustained but slight injuries. Every London morning paper contained an obituary notice, *The Times* alone excepted. A few hours later it was discovered that a hoax had been perpetrated, and it has always been believed that Brougham himself caused the report to circulate, in order that he might anticipate the verdict of posterity. He himself, of course, stoutly denied any complicity in the affair. He wrote to Lord Lansdowne, "The late hoax (scandalous and cruel towards Lord Wellesley,[22] whom it nearly killed, towards the press and the public I care not a pin) has shown me the public and the party in so kind and amiable a light that it confirms if it does not create an intention in me for next session which will tend to terminate hostilities on my part towards old allies".[23]

In 1848 he again succeeded in making himself the object of general ridicule by applying to be made a naturalised French citizen in order that he might be elected as a deputy for the department of the Var to the National Assembly at Paris. His friend Lord Althorp had long before noticed his eagerness to be thought a Frenchman, which, said Althorp, was neither sane nor respectable. In 1835 he had written a letter in which he had spoken of "my French fellow-countrymen", but he had been induced to correct it and to substitute the words, "fellow-citizens". When, in reply to his application to the Minister of

Justice at Paris, he was informed that if he desired to become a French citizen he would have to cease to be an English citizen and would have to lose his title of nobility and all his privileges, he at once withdrew his application. But the story leaked out, and Brougham in the House of Lords severely castigated the Republican Government whose favour he had just been attempting to court. *The Times* wrote a characteristic appreciation of the affair:

> It is not sufficient for him to have played the Edinburgh Reviewer, the English barrister, to have propounded startling theories in science, to have been created an English peer, to have translated Demosthenes, and to have passed himself as the greatest orator of his age; like Alexander, he sighed for other worlds, not to conquer, but in which to display his eccentricities. . . . A National Convention is still open to the *Citoyen Brougham*. He may yet rival Vergniaud in eloquence, and employ the remainder of his life in reconstituting civilisation in France. . . . When sacrificed at last before the rising demagogues of the new Mountain, and led off to the Place de la République in a cart, he will devote the brief minutes of his passage to chanting, with sincere enthusiasm and strong Northumbrian burr,
>
> —mourir pour la Patrie,
> C'est le sort le plus beau et le plus digne d'envie.

During his later years he devoted much of his time to literature, publishing his speeches, lives of statesmen and men of letters of the eighteenth and early nineteenth century, and writing his autobiography. He kept up his Parliamentary attendance, and busied himself with all the affairs of the House of Lords. During the winter of each year he went to reside at his hermitage at Cannes, returning to England for the opening of the parliamentary session. He became a confirmed spiritualist, and spent many a Saturday and Sunday in

The Citizen of the World, or, Lord Brougham Naturalised Everywhere, from Punch, *1848*

London with Robert Owen, getting into communication by means of a boy medium with the departed spirit of the Duke of Kent, the father of Queen Victoria.[24]

It is pleasant to think that not only Melbourne was reconciled to Brougham before death divided them, but also *Punch,* which had for years tormented him with its satire. In 1851, after Brougham had told the House of Lords that bodily infirmities had brought him to such a state that he could struggle no more to help on a measure of law reform to which he had long devoted himself, *Punch* wrote the following palinode to him:

> And is the busy brain o'erwrought at last?
> Has the sharp sword fretted the sheath so far?
> Then, Henry Brougham, in spite of all that's past,
> Our ten long years of all but weekly war,

Let Punch hold out to you a friendly hand,
And speak what haply he had left unspoken
Had the sharp tongue lost naught of its command,
That nervous frame still kept its spring unbroken.

Forgot the changes of thy later years,
No more he knows the Ishmael once he knew,
Drinking delights of battle 'mongst the peers—
Your hand 'gainst all men, all men's hands 'gainst you.

He knows the orator whose fearless tongue
Lashed into infamy and endless scorn
The wretches who their blackening scandal flung
Upon a queen—of women most forlorn.

He knows the lover of his kind, who stood
Chief of the banded few who dared to brave
The accursed traffickers in negro blood,
And struck his heaviest fetter from the slave;

The statesman who, in a less happy hour
Than this, maintain'd man's right to read and know,
And gave the keys of knowledge and of power
With equal hand alike to high and low;

The lawyer who, unwarped by private aims,
Denounc'd the law's abuse, chicane, delay:
The Chancellor who settled century's claims,
And swept an age's dense arrears away;

The man whose name men read even as they run,
On every landmark the world's course along,
That speaks to us of a great battle won
Over untruth, or prejudice, or wrong.

Remembering this, full sad I am to hear
That voice which loudest in the combat rang
Now weak and low and sorrowful of cheer,
To see that arm of battle all unstrung.

And so, even as a warrior after fight
Thinks of a noble foe, now wounded sore,
I think of thee, and of thine ancient might,
And hold a hand out, arm'd for strife no more.

Lord Brougham died in his sleep on May 7, 1868, at Cannes, in his ninetieth year, and was buried in the cemetery there. The inhabitants of Cannes, grateful to him for having done so much to transform a small and unknown fishing village into a great and prosperous fashionable watering-place, erected, in 1878, the centenary of his birth, a statue to his memory.

1. Lambton MS.; Durham to Lady Durham, Feb. 18, 1835.

2. *Ibid.*: Joseph Parkes to Lord Durham, April 11, 1835.

3. Add. MS. 34617, fol. 132.

4. For the formation of Melbourne's second ministry: Lambton MS.; Hatherton MS.; Add. MS. (Wellesley Papers); Russell, *Early Correspondence*; Torrens, *Melbourne*; Sanders, *Melbourne Papers*.

5. Now appointed Under-Secretary for Ireland, Drummond, a very able man, had been Althorp's private secretary.

6. *Melbourne Papers*, p.241.

7. Torrens, *Melbourne*, ii. 111; *Runnymede Letters*, p.64.

8. *Melbourne Papers*, p.257.

9. *Ibid.* p.262.

10. Napier, *Correspendence*, p.157.

11. Althorp MS.

12. Hatherton MS., Diary, April 15, 1835.

13. Melbourne's brother and sister.

14. Althorp MS.

15. *Greville Memoirs*, iv. 35.

16. *Life of Delane*, ii. 11.

17. Add. MS. 34617, fol. 121, 152.

18. Add. MS. 37297, fol. 420.

19. Althorp MS.

20. *Ibid.*

21. Althorp MS.

22. His closest friend.

23. Lansdowne MS.

24. The following letter from Owen to Brougham is of sufficient interest to be introduced here. It is dated April 30, 1853.

> "You will, I have no doubt, remember our séance with the boy medium at Cox's hotel one Saturday afternoon. On the following morning I had an engagement at Mr. Seaton's to have a séance with his niece, who is often with me and boasts a good medium for superior spirits.
>
> "I had previously prepared a long list of questions to which, if the spirit of H.R.H. the Duke of Kent announced his presence, I intended to ask replies. My engagement was at 10 A.M. and at that hour to a minute the spirit of the Duke was announced by raps through the alphabet. I put the written questions folded on a table and asked if he saw and understood them. Yes. Would he answer each question separately? Yes. And the reply to each was prompt and very satisfactory. They were questions of interest to us.
>
> "I then asked, Were you present last afternoon at Cox's hotel with Lord Brougham, myself, and the boy medium? Yes, and I replied to Lord Brougham's two questions. Was the other spirit present, Daniel the prophet? No. Do you know what spirit it was? Yes. Will you inform me its name? Yes, it was the spirit of Evan's wife who assumed the name of Daniel the prophet; she added you must be very much on your guard for many will attempt

to deceive you. I thanked H.R.H. and asked if he wished to say anything to me? Yes, bring Lord Brougham with you the next time you come here. I said I would endeavour to invite you to come, but I had no opportunity of seeing you before I left London on the 12th May and to make an engagement with the medium at Mr. Seaton's for 10 o'clock on Sunday this day fortnight. If you are not engaged at that time and will accompany me to the medium, I think it probable you may have a satisfactory séance with the spirit of the Duke.

"I write now to give you time to make your arrangements, and I could, if you should be disengaged, see you on Saturday morning, May 13, and arrange questions for the next morning's séance." (Owen MS.)

XII

Brougham's Economic Thought
and his Work as a
Social Reformer

To diffuse useful information—to further intellectual refinement, sure forerunner of moral improvement—to hasten the coming of that bright day when the dawn of general knowledge shall chase away the lazy, lingering mists, even from the base of the great social pyramid—this indeed is a high calling, in which the most splendid talents and consummate virtue may well press onward, eager to bear a part.

—Brougham, at Glasgow University, April 6, 1825

I. ECONOMIC THOUGHT

UNTIL 1819, in which year David Ricardo entered Parliament for the Borough of Portarlington, the Opposition was badly in need of an expert political economist. The Whig party had talent and eloquence enough at its disposal when the ordinary political topics of the day were being discussed. Its members could deliver admirable speeches on the virtues of our glorious constitution, on the blessings of political liberty, on the reactionary policy of continental despots, and on the wholesome effects of the existence of a free press. But when they came up against thorny questions of currency, finance, national and international trade, they found themselves under a palpable disadvantage in attempting to stand up to such economic experts as Huskisson and Wallace. In 1816, however, Brougham, who had already arrogated to himself the position of chief Opposition expert on legal, constitutional, and philanthropic subjects, deciding that such a variety of fields of activity was not sufficiently comprehensive for a man of his capacity and energy, determined to strike out boldly as an expert on the burning economic questions of the day. Thirteen years before, he had written much, in his *Colonial Policy*, on economic matters, and had attempted, with some hardihood and much confidence, to refute the theories or propositions of such a master of his subject as Adam Smith; but it must be confessed that he had somewhat overstrained himself in the attempt. A little later, in the pages of the *Edinburgh Review,* he had taken up the subject of the National Debt, and had endeavoured to destroy the arguments put forward by Dr. Watson, the Bishop of Llandaff, for its speedy liquidation.

In 1816 he set to work with characteristic zeal to equip himself for his new and self-imposed task; and during the session of that year he went through the departmental estimates and pulled the Budget to pieces with a thoroughness and pertinacity that were exceeded in later years only by Joseph Hume. On April 9 he delivered a great speech on the alarming situation of the agricultural interest; and on March 13, 1817, he made another remarkable speech on the state of our industries.

The most casual reference to these two outstanding performances is sufficient to show with what extraordinary persistence, with what indefatigable energy, he set out to master the subjects he took upon himself to expound. His information (which was not much inferior to that which the Government itself, with its infinitely greater resources, could obtain) was derived from hundreds of correspondents in the provinces. "He is apprised", wrote Hazlitt, "of the exact state of our exports and imports, and scarce a ship clears out its cargo at Liverpool or Hull but he has notice of the bill of lading".[1]

But his knowledge of the general principles of political economy was lamentably inferior to his knowledge of practical detail; a deficiency which was never more strikingly displayed than in his speeches in 1822 on the subject of agriculture. Ricardo declared with evident truth that Brougham was "Not even perfect in Adam Smith's work, and really appears not to have paid any attention to the works which have been published in our day".[2]

In 1816 Brougham supported the protective Corn Law which had been passed the previous year, and which imposed prohibitive duties on the importation of foreign corn until the price of home grown corn had reached eighty shillings per quarter. But in 1817 he strove to convert his party and the country to free trade. He demanded the repeal of the obsolete and obstructive navigation laws, and of the laws (passed in the interests of English iron-masters and English shipping companies) which imposed prohibitive duties upon imported Scandinavian ore and timber. It is not easy to see upon what principle Brougham could support protection for farmers and landowners, and denounce protection for shipowners and manufacturers.

His speeches in 1816 and 1817 on the industrial situation made a certain impression, but on February 11, 1822, he completely ruined his reputation as an economist. His speech on that occasion was mercilessly dissected by Huskisson from the Government benches and by Ricardo from the Opposition side of the House. Its failure was so complete that years elapsed before he ever opened his mouth again on an economic question.

His statement was grounded on the assumption that the cause of the evil plight in which the agricultural interest still found itself in 1821 was high taxation. He quoted official figures which proved, as he said, that "In the fifth and sixth year of peace, after a war of unprecedented magnitude, they were draining from an impoverished people last year the same amount of taxation, and this year one million more, than was raised in 1806, which was the fourth year of war". Huskisson blandly reminded him that he was proving that the farmers flourished during the war notwithstanding the fact that they had paid in taxation a sum at least equal to that which they paid in 1821. Taxation, therefore, could not be the cause of the distress that existed in 1821 and 1822. Brougham admitted, too, that heavy taxation increases the costs of production. But he had also to admit that the price of corn was twenty shillings less than the cost of production.

He went on to argue, in a most extraordinary manner, that it was a "known and acknowledged axiom of political economy, as old as the science itself, that one effect of taxation was to raise prices by increasing the profits of capital". Huskisson dryly remarked that it had always been his opinion that taxation diminished profits; and he added, "If it *increase* profits, how can it produce this effect without increasing the powers of employing industry, without increasing the means of consumption and enjoyment, without adding to the accumulated wealth of the country?"

Brougham again blundered most lamentably when he proceeded to complain that the farmers were suffering because the people had taken much to thinking tea instead of good old English beer, and that the consumption of malt had accordingly not increased since 1792, in spite of the great increase of the population. But in complaining that the people's changing habits did not tend to promote employment at home, he apparently overlooked the simple fact that the tea imported from China and India had to be paid for in British goods, and that British shipping had to be employed in carrying the tea from the East.

He again went far to destroy his own argument when he declared that leather manufacturers protested against the abolition of the tax on leather, since they increased the price of their leather to their customers over and above the amount of the tax. He vainly attempted to save himself by stating that though one class of producers—the leather manufacturers—could pass the tax on to the consumer, another class of producers—the farmers—were unable to do so.

In truth, the post-war distress of the agricultural interest was due, not, as Brougham most erroneously supposed, to excessive taxation, but, as Huskisson and Ricardo pointed out, to over-production encouraged by the mistaken system of protection; and it was clear that the only positive remedy for that distress was, not diminished taxation, but the abandonment of the poorer lands that the long war and the corn laws had caused to be put under the plough, and the cultivation of which had raised the cost of production to an unremunerative level. Many years, however, elapsed before Brougham (and many of the Whigs too) was converted to the view that the Corn Law ought to be repealed.

Whilst he had been growing up the factory system had been rapidly introduced into Great Britain. The new methods of production increased the wealth of the country by leaps and bounds; but the workers were becoming poorer and more degraded whilst their employers were amassing fortunes. The widespread poverty, distress, and unemployment that existed for years after the conclusion of the Napoleonic War, convinced Brougham that the introduction of machinery, by throwing thousands of people out of work, was a misfortune which deserved the serious attention of Parliament.

In common with the vast majority of Whigs and Tories alike, Brougham believed that the interests of the country would be best served if the Government would totally abstain from interfering with the economic pursuits of the population, and allow complete freedom to individual enterprise and energy. He therefore offered a strenuous opposition to the legislation of the 'forties which marked the transition from *laisser faire* to State regulation of industry. It was with reluctance that he accepted the Bill brought forward in 1842 to exclude children under ten years of age from the mines. He condemned the Factory Bill of 1844 which regulated the working hours of women and children, on the grounds that the former were well able to look after their own interests and make favourable bargains with their employers, whilst the interests of the children were fully protected by their parents.

Brougham made great use of his own creation, the Society for the Diffusion of Useful Knowledge, for the purpose of broadcasting his economic ideas. Several of its text-books on economics were almost certainly his work, though they were published anonymously. Those who criticised these tracts took his authorship (which he never denied) for granted, just as his Tory critics took for granted the authorship of the famous Whig pamphlets which agitated the political world in the summer and autumn of 1830.

There was no more stability about his economic views than there was about his political principles. He adopted and abandoned his opinions with as much ease as he changed his political colours. At one time he was the chief organiser of the campaign against the income tax; at another he voted for that "odious imposition". At one moment he urged the repeal of the obsolete navigation laws, whilst at a later moment he strongly condemned an attempt to repeal them. In 1816 he supported the corn laws; in 1830 he demanded their drastic modification; in December 1845 he was preparing to lead the protectionists against Peel; and a few months later he declared himself boldly for free trade.

His views on the subject of population, did, however, remain consistent throughout. He always maintained, with Malthus, that the increase of the population since 1790 was a misfortune for the country, and he believed that its excess was one of the main causes of the distress which periodically afflicted the nation.

Brougham's speeches on economic subjects were primarily intended to serve personal and party ends. They afforded him excellent opportunities of advertising his cleverness and industry, and he turned them to political account by making them the vehicle of attacks on the Government. In 1817 he ruined his chances of effecting useful reforms of the commercial code, by appending to his exposition of free trade doctrines a factious attack on the Government. In 1822 his persistent attribution of the existing agricultural depression to unwarrantably high taxation recklessly imposed by an extravagant Ministry was prompted by the idea that a successful speech in which that argument was put in the forefront would do much to damage the Government and to clinch his own reputation as a trenchant and popular advocate of economy.

II. SOCIAL REFORM

As we have seen in an earlier chapter, the Whig party emerged from the great conflict with Napoleonic France almost without a programme with which they might appeal to the country for support. Brougham oft repeated his well-founded complaint that the leaders of the Whig Opposition were content to live on in the atmosphere of the eighteenth century, regardless of the patent fact that the England of 1815 was vastly different in its social aspect from the England of the days of Lord North and the American War. They hardly seemed to perceive the fact that the old party cries that had served to distinguish Whig from Tory in 1780 were no longer applicable to the changed condition of the country. Brougham had the solid merit of seeing, with greater clarity and insight than any other member of his party, that at the beginning of the nineteenth century Great Britain was ripe for extensive measures of political and social reform.

Brougham began his career as a Reformer several years before he joined the Whig party; and the first cause which he set himself to promote was that of the abolition of the slave trade. He exposed the iniquities of that traffic in human flesh, in the pages of the newly-founded *Edinburgh Review,* in the first pamphlet he ever wrote, and, later, in the House of Commons, where, as we have seen, he introduced a Bill to make slave trading a felony. It was not, indeed, until 1830 that he declared himself strongly for an early abolition of slavery itself, but he was a member of the Government which passed the Abolition Bill in 1833.

As a legal reformer, Brougham stands high among the lawyers of his day. He laboured hard to mitigate the severity of the criminal code, to simplify the laws, and to improve the administration of justice. His creation of the Judicial Committee of the Privy Council, now, with one exception, the most wonderful court of justice in the world, was perhaps his most splendid and useful achievement as a lawyer. Had his Bill to establish a provincial system of county courts not been defeated by his political opponents, it would have set the seal on his fame as a judicial reformer. Bentham, to whom he was much indebted for legal information and ideas, though occasionally critical of his pupil's proposals, acknowledged that he had done "most valuable service to this country".[3] Brougham himself gave noble expression to his ideals in his famous 1828 speech on law reform.

> It was the boast of Augustus—it formed part of the glare in which the perfidies of his earlier years were lost—that he found Rome of brick and left it of marble; a praise not unworthy a great prince, and to which the present reign also has its claims. But how much nobler will be the sovereign's boast when he shall have it to say that he found law dear and left it cheap; found it a sealed book, left it a living letter; found it the patrimony of the rich, left it the inheritance of the poor; found it the two-edged sword of craft and oppression, left it the staff of honesty and the shield of innocence.

Of even greater importance was his educational work. Throughout his active career he devoted himself untiringly to the stupendous task of breaking down the barriers that stood in the way of universal education, and to the work of liberating the minds of the masses from the bondage of ignorance and prejudice. Reformers like Bell and Lancaster interested themselves in only one branch of education; Brougham, with greater intuition and more systematised thought, perceived the importance of correlating infant with juvenile, and juvenile with adult education. He was thus a pioneer in many fields. He was the driving force in the movement for establishing infant schools in London in the years after 1815, Robert Owen of New Lanark fame, Lord Lansdowne, and the two Macaulays, giving him much assistance. Before that time, he had become prominently connected with Joseph Lancaster's endeavours to provide schooling for the poor children of London and Westminster. He co-operated with Mill and Bentham in the unsuccessful attempt to establish a "Chrestomathic" or Secondary school in the Metropolis. In 1825 he set on foot the project which in a few years developed into the London University. The poet Campbell was the first to conceive the idea of a non-sectarian college for London; but it was Brougham, a man of greater influence, energy, and capacity, who did most to carry the scheme into execution. University College is one of his most impressive memorials. The University of Glasgow recognised his services to education by electing him its Lord Rector for the year 1825.

In 1823 he began to concern himself with adult education. He shared with Dr. Birkbeck the honour of founding in that year the London Mechanics' Institute for the education of the artisans of the capital. He was one of the four trustees of the building, which was the first of its kind. Its success stimulated the foundation of similar institutions all over the country; they did much to promote the social well-being of the artisan classes of the community.

Francis Place, who was also in the van of the educational movement, and who at times differed violently from Brougham on political questions, handsomely acknowledged the value of his services to the cause of popular education. "There is not a man living," he wrote, "who has a stronger desire to have the people instructed than Mr. Brougham, nor one who has exerted him more than he has to promote that object."[4] Coming from one who had repeatedly written and spoken of Brougham in terms of the severest censure, that is high praise indeed.

In 1827 he continued his work for adult education a step further by founding the Society for the Diffusion of Useful Knowledge. It was the natural outcome of the Mechanics' Institutes. Working men had discovered that they were handicapped in their endeavours to obtain instruction, by the lack of suitable text-books, and by the almost prohibitive price of the few that were available. In April 1825, a month or two after he had published his pamphlet on the education of the working-classes, Brougham, with the assistance of Lord John Russell, Dr. Lushington, William Allen, and others, began to make preparations for meeting the deficiency. But difficulties sprang up, and nothing could be done except to make inquiries and to raise funds. In March 1827, however, the Society for the Diffusion of Useful Knowledge was in a position to publish the first of its treatises, which was written by Brougham himself. It was characteristic of him that he undertook to show mathematical scholars, whose knowledge of their own subject was far more profound than his own, how scientific treatises ought to be written. In a private letter he thus sketched the objects of the Society:

> The original design was that of diffusing knowledge among the *People* (whom having taught to read and to desire information we were bound to supply with wholesome food, as you will admit when you are told that there were cheap circulating libraries of obscene publications). That first plan was, however, found to be too limited—first because improvement naturally goes downwards and the upper and middle classes wanted it—secondly, because of late I have observed with surprise and, I must add, shame the degree in which those upper classes are ignorant of much that their inferiors know. There are subjects and places, too, which I need not name, abounding in sense-less clamour and in stupid prejudices only to be explained by referring them to the great root of evil—ignorance.
>
> This being the case, we felt that a better education for all ranks was necessary, and my own opinion being very decided, that much of the prevailing ignorance arises from want of elementary treatises, which would enable those who had neglected their education at a time when knowl-edge was less in vogue to make up for the want of it by private reading, we conceived that if we could supply a series of such treatises, every point would be gained—for the upper classes who could not afford to pay for teachers might also be instructed in the same way.
>
> This, in a few words, was the origin of the scheme in which our Society is now embarked. It is our first and will certainly be our most important operation. . . .[5]

The Society solved the problem of supplying the people with suitable text-books by employing experts to write popular and easy treatises on scientific, literary, historical, and ethical subjects, to be published at the reasonable price of sixpence. A much more difficult task had then to be solved: the task of stimulating the people to read them. The problem, as Brougham beheld it, was this. A considerable proportion of the population was now sufficiently educated to be able to read; but comparatively few took full advantage of their opportunity of acquiring knowledge. The majority read little, and that which they did read was of little use to them. The poverty of many prevented them from obtaining the knowledge they would have liked to acquire; whilst the disinclination to study was a fatal obstacle to the mental improvement of others. Text-books and serious works in general repelled them; they would read only what was amusing. For this class of people Brougham provided the *Library of Entertaining Knowledge,* which comprised "As much entertaining matter as can be given along with useful knowledge, and as much knowledge as can be conveyed in an amusing form". People who would not read at all—and here Brougham was referring particularly to the farming class and the agricultural workers—were to be induced to read by providing them with books that had a direct bearing on their occupation. Thus he included a Farmers' Series of treatises in the *Library of Useful Knowledge.*

The attitude of the governing class towards the movement for educating the masses had, in general, been one of deep distrust. Thomas Love Peacock, one of the irreconcilables, ridiculed the activities of the Useful Knowledge Society and of its founder in *Gryll Grange,* where he declared that he would rather hear the cook lecture on Bubble and Squeak than hear one of the Pantipragmatics lecture on the difference between a halibut and a herring; and in *Crotchet Castle,* in which Brougham appears as the Learned Friend, and the Useful Knowledge as the Steam Intellect Society.

> "God bless my soul, sir!" exclaimed the Rev. Doctor
> Folliott, bursting, one fine May morning, into the break-

fast-room at Crotchet Castle. "I am out of all patience with this march of mind. Here has my house been nearly burned down, by my cook taking it into her head to study hydrostatics in a sixpenny tract, published by the Steam Intellect Society, and written by a learned friend who is for doing all the world's business as well as his own, and is equally well qualified to handle every branch of knowledge. I have a great abomination for this learned friend; as author, lawyer, and politician, he is *triformis,* like Hecate: and in every one of his three forms he is *bifrons,* like Janus; the true Mr. Facing-both-ways of Vanity Fair. My cook must read his rubbish in bed; and, as might naturally be expected, she dropped suddenly fast asleep, overturned the candle, and set the curtains in a blaze.

Very different from Peacock's pleasant and good-humoured wit was the vulgar abuse with which Brougham's endeavours to educate the people were assailed by the gutter Tory press. On one occasion that notorious paper, *John Bull,* wrote of him:

To see Squire Brougham active, is to know that mischief is busy; to see him associated, as he is, in the dirty work of inflaming the minds of the lower orders, under false pretensions, is quite enough to proclaim the truth. Not more surely does the fluttering lark betray her brood by anxious care, than this squalid hypocrite marks to the watchful eye the point of treachery and deceit by his baleful presence. His object is clear as day to those who know the workings of his crooked mind; and the liberality which will concede to his measures seems to us of the same species as that which induces a coward to give up his money to a highwayman rather than run the risk of a beating. But the season for such liberality must soon expire; in incautious hands the flame which the incendiaries have been fanning has been too violently blown upon, and the blaze is premature—thank God it is.[6]

The *Library of Useful Knowledge* proved an immediate success; the circulation, great though it was, would have been still greater but for the tax on paper, which prevented the reduction of the price from sixpence to threepence. "When this great work is completed," wrote Brougham, "if finished as it has been begun, it will undoubtedly form by far the most important of the contributions from men of science and letters to the instruction and improvement of mankind." Much to Napier's secret annoyance, no doubt, Brougham for several years, made frequent use of the pages of the *Edinburgh Review* to advertise the proceedings and publications of the Society, and to defend it from the abuse of the enemies of popular education; and in the July issue of 1830 he announced his intention to devote an article every year to the Society's activities.

Other admirable series of books followed the appearance of the *Library of Useful Knowledge* and the *Library of Entertaining Knowledge*. In 1832 the highly popular *Penny Magazine* was begun, being issued in weekly parts; and the *Penny Cyclopaedia*, begun in 1833 and completed eleven years later. Miss Harriet Martineau, the Radical friend of Lord Durham, and who hated Brougham, complained, with some show of truth, that the long-promised books on political subjects, which working men, in their new eagerness to learn something of the recent history of their country, would have been delighted to study, never appeared. The people, she said, were put off with treatises on dynamics and the polarisation of light, and became convinced that the Whigs desired to withhold political knowledge from them. Nor was the fact forgotten that even Brougham was opposed to the decision made in 1835 by the Melbourne Ministry to permit the sale of parliamentary papers and reports.

The Useful Knowledge Society became bankrupt in 1844, not because, as Lord Campbell malevolently declared, it was ruined by the failure of Brougham's *Political Philosophy*, which it had undertaken to publish, but solely by reason of the enormous expense which the preparation of that vast work, the *Penny Cyclopaedia*, entailed.[7]

During the years after 1815 when Brougham was actively engaged as *de facto* leader of the Whig Opposition in the House of Commons, his efforts to dislodge a spendthrift and reactionary Government had, as we have seen, met with little success. But though, at this time, he failed to a large extent in the strictly political warfare, he was far more successful in moulding the opinions of both the Ministry and the Opposition on the question of the education of the people. He did more to convert the members of both Houses of Parliament from their hostility or indifference to the instruction of the masses, and to make them realise the importance and urgency of the educational question, than any other man in the country. Whitbread had already introduced the subject into Parliament, but Brougham was the real pioneer in the movement in the House of Commons, as he was one of the most active and successful pioneers in the movement out of doors. It was in 1816 that he first brought forward the question of education in the Lower House. In that year he obtained the appointment of a Select Committee to inquire into the state of popular education in London, Westminster, and Southwark. He proved that the voluntary system had but touched the fringe of the problem, and he urged that the State ought to intervene and supplement the praiseworthy but inadequate efforts of voluntary organisations to educate the children of the poor. In thus advocating even a small measure of State interference, he showed himself capable of penetrating beyond the narrow boundaries of thought within which he and his generation had been brought up. True to the reigning tradition of *laisser faire*, he did, indeed, make it clear that the voluntary system was infinitely to be preferred to an all-embracing State system of education, and he was opposed to the idea of giving annual grants-in-aid from public funds to educational institutions. He would give State aid only for the purpose of building and equipping new schools; they ought to be maintained by voluntary effort. That dual system—the co-operation of the State and voluntary organisations—he continued to advocate throughout his life.

Of the Select Committee of 1816 he was the very soul. Its report, written or inspired by himself, showed that grave abuses existed in the administration of scores of charitable funds devoted to educational purposes. Largely as a result of his endeavours, an Act was passed in 1818 by which a commission was set up to inquire into the administration of such funds; and although he complained, in a pamphlet addressed to Romilly, that the powers of the commission were unduly curtailed, it did useful work, and was the parent of the later Charity Commissions.

Two years later, Brougham found time, even amidst the bustle and excitement of the Queen's case, to prepare an Education Bill, on lines which he had laid down in the various reports of the parliamentary select committee. But his scheme was wrecked by his proposal to work it in connection with the Church of England. The Dissenters sounded the tocsin of alarm, and their agitation against his Bill assumed such proportions that he found it prudent to withdraw it. In 1820, and, indeed, throughout the century, the question of religious instruction played havoc with educational progress. Six years later he again introduced his Bill, but the Dissenters again raised up such a storm of opposition as compelled him to abandon it.

His advocacy of State aid for education reached its high-water mark in the Bill which he introduced in 1820. He had then favoured the levying of a compulsory rate for educational purposes; but by 1833 (the first year in which the Cabinet, of which he was then a member, proposed to set aside £20,000 a year for education) he had abandoned that plan. He declared that

> ten years' experience had shown that perfect reliance might be placed on these voluntary contributions, and that it was rather to be expected that they would increase than decrease. Trusting to these voluntary supplies, he did not think it would be advisable to turn legislative attention to the subject; and, therefore, he had abstained from bringing it forward.[8]

But though he was forced to admit that a great deal of leeway had still to be made up under the voluntary system (in 1833 there were, he thought, 1500 parishes without any day school, apart from the fact that many large towns were inadequately supplied) he still thought that private enterprise would be able to fill the gaps. In the following year he declared in the House of Lords:

> The voluntary principle . . . should always be adhered to; nothing like compulsion should enter into the system. . . . He did not think that any one measure could be devised by the mind of man so admirably calculated to make a system of education unpopular as that of compelling people to send their children to school. He was, therefore, decidedly adverse to the introduction of a compulsory system in any sense whatever, either by forcing parents to send their children to school under certain penalties, or depriving them of certain privileges if they refused to let them attend. A knowledge of the benefits that were to be derived from education—a knowledge of its great usefulness in every rank and condition of life—ought to be the great incitement to seek it; and every effort ought to be made to disseminate that leading principle, in order that all might profit by it. As to another species of compulsion—that of a rate—he would not consent to it; for he would never sanction any proposition which coupled the word education with the word rate.[9]

He referred to the subject again in 1835, when he told the House of Lords that they had "a right to conclude against any general interference of the legislature, until the efforts of individuals shall be found insufficient, and the seminaries which they have established shall be seen going to decay".[10] But though he pronounced against the establishment of a State system of education, he did not wish it to be inferred that he was opposed *in toto* to Government interference and Government aid. He declared that there were still insufficient numbers of schools, that they were provided for children of too advanced an age, to the exclusion of infant schools, and that the quality of the instruction that was given was far too poor.

I shall call upon your lordships, therefore, with the view of remedying this great evil, to adopt the principle sanctioned by the report of the Education Committee of 1818. I am of opinion that the only safe course which we can take for the supplying the lamentable deficiency which I have described is to furnish the great towns with the funds now wanting, and to apply this public aid so as not to interfere with the exertions of individual zeal, or cut off the supplies of private munificence. This is to be done, in my opinion, by acting upon the principle recommended in the second report of that committee.[11]

He was under no illusion about the quality of the teaching that the children were receiving.

The instruction they bestow hardly deserves the name. You can scarcely say more in its praise than that it is better than nothing, and that the youth are far better employed than idling away their time in the streets. They learn reading, some writing, and very little arithmetic—less it is nearly impossible to learn. . . . Learning of that scanty kind is only another name for ignorance; nor is it possible that it should be better; for the schoolmasters are uneducated themselves; they know little of what they ought to teach, still less of the art of teaching, which every person who is only a little less ignorant than the children themselves thinks he is quite capable of exercising.[12]

Brougham was one of the first to suggest the establishment of training colleges for teachers, so that the defects in the teaching described in the course of this speech might be remedied. In 1837 he urged that a new department of State should be set up with adequate powers to extend education throughout the country, to administer the annual grant provided by Parliament, and even "to superintend the distribution of such other funds as might be raised by local taxation for this purpose". But it was highly characteristic of the individualist thought that was still current for Brougham to descant once more on the evils of collectivist action, which he denounced as a violation of individual liberty, and as an unwarrantable attack on the sacred rights of parents. He spoke as follows on the question of making education compulsory:

> . . . He would ask . . . how dangerous a thing it would be, upon whatever grounds they put it—whatever temptation there might be for extending education—whatever risk there might be in the continuance of ignorance—whatever might be the duty on the part of the parents to educate their children—whatever mischiefs might arise, or whatever consequences might infest the whole community, from the breach of that duty of parents—he would ask that man to consider how delicate, how perilous a matter it would be to usurp the parental office by public authority, and prescribe, by a command of the State, fortified perhaps by the penalties attached to a civil offence, the line of parental management which the father and mother should pursue in taking care of the offspring which Providence and nature had committed to their care? Another answer against the compulsory principle, if indeed any other were wanting, would be that it was a violation of individual liberty, that it was a tyranny, introduced no doubt, and he admitted it, for a laudable purpose, but nevertheless declaring that in order to educate people they would enslave them, that in order to diffuse instruction amongst them they would contract their liberty, and introduce a system which would be intolerable to the citizens of a free State, and only fit (if fit at all) for a country ruled by a despotic Government, where, liberty being little known, slavery was the more bearable.[13]

Brougham was far from being a mere theorist. He had visited New Lanark, where he saw Owen's famous infant school. He had inspected Fellenberg's educational institution in Switzerland. The leading part that he had played in the foundation of the Mechanics' Institutes, London University, and the Useful Knowledge Society, had enabled him to gain practical knowledge of the problems that confronted educationists. But at the same time, in common with most contemporary educational enthusiasts, he held grossly exaggerated opinions of the efficacy of education. Like the eighteenth century philosophers, he over-emphasised the importance of post-natal circumstances in the formation of character. He regarded education as an insurance against social convulsion. He believed that education, and by education he meant the acquisition of knowledge, would abolish not only ignorance but crime; it would do more than anything else to secure peace and order and to maintain the stability of the Government. But it would not only instil into the minds of the masses a wholesome respect for property; it would better their hearts and improve their worldly condition.[14] In the *Edinburgh Review* he showed how a perusal of the Useful Knowledge Society's treatise on brewing would enable the poor to get their beer at a fourth the cost of the article obtained from the brewer.

There is undoubtedly another side to Brougham's multifarious activities for social reform. It is certain that his efforts were prompted, partly, at any rate, by a desire to make personal capital therefrom. He found them a most useful form of advertisement, and it was upon them that his influence in the country, of which he was so proud, was founded. People pointed to the significant fact that he first came out strongly for an early abolition of slavery on the very eve of the Yorkshire election of 1830, and he himself acknowledged that the election turned largely on that subject. In 1818, when Brougham was busying himself with inquiries into charitable foundations, the Tories did not hesitate to assert that his object was to ingratiate himself with the multitude, to throw discredit on the Government, and to bring Church and State into contempt. They pointed out that his activities on the select committee were reaching their height at the very time when a General Election might be expected, and that he might not be unwilling to bribe the electors by disposing of charitable funds in ways other than those originally intended, and by so doing to win political support for himself and for the Whig Opposition. "His Majesty's ministers", wrote one anonymous pamphleteer,

> "know indeed that 'the season has passed away when the country could be frightened out of a necessary attention to the management of its affairs', but they are afraid that the season still exists, in which a popular leader may employ public reform as the pretext for general innovation, and whilst he comes forth as the champion of public abuses, may rally round him a party to assist him in the objects of his personal ambition".[15]

Brougham himself declared that he published his letter to Romilly on the abuses of charities, in order to "Blow up the coals".[16]

But he was at least disinterested in his lifelong advocacy of Poor Law reform, for it brought him much unpopularity in later years, and it contributed to alienate the support and favour of the *Times*, which was until 1834 his most powerful ally in the press. Since 1795 the practice had grown of supplementing the wages of labour from the poor rates in proportion to the number of children in the workman's family. That disastrous policy had had the effect of reducing all wages far below the subsistence level, of creating a pauperised population, and of imposing a crushing burden of taxation upon the ratepayers. Brougham there-fore regarded the Poor Law as a kind of vampire that was insidiously sucking the life-blood of the country. He first turned his attention to the subject of Poor Law reform in 1816, when, in the course of his speech on agricultural distress, he made the proposal that after a certain period no outdoor relief should be given to able-bodied work-ers, or on behalf of children born of future marriages. He deplored the enormous increase in the poor rates, but his chief concern was the blow to the status of the labourer which the "Speenhamland" system had been administering. It was this feature of poor law policy that he continued to emphasise.

> As the law is now administered, he said, under the influence of the habits which have unfortunately grown up with the abuse of it, the lower orders look to parish relief, no longer with dread or shame; but they regard it as a fund out of which their wants may at all times be supplied. To say nothing of the effects of this feeling upon their habits of industry and economy; to pass over its fatal influence on their character, and especially on their spirit of independence; only observe how it removes all check upon imprudent marriages, and tends to multiply the number of the people beyond the means of subsistence. . . . It is truly painful to reflect that our peasantry who, some time ago, used to regard such a supply with dread—used to couple every notion of ruin, misery, and even degradation with the thought of coming upon the parish—should now be accustoming themselves to receiving relief almost as if it were a regular part of their wages.[17]

Nothing but the pressure of his work on educational charities prevented him from bringing forward the subject at length during the session of 1818. In 1834 the Whig Government passed the Poor Law Amendment Act, which prohibited outdoor relief to the able-bodied, and set up workhouses as an alternative. The clauses establishing workhouses and abolishing outdoor relief to the unemployed were strenuously opposed in Cabinet by the Duke of Richmond, one of its Tory members, who objected that a man when once in a workhouse would never get out of it, and that it would virtually mean imprisonment for life; and he believed that any attempt to put these clauses into execution would bring about a rebellion. Sir James Graham, who was also soon to join the Conservative party, was the only other member of the Whig Cabinet who agreed with the Duke of Richmond's views.[18] Brougham himself took little or no part in the Cabinet discussions, but it was he who on July 21, 1834, moved the second reading of the Bill in the House of Lords, taking the place of Lord Grey, who had resigned some days before. In the morning of that day, the Chancellor had read over the notes of his speech to Melbourne and Althorp. They found it so opposed to their own views and to the principles laid down in the Bill that they begged him 'for God's sake' to say nothing of what he intended to say. In the afternoon he went over his speech with Nassau Senior, who, with Chadwick, was mainly responsible for the framing of the Bill; and Senior, too, strongly urged him to re-write his speech. But his representations, and those of the Prime Minister and of the leader of the House of Commons, failed. In the evening, wrote Nassau Senior:

> the speech then was made, and as a speech, indeed, as a philosophical disquisition, it was admirable. The description of the evils of the existing system had a very powerful effect on the House, and it did not appear, as far as the House was concerned, that the doctrines to which I had objected did any harm. Out of doors they excited a great clamour against Lord Brougham, but they were so clearly opposed to the sentiments of the report and to the enactments of the Bill, that the papers failed in their endeavours to connect the measure with Lord Brougham's views. Indeed, as those views, though perhaps more guardedly expressed, are in a great measure, indeed almost to the whole length, founded on truth, I am not sure that this powerful exposition of them, by suggesting to many persons doubts as to the justice and expediency of the whole system, did not induce them to concur more readily in its restriction and modification.[19]

Whereas the Ministry was legislating on the assumption that the principle of poor laws was sound, and that the trouble lay in the maladministration of those laws, Brougham categorically maintained that the evil lay in the maladministration of bad laws, and that the right to be supported out of the industry and property of other individuals was destructive of frugality and diligence. He declared that every permanent fund set apart for the support of the poor and the unemployed, from whomsoever proceeding, and by whomsoever administered, must needs multiply the evils it is destined to remedy. Hitherto, any unemployed man had enjoyed the right, by act of parliament, of compelling the parish in which he resided either to find him work or, alternatively, to feed him. It was, said Brougham, a provision destructive of all self-reliance, all provident habits, and independence. The Act of 1796 had increased the pernicious consequences of this earlier legislation, for it had given the poor the right to be supported in their own homes, although workhouses for their reception should have actually existed.

Brougham, however, did go so far as to admit that people unable to work, either through old age, sickness, or other incapacity, were entitled to be supported by the community; but even in the case of these individuals, he preferred that their support should be left to private charity, in order to prevent abuses from arising.

> I do not, he said, object to compulsory provision in such cases as I have mentioned, so it be subject to proper regulation, in order to prevent the abuses it is much exposed to. That species of charity is the least safe which affords a constant fund, known by the community to exist for charitable purposes. . . . If the fund is known to exist, however it be constituted, whether by voluntary or by compulsory subscription, the poor immediately calculate upon it, and become less provident, forsaking every habit of frugality, taking no care to provide against the ordinary calamities of life, or the inevitable infirmities of old age. They no longer strive for the means of maintaining their children, but heedlessly, recklessly, count upon that fund,

out of which, whether in sickness or in health, in youth or in age, in impotence or in vigour, they know that they may claim the means of support; and, setting the pains of labour against those of a scanty subsistence, they prefer idleness and a bare subsistence to plenty earned by toil. Hence men's minds become habituated to the fatal disconnection of livelihood and labour, and ceasing to rely upon their own honest industry for support, their minds become debased as their habits are degraded.[20]

Brougham did not quail before the storm of abuse that greeted this expression of such unpopular opinions. Whether his analysis of the motives that guided the conduct of the poverty-stricken workers of his day was fair and just towards the poor is perhaps doubtful. The circumstances of the time were exceptional, forcing thousands of workers to apply for poor law relief who would, had they possessed a living wage, have felt shame at the idea of throwing themselves on the parish. Brougham, however, intended his analysis to apply at all times and in all circumstances, and he believed his view of the motives underlying the conduct of the poor and the unemployed to possess a validity at least as universal in its application as the law of gravitation. But to suggest as he did that the poorer classes of the community always did, and always will, prefer to live in idleness on the earnings of industrious people, rather than support themselves by the toil of their own hands, was in truth to libel in a peculiarly gross and calumnious manner the characters of the vast majority of his countrymen.

1.   Hazlitt, *The Spirit of the Age*: Mr. Brougham.
2.   Add, MS. 34545, fol. 80.
3.   Bentham MSS. at University College: Bentham to Lord William Bentinck, April 10, 1829. Bentham's extreme detestation of jobbery

caused him to be unduly critical of Brougham's Local Courts Bill (1830). He wrote: ". . . Samson (the Agonistes) was one giant; our learned Bill-builder, another; and, with the whole strength of his learning, such as it has been seen, we shall be more than a little surprised, if this Bill of his be not pulled down about his ears, and the whole congregation of the judges, registrars, clerks, ushers, court messengers and extra-messengers, buried in the ruins of it. Such a catastrophe of this sort presented itself to us as a desirable one; and we have accordingly lent our humble endeavours to the production of it . . ." (Bentham MSS. Box No. 4.)

4. Add. MS. 27823, fol. 248.

5. Add. MS. 38749, fol. 152.

6. Add. MS. 27824, fol. 81. This particular attack was directed against the Mechanics' Institutes.

7. A complete set of the volumes published by the Useful Knowledge Society occupies a prominent place in the library at Brougham Hall.

8. *Parl. Deb.*, Third Series, xvi. 635.

9. *Ibid.* xxii. 848.

10. *Ibid.* xxvii. 1302.

11. The principle that the State should contribute only to the cost of new buildings, not to their upkeep.

12. *Parl. Deb.*, Third Series, xxvii. 1319.

13. *Ibid.* xxxix. 436.

14. *Edinburgh Review*, xxx. 191; speech in the House of Lords on prison discipline, June 20, 1834.

15. A Letter to Sir William Scott, in answer to Mr. Brougham's Letter to Sir Samuel Romilly, p.99.

16. Lambton MS.: Brougham to Lambton, undated.

17. *Parl. Deb.*, xxxiii. 1115.

18. Nassau Senior's MS., p.48.

19. *Ibid.* p.204.

20. *Parl. Deb.*, Third Series, xxv. 220.

XIII

Conclusion

"His life ought to be generously written, not without a sufficient mention of his many failings, but with a handsome
recognition of his great merits and greater aspirations."

Delane on Lord Brougham, 1852

THE portrait of Lord Brougham which hangs in the ancestral mansion,
was presented to him by the freeholders of the county of Westmorland,
as a token, no doubt, of their admiration for his efforts to win the
representation from the clutch of the Lowthers. It is one of the best that
exists. Tall and slenderly built, his figure was awkward and ungainly in
the extreme. His face was thin and pale, his cheek bones prominent,
his hair dark. "His eye," said Haydon, who painted his portrait in 1833,
"is as fine as any eye I ever saw. It is like a lion's watching for prey." But
his most prominent feature was not his piercing, aquiline eyes, but his
long, turned-up nose, whose twitching betrayed his highly-strung state.
His countenance was too remarkable not to be seized upon with avidity
by the caricaturists, and to this day his nose figures prominently on the
front cover of *Punch*. The versifiers also delighted to make sport of him
and to exaggerate his peculiarities:

> A meagre form, a face so wondrous thin
> That it resembles Milton's Death and Sin;
> Long arms that saw the air like windmill sails,
> And tongue whose force and fury never fails.

Brougham, by universal consent, made himself the most powerful orator of the day. Disraeli writes his *Runnymede* letter to the ex-Lord Chancellor, "whose scathing voice, but a small lustre gone, passed like the lightning in that great assembly where Canning grew pale before your terrible denunciation, and where even Peel still remembers your awful reply". Dickens, who, as a young journalist, reported the parliamentary debates for the *Morning Chronicle*, declared that Brougham in his prime was by far the greatest speaker he had ever heard.[1] Lord John Russell said that Brougham's speech in opening the defence of Queen Caroline was the most wonderful effort of oratory to which he had ever listened.[2] Of his celebrated speech delivered on October 7, 1831, in the House of Lords in support of the Reform Bill, Althorp wrote: "All agree that it was the best he ever made. Grey and Holland both say it was superhuman—that it united all the excellencies of the ancient with those of modern oratory, and that the action and delivery were as much applauded as the speech itself".[3]

But though his eloquence was of a high order, his speeches have long since ceased to have any but an historical interest. They lacked the charm, the imaginative touch, the philosophical insight that might have made them live. There was nothing elegant, nothing graceful about them; but what they lacked in charm they gained in force and effectiveness. They were for the most part 'fighting' speeches, blows struck in many a fierce party conflict; and speeches of such a kind are, after all, to be judged mainly by the effect they produce. Gauged by such a standard, they fully accomplished their purpose, and always hit the mark. They crushed an adversary by their overwhelming force. Canning once declared that there was no one like him who could pound and mash with such effect. Thus it was the trenchant style of oratory in which he excelled; it was modelled on Demosthenes, and in Demosthenic force and vigour it has rarely been surpassed. His powers of sarcasm and irony were very considerable; but he used them too frequently and unsparingly ever to make himself really popular as an orator. Unlike Palmerston or Peel, he never succeeded in winning the heart and commanding the allegiance of the House of Commons; though he made himself feared, he never made himself loved. His extraordinary fluency and readiness of speech often caused his language, in moments of excitement, to become recklessly extravagant; and a dozen of his electioneering speeches could be quoted to show how his passions, which were easily kindled, hurried him beyond all the regular bounds of oratorical expression.

His technique was as uncouth as his eloquence was forceful. He usually spoke in a loud and commanding voice, but sometimes it was thunderous and even deafening; and his wild and absurd gesticulations, some of them perhaps borrowed from ministers of the Scottish Kirk, excited ridicule when they ceased to intimidate. People used to complain that he almost split the drums of their ears by his roaring.[4] On one occasion Western wrote: "He could not have roared louder if a file of soldiers had come in and pushed the Speaker out of his chair. Where the devil a fellow could get such lungs and such a flow of jaw upon such an occasion as this, surpasses my imagination. . . . He made my head spin in such a style, I thought I should tumble over. He quite overcame one's understanding for a time".[5]

Although Brougham was for years the most conspicuous member of the Whig party, he was never accepted as its leader, nor did he ever succeed in gaining the support of a personal following, as did Grey, Melbourne, and Palmerston. Aristocratic prejudices were to some extent responsible for his exclusion from the party leadership; but, on the other hand, Tierney, who was elected to that position, and who, like Brougham, was not born in the purple of the governing class, was almost as much an outsider as he. Faults of character and temperament, which time did little to efface, were even more important in inducing the Whig magnates and party managers to keep him at arm's length. At no period of his life was he devoted to party. With the party system as he saw it working at the beginning of the nineteenth century he was entirely out of sympathy; and a conviction of its essential unreality, combined with much more personal motives, made his allegiance to either party or creed essentially precarious and uncertain. Party connection, he was wont to declare, was merely a cloak for selfishness and hypocrisy, a means of getting into, or retaining, place. It was an evil and an absurdity that half the great men of the day were excluded from the service of their country; that one half was engaged in carrying on the Government whilst the other half was solely occupied in thwarting its proceedings. Interest, not principle, was at the bottom of party; and the history of political party in England had been nothing more than the struggle for place and power between a few great families. In office, a Whig became virtually a Tory; in Opposition, a Tory became virtually a Whig. In Opposition, a Whig clamoured loudly for retrenchment and denounced as iniquitous measures for suspending the liberties of the people. In office, a Whig would increase the army estimates and pass the most stringent coercion bills. Not individuals, however, but the system, was to blame. It was injurious to the interests of the country, it corrupted and spoon-fed the people, it sacrificed principle to expediency and self-interest, and it caused the administration of public affairs to be carried on in the most clumsy and inefficient way. The party system could only be borne during the preliminary stages of a nation's political growth; and the time would soon come when the universal diffusion of knowledge would emancipate the people from the thraldom of political factions and give them both the right and the power to manage their own affairs themselves.

"No man is less exclusive in his political propensities than I am," he wrote in 1831; and, in truth, both his principles and his personal predilections were guided by his interests. With equal facility he could co-operate with Whig, Tory, or Radical. When he was hoping to receive employment from Pitt, he would praise him as a great statesman who had saved the country from the horrors of Jacobinism; when it was his interest to throw stones at the Tories, he would attack the memory of that same 'immortal' statesman who had plunged Great Britain into a ruinously expensive and wholly unjustifiable war with France. When it was his game to do so, he fulminated against the enormous influence of the Crown and against our huge naval and military establishments; and at the dictation of his personal interests he complained that the Government was not spending enough on naval defence, and declared that to cut down the patronage at the disposal of the Crown would be a policy fraught with danger. Out of office he protested with great vigour against the Government's harsh treatment of the Luddites and the Radical Reformers; while as Lord Chancellor he as vigorously defended the merciless repression of the starving west-country labourers who had taken to rioting as the only means of drawing the attention of the authorities to their intolerable condition.

Since he was never for long able to win the confidence of those with whom he was politically connected, he remained in a comparatively isolated position. It was therefore natural that he should concentrate his attention in Parliament on subjects that had little to do with party as such. Thus he had comparatively little to say about such hackneyed party topics as Parliamentary Reform and Catholic Emancipation, which he took up in earnest, in the summer of 1830 and in 1825 respectively, only because they were likely to bring him into power. Referring to the Reform Bill he declared: "I feel only anxious for the plan, because the peace of the country and safety of the constitution. . . . seem to me to require it. I care not half so much for Parliamentary Reform as for many other improvements, and were I left to my own wishes, and to follow my own Reform doctrines, I should certainly be a very moderate and very gradual Reformer". It was just because it was a question he had so little at heart, that his opinions on it underwent such frequent and startling changes.

Nor did he ever attempt to make himself a specialist on Foreign Policy. Sometimes his interventions in debates on questions of Foreign affairs were intended to serve personal ends. In 1816 he denounced that terrible bogy, the Holy Alliance, because the Ministry, which he was bent on destroying, had to some extent identified itself with the proceedings of the continental despots. His speeches on the same subject in 1823 and subsequent years formed part of his design to precipitate a rupture between Canning and the ultra Tories. The French Revolution of 1830 came at an opportune moment—in the midst of his Yorkshire election campaign; and he welcomed it not only because it was a victory for continental Liberalism, but also because it encouraged the success of the Liberal movement at home, and helped to turn out the Wellington Ministry.

His attitude towards questions of Foreign affairs was full of the same strange inconsistencies that characterised most of his utterances and writings. During the years after 1815 he vigorously denounced the repression of resurgent Liberalism on the continent; but in 1849 he welcomed the intervention of Russian Armies in Hungary, and the merciless repression of the Magyar insurrection against the Habsburgs. In 1827, in his anxiety to see the Turks driven out of Europe, he was quite prepared to allow the Russians to succeed to Constantinople and the Turkish Empire, and had no fear of the Russian Colossus bestriding the Near East. "It brings them only more within the power of England and France," he said. Very different were his views ten years later, although the situation had undergone no fundamental changes. Russia, he wrote in June 1838, had hitherto been a safe member of the European community of states only because of the remoteness of her position. But he now viewed the possibility of the conquest of Turkey and Constantinople with the utmost alarm. With Russia mistress of the Bosphorus and the Dardanelles, he said, the Mediterranean would become a Russian lake, and the independence of Egypt would be seriously threatened. He then proceeded to overwhelm with ridicule his own argument of ten years before. "The view taken by some that there will be an advantage gained over Russia, inasmuch as she will be brought into the circle of the other European powers, and exposed to be attacked in her new dominions, appears a refinement too absurd to require a serious refutation. She still has her vast and inaccessible empire behind on which to retreat; and, admitting the utmost weight that can be assigned to the argument just stated, it would only follow that she might always run the risk of losing her new acquisitions, in an attempt still further to extend her encroachments; thus playing the safe game of either winning universal monarchy or remaining where she was before she seized on the Dardanelles."[6]

On the other hand, he retained his opinion that the danger to our empire in India was remote. Writing of Russian expansion eastwards, he said:

> Persia may be said to exist at her good pleasure. But of such a mighty operation as a march to the northern provinces of India, where, independent of the distance, and the barren and difficult country through which the route must lie, there would be found a powerful army, inured to the climate, admirably commanded, strictly disciplined, and amply appointed in all respects—we really cannot entertain any very serious apprehension; as long, at least, as the justice and lenity of our Indian administration shall avoid all collision with the natives, and our grasping spirit after territory and revenue shall not throw the country powers into the arms of the first adventurer among themselves, or the first European rival, by whom our immense dominions may be assailed. Besides, long before England could have to contend for her Eastern dominions at Delhi, Cabul, or Lahore, Russia would have to encounter our fleets at Cronstadt, and to defend Petersburg itself. Miserably ill-informed must our Government be of her movements on the east of the Caspian, if she would make any advance towards India before an overpowering armament laid Petersburg in ashes.[7]

His lucubrations on the future of the new world are also of some interest. He believed that Canada would follow the same line of political development as the American colonies, and would eventually become an independent state. In all probability, he added, it would throw in its lot with the United States. He disagreed with the opinion, widely held in England in the 'thirties, that America was seriously threatened with the prospect of a civil war over the slavery question, and of the break-up of the Union. He foresaw, indeed, that the southern planters would eventually be forced to emancipate their slaves; but he believed that the "powers of discussion and the energy of truth" would prevent the outbreak of civil war.[8]

Brougham's policy of concentrating on non-party objects enabled him to put himself at the head of the middle class, which, deprived of political power, was bent on obtaining large measures of political and economic reform. With a singularly unerring judgement, Brougham selected such causes as popular education, law reform, the abolition of slavery, the skilful advocacy of which would not only be of incalculable benefit to the people, but would also redound to his personal advantage, gain him the support of middle-class opinion, and bring him great political power. His devotion to such subjects, and his careful fostering of what he proudly called his "influence in the country", filled the party politicians with astonishment. They could not understand how a man was to push his way in politics by employing such a large portion of his time in writing educational treatises for the people; in attending innumerable meetings of the Useful Knowledge Society and of the Council of the new London University. It was his untiring advocacy of measures of social reform that gave him a sufficiently great reputation in the country and a personal ascendancy in the House of Commons to enable him to negotiate as an equal with the aristocratic Whigs, who, when once more, after an interval of over twenty years, they had at their disposal all the great offices of State, would dearly have liked to keep in the background the man who had done more than any other to bring them to victory.

Brougham was essentially a middle-class statesman. Though, during the course of his long connection with the movement for reform in all its branches, he did much for the masses, he never was a democrat. He never advocated universal suffrage, although in 1837 he professed to be a convert to the ballot. He was seriously alarmed at the progress of the democratic movement during the struggle for the Reform Bill. He thought trade unions were dangerous to the community. Like all men of his class he held exaggerated views of the importance and sanctity of property; and he condemned trade unionism not only on the ground that it encouraged the holding of large public meetings, which he regarded with extreme distrust, but also because it had a tendency to menace the security of property. The growth of an anti-aristocratic spirit in the country filled him with dismay. He had to share with the other members of the Grey Ministry the odium attached to their harsh and cruel repression of the starving labourers who took to rioting in 1831. He vigorously defended the execution of several of the convicted men and condemned the great outcry against such measures which was raised by the press and the public as "incredibly absurd", founded on the "falsehood and delusion that the people convicted were poor, innocent, ignorant folks who were in great distress and thought their calamities would be relieved by destroying machinery. This is not true, but the very reverse of true".[9] Six months later the ministers had to acknowledge that facts which they had brought forward to justify death sentences and executions were false.[10] The rest of Brougham's letter quoted above sufficiently illustrates his attitude at the beginning of 1831 towards the peasantry:

> Is it now meant to be said that all property is henceforth to be in common and that no man shall henceforth sleep secure in his bed or employ his assistants in manufactures, or keep his money in his pocket? Is it not a gross abuse of language to call these villains *misguided* men?
>
> They are violent felons who desire to seize all they can, and don't care what blood they spill in getting hold of money. Is it to be said that unless life be taken no capital punishment shall be inflicted? Then change the law—but this will spill more blood . . . for all felons will speculate on it and go as near the wind as they can. They will go armed and ready to threaten, and will *intend*

not to kill. But killing will ensue, and far more than at present, when men dare not do these things which lead to murder.

People forget *now* what alarm they were in, and how they called on Government to pacify the country. *It is pacified*, and now the self-same people cry out against the very means by which peace has been restored. If the worst criminals escape, the burnings, etc., will begin again, and far more punishments will be necessary from ill-judged lenity now. It is *true mercy* to make timely examples, not going beyond what is necessary. In 1813 seventeen men were hanged at York by the Special Commission, yet all the Luddite riots were over months before. Fourteen of these were for cases of no blood and very little violence, mere burglaries and robberies. Here, though the disturbances have been infinitely greater, only three *suffer*.

The petitions in several places (Newcastle) pray that the "unfortunate *incendiaries*" should not even be tried. "Unfortunate *incendiaries*!" Murder will next be called unfortunate. In truth any interference by public meetings and debates on *individual cases* of malefactors seems of very doubtful prudence and efficacy. The state of the criminal law or even the general conduct of judges and Government as to mercy and prosecutions may well be so canvassed. But what will be the consequence of debates and canvassing for petitions and signatures every time a felon is condemned? Bringing the law into hatred and making only felons the object of compassion; nay, vindicating all felons. Besides, those who so discuss *must* proceed in the dark and on the most scanty knowledge of the facts—newspaper reports and rumours afloat in the public. Cases tried on oath by judges will be tried again by mobs without any evidence at all, and nothing can result but the encouragement of crimes.

> Till the disturbances be put down, not one step *can* be
> taken, either to amend the poor law or relieve the existing
> distress, and improve the law or reform the Parliament.[11]

Few statesmen have spent so long a period of their active political life in Opposition. Whereas Palmerston was in office for about forty-eight years and unemployed for a mere ten, Brougham, though engaged in politics for half a century, held office for only one brief spell of four years. But although fate (and his own imprudent conduct) willed that he should for such a length of time be "cast away with other mournful ghosts on the tempest-beaten coasts of Opposition" (to use one of his own phrases), his career affords a striking illustration of the amount of good that an able and energetic politician can accomplish

"*SWING CAUGHT AT LAST*". *Brougham (Swing) is brought before the King. Peel (the policeman) explains: "Please, your worship, the prisoner at the bar is accused of incendiarism. He was often strongly suspected in 'Times' past of inserting inflammable matter in the night, his progress everywhere being marked by* Columns *of smoke; but we have positive evidence of his having within the last few months actually set Barnes on fire."*

without office. The fifteen years and more during which he opposed the Liverpool Ministry were only apparently futile. As an unofficial leader of the Whigs, he did little, indeed, to heal the dissensions and disunion which stultified all their efforts to obtain power. But it was during this period that his influence in the country was almost at its height. It was during these years that he was most successful in forcing his views on the Ministry, in giving shape to the opinions of the middle-class of the nation, and in moulding the ideas of the Whig party.

In this supremely important work he derived his most valuable assistance from the press. There was no other statesman of his time who perceived so clearly as he the immense value of such an organ of public opinion. There was no other politician who made such use of the press, and wrote so copiously both in periodicals and in newspapers. At the beginning of the century, parliamentarians were almost unanimous in regarding it as a disgrace to be connected with the daily press. Brougham did much to break down that tradition, which, one may perhaps say, was finally destroyed by Disraeli. It was Brougham, as we have seen, who was largely responsible for making the *Edinburgh Review* the accredited organ of the Whig party. It would have perished, he on one occasion declared, but for the political articles that it inserted at his own instigation. He popularised his views under the mask of anonymity not only in the pages of the *Edinburgh* but in many pamphlets; and the "musings of Jenkins and the meditations of Tomkins" were no doubt identical with the lucubrations of the Lord Chancellor on the great political controversies of the day.[12]

Great as were his achievements, they might have been still greater had he not tried to excel in too many spheres. He dissipated his energies over too wide a field. Neither to science nor to letters nor to philosophy nor to theology nor to politics did he make such original contributions as many a less gifted man has done in one single sphere before and since. Rogers' witticism has often been quoted. "This morning," he remarked on one occasion when Brougham was leaving a country house, "This morning Solon, Lycurgus, Demosthenes, Archimedes, Sir Isaac Newton,

Lord Chesterfield, and a great many more went away in one post-chaise." "Is Foaming Fudge to come in for Cloudland?" asks one of Disraeli's characters. "Doubtless. Oh, he is a prodigious fellow. What do you think Booby says? He says that Foaming Fudge can do more than any man in Great Britain: that he had one day to plead in the King's Bench, spout at a tavern, speak in the House, and fight a duel, and that he found time for everything but the last."[13] Lord Holland once assured him that he believed that if a new language was discovered in the morning he would be able to talk it before night. Campbell, his biographer, declared that if Brougham was locked up in the Tower of London for twelve months without being allowed a single book, the year would not elapse before he had written an encyclopædia. He prided himself on his 'universality'; and his amazing number of gifts indeed completely dazzled and astonished the people. But, Cobden justly observed:

> It is this attempt at universality which has been the great error and failing of Lord Brougham's public life. He has touched everything and finished nothing. Had he given his vast powers to one thing at a time, he might have codified our laws, and endowed every village with a good school, besides leaving nothing for me to do in Free Trade. But he made a speech for five hours on law reform forty years ago nearly, and another as long on national education, and then he left those questions for something else. The result will be that in fifty years he will be remembered only for his herculean mental powers and his unrivalled intellectual industry; but his name will not be specially associated with any reforms for which posterity will hold him in grateful remembrance.[14]

Thus his qualifications for a statesman were limited as much by the fact that he attempted too much and therefore knew too little about all the many subjects in which he tried to specialise, as by the many and glaring defects in his character. His attitude towards the

Dorchester labourers shows how little he really knew of the dreadful conditions under which they lived, how little he appreciated their difficulties and aspirations. His advocacy of the famous Poor Law Amendment Bill was based on the wholly gratuitous assumption that the people preferred to live in idleness to earning their own bread. What did he know of Ireland, of the social misery, poverty, and wretchedness that everywhere abounded in that unhappy country which he had never visited, when, as Lord Chancellor, he declared that the last chapter would soon be torn out of the book of Ireland's wrongs?

The gravest charge that can be brought against him is his faithlessness and egoism. There is abundant evidence to prove that he used the Royal Divorce as a grand opportunity of promoting his own ends, and that he was willing to betray the Queen to the ministers for his personal advantage. Had he been as astute as he was unscrupulous, his success would have been assured. There can be no doubt that if he had really been anxious to settle the question satisfactorily from the point of view of both his client and the King, he could easily have settled it; and it is certain that had the affair been in Canning's hands, no crisis would ever have arisen.

His weaknesses became apparent at an early period of his life. From the first they seriously impeded his progress, and he was never destined to overcome them. One may point to his unsteadiness and unreliability—to his jealousy of all those whom he could possibly regard as rivals—to his recklessness which got him into innumerable scrapes and which hurried him beyond all the bounds of prudence—to his perpetual interference in matters with which he had no concern—his contempt for those whom he deemed his inferiors in intellect—and his overweening vanity. Greville wrote of him in 1828:

> Brougham is only a living and very remarkable instance of
> the inefficacy of the most splendid talents, unless they are
> accompanied with other qualities, which scarcely admit
> of definition, but which must serve the same purpose

that ballast does for a ship. Brougham has prospered to a certain degree; he has a great reputation, and he makes a considerable income at the bar; but as an advocate he is left behind by men of far inferior capacity, whose names are hardly known beyond the precincts of their courts or the boundaries of their circuits. As a statesman he is not considered eligible for the biggest offices, and however he may be admired or feared as an orator or debater, he neither commands respect by his character nor inspires confidence by his genius, and in this contrast between his pretensions and his situation more humble abilities may find room for consolation and cease to contemplate with envy his immense superiority.[15]

In the House of Lords on August 3, 1838, replying to Brougham on the question of Irish tithes, Melbourne alluded to the character of Burke as a reflection of that of the ex-Chancellor. With all his great gifts none dare employ him:

He was a man of the greatest natural abilities, cultivated in a degree worthy of such gifts; but the noble and learned lord should have, at the same time, remembered that Mr. Burke was a man of violent, of intensely violent passions; that he was a man as unmeasured in his invectives as he was profuse in panegyric, that he disregarded the moral maxim *ne quid nimis*—that such was the extreme recklessness, such the unequalled eccentricity of his conduct, that he often proved a most pernicious and dangerous guide.[16]

Political partisanship caused Brougham to be hated and feared by some as intensely as others admired and respected him; but in private life almost every one fell under his spell, and was charmed by his good humour, his racy and entertaining conversation, his generosity

Brougham as a Frenchman, another cartoon from Punch, *1848*

and kindliness, his wit and learning. "Even his greatness," wrote Whitwell Elwin, one of his many Tory friends, "was surpassed by his kindness. His warmth, tenderness, and constancy of friendship were wonderful."[17]

1. Elwin, *Men of Letters*, i. 249.
2. *Recollections and Suggestions*, p.137.
3. Le Marchant's *Althorp*, p.352.
4. Elwin, *Men of Letters*, i. 153.
5. *Creevey Papers*, i. 249.
6. *Edinburgh Review*, Jan. 1839, Art. ix.
7. *Ibid.*

8. *Ibid.*

9. Add, MS. 34615, fol. 4.

10. Hammond, *The Village Labourer* (ed. 1920), p. 295.

11. Add. MS. 34615, fol.

12. Jenkins and Tomkins, whom Disraeli thus mentions in his *Runnymede* Letter to Lord Brougham, are two characters introduced by Brougham in his treatise *On the Objects, Advantages, and Pleasures of Science*. It is practically certain that Brougham wrote the much-talked of pamphlet which appeared in 1835, entitled, *Thoughts upon the Aristocracy of England*, by Isaac Tomkins, and which he reviewed in the *Edinburgh Review*.

13. *Vivian Grey*, Book ii. oh. 12.

14. Morley, *Life of Cobden* (ed. 1906), p.848.

15. *Memoirs*, i. 121.

16. *Parl. Deb.*, Third Series, xliv. 976.

17. Elwin, *Some Eighteenth Century Men of Letters*, i. 262.

Appendix A

Brougham's Contributions to the *Edinburgh Review* 1802–1846

I AM indebted to Mr. Harold Cox, the present editor of the *Edinburgh Review,* and to Messrs. Longmans, Green & Co., Ltd., for an authentic list of the articles which Brougham contributed to that periodical from its foundation in 1802 to 1830. A list of his later contributions is readily obtained from the printed volume of Macvey Napier's correspondence, and from the catalogue of the Napier MSS. in the British Museum. That collection contains the articles in manuscript. (Add. MS. 34627, 34628.)

Brougham claimed a great number of articles which were really not his own; on the other hand, he wrote several to which he laid no claim. In his *Memoirs* he declared that he contributed eighty articles to the first twenty numbers of the *Review,* and his statement, which the truth does not bear out, has always been accepted. That he laid claim to so many that were really the work of other contributors need not necessarily be ascribed to his vanity; for Jeffrey himself experienced great difficulty when in his later years he attempted to sort out his own contributions. There is abundant evidence in the Napier MSS. and elsewhere that Brougham was in the habit of adding the seasoning to other people's dishes (putting a little salt in them was his own phrase) before they were sent to Jeffrey or Napier. There is, therefore, something substantial in the tradition that he acted as a kind of sub-editor. Under these circumstances, then, it is hardly a matter of wonder that in later life he claimed a considerable number of other people's contributions.

One illustration of how he tended to usurp the editor's functions will not be out of place. Writing to Napier on September 21, 1832, he said:

> This parcel contains the article on English Church Reform and the extracts, and also one on the Records, which last I have carefully read and struck out some passages. It is a very learned paper . . . its value and importance make it most desirable that it should come out *now,* when it may be read. I particularly beg that you would *not* print the complimentary passage which I have struck out and altered.[1]

No. I. *Oct.* 1802

Art. 23.   Wood's "Optics".

    24.   Acerbi's Travels.

    27.   The Crisis of the Sugar Colonies.

No. II. *Jan.* 1803

Art. 9.   Politique de tous les cabinets de l'Europe.

    12.   Woodhouse on Imaginary Quantities.

    14.   Mrs. Hunter's Poems.

    15.   Herschel on the new Planets.

    17.   Bakerian Lecture on Light and Colours.

    18.   Young on Colours not hitherto described.

    23.   Transactions of the Royal Society of Edinburgh.

No. III. *April* 1803

Art. 8.   Woollaston on Prismatic Reflection.

    9.   Woollaston on Iceland Crystal.

    10.   Hatchett's Analysis of a new Metal.

    13.   Ritson on Abstinence from Animal Food.

    20.   Memoirs of the Literary and Philosophical Society of Manchester.

    26.   Stewart's Life of Robertson.

No. IV. *July* 1803

Art. 6. American Philosophical Transactions.

8. Dallas's History of the Maroons.

12. Walker's Defence of Order.

17. Moore's Translation of Anacreon.

19. Pownall's Memorial.

No. V. *Oct.* 1803

Art. 1. Dr. Black's Lectures on Chemistry.

18. Wheatley on Currency and Commerce.

No. VI. *Jan.* 1804

Art. 5. Karamsin's Travels in Europe.

12. Izarn's Lithologie atmosphérique.

17. Hatchett on the Gold Coin.

19. Bishop Watson on the National Debt.

No VIII. *July* 1804

Art. 8. Lord Lauderdale on Public Wealth.

11 Rumford on the Nature of Heat.

12. Rumford on a Phenomenon in the Glaciers.

15. Barrow's Travels in Southern Africa.

16. Dr. Hill's Latin Synonymes.

No. IX. *Oct.* 1804

Art. 5. Kotzebue's Travels to Paris.

7. Dr. Young's Bakerian Lectures.

8. O'Connor's Present State of Great Britain.

No. XI. *April* 1805

Art. 2. Venturi, Sopra i colori.

4. Fontana, Sopra un problema Euleriana.

6. Talleyrand, Sur les colonies.

8. Memories de l'Académie de Turin.

No. XII. *July* 1805

Art.   2.   Lord Lauderdale's Hints to Manufacturers.

        8.   Examen de l'esclavage.

        11.   De Langes, Statici per i tetti.

No. XIII. *Oct.* 1805

Art.   4.   Leslie's Inquiry into the Nature of Heat.

        15.   Thiebault, Memoirs de Fred. le Grand.

No. XIV. *Jan.* 1806

Art.   1.   Lord Liverpool on the Coin.

        8.   Life of Dr. Johnson.

        10.   Kotzebue's Travels in Italy.

No. XV. *April* 1806

Art.   15.   An Inquiry into the State of the Nation.

No. XVI. *July* 1806

Art.   2.   Lemaistre's Travels.

        8.   Dutens—Mémoires d'un voyageur.

No. XVIII. *Jan.* 1807

Art.   1.   Gentz on the State of Europe.

        3.   Dr. Pinckard on the West Indies.

        5.   Turnbull's Voyage round the World.

No. XIX. *April* 1807

Art.   13.   Wilberforce on the Abolition of the Slave Trade.

No. XX. *July* 1807

Art.   1.   Thornton's Present State of Turkey.

        8.   Dumouriez, Jugement sur Buonaparte.

        11.   Burnett's View of the Present State of Poland.

        13.   Savage's Account of New Zealand.

The Bear and the Bees, from Punch, *1848*

1. Add. MS. 34615, fol. 411.

Appendix B

Notes on Manuscript Material

Chatsworth MSS.

The very extensive collection of manuscripts at Chatsworth Hall includes a large mass of the papers of the sixth Duke of Devonshire, dating from 1819. Of Brougham's letters there is a very considerable number, written between 1819 and 1833 or 1834, about which time the correspondence suddenly ceases, Brougham apparently quarrelling with his old friend and patron, as he did with so many others. Brougham also corresponded with B. Currey, who succeeded Abercromby as the auditor of the Duke's accounts. There are important letters from Lord Grey, Lord Lansdowne, Lord Essex, Macdonald, Duncannon, Russell, Lord Holland, Lord Dover, Melbourne, Lord Carlisle, and others; whilst there is a whole series of letters that passed between the Duke of Devonshire and his sister Harriet, Lady Granville. The letters are particularly valuable for the history of the rise and fall of the Coalition Ministries of 1827.

Lansdowne MSS.

Of the papers of the Marquis of Lansdowne I have seen only the correspondence of Brougham, ranging between 1799 and 1863, and comprising about ninety letters, twenty-five of which are undated. These again are very useful for the negotiations of 1827.

Holland House MSS.

Of the rich collection of papers at Holland House I have, again, seen only the correspondence of Brougham with the third Lord Holland, with Lady Holland, and with John Allen. The series begins in 1807, and is a very extensive one. It is particularly useful for the light that it throws on Brougham's relations with the Whig party, with Jeffrey and the *Edinburgh Review*, and on his connection with the party press.

Lambton MSS.

Portions of the correspondence of the first Earl of Durham have previously been used by Stuart Reid, by Mr. J.R.M. Butler, and by Mr. G.M. Trevelyan. Lord Durham did not preserve many of his letters, and there are great gaps in the correspondence as a whole. There are, for instance, no letters at all dating from 1821 to the middle of 1827. Brougham's letters are surprisingly few in number, dating apparently only from 1817 to 1818 and from 1830 to 1831. Several, however, are highly important, and are noticed in the text. Sir Robert Wilson corresponded with Lord Durham almost as frequently as he did with Lord Grey, to whom he was, as his collection in the British Museum shows, in the habit of writing two or three times a week. Wilson wrote much more freely to Lambton than to Grey, and his letters contain more scandal and small talk, and rather less political intelligence. There is a great mass of correspondence from Edward Ellice dating from 1820 to 1838 or 1839. His handwriting, however, is like Brougham's, very difficult to decipher, and nearly all his letters are, like Brougham's, undated. Stuart Reid attempted to assign dates to some of them, but not with any great success; and in some cases his estimate was out by several years. He stated, too, that the series began only in 1826, whereas it really began in September 1820. Ellice's correspondence in 1827 is of much interest. After 1833 he appears to have begun to write regularly once or twice a week, and his letters of 1834 and 1835 in particular, are of considerable importance for their political information. They show in striking fashion the complete dissatisfaction of the Liberal and progressive wing of the Whig party with the Conservative leadership of Lord Grey. Ellice and others, for instance, were overjoyed to hear that Grey was not again to be Prime Minister after the defeat of the Tories in April 1835.

There is a good deal of private correspondence between Lord and Lady Durham. Lord Durham's letters contain much political news, but Lady Durham was much more concerned with the welfare of her children than with affairs of State, and, unlike Lady Grey, wrote little on political topics.

There are many letters from Grey and Russell on the subject of the Reform Bill and the quarrel between Durham and Brougham in 1834; and a number of useful letters from Duncannon, Althorp, Lord Darlington, Sefton, Sir James Graham, Lord Stanley of Alderley, and others. With the large mass of papers concerning Durham's embassy to Russia we are not concerned; nor with the Canadian correspondence, which is at present in Canada. Lastly, there is a long series of letters from the Radical Reformer, Joseph Parkes.

Althorp MSS.

The correspondence of Lord Spencer preserved at Althorp consists largely of Althorp's letters to Grey (68), Althorp's letters to Brougham (110), Grey's letters to Althorp (30), Brougham's letters to Althorp (about 60), and a smaller number from William IV. and Sir Herbert Taylor to Althorp, and from Althorp to William IV. These series of letters were some years ago privately printed for Lord Spencer, but so far as Brougham's letters at any rate are concerned, the printed copy is unreliable and the excerpts from his letters printed in the present volume are taken from the actual manuscripts. The many errors that have crept into Lord Spencer's printed copy are, of course, to be ascribed to Brougham's atrociously bad hand, which presents difficulties even to the expert. A number of his manuscript letters, of considerable political importance, do not appear in the printed volume at Althorp. He wrote, too, a very long and interesting Memorandum on his friend, Lord Althorp. Althorp's biographer, Le Marchant, made use of the collection, but he was not allowed to print some of Brougham's letters written in 1835 and 1836, at a time when he was keenly feeling the blow which Melbourne had given him in April 1835, and when his hatred of and bitterness against his old colleagues was being freely expressed in his correspondence. Lord Spencer's objections to the publication of these letters appear in some instructions which he drew up, apparently for Le Marchant's benefit. Commenting, for instance, on Brougham's letter of April 4, 1835, Lord Spencer wrote:

> The two first pages are unobjectionable. . . . All that follows
> down to page eight cannot be printed, for it is written in
> a spirit of painful soreness and of bitterness against his old
> colleagues and party. However well founded may be his
> complaints of ill-treatment, by those who owed everything
> in political life to his unwearied labours—the publication
> of such grievances would do no credit to his memory—and
> really the objectionable pages are not material, in a life of
> Lord Althorp—and therefore I trust you will agree with me,
> that they are better suppressed.

The letters that Le Marchant accordingly suppressed have been printed in the volume preserved at Althorp. The reasons against their publication no longer, at this distance of time, apply, and to my making use of them the present Lord Spencer has no objection. The collection also includes valuable letters from Duncannon, Holland, Abercromby, Tavistock, and others.

Hatherton MSS.

Like the papers of the sixth Duke of Devonshire at Chatsworth, Brougham's letters to Lord Lansdowne and to Lord Holland, the large and valuable collection of manuscripts in the possession of Lord Hatherton at Teddlesley, has never hitherto been used. It consists of the private journal and correspondence of the first Lord Hatherton, the Secretary for Ireland from 1833 to 1834.

Edward John Littleton's private diary was begun on November 25, 1817, and was originally intended to be kept for one year only. But not only was the journal not discontinued after a twelvemonth, but its last entry was not recorded until August 25, 1862—within a few months of his death.

The journal is preserved in 95 volumes and note-books varying much in size. For the period 1817–1835 there are but eleven volumes, but they are much larger than those which follow. The entries are for the most part daily and continuous; but there are several gaps, some of them extensive. For example, the diary was not kept between March 25, 1825, and January 1828; between February 27, 1828, and June 27, 1831; and between August 28, 1833, and March 3, 1835, during which period, official duties occupied most of his time.

The diary is by no means exclusively political in character. No better picture of the life of a "country gentleman" is to be found than in the early volumes. With the continent Lord Hatherton was well acquainted, and he gives many full and admirable descriptions of French, German, Austrian, and Italian scenery and society. Like Greville, he recorded many conversations that took place in high political circles. There are entertaining stories of Brougham being once arrested for horse stealing, and of the extraordinary conduct which he periodically exhibited in later life; anecdotes of Lord Wellesley's brilliant career in India, and of the famous campaigns of Wellington; accounts of Warren Hastings's trial in Westminster Hall, of Castlereagh's first election campaign in Ireland; of George III.'s intended abdication of the throne in 1783 when faced with the Coalition Ministry of Fox and North.

Lord Hatherton's correspondence begins in 1812 and extends to the year 1862. In all, it occupies 63 substantial volumes, containing approximately 5500 letters, memoranda, and copies of official secret despatches from Ireland. About 30 volumes contain the correspondence after 1835. One volume consists of Littleton's letters on the subject of his candidature for the Speaker's chair (1832–1833); another of copies of Lord Anglesey's despatches from Ireland in 1832 and 1833 privately furnished by the Lord Lieutenant to Littleton at the time of his acceptance of the Irish Secretaryship. Others deal with his Staffordshire election contests, and family correspondence. Thirteen volumes contain his letters while in office; one of these, containing his "Memoir of 1834" relating to the O'Connell episode, was published by Henry Reeve after Lord Hatherton's death.

At the end of one of the early note-books there is a brief but valuable autobiographical sketch, occupying some twenty pages.

Lord Hatherton's most important correspondents were the following. The number of their letters is also given:

Aberdeen (12); Althorp (23); Anglesea (82); Brougham (24); Canning (8); Dudley (26); Duncannon (43); Ellice (33); Gladstone (3); Granville (12); Grey (25); W. Horton (40); Lansdowne (19); Melbourne (128); Palmerston (44); J. Parkes (*c.*150); Russell (30); Seaford (8); Spring Rice (16); Stanley (27); Wellesley (several hundreds).

The Pitt Papers at the Public Record Office.

Brougham never made the acquaintance of Pitt, although he heard him speak in the House of Commons. Since Pitt died in 1806, when Brougham was still on the threshold of his career, and had only recently taken up his residence in London, we could hardly expect to discover much information about Brougham in the papers of the Prime Minister. Brougham's letter to Pitt (1803) enclosing a copy of the *Colonial Policy*, has not been preserved; but the collection contains Brougham's unpublished Memorandum to the Premier on the subject of the Edinburgh Volunteers.

There are no references, to Brougham in the correspondence of Lord Harrowby, who was in communication with him in 1804; but one of Wilberforce's letters (packet no. clxxxix.) refers to Brougham's continental tour in 1804 and to his important pamphlet on the slave trade. He wrote:

> . . . One very powerful and important reason for your abolishing the Guiana Sla. Trade *by an act of government*, not by, or in consequence of, a vote of Parlt., is that it would tend to confirm the disposition so strongly manifested by the Dutch to abolish the Sla. Trade, and give them the sort of satisfaction they desire, that the subject of the restoration of their colonies *for an equivalent*, or at least of a part of them, should be left open to discussion, and not be precluded. Mr. B. was assured by some most knowing men that the French influence wo'd not prevent this—and the publication of the translation of Mr. B.'s summary of the case of the abolitionists, by a man of leadg. influence, and its circulation thro' the country are strong confirmations of the disposition which Mr. B. stated to prevail.
>
> If there be any part of this which you do not distinctly recollect, for I imagine Ld. Harrowby made you acquainted with it all, had I not better see you for a few minutes? . . .

Nassau Senior's Narrative.

George Nicholls, the historian of the Poor Law, wrote on the fly-leaf of this manuscript volume of over two hundred pages:

> This very interesting account of what occurred in connection with the passing of the. Poor Law Amendment Act, was given to me by Mr. Senior. The detail is valuable and instructive, and I trust Mr. Senior will some day make it public. He has given me permission to make use of it in the work I have commenced, but I purpose doing so in a way that shall not anticipate or interfere with his publishing of the entire, whenever he may determine on doing so.
>
> GEO. NICHOLLS. March 1851
>
> *N.B.* The book was afterwards given to me absolutely by Mr. Senior.—G.N.

With the framing of the new Poor Law Brougham had little to do, and he took little part in the Cabinet discussions on the subject. But Nassau Senior gives an interesting account of a conversation he had with the Chancellor on July 21, when the Bill was introduced into the House of Lords, and when Brougham made a speech that gave his colleagues much uneasiness. Whilst he was opposed to Poor Laws altogether, the Cabinet was opposed only to their maladministration.

The British Museum Additional Manuscripts.

The most useful collections for the present theme are the papers of Sir Robert Wilson, Francis Place, and Huskisson.

The correspondence of SIR ROBERT WILSON is so fully noticed in the text that any detailed statement of the contents is here unnecessary. Though much of it concerns Wilson's career in the army during the Napoleonic Wars, eleven out of the fifty odd volumes in the collection contain his political correspondence with Grey, etc., from 1814 to 1830 and beyond. There is a considerable number of Brougham's letters, of varying importance, but written in a very difficult hand, and, what is worse, the majority of them are undated. Thus the task of attempting to assign an exact date for each is a very heavy one; but from the internal and external evidence and the application of the methods of the higher criticism, it is possible to overcome this difficulty in the case of practically all the letters that are of any importance.

From the PLACE PAPERS, of which huge collection Mr. Graham Wallas touched only the fringe, a great deal of new and valuable information is to be derived on the subject of Brougham's relations with the Westminster Reformers from the year 1814. These manuscripts enable us to give for the first time a connected and detailed account of Brougham's career as a Whig-Radical from 1814 to 1816.

THE HUSKISSON PAPERS, which have only recently become available, and which have not yet been thoroughly explored, are of immense value for the light they throw on the history of the Canningite party up to its absorption by the Whig party in the autumn of 1830. There is, in particular, a large mass of Canning's correspondence (practically all unpublished) with Huskisson, which admirably illustrates his motives and conduct during the critical period after 1820, end which points definitely to the conclusion that he was not working for an alliance with the Whigs. There is, too, a useful correspondence with the chief members of the Canningite party, especially with Granville. That there are no autograph letters from Palmerston till 1827 or 1828 shows how loosely connected was Palmerston with Canning and his party.

THE WINDHAM PAPERS contain Brougham's letter to Windham of June 1, 1803, in which the latter was asked to accept a copy of the *Colonial Policy*. There is also the draft of Windham's reply.

THE BENTHAM PAPERS, too, contain no important letters of Brougham.

Brougham's letters to JOHN CAM HOBHOUSE (LORD BROUGHTON) are of no great significance, but the Broughton collection includes several valuable letters from Lord Tavistock which throw light on the attitude of the Whigs towards the Coalition Ministry of 1827.

In the drama of April 1827 LORD AUCKLAND was one of the Whig peers who played a minor part, but his correspondence contains no reference to the negotiations that preceded the formation of Canning's Ministry. One or two of Lord Lansdowne's letters written in 1816 refer to Brougham's activities on the continent.

There is not much to be gleaned from the correspondence of the third EARL OF HARDWICKE. The few useful letters are mentioned in the text.

Many of Brougham's letters to LEIGH HUNT have been printed in the first volume of Hunt's correspondence. But several of high importance, not hitherto printed, are to be found in this collection They are quoted *in extenso* in the text.

The printed volume of MACVEY NAPIER'S LETTERS contains most of the important letters in the manuscript collection of Napier's papers. Brougham's letter, which is dated March 27, 1830, in the published volume should be dated March 7, 1830. The manuscripts throw little additional light on Brougham's relations with Napier and with his connection with the *Edinburgh Review*, but there are several interesting letters dealing with his quarrel with Lord Durham in 1834.

The most important of the papers of the MARQUIS WELLESLEY have already been published, and Mr. Trevelyan has made use of Grey's letters to Wellesley in his *Lord Grey of the Reform Bill*. But quite a considerable number of letters dealing with Lord Wellesley's Irish administration and with the Cabinet crises of 1834 were excluded from the two printed volumes.

The bulk of the enormous mass of the papers of the first and second EARL OF LIVERPOOL consists of strictly official correspondence of little value. The correspondence of Canning, Peel, and Palmerston with the Prime Minister is arranged in separate volumes, but only Canning's is important, and the more significant portions are noticed in the text. Most of the correspondence relating to Queen Caroline is also bound up in separate volumes, and much has been printed by Yonge, who, however, strangely enough, apparently failed to notice some of the most important letters.

Brougham's letter to WILLIAM ROSCOE, of Liverpool, on the subject of the slave trade, is included in a volume of miscellaneous letters purchased at Sotheby's in 1891, and is fully noticed in the text.

Volume 34545 contains important unpublished letters of RICARDO, written to M'Culloch and others, on various economic subjects. Ricardo criticises several of Brougham's speeches in the House of Commons on the question of agricultural distress.

Volume 38080 contains some of LORD JOHN RUSSELL'S CORRESPONDENCE with Grey, Moore, Durham, etc., and extends from the year 1819 to the year 1860. Some interesting letters passed between Russell and Durham on the subject of the latter's quarrel with Brougham in the summer of 1834, and on the framing of the Reform Bill.

Robert Owen MSS.

The Robert Owen papers in the possession of the Co-operative Union include a number of letters that passed between Owen and Brougham from about 1830 to 1855. The chief topics discussed in this correspondence were spiritualistic séances, in which both these remarkable men were wont to participate during the later part of their lives; and Owen's multifarious schemes for the "permanent improvement of society," and his attempts to induce the various Governments of Europe seriously to take them up. "The literary Liberal party (political) in this country and throughout the civilised world look to you," wrote Owen in June 1835, "to lead them wisely out of the difficulties in which their old learning and principles have involved them. Nor is there any other individual to whom they will listen with the same attention or by whom they will be so readily directed."

Bentham MSS.

A catalogue of the Bentham papers at University College has been published, and it is therefore unnecessary to say anything here about their contents.

There is not much material that bears on Brougham's political career; but, in an unpublished and uncompleted pamphlet Bentham sharply criticises Brougham's proposals for the reform of the judicature. Bentham gives an interesting account of Romilly in his unfinished Letter to Lord Erskine, 1819.

John Rylands Library MSS.

References are made in the text to one or two of Brougham's and Macaulay's letters in the possession of the John Rylands Library. An unpublished letter written by O'Connell to B. Boothley, of Nottingham (July 17, 1834), is worth quoting for his views on the policy of the Whig Government, which was at the moment being reconstructed by Melbourne. He wrote:

> You did me the great honour to consult with me previous
> to the last election on the subject of the fitness of Lord

The Political MacHeath, from Punch, *1848*

Duncannon to represent your town. I hope, therefore, you will not deem me presumptuous if I initiate—as the Americans say—the correspondence on the present occasion. The fact really is that we are now in a much more critical situation than we were at the former election. The Whigs have been such cruel *drags* on the wheels of rational improvement that many of their Cabinet have been compelled to yield and fly before the force of public opinion repressed as it has been by a multitude of causes. But the remnant of that Cabinet want sufficient energy to meet the national exigencies, or to give that substantial relief which would alleviate public distress and secure the enjoyment of popular rights against the perpetual spirit of invasion of a worthless aristocracy for whom alone mean courtiers have hitherto been governed.

At such a moment it is the duty of every honest radical reformer who is equally desirous to prevent any approach to a social revolution as to carry into practical effect salutary changes and needful improvements in the political system to come forward and send to Parliament men who are totally free from the bias of *personal* party, and determined to do their duty to their country and to the cause of civil and religious liberty, fearlessly, perseveringly, and disinterestedly.

Appendix C

Excerpts from Manuscript Sources

Chapter I

Brougham to Allen [of Holland House]. Wednesday [1807]

You will see a curious detection of Sir H. Popham in this day's *Chronicle*. It occurred to me after I had written to you yesterday. Also in to-morrow's *Press and Globe*—another statement of Sir H. Mildmay's business. I shall send a paper of the former to you, that you may see the job in all its lights, and help me in attacking it. The statement in the *Morning Chronicle* has already produced a considerable effect—for the job is everywhere talked of and with general reprobation. This shows the use of having some one always ready to give publicity to what is hid in the Reports of Committees. Something on the York election will also appear to-morrow—but you are wrong in your idea of my having attacked the Saints in Monday's *Chronicle*. I think the article was very well done, and on the whole, just—but I differ widely from the author of it (Perry or Spankie, I presume) in allowing Wilberforce so little share in the abolition. That is their opinion—and I have mine, and so it must remain. With the exception of that article, and Jekyl's squibs, I think every prose article or paragraph of late weeks inserted in the *Morning Chronicle* has come either from Lord Holland or you or me. Such as are not put in there, go to the *Pilot, Globe*, etc.

(Holland House MS.)

CHAPTER II

Brougham to Holland. Saturday, April 6 [1811]
[Ex officio information for libel, and the liberty of the Press]

. . . It has grieved me beyond expression to see the accounts in the newspapers of the division and debate on Lord Folkestone's motion,[1] but as I have had no very correct private accounts of the matter (indeed none except a note of the conduct of two or three individuals) I am still in hopes there may be some mistake, and that the seeming wish of the bulk of our friends to wash their hands of the question may have been only accidental.[2] It certainly, however, wore a very unpleasant appearance, and if the leaders of the party really absented themselves or voted with the Government on purpose to discourage the motion and to manifest an indisposition towards such salutary and popular courses, I confess I should apprehend that an open splitting of the Whigs is near at hand, and that those (strange) WHIGS OR FOXITES who love State prosecutions, and neither care for the people nor can bear the occasional personalities of the Press, and on account of such trifling injuries hate the Press itself, will find themselves deserted by the friends of liberty everywhere, and despised by the real, thoroughbred courtiers—for after all, do what they will, they must prove at the best a second-rate kind of Tories, and can't fail to be outwitted by your Jenkinsons[3] and Castlereaghs who are born and bred to the trade.

(Holland House MS.)

Canning to Huskisson. August 17, 1812

[The Ministers] . . . have a notion that it is as well my disposition as my interest, however treated by the Government, rather to keep them in, with the hope of joining them sometime or other, than to help to bring in Opposition. It is neither my disposition nor my interest to make this foolish option. Certainly, it is not my inclination and it is not my *game* to join the Opposition on Tierney's proposed terms '*in* together, *out* together'; but, being out myself, I have not the slightest hesitation to say that I would *rather* have the Opposition *in* than these people as they are.

My objection to the principles of the Opposition as regards the Crown is answered by what I have *seen* of the Prince Regent's situation in the hands of the present Cabinet.

As to their politics, better to *oppose* Brougham's surrender of the Orders in Council than to support Castlereagh's. Better, if Opposition are to dictate the measures of the Government and to be in fact our rulers, that they should dictate them in office and on their own responsibility.

But there is a still stronger and more favourable point of view in which I look at the Opposition in power. They *in*, and the present people *out*, the state of parties will be wonderfully simplified. Between Castlereagh in office, and me where I am, the Pittites, with Charles Long for their guide, probably will not hesitate to choose Castlereagh as their leader. Let us be *both out*; and *then* let them make their choice and let Lord Castlereagh *then* state his pretensions.

That state of things is all that I desire. And that state of things, if the *present* remains unaltered *till the meeting of Parliament,* neither interest nor inclination will then prevent me from co-operating with—I care not whom—to bring about.

The Prince Regent *cannot* be in greater thraldom in the hands of Opposition than I find him to be in the hands of Lords Westmorland, Sidmouth, Bathurst, and Buckinghamshire, and Mr. Bragge.

In Whitbread, Secretary of State, I shall at least have an open and worthy antagonist. . . .

(Add. MS. 38738, fol. 316.)

Chapter III

Canning to Huskisson, Plymouth Sound. November 19, 1814

. . . There is certainly no want of 'acrimony' in the Opposition with respect to me, and to those connected with me. But this neither surprises nor now, to say the truth, grieves me. It is a satisfaction to me, on the contrary, that those most inclined to them among my friends must now see (what I have never myself doubted for a moment since 1809) that the hatred of the Whigs to me is tenfold greater than that of any part of Opposition to the Government or than that of any part of the Government to us. The change in their tactics is perfectly intelligible and exactly what I expected. During the last two years they have avoided pressing the Government hard, lest distress should drive the Government to make overtures to us, but they have never declined a division, however contemptible they knew their own numbers to be, when they could force us into the minority with themselves. Now they have no longer any motive for forbearance; they will probably distress the Government as much as they can in debate, and they will at the same time naturally avoid a division, which may only expose their own smallness of numbers without embarrassing anyone else, or committing anyone else against the Government.

Undoubtedly they may make inconvenient debates and excite a certain degree of dissatisfaction out of doors, upon the topics which you mention: but as to changing the Government—as to forcing themselves in—I believe the distrust and detestation of them throughout the country to be effectual safeguards against that result. Not that it would be a result which, individually, I should much deprecate. It is perhaps the only one in which I should ever *wish* to resume my place in the House of Commons. But I am satisfied that it is wholly out of all reasonable calculation.

(Add. MS. 38739, fol. 272.)

Extracts from Brooks's Club Rules, 1817. [Printed]

1. That the Club shall not consist of more than 550 members.

2. That the subscription shall be eleven guineas per annum, and to be payable on the first of every January for the current year.

3. That every new member shall pay twenty guineas for his first year's subscription, and sign his name in the book containing the rules of the Club.

4. That no person shall be admitted but by ballot.

5. That no ballot shall consist of less than twelve members, and that when any candidate has but one black ball, he shall be balloted for again; and unless he has two or more black balls upon the second ballot, he shall be duly elected.

16. That there shall be six managers appointed on the first of every May, who are to continue one year; each manager to appoint his successor, and if any manager neglects naming such successor before the first of June, a majority of a General Meeting of the said managers, which shall be called on the occasion, shall fill up the vacancy, and they shall have full power to settle any complaints, and take care that the rules and regulations of the Club are complied with. And that the managers of the preceding year should meet their successors, and give over to them the accounts of the Club.

17. A dinner for six members, at 15s. per head, including waiters and dessert, to be furnished daily, during the sitting of Parliament; the dinner to be on the table at 7 o'clock precisely, under a penalty of one guinea from the House, and to be deducted from the bill; and the bill brought in at half-past nine exactly: those members who intend to dine, to give notice before five o'clock, and any member putting down his name after that hour, to pay 5s. extra; and any member putting down his name to dine on any particular day, and withdrawing it after 4 o'clock on the day named, shall be liable to pay 10s. for the dinner. Port, claret, madeira, and sherry, only, to be provided in the room.

Members wishing to dine during the prorogation of Parliament, to have dinner sent up agreeable to the above rules, they giving four hours' notice to the House.

18. A supper, consisting of hot and cold dishes, fish excepted, at 7/6 per head, to be furnished, if required, every night during the sitting of Parliament.

19. That no hot dinners or suppers be allowed but in the dining-rooms.

20. The papers of the day are not to be sent out of the House at any hour or upon any application.

The Managers, finding the necessity of increasing the size of the Coffee-room for the accommodation of the members of the Club, have ordered three plans to be put up in the Morning-room, and are induced to recommend plan iii. as the most commodious, to be carried into execution; and as that plan will amount at least to the sum of £457:5 it is proposed, with a view of not encumbering the Club with an addition to the present debt, to resolve by ballot that each member shall be called upon for one guinea (for this express purpose) to be paid on the first of January 1818.

The new Coffee-room will be opened on the first of October 1817; and during the alteration, which will commence on the first of August, the Coffee-room will be kept in a room upstairs.

This was balloted for and admitted the fourth May 1817:

For it	67
Against it	1
	66

(Signed) ESSEX.
DUNCANNON.
W.J. FERGUSON.
WENTWORTH FITZWILLIAM.
FOLEY.

(Althorp MS.)

CHAPTER IV

Brougham to Leigh Hunt. Temple, Wednesday [about 1815]

[On Voltaire.] . . . I need not tell you how much I admire that astonishing genius—whom I should call second to Newton if his line were not so different.

You can hardly class them by reference to one another any more than you can compare them together. It is equally unnecessary to add how heartily I pity those who rail at him—in their ignorance certainly—and abuse him as superficial—because, judging of superior natures by their own, they cannot conceive how a man can be both lively and profound. I will even go so far as to admit that there is in his writings much real natural piety—and that he had really some religion in his composition is certain—though he was quite sceptical upon the immortality of the soul—Condorcet states this in his life of him. But taking his whole writings together, I consider them as not merely directed against Christianity but all religion whatsoever. This is their tendency—if not their aim—and a powerful effect they have had both upon Theists and Christians.

But let us pass over their effects on the former class of believers. I think he who attacks Christianity does a great and serious injury to mankind. I say so independent of all faith or reasonable belief in that system—and I hold that a pure and philosophical deist may in perfect consistency reprobate and deeply lament whatever tends to vilify Christianity in the eyes of the world. First, because so long as the bulk of mankind believe it, he who *laughs and rails* at it is guilty of the same offence with those who should laugh and rail at our near relatives—and expose them to us who see them with the blindness of affection. But next, because I am firmly convinced that the real good operated by that religion is a thousand-fold greater than the evil its abuses have worked—and lastly—because it really approaches as near to pure theism as the bulk of men can go, in their present state of information. . . .

(Add. MS. 38108, fol. 125.)

Brougham to Leigh Hunt. Thursday [probably February 29, 1816]

. . . I have been extremely occupied in the fight against arbitrary power in its . . . worst shape—the military establishment and the income tax. I think we have given the first a blow and the second a complete defeat—or what in the end will prove such if the country backs us. My voice has been directed to this and to rouse the popular feeling—which alone can keep the House right. It is needless to observe that one has had all sorts of clamour and official petulance to encounter—and a dangerous experiment has been tried by the adherents of Government of representing me as the leader of the Opposition. The success of the threat on Tuesday which stopped the Bill effectually, led them to this effusion of spleen, and to-night they followed it up with an effort not very consistent to represent me as of no weight or influence in the House. These are poor tricks.

The Government are sorely pressed, and I have great hopes that they will be beaten out of their worst measures.

The blackguard conduct of Hunt at the Westminster meeting failed entirely, as it merited. All the reputable part of the meeting were disgusted and highly approved of our withdrawing. Burdett's conduct in not silencing the fellow is generally reprobated—indeed it was very bad, and he is damaged by it.

(Add. MS. 38108, fol. 158.)

CHAPTER V

Brougham to Holland. Brougham, August 1, 1817[4]

. . . When I left it [London] a fortnight ago, there was such a clatter of abuse against me for attacking Castlereagh on Ireland (I suppose, I could fancy no other ground) that you might have heard it across the Channel. I believe no similar instance of violent and persevering abuse in all the Government papers has lately occurred—so much so that some of the people the *least likely* to give such advice seriously insisted on my proceeding against the vermin. This I have refused on the ground that the gratification (I admit a most rational one) of imprisoning all the Treasury editors, printers, and for six months, would be too dearly bought—as it would make the enemy retaliate and thus all the Press and all discussion of public men would be abridged. Besides, I don't mind it. The enemy proceeds in this on an observation of what I fear is fact—that when one of ourselves is severely attacked, the others among us have an itching to give him up. This, too, one ought not to mind—though it is worse to bear by far.

I must add—that in this affair—the Russells behaved as they always do. The Duke took a warm interest in my motion—remained in town on purpose—and Tavistock sat till the very end to give it countenance. . . . I really never spoke so moderately in my life, both in opening and in reply.

(Holland House MS.)

Brougham to Lambton. Friday [probably about the end of February 1818]

I warn you that you will soon grow into a regular country gentleman, which is one degree above a parson. Indeed your letters contain symptoms already, though it may be owing to the reports of the debates (which I never read) being inaccurate. I assure you Canning made the very worst speech I ever heard him make. It was all dead flat, and not a single flash or cheer from beginning to end, and Tierney gave him such a licking as made one pity him. It was a capital speech in every respect, and in a much higher and more *pummelling* style than the Citizen generally deals in. For me to have said a word that night would have been quite superfluous and indeed preposterous. So the night of Archy's [Lord Archibald Hamilton] motion. The debate was wholly with us—and we never could have made it better. The only moment at which I felt a doubt was when the Attorney-General sat down, having made some little impression, but that would have given *them* Canning and the Solicitor-General, who were capable of doing them far more service than had been done by anybody that night. The last debate (on Folkestone's motion) was not so favourable to us. We had full warning that we should be beaten upon our petitions—I mean those already presented by Bennet and F., and which were rather rotten. I, therefore (all means having been used in vain to make F. put it off), flung in a real good case, which I knew would bear sifting, and which I brought forward with great ceremony. Having spoken upon it in presenting the petition, I thought it better not to speak again. I am very lazy, I admit, but I shall not be wanting where I see any good to be done. Hitherto there has not been the smallest occasion for my saying a word. . . .

(Lambton MS.)

Sir Robert Wilson to Grey. February 18, 1818

. . . The House of Commons is rapidly making proselytes for Reform, and I hope you will feel something more disposed to amendment as the basis of your redeeming system. Unless some change does take place to restore character to the legislature, *perilous danger*, as Castlereagh said last night, will not be very remote.

(Add. MS. 30122, fol. 166.)

Sir Robert Wilson to Grey. April 5, 1818

. . . If you could but persuade the big Whigs to repeal the Septennial Bill and regulate the elective franchise I am positive you would find yourself in command of an irresistible power. There is more public spirit than many of your correspondents presume upon, and there would be a redundance if proper example was given. . . .

(Add. MS. 30122, fol. 204.)

Brougham to Holland. Brougham, Friday night [c. Sept. 1819]

. . . The language of our friends in London is *against* meetings, etc. I hear George Lamb quoted repeatedly for this—and Scarlett. I hope the latter was changed in his opinion at Wentworth—the former deserves every degree [of] blame for not running up to the Westminster meeting by the mail coach, the moment it was summoned.

(Holland House MS.)

Grey to the Duke of Devonshire. Doncaster, September 23, 1819

After the communication which Lord Fitzwilliam has made to me this morning, of your having declined to sign the requisition to call a meeting of this county, I am apprehensive that you may think me improperly importunate in attempting to urge you further on that subject. Yet I must trust to the importance of the occasion, and to the kindness I have always experienced from you, to excuse me for submitting, as shortly as I can, to your consideration the motives which influence me in anxiously recommending a measure which I have this reason to fear you do not approve.

The evil which has for some time been increasing, the greatest surely to which any country can be exposed, and which the violence of the Radical Reformers on the one hand, and the policy of the Government on the other, have been urging on to the crisis which the late unfortunate occurrences at Manchester have at last produced, is that of a separation between the higher and lower orders of the community. Such a division never has taken place in any country, and certainly cannot take place in this, without proving fatal either to its peace or its liberty. But this must happen whenever, in a case of real injury, the people find themselves abandoned by their natural protectors, and left without defence or support against a lawless execution of power.

It is with this view that I think it absolutely necessary, to prevent our losing every hope of preserving at once the tranquillity of the country and its Constitution, that upon an occasion in which the principles of the latter have been so clearly violated the Whig party should now take that post, which it is equally their interest and duty to maintain, in their defence. Their character as a party, their interest as individuals, deeply involved in the maintenance of the Constitution as the only safeguard of their property and their rank, equally prescribe a firm and active discharge of their duty.

In recommending meetings to assert the right of meeting for public objects whilst such meetings are legally assembled and peaceably conduct[ed] and to call for a strict inquiry into proceedings hitherto without explanation or defence, which threaten to establish a precedent fatal to the future exercise of that right, I am sure you will not suspect me, still less Lord Fitzwilliam and those who have set the Yorkshire requisition on foot, of any disposition to give countenance to the opinions and the practices of Mr. Hunt and his associates. . . .

(Chatsworth MS.)

Lord Darlington to Lambton. Raby Castle, September 24, 1819

In reply to the favour of your letter of the 22nd. I am desirous of assuring you of my perfect conviction of the impropriety and illegality of the proceedings at Manchester, which I condemn as much as any man in what relates to the magistrates and the yeomanry cavalry. Their conduct requires strict and minute investigation, and demands parliamentary inquiry, and the condemnation of the Ministers for their advice to the Prince Regent to approve of the very reprehensible measures adopted at Manchester.

With this conviction so strongly impressed upon my mind, I can not, however, coincide with you in the necessity or benefit to be derived from a County Meeting of Durham, where past experience has proved to me the inefficacy of provoking political discussion which always branches out to different topics totally irrelevant to the object.

I also conceive it highly improper to be the first County to take the lead on such an important subject, when no other county has already held a meeting, and it is doubtful, I believe, whether Yorkshire will succeed. I certainly can have no hesitation in saying that if a County Meeting should be held and that a moderate tone is adopted, with equally moderate resolutions, explanatory of what I consider to be requisite at the present extraordinary crisis, I shall then have much satisfaction in affixing my signature and readiness to further the object, but must decline to take the lead in promoting a meeting which for some substantial reasons I conceive, as I have already named, to be objectionable.

(Lambton MS.)

Lambton to Milburn (of Stockton). September 27, 1819

. . . As you have asked my opinion respecting the measure alluded to, I will fairly state to you that I conceive you will be doing a greater public service by confining your resolutions and address to the subject of the Manchester proceedings, and the right of the people of England to meet together . . . than by entering into the larger field of discussion announced in your communication to me.

I do not mean to dispute any of the facts advanced by you, such as the alarming state of the country, the depression of commerce and agriculture from the severe weight of taxation, the necessity that exists for practising the most rigid economy and retrenchment, and the glaring abuses which manifest themselves in the present system of our representation. All these are too notorious to be denied, and should undoubtedly be asserted and reprobated by the people at large, but I must contend that by entertaining them at the present moment you would weaken the effect which an undivided and energetic appeal with respect to the Manchester proceedings must inevitably produce.

(Lambton MS.)

Brougham to the Duke of Devonshire. Carlisle, Tuesday [Sept. 1819]

I have been attending the races here—and as there was a strong muster of political friends (Lord Thanet among others) we naturally conferred upon the propriety of calling a County Meeting—on the same plan with the Yorkshire one, for which I conclude you have signed the requisition which Lord Fitzwilliam sent to Lord Thanet among others.

There prevails the strongest inclination to have such a meeting in Cumberland—and those who above all things dread the influence of such people as Hunt and Co., see in the strongest light the necessity of persons of respectability coming forward and taking the management of such meetings.

I am desired by the friends in question—Lord Thanet, James Graham (of Netherby), Wilfrid Lawson, Crackenthorpe, etc., etc., etc., to write to ask your leave to sign the requisition which is the same with the Yorkshire one and only goes to asking the Prince to assemble Parliament—*to inquire* into the circumstances of the Manchester business.

P.S.—Of course you are *not* expected to attend the meeting in consequence of signing the requisition.

(Chatsworth MS.)

Sir James Graham to Lambton. Netherby, October 23, 1819

. . . These County Meetings are salutary in a double point of view: they prove the real insignificance of the Radicals, and disprove the necessity of those coercive measures which a Government disposed to despotism would seek to carry in a moment of groundless terror: moreover, they ought to teach our friends that it is the apathy of the Whigs which has of late estranged the people, and that if they be willing to resume the lead, and boldly stand forward on popular grounds, the people are by no means indisposed to follow; and it is true that Hunt and his crew would relapse into contempt, from which our indifference to public meetings and the unjust suppression of them by the Government has for an instant raised him.

. . .Parliament never met under circumstances which claimed more strongly a full and regular attendance; and we shall either help to establish a new Administration, or we shall be called on to resist to the last extremity the growing spirit of despotic innovation too fatally evinced by the wretches who now govern us.

(Lambton MS.)

CHAPTER VI

Brougham to the Duke of Devonshire. Hill Street, Berkeley Square, Friday
[February 4, 1820]

The dissolution, which we now expect confidently in March, induces me to lose no time in mentioning to you that I feel under the necessity of standing again for Westmorland. The many applications made to me to come forward for *Westminster*, with the assurance that the Burdettites would agree to that arrangement, have hastened my determination, and I have at once put an end to all such measures by coming forward for the County. I am peculiarly anxious to have your and Lord George's countenance and support in this contest—aware of how much use it will be to us—and I assure you that the want of it last time was most seriously aggravated by the part I took in Lord

Morpeth's behalf in Cumberland. One of the charges brought against him was that his connections had done nothing in Westmorland for the Blue interest, and I stepped forward to prevent him from giving any answer to the inquiry, and said that everything had been done which I wished, and that I being satisfied, they might be too. I feel that the great odium I have since encountered in Cumberland, and which tells exceedingly against me in both Counties, is much owing to this declaration—followed as it was by Lord G., etc., taking no part—and I am most anxious to have something to show this time in favour of the assertion above mentioned.

[*P.S.*] The King is certainly out of danger—but he has been terribly bled and his life is a bad one.

(Chatsworth MS.)

Edward Ellice to Lambton. September 14 [1820]

. . . Nothing is thought or dreamt of except Her Majesty, and the interest of some and the fears of others seem to increase rather than decline, as many prophets on this subject in the commencement of the business foretold. The road from town is nearly impassable towards the middle of the day, from the crowds of addressers, and yesterday I was detained fully an hour between Kensington and Hammersmith by a corps of about 5000 stout, able-bodied, and *well-dressed* sailors, headed by the masters and mates of the vessels in the river; and be assured there is more than a *Radical* fever raging through all this part of the country. The middling classes, the shopkeepers and their families, are as much devoted to her cause as the rabble, and Wilson assures me, although I have no other knowledge, that the soldiers are equally so. At Brighton *on his birthday*, the manager told Lord Darlington that he dared not desire the performers to sing God Save the King, and if all one hears of the violence of the people there is true, His Majesty would have been better off in the Cottage in Windsor Park, than he is likely to be at the Pavilion. What it will end in, God only knows. If all parties, as the saying is, had their deserts, the Ministers should be taken to Tower Hill, or rather as they have been merciful to the Radicals at York (for which I acknowledge some obligation), transported to Botany Bay, and His Majesty carried to the horse pond.

But guilt or punishment is now out of the question, and the cry is, show us the way out of it, how are we to escape? . . .

(Lambton MS.)

CHAPTER VII

Huskisson to Granville. March 9, 1826

. . . In the House of Commons, we have had nothing to complain of. All party distinction, at least for the present, appears at an end. The Opposition have been very true in supporting our measures; whilst, on the other hand, some of our ultra friends are disposed to growl, but they are too cowardly to bark out. I do not say that this is a very comfortable, or a very secure state of things; but I do not see how, for the present, we can mend it. The King is more reconciled to the general system of the Government; public opinion (at least all that portion of public opinion which is worth having) is decidedly with us; and if the Opposition support us because we have ventured upon a course of improvement, instead of incessantly attacking us for being hostile to all improvement, we cannot help it. We must bear, as well as we can, the sulkiness of those who think that a posture of inert disgrace is most befitting the Government; and that the Treasury bench should never take a step towards improvement, without the apology and discredit of compulsion, and without sustaining a previous defeat in an unavailing attempt to oppose it.

(Add. MS. 38747, fol. 208.)

CHAPTER VIII

E.J. Littleton to the Rev. W. Leigh. May 19, 1827

Everything regarding the Administration goes on well, except in the House of Lords. But even there I do not see what they will have to differ about, except the Catholic question, *when* the friends of it choose to bring it forward. The old Tory Peers always cling to the Court; and their confidence in their numbers, and in the scruples of the King about the Catholic question, make them think opposition the winning game. But I do not see how even the Catholic question is to turn out the Government. If the question shall succeed or gain ground, they are strengthened. If it fail, why should they resign, for they do not pledge themselves to it as a Cabinet measure? At the same time it is impossible not to own that the Government has difficulties to contend with, and that there are defects in its construction which endanger its continuance. For instance, were Canning to die, there is not a soul on the Treasury bench who could succeed him. No Party would follow Brougham as a leader; Mr. Lamb, who is competent, is the elder son of a peer who is 82, and Mr. Stanley, a young man, competent to any post, is not brought into office. Canning's health is not bad, and would be firm if he would take exercise and keep regular hours, all which is impossible. With respect to the situation of the Government in consequence of the King's scruples, there is this to be remembered—that his life is a very precarious one, and the Duke of Clarence is rather inclined to the Liberal side in questions of religious liberty.

The Apostolicals in both Houses have acted unworthily. They have blustered, insinuated and maligned, but will not come to the point, and will afford the friends of the Ministers no opportunity of an engagement with them. . . . While he [Peel] is professing neutrality in the House, he is doing all he can covertly to organise an Opposition. But I really do not see what he will find to quarrel about—he is so pledged by his past conduct, nor will he any longer enjoy the exclusive popularity of his Consolidated Bills. He opposed all Romilly's and Mackintosh's attempts to soften our criminal law, and only took up the work when the public mind was prepared by them to demand it. It will be odd if Lord Lansdowne and they who concurred with him in suggesting the improvements Peel has been the instrument of making, do not take up the system and pursue it. It is a child of their blood, which he was rearing. . . . The revenue is improving at this moment, and manufactures *generally* in a better state.

(Hatherton MS.)

Abercromby to Huskisson. Stubbing, near Chesterfield,
August 26, 1827

. . . When we negotiated with Mr. Canning I was of opinion that the share of power assigned to his new allies was a matter of secondary importance. Our security consisted in our reliance on his inclination, his power, and his talents, which gave every reasonable assurance that our opinions would be properly assented and maintained with efficiency and credit. Now the case is most materially changed. It is no disrespect to Lord Goderich to say that he is in all these particulars greatly inferior to Mr. Canning; he is most especially so, I fear, in his influence and authority at Court, a point to which all his adherents ought to look carefully because it involves so essentially the character and conduct of the Administration. With such a chief, the arrangement of the Cabinet and the distribution of power became questions of vital importance. Of Mr. Herries I personally know nothing except that by common report he is an excellent man of business, and I must add, an enemy to many principles to which I attach the greatest importance. . . . The admission of Lord Holland would have brought much strength in the Lords, where it is much wanted, and would have been most acceptable to a large portion of the popular party. But that request, apparently a very reasonable one, is positively refused for the present, and the expectation for the future is so vague that no reliance can be placed upon it. With an amiable but powerless chief, with the inferences that necessarily arise from the admission of Mr. Herries and the exclusion of Lord Holland, I must honestly say that I have never been able to convince myself that it would be either creditable or desirable for Lord Lansdowne to continue a member of Lord Goderich's Government. Those who are disposed to support Lord Lansdowne would be entirely alive to the difference between Lord Goderich and Mr. Canning. They would feel that the security for the maintenance of their opinions had been materially diminished, for much has been lost and nothing gained. They would not fail to think that Lord Lansdowne was a member of the Cabinet in which he had no real power, because they must he aware that he would have wished to exclude Mr. Herries and to have introduced Lord Holland. Their support would depend on the character of the measures proposed, and never would Lord Lansdowne expect, in such a state of things, to have any real influence on the decision of the Government in public affairs. The only ground on which Lord Lansdowne could possibly defend his continuance in office, would be to assert that the present Administration was better than that by which it would be replaced. There may be some truth in this view of the case, but it is not surprising that others should be reluctant to concur in their friends remaining in office on such a negative principle. This has all along been and is my private opinion. It is perhaps indiscreet to avow it so frankly, and I shall add to the indiscretion by frankly stating that except in yourself I have no confidence in any other member of Lord Liverpool's Government. . . .

(Add. MS. 37850, fol. 97.)

Ellice to Lambton. December 6 [1827]

One word—for fear of your interpreting my silence as consent to your supposition that Lord D. was the Minister who told me he heard you were already threatening opposition, in despair of your peerage. He was not the person, I assure you; and it is of the less consequence who was, as I suppose I am now writing to the *late* Mr. Lambton. Your friends will require your services in the House of Lords, and more particularly to justify this Navarino affair, which you *so certainly* approve of. I do not think from what I could collect in town, there will be any opposition in the House of Commons—at least any that can give Huskisson much trouble, and I feel more for him than all his other colleagues. If I have any politics *now,* I am with him and the Liberal Tories. The Whigs are gone by, and Lord Lansdowne is by common consent *Goody* Lansdowne all over the country, and with all descriptions of parties and persons. But I suppose we shall all in our turn be converted from our old sinful paths, and follow the old Scotch doctrine of the *King* and *his* Government, either from a conviction of its soundness, or in despair of being able to do better. He has it all his own way with a vengeance, and the only thing wanting to his absolute Government (although, to be sure, the two parties might then dispute for it) is the appointment of Bruffam as maire du Palais in the room of Knighton. . . .

(Lambton MS.)

Brougham to Lansdowne. Hill Street, Monday [1827]

My reason for mentioning Hamilton was that I well knew he would never mention himself. He is a moderate Tory and thinks that he has no right to apply to you. [Sir Walter] Scott, who libels you and me every day (and will, I have little doubt, get the place by dint of *pertinacity* and *impudence*) has no such scruples. All the Clerks of Session are Tories, as well as Hamilton. But he never was offensive—he never libelled us—he quarrelled with Scott's gang by refusing to be one of the *Beacon* Bondsmen.[5] Surely this is some claim when almost all the other Clerks of Session did sign and pay their money—you recollect that concern—how it every week libelled all our families—*female* as well as male—how our wives and sisters and even mothers were slandered weekly by Scott's son-in-law, Lockhart and Co., and by Scott himself. Out of their villainy arose two duels—both fatal. Mr. John Scott (an excellent author and most zealous Whig) was killed here—in consequence of Lockhart's libels—who fought that duel by proxy. Stuart being libelled as a coward weekly in the same paper by the men who met him as a friend daily in society, went out with one of the gang (not at all the worst) and killed him—which abated the nuisance. But I put it to you whether he who originated this system (W. Scott), merely because he writes novels, still read, and once wrote rhymes, no longer read, deserves your patronage even if there were no other man to promote. . . .

(Lansdowne MS.)

Brougham to Allen. August 26, 1827

. . . As for widening the breach with Lord Grey, God forbid. You know how I stopped the newspapers expressly on this score before leaving town. On the same score I defended him at my own great risk at Liverpool, and I am in correspondence with this worthy Whig of 1784 at this moment, and I am amused if not edified to find him talking like old Mrs. Bourne[6] as if all things had stood stock still since the American War, though there has been French Revolution, Bonaparte, and Bolivar since. I abhor Herries—I love

Palmerston—an excellent honourable Liberal man and of a good Whig stock. . . . But if we must take Herries for the present—why, we must, if he washes himself clean.

(Holland House MS.)

Brougham to Allen. Lancaster, Wednesday [September 5, 1827]

I can't help, after hearing the *rights* of the late fracas, saying a word or two— that Lord Holland may take his opportunity of preaching wisdom—or at least common sense to our friends. I was first told by Abercromby that there were very bad symptoms—that our affairs were going very [badly], that the King was behaving ill—that he was insulting and lowering us, and after further disgracing us would turn us out! All turns out to be a mere fiction—a pure fancy, and theory, and refinement. Good God! that great concerns should be the sport of such dreaming—all the foundation being a bare possibility!

For this we were to have gone before the country with a case which was utterly untriable, and not a human being could have comprehended why we went out. It turns out that Herries did not wish to come in, nor the King to bring him in, nor had the least desire to turn us out! . . . Now, however, it turns out that by Lord Goderich's blundering *he got* the King to ask Herries to take the place in spite of his disinclination from bad health, and that then when the King had asked him, the whole objection was made.

. . . *I* am in fact the only one of the whole Party who am excluded by the King's prejudices, but I therefore am the more anxious to keep all right. My reward is to be the vast improvements in the Law, etc., which I am sure I can carry next session in the present happy juncture of affairs—and for the prospects of which and for the good of our Party I have refused the most brilliant and secure emolument, and in my profession too—but out of the House of Commons—and therefore I thought forbidden to me in Canning's precarious health—a presentiment too soon realised.

(Holland House MS.)

Brougham to Lansdowne. Lancaster, Thursday
[probably September 6, 1827]

I heartily congratulate you and all our friends on the happy escape from one of the greatest of all scrapes—breaking up the Government and going to the country upon unintelligible grounds. Indeed, all seems to have been cross-purposes and misunderstanding from first to last, and the King never to have harboured the thought of turning any one out or degrading any body, much less putting the existence of the Government in hazard, as some of our too suspicious friends were so sure of. His (the King's) letters to town since his interview with you are full of your praises, as I learn from one who knows it, and nothing can exceed Huskisson's relief at all having gone well in the end. . . .

(Lansdowne MS.)

Brougham to the Duke of Devonshire. Lancaster, Saturday
[probably September 8, 1827]

I very heartily rejoice that the *difficulty* has been got over—and the arrangement is not to be broken up upon a trifle. I dare say our friends are all right—but I own my weak judgement can see no common sense in seeking occasions of quarrel with the King. I shall not easily, I suppose, be accused of over partiality to him and the Court, but it is with coming into office as with holy matrimony—you take one another for better—for worse (in some sort) and should put up with things until you have good grounds for a split, and then break off altogether. I own I had infinitely rather you got no victories over the King—where your honour and the public good absolutely requires you to break with him—do so—but unite hard at all other times—and don't lay in materials of future quarrels. However, I hope it is all well now—and I trust nothing of minor importance will cause a split or squabble again

(Chatsworth MS.)

Brougham to Lansdowne. Lancaster, Monday [? September 10, 1827][7]

I am unable to divine the hand of crazy-brained mortal that can work him-self into the revené (?) or whimsy of doubting you do right to remain in power. Many will be doubting whether you had ground for resigning after the explanation showed that all was mere misunderstanding and that the King by Goderich's blundering was in a situation, *not of his own seeking*, when no man of common candour and fairness *could* think of leaving him to pay the costs of another's mistake. But I am glad you did because it has produced the best effects, both silencing all clamour (if any could ever have arisen) as to you—and making the King so satisfied as he is and behave so well as he certainly did. My objections to Herries were very truly, as you said, great and strong. The stock business required to be cleared up, and his hostility to the Liberals, his Lowther and ultra habits, were very distasteful. But it is one thing to say 'Don't take Herries if you can possibly help it', and another to say 'Break up the Government rather than take him'. I certainly am the furthest thing from saying Herries was a right man, and the furthest from making a *sine qua non*. However all is now as right as heart can wish with us and as wrong as can be with the ultras. . . .

(Lansdowne MS.)

Brougham to Lansdowne. London, October 22, 1827

I know not if Lord Holland has written to you the fact (on the authority of Lord Darlington far too accurate to leave any hope of its being untrue) that Lord Grey's ground of difference resolves itself into the Government being popular and consulting public opinion instead of the feelings of the aristocracy, which he thinks requires support and is resolved to stand by as against the Government. It was not speculatively put, but on the practical question of Howick's seat. It is really as if he had taken up his own party expression of 'his order', and was determined to make it his creed merely because it was attacked. I never have felt in my life more pain than in making the avowal which such conduct wrings from me, viz., that I no longer feel anxious as before about the line he takes.

But there are others not so situated and who never will follow him on such ground—*e.g.* Lord Rosslyn and Duke of Bedford. The former writes to me this day in answer to my saying something about his factious proceedings—in half joke—as follows—"You are entirely mistaken with respect to Grey and me—we are engaged in no Opposition or other political party, but disposed to persist in supporting the principles upon which we have been acting for so many years". He adds that *his* objections arise from not seeing sufficient weight given to our friends in Government and particularly as to the law appointments.

(Lansdowne MS.)

CHAPTER IX

Althorp to —. January 25, 1828

As you have done me the honour of asking my opinion as to the course which the Catholics ought to pursue at the present time, I have no hesitation in giving it to you. . . . I do not think that the cause of Catholic Emancipation has lost anything by the dissolution of Lord Goderich's Administration. . . . If you will look at the promotions made by the last Ministry I think you will see that with one solitary exception the whole patronage of the Government in the Church has been given to men marked as opponents of Catholic Emancipation. I speak of England where only the cause wants support. I say then that the loss of the last Ministry is no loss to you, because it was not advancing your cause in the least, and that it ought not, therefore, to produce any extraordinary irritation on your parts. The new Administration must, I think, be considered by all as decidedly hostile to your claims; they may put forward a semblance of neutrality, but Mr. Peel explained to us last year what the meaning of a neutral Government with an anti-Catholic chief was. Your course, therefore, I conceive to be very easy. You will, of course, send a petition over to Sir Francis Burdett that he may bring the question forward and take a division upon it; this ought to have been done in any circumstances as well under the last as under the present Administration, and till the result of that division is known I should strongly recommend to the leaders of the Catholics to be as moderate and conciliatory in their language and conduct

as is possible, consistently with retaining their influence over their brethren.
. . . After you have been beaten, as of course you will be, I think your object
ought to be the destruction of the new Ministry; their continuance in office
can do you no good. . . .

(Althorp MS.)

Althorp to Brougham. June 17, 1829

I have been thinking that it might be desirable for you to say something before
the session closes as to the state of the Ministry. I do not feel at all confident
that you ought; but, the thing having occurred to me, I do not think I can be
wrong in stating my doubt to you. They are so weak that they are quite unfit
to govern this or any other country, and I am doubtful whether it might not
be expedient to say that, with every wish not to oppose them, yet that unless
something is done to strengthen their hands before next session, we shall feel
it our duty not to allow the country to remain any longer in such inefficient
hands, if we can prevent it. You are much better able to decide whether this
is desirable than I am. A great deal depends on the real wishes of the Duke of
Wellington. If he wishes to form a junction with us, and is only prevented by the
bad humour of the King, it perhaps is the most prudent thing to say nothing.
If, on the other hand, he is absurd enough to fancy he can govern without the
House of Commons, a gentle notice of this kind might tend to bring him to his
senses. I conclude, if you think fit to do this, you can easily find an opportunity,
if it should be even on the day of the prorogation. I am rather, on the whole,
inclined to think they are favourably disposed. The appointment of Rosslyn can
be accounted for on no other grounds; yet the supporting of Bankes against
Cavendish amounts nearly to a declaration of war.

(Althorp MS.)

Palmerston to Littleton. September 16, 1829

. . . I suspect that the Russians look upon the Turk somewhat in the same
way that somebody did upon our gracious sovereign, when they said he was
the best king we ever had, because he was almost as good as no king at all;

the Russians think the Turks the next best thing to having no neighbours at all, and they well know that Europe would not permit them to be what Sheridan said George III. was, in that house which he built at the gate of Windsor Castle, next door neighbours to themselves. I confess I should not be surprised some day or other to see the Turk kicked out of Europe, and compelled to go visit (?) crosslegged, smoke his pipe, chew his opium, and cut off heads on the Asiatic side of the Bosphorus: we want civilisation, activity, trade and business in Europe, and your Mustaphas have no idea of any traffic beyond rhubarb, figs and red slippers; what energy can be expected from a nation who have no heels to their shoes, and pass their whole lives slipshod?

Our Government seems to have got their friend Charles X. into no slight scrape by urging him to take in Polignac, which, deny it as they may, they certainly did; although I believe they would have preferred having him only, so as to get the foreign policy of France into their hands, and did not wish for the Bourmants and Labourdonnayes. The plan of not paying taxes is too tempting not to spread, and would, if adopted by the greater part of a people, puzzle the Government considerably.

It seems likely, however, that the Duke will be disappointed even in the object for the attainment of which he has brought France to the brink of a revolution, for Polignac and Charles will probably give way to public feeling in France, in their foreign policy, in order to have a chance of being able to have their own way at home; and the French are just as strongly for the Greeks as our Cabinet is against them. . . .

(Hatherton MS.)

Brougham to Lansdowne. Wednesday [probably July 21, 1830]

. . . When I left town on Thursday evening, no doubt seemed to be entertained that the Polignac concern was as good as at an end, but I find it now doubted, and Lord Grey writes that Lord Ponsonby (who is at Paris) thinks the violence of the Liberals will enable P. to keep his ground. In fact our Liberal friends have not of late been very wise, and their hankering after war is a great damper to one's love of them. But I still cannot persuade myself of P. being able to stand. Indeed it does not seem much easier to perceive how our own Ministers are to keep their position, but one believes they will without knowing how they can. Not the least advance of any sort *direct* or *indirect, Irish* or *English*, has ever been made to Lord Grey—*of that be assured.* The Duke of Wellington is either very bold or very blind, or very secret. . . .

(Lansdowne MS.)

Althorp to Brougham. October 5, 1830

. . . I am inclined to ground our opposition to the Government mainly, if not entirely, on their total inefficiency. I think the greatest danger which we run, and the thing most to be avoided, is the giving people the opportunity of saying that we were very moderate and mealy-mouthed as long as there was a chance of the Duke taking us in; but that now we despair of this, we are become violent. We, who know the accusation not to be true, will not be believed; and it is of importance, therefore, if possible, so to conduct our mode of proceeding as not to give a colour to it. I think with this view we ought to be cautious how we urge anything against the Ministers which might have been equally well brought forward last session. I should also be for giving them some credit for the quickness with which they acceded to the wishes of the people in acknowledging Louis Philippe. I think they deserve credit also, it being better to do a thing late than never, for having at last removed Lord O'Neill from the office of Postmaster-General. With respect to the Regency question, I conclude the Duke will propose the Queen as Regent, either with or without a Council. I should prefer the Duchess of Kent; but they are both very well fitted for the office, and, provided they are not either of them to be saddled with a Council, I should not be inclined to run into the trap which in this case will be set, and to give him the popularity with the King which his fighting the battle of the Queen against the Duchess of Kent would undoubtedly give him. These are my present views; but I shall be very glad to talk them over with you, and to hear what you think about them, being by no means wedded to my own opinions.

(Althorp MS.)

Durham to Lady Durham. November 8, 1830

You will see by the papers that the King's going to the City is put off. Nothing can equal the confusion in which the Ministers are. They sat in council yesterday from three to nine and again from eleven to half-past twelve. The universal opinion is that they must go out. The Duke is execrated by the mob, who openly threaten to tear him to pieces, most unpopular with the monied men in the City, who see the funds going down every day and their property not only diminished but in danger from a panic; and almost abandoned by his own party, who openly say (even his subalterns Ashley, Wortley, etc.) that he ought to give it up, and make way for Lord Grey. All classes seem to look to him as the only person likely to save the country. . . . The language of the workmen is open and undisguised. They say if they don't get reform they will imitate the French and Belgians, and at such a moment the Duke is insane enough to say that he never will grant any reform!

(Lambton Papers.)

CHAPTER X

E.J. Littleton's Diary. October 8, 1831

The Lords divided this morning at six o'clock, after Lord Brougham had delivered one of the most splendid speeches conceivable—flaming with wit and irony and eloquence, and nerved with argument and admonition to a degree that made one tremble. He was three hours and a quarter on his legs, and during the effort drank three immense soda water tumblers of hot negus. His fun never deserts him even in the most serious occupation. After tasting his negus, he had put it down on the bench behind him next *Lord Bathurst,* when, thinking it in danger, he stopped in the middle of his sentence and removed it to the table in front of him, amidst some laughter. The House crowded to suffocation—the thermometer at 85.

(Hatherton MS.)

E.J. Littleton's Diary. May 19, 1832

Rode with Lord Grey. . . . I congratulated him on his triumph over the King's reluctance and the pride of the Lords, and earnestly exhorted him, as it was clear the House of Lords would still be in conflict with the Commons, as long as the Tories were out of power, to throw himself solely on the people, and maintain by all means the alliance that so happily subsisted between him and them. He answered, "There is nothing else for it". He told me that the Duke of Wellington had seriously proposed to the present Speaker to take the post of Prime Minister!—and that this was the meaning of the audience of two hours which the Speaker had had of the King! Gracious Heaven! How infatuated must the Royal Family be, and how ignorant of the prevalent feeling! If there is one man in the country it would absolutely forbid to take office, and whose appointment would drive it into rebellion, it is the Duke; and if there is a public man whose mind is utterly incapable of conducting a Department, it is the Speaker! A perfect old woman! Lord Grey, speaking of the Peers, said, "Good God, where do they live? What do they do in the country, that they are so ignorant of what is passing among them?" I told him that in my County [Staffordshire] I did not believe Lord Talbot, who is Lord Lieutenant, had a single correspondent in the manufacturing districts, and I remembered to have been at a large meeting of the Parish of West Bromwich, when I had actually introduced Earl Dartmouth to all his principal parishioners, among whom he had been living twenty years!

(Hatherton MS.)

Brougham to Althorp. Private and Confidential. House of Lords, Monday
[1834]

From what Lord Grey dropt yesterday, and from something you said, I really feel it necessary to come to an immediate understanding. I think you will admit that a sillier thing cannot be done by any Government, than risking its existence on any question unnecessarily. Stanley got us once into this scrape for the sake of his darling Irish Church, and we all said we should not easily be led to do so again. But yesterday, to my utter confusion, Lord Grey avowed that now *every one question, great and small*, is a question of existence; in other words, that the first vote of any kind the Lords pass, we go out. This is a piece of insanity at the best. But I think it is liable to a worse charge. I regard it as lending ourselves to the conspiracy of Tories—and doing so against our own friends in and out of Parliament. Lord Grey is in a humour to risk a civil war, in order that he may get to Howick a fortnight earlier than by doing his duty and standing by his friends. You have a strong desire to get to your cattle. But *I* must at once wash *my* hands of all such designs; and as I see you are resolved to carry the Coercion Bills on, and drag your friends through the mire, in order that you may afterwards throw up the Government by letting them defeat the Tithe Bill, or, what is as bad, go out if they do defeat it, I must fairly warn you that I hold it the bounden duty of the Commons, and of any honest man in both Houses, to let the Coercion Bill hang over till the Lords pass the Tithe Bill.

As for resigning because I can't get a measure carried for the Irish Church, if I stand alone, *I will refuse* to go out on any such grounds, and I will tell the King that if he sends for the Great Seal, I will most reluctantly give it up, being determined to show the country that nothing but compulsion shall ever make me hand over power to the Tories, or deliver up the country to confusion.

The black ingratitude, and even treachery of the conduct I am speaking of towards our friends, whose seats we are endangering, exceeds all belief, and it never will and never ought to be forgiven. Lord Grey had made a speech of much proper spirit as to the Lords. He no sooner gets anxious for Howick than he is ready to eat it all up, and turn his back on the enemy and desert his friends.

(Althorp MS.)

Brougham to Althorp. Private and Confidential. Monday [1834]

I allow that there is much in what you say; but, first, I am for the conciliating of O'Connell clearly; and second, I wish you to ask yourself if the Tories would find it easier to collect tithe and govern Ireland without bloodshed (*i.e.*) by the Orange faction, into whose hands they must throw themselves (than we should do). If not—if, on the contrary, there would be instantaneously a great and frightful convulsion in Ireland; seeing this, makes an additional reason against the folly of Lord Grey's course. He really is incurable. If he would keep his own counsel, and say nothing, and *face the Lords*, and show them he did not mind them, I'll answer for it, they never would venture to fight. But ever since we came in, he has been encouraging them, and everyone, to attack us.

[*P.S.*] I almost as widely differ from you as from him, though on far other grounds. Convince me the Tories can keep Ireland quiet, and England too, and I agree with all you say; at all events, we are bound not to keep our friends in the dark.

(Althorp MS.)

Brougham to Althorp. Private. Saturday [1834]

. . . I am yoked to men who are resolved to throw me overboard to be devoured by the Lords. Lord Grey avows that now every question is vital, and in the House of Lords. Vital!!! That is, that the instant the vile and despicable Lords choose to bid him, out he goes, that he may not be bullied by Lord Wicklow and Lord Londonderry, and that he may get to Howick a week sooner.

I am, therefore, left in the lurch, but I won't die without a struggle; and I have the satisfaction of knowing that whatever the Lords and the Court may feel, the people is with me still, just as much, indeed more, than when I was member for Yorkshire. With them to back me, I care little for the poor Lords, and they will have to beg their life of me before I do so from them.

(Althorp MS.)

O'Connell to B. Boothley (of Nottingham). London, July 17, 1834

You did me the great honour to consult with me previous to the last election on the subject of the fitness of Lord Duncannon to represent your town. I hope, therefore, you will not deem me presumptuous if I initiate—as the Americans say—the correspondence on the present occasion. The fact really is that we are now in a much more critical situation than we were at the former election. The Whigs have been such cruel *drags* on the wheels of rational improvement that many of their Cabinet have been compelled to yield to and fly before the force of public opinion, repressed as it has been by a multitude of causes. But the remnant of that Cabinet want sufficient energy to meet the national exigencies or to give that substantial relief which would alleviate public distress and secure the enjoyment of popular rights against the perpetual spirit of invasion of a worthless aristocracy for whom alone mean courtiers have hitherto been governed.

At such a moment it is the duty of every honest Radical reformer who is equally desirous to prevent any approach to a social revolution, as to carry into practical effect salutary changes and needful improvements in the political system, to come forward and send to Parliament men who are totally free from the bias of *personal* party and determined to do their duty to their country and to the cause of civil and religious liberty, fearlessly, perseveringly, and disinterestedly.

(Rylands Library MS.)

Joseph Parkes to Durham. July 20, 1834

. . . The more I think, the more I think you are right in the opinion that the Chancellor is the man who will go on and *through* the Lords. But whether he will be the Moses or the Pharaoh of the Red Sea, God in Heaven only knows.

(Lambton MS.)

Joseph Parkes to Durham. July 1834

. . . I don't think it looks as though the Tories will come in. Brougham says he is not out. Nothing but an ejectment will get *him* out.

(Lambton MS.)

Brougham to Wellesley. House of Lords [July, 1834]

I have as you see stood firm and I am rallying our scattered troops. We shall, I think, do, after all. The King *will* have a coalition honestly tried, and it has so far failed that the only two he has consulted about it, Melbourne and myself, have declared it won't and can't do. Melbourne was commissioned to communicate with the Duke, Peel, Stanley and our own Cabinet, and he gave a formal and most excellent written answer, that he could not undertake it.

I have in writing stated to the King that I would not resign, because I *knew* full well that there is no kind of difficulty in re-forming the Government without Lord Grey. I have, however, repeated this, and I think it will end so. The King is very kind and gracious and must now see that coalition at present is hopeless.

The House of Commons are all recovered, having at first been horror struck. I believe from all I hear that my attack on the Duke (which his *very very false* movement gave me an opportunity of making), and my firm declaration, has rallied the House of Commons. They are all addressing Althorp to take office and they will not suffer for a day any other Government than ours. Even Tories talk in this way. . . .

(Add. MS. 37311, fol. 251.)

Durham to Joseph Parkes. October 19, 1834

I don't think I have deserved such treatment from Black. Why does he insert anonymous articles on me—coming as he knows they do from the Chancellor, who is engaged in a public contest with me? This is not fair—and, coming from one with whom I was on terms of private intimacy, is too bad.

Now for yourself—if you will really buckle on your armour and go out against him, you will be followed and supported by hundreds. It wants only the first blow to bring down a shower that shall leave him black and blue, instead of buff and blue. His abominable treachery should be fully but quietly explained to Fonblanque, Rintoul, and others who may assist in the good work. Surely he has bullied, and lied, and humbugged long enough. Is the day of retribution never to come? He shall find me an awkward customer too; if once I get him on the ropes I shall not let him drop till I have made him feel what a north-country blow is.

(Lambton MS.)

CHAPTER XI

E.J. Littleton's Diary. March 5, 1835

. . . [Thomas] Drummond, R.E., called on me to-day. . . . We had a
good deal of conversation about Lord Spencer, whose private secretary
Drummond was. We both agreed that Lord Melbourne, though one of
the shrewdest of men, was not the most likely person to lead the Whigs
back to power, and that the only person who could rally the party in the
country would be Earl Spencer. His mind and character had more to do
than that of any other man with the creation of that spirit that carried
the Reform Act—whereas Lord Melbourne, though a man created by
the times, is hardly equal to them. I hazarded an opinion that the King
might in an emergency still send for Lord Grey (his honour would forbid
his sending for Melbourne again, whom he had dismissed, or for Lord
Spencer, to whom he had almost gone on his knees last summer to implore
him to stay in the Government, though he hated him (a humiliation
a King is not likely to forget)), and that Lord Grey might place Lord
Spencer at the head of a new Government. Drummond answered, "Not
under Lord Grey. Lord Spencer's deference to Lord Grey was such that he
had no will of his own in his presence, though of very decided opinions
with all others among his colleagues—so much so that they all submitted
to him". I had many opportunities of remarking the same thing. I never
knew an ascendancy over a powerful and vigorous understanding and
manly character, so complete as Lord Grey's over Lord Spencer. It was
this that made Lord Spencer fail to keep his voluntary pledge to me in
July 1834, that he would resign if the clauses about public meetings in the
Coercion Bill were not given up. It was the positiveness of his expressed
assurance that the clauses must be abandoned, as Lord Grey would not
hear of his resignation, that induced me to be so open with O'Connell.
But in Lord Grey's presence at Cabinet, he said not a word, and there I
was in a scrape.

(Hatherton MS.)

Ellice to Durham. Lyons, March 5, 1835

. . . Lord Grey writes in such a humour that I begin to think my correspondence troublesome to him. In answer to some observation on the breaking up of his Government, and the obligations he and the country were under to Stanley and Graham as the principal cause of it, he turns round on his other colleagues for their refusal to support him and the obnoxious clauses of the Coercion Bill, and calls our conduct a 'cowardly' desertion of him. I should have answered this to any one else. To *him* I can only pass it over in silence.

. . . From the accounts in the papers, matters appear to be taking the turn, and even a better turn than I dared to anticipate. At least there has been spirit enough to resist the Tories, and the public has not been disgusted by any great division amongst the popular party on that point. . . . Stanley's conduct is more capricious and unaccountable than ever. Why abuse the people, and support them? It appears necessary to employ Baring's example—to make a speech one way, and act another. The attempt to persevere with the Government appears even to exceed the dissolution in folly and insanity! However, while the House of Lords lasts, a Tory Minister is safe from responsibility and the consequences which in other times would have followed such an attempt. It surely cannot last long, and is practically over by this time. What is to follow is a point of greater difficulty. If Peel had resigned on the amendment being carried, the chances, from what one can collect from the papers, are that the King would have been obliged to send for him again, after the Whigs had been appealed to and failed in forming an Administration. Who is to be Minister? Who are [to] be his colleagues? Are Dan and Co. to be parties? How can the old Whigs get on with a House of Commons in which they are the smallest of these minorities? . . .

(Lambton MS.)

Ellice to Durham. March 19 [1835]

. . . It is difficult even on what I have hitherto heard and seen to give any very decided opinion, but my impression is that Peel's fate depends rather upon the incapacity and unpopularity of his colleagues and supporters than upon any union and energetic action on the part of his opponents.

He fights his battle well; pleads his duty to the King as a justification for submission to the personal mortifications which his position necessarily exposes him to; takes a bolder and better line in the measures he brings forward than Lord Grey's Government did, and hopes to escape attack on the points on which he is prepared to make no concession. . . . His Dissenters' Marriage Bill is like their Bill for Catholic Emancipation. How often did we in vain press upon Lord Grey and the Cabinet to propose a measure in these express terms, and were always answered that they could not run the risk of collision with the House of Peers!

It is impossible, however, to see how they can escape the Irish Church. My calculation is that our majority on that question will be 200 less in this than it would have been in the last session, the Government having gained in direct voters and trimmers more than 100 men of all ranks, but still we shall beat them. We are hampered, however, in our manner of bringing on the question by our own commission, and they have also the advantage of object-ing to our affirming an abstract proposition, which there are no immediate means of applying. If we could depend upon their bringing forward their Irish Tithes Bill, the most simple proceeding would be to insert clauses of appropriation, giving them notice, that if those clauses were rejected in the Lords, we would throw out the Bill, and swamp the Church entirely, being of opinion that its entire destruction would be, if any evil, a less evil than maintaining it upon the principle insisted upon by Stanley, Graham and Peel. This would also be a tolerably practical illustration of the power of a reformed House of Commons, without reference to the Lords. We shall be involved in all kinds of difficulties with the other course, which gives shabby people the means of avoiding, which it is evident they desire to avoid, a direct vote against Peel.

The Corporation Report will be presented on Monday, and a vote on that might be the preferable point of attack. The country takes an interest in the one, and very little in the other. My impression on the whole is that the Government are in no immediate or pressing danger, and that if they choose to submit to votes of majorities without thinking it necessary to resign, and can keep the peace amongst themselves, they may yet have a year's tenure of office. The Radicals behave as they have always done, most honestly and cordially. They repent them a little of former follies, although they have not to answer for the greater share of those committed by all parties. Lord Grey is come up in the worst possible humour; apparently as angry with Howick as he is with me, and vowing that he will have nothing to do with any person *in communication* with the Radicals! Who carried his Bills, and who established his fame? But this is only the folly of the moment, and as for Radicals, I know few who really differ in opinion with him, or who would not be satisfied with measures which he has always professed his readiness to support.

(Lambton MS.)

Ellice to Durham. Tuesday, March 24, 1835

We are *apparently* approaching the *commençement de la fin* here. Peel will go out if he is beaten on the 30th, and he must be beaten unless there is a greater desertion and more shabbiness than our people, who have been watching the motions of their friends and are better acquainted than I am with the opinions of the imbecile *section*, are at all prepared for. . . .

But if we were to take no step to drive them out, I really believe they would fall to pieces themselves. The whole labour is thrown upon Peel, and he is getting jaded and losing his temper with it. . . . Lord Grey is growling at the Radicals, talking of going to Paris, but, according to my observation, quite willing to entertain a proposition which I have no doubt the King will make to him before another month. Howick and Wood keep aloof from their friends. The former, forsooth, will not attend a meeting at which Dan [O'Connell] and the Radicals are present—and these old women and children think they can regulate the House of Commons and the affairs of the country. How much they know about them! I have endeavoured to persuade Howick to conciliate people. He has more talents and capacity than any of the young ones, but a most foolish estimation of his place, and influence with other men. As to poor Wood, he is only making himself unpopular, and destroying his chance of employment in the class of office for which he is so humbly qualified. They will not be advised by me—think with Lord Grey that I am Radical, and do not intend to be compromised with either of the aristocratical *sections*—by any Radical contamination. I don't believe that any set of men could be found to encourage Lord Grey in destroying his reputation by engaging in this mess. *I will not be one of them.*

(Lambton MS.)

Ellice to Durham. Saturday, March 28, 1835

. . . After ascertaining yesterday that Peel had made up his mind to cut and run, I went to Lord Grey and found him alone with H. I told them, what I had no doubt would follow in the course of the week—an application to Lord Grey, and that I entreated he would in that case recommend to His Majesty to transfer the honour to Lord Melbourne—that, at all events, I had made up my mind not to encourage by any advice or assistance I could give the rash speculation of Lord Grey's risking the character and reputation he had established, by again mixing himself up in affairs which his age neither enabled him to manage, or any means he had could enable him to control—that their great object should be to get Howick into any arrangement which might be made, and to reconcile him to our friends, from whom his conduct has lately estranged him. Of course my advice was received in the manner in which all advice is received by people who think no persons capable of forming a judgement on any subject except themselves. We shall see the result. Melbourne has in the handsomest manner told Lord Grey that he certainly does not wish him to embark again in political life, but that if he does, he is welcome to his support and assistance in any situation in which it can be useful. I will not be party in any arrangement at first—but I will support *any* that can be made—and wait my time, if ever that arrives, after another southern winter shall have completely set me up again.

(Lambton MS.)

Ellice to Durham. Confidential. Saturday, April 11 [1835]

Nothing yet settled, or likely to be settled. Lord Melbourne, Johnny, [Lord John Russell] and *even* Lord Lansdowne quite right and stout— and Dan [O'Connell] had announced, as he saw his admission might divide our friends, his determination not only to give no embarrassment, but his warmest support to a Liberal Government—when Mr. Spring Rice declares his objection to join a Government to be dependent upon Radicals for support, or which may have the appearance of a provisional Administration!! This leads Lord Lansdowne back—he is at this moment in consultation with Melbourne upon their answer to the King—and nothing would surprise me less—although it may end otherwise—than their declining the task of forming a Government.

The case stands thus. A committee consisting of Melbourne, Lansdowne, Johnny, Rice and Hobhouse, have constantly met to arrange the course to be taken by the Opposition in the House. They consult public meetings of members of all shades of opinion, who consent to adopt the course and to follow their advice. This ends in the resolution being carried which made the Government impossible by the Tories. It is offered to the victors. They refuse to undertake it. It is thrown back upon the Tories. They have no scruples, and as they can neither ask the House to rescind the resolution or consent to act upon it, dissolve the Parliament and send Rice and his supporters and others back to their constituents, amidst the jeers and contempt of the country!!!

Oh for some masculine mind to save us from the councils of these small-beer statesmen!

You will observe I have only attended one meeting, giving notice to every one of my determination in any event not to take office, and I have not spoken once in the debates. Rice has taken the lead, and if not with the intention of assisting in the formation of a new Government, why for the destruction of the old one?

The truth is, that he hoped Stanley would strike, and join them. He has no such intention, and Rice thinks it safer to throw off his Radical and Liberal friends, than his religio-Conservative ones.

The case about Dan was that 250 of our people wished him in office, about 60 or 70 objected to it, especially as Attorney-General; and in such cases when we have to come and go on a majority of 27, the minority must have their way.

. . . Lord Grey was not offered the Government. He was only asked *for advice*. If he had been pressed by the King, the family were quite willing to force it upon him. Thank God he is to be out of it. If Peel is again sent for, he will, I have no doubt, apply to Lord Grey, but from the insanity with would dictate any coalition between them, with the Irish Church resolution on the Journals, the Lord in His mercy deliver us!

(Lambton MS.)

Joseph Parkes to Durham. April 13, 1835, 7 o'clock

. . . There was an extraordinary and confident rumour prevalent in the House that Brougham will have the Seals again! Hume and others asserted that they knew it. But it is so contrary to all I have heard the last two days, so little expected by his set, and in itself so incredible, that I can't believe it, though more miraculous things have happened in politics. If he is again Chancellor it will be childish fear of an impotent public man. I don't mean to say that Brougham will not always be an active and perhaps a resurrection public man, but for himself and his late friends, he is better placed in quarantine.

(Lambton MS.)

Lord Hatherton's Diary. April 28, 1835

I this evening being in Brooks's Club, at the windows, saw Lord Grey standing opposite the window of the caricature shop on the other side of St. James's Street, looking at the excellent caricatures of Brougham by H.B., and at some also of himself. He stood among the crowd for about ten minutes. All Brooks's ran to the windows to observe him, which, when he turned round, he saw with a smile.

(Hatherton MS.)

Lord Hatherton's Diary. July 3, 1835

[Talk with Lord Melbourne.] I enquired of him whether Lord Grey had ever been in the House of Lords this year. He answered, "Only once". I enquired why not? He replied, "He is still very sore. The thing that offended him most was that when Althorp retired last July, and he followed, the House of Commons members supporting the Government addressed Lord Althorp to return, but did not ask him, Lord Grey. It made a deep impression on his mind, and although we, who form the present Cabinet, did all we could the other day to induce him to take office, he is still sore, and perhaps a little jealous of our present success". He added that he "even doubted whether he would attend the Committee in the Lords on the Irish Church Bill". I believe he fears meeting Brougham, whose sight he loathes, and whom he considers to have been engaged in a continual plot against him, when in the Government. Certain it is Lord Grey refused to the very last moment to make him Chancellor, and only consented when Brougham had begun to take a hostile attitude in the House of Commons.

(Hatherton MS.)

Lord Hatherton's Diary. August 17, 1835

. . . Sharp debating between Lyndhurst and Brougham . . . Lord Lyndhurst's manner admirable for a Committee—slow, considerate, perspicuous, and decided. Nobody more briefly makes his view comprehensible to others—the statement always sufficiently eloquent—without any attempt at figurative eloquence. In short, his manner is judicial. . . . Brougham on the contrary is distinguished by acuteness, and what is called debating power—finding weak places, enforcing strong points, gathered accidentally while speaking, the whole uttered with the eagerness of a mind exuberant in matter, agitated by extraordinary fervency of feeling, his language always strong and highly eloquent—impatient under reply from unceasing irritability of temperament, and always rising five or six times in the discussion of one point—besides divers audible interruptions by remark while his opponent is speaking. I was amused with watching him all night—while seated he scratched the top of his head with his fingers or picked his nose continually. His brain works so actively, he can never allow himself time to attend to his person, and is accordingly not cleanly. While Chancellor he seemed to pride himself a little on attention to his dress. He rendered himself singular by wearing a broad green and red Scotch-plaid pair of trousers and a round hat—for the latter, Lyndhurst had set him the fashion—and the judges generally are now growing less quizzical in dress.

(Hatherton MS.)

Lord Hatherton's Diary. May 3, 1838

[Talk with Wellesley.] . . . Observing he said nothing about Brougham, I alluded to him as being in Paris, and his singularity in building a house near Cannes. Lord Wellesley immediately defended him against any charge of singularity, and burst out into an eulogium of his character and powers. "Nobody in the House of Lords dare look him in the face", which is nearly true; but the fear of him is like all men have of a violent madman. I did not deny that as one who had been slighted by Melbourne, Lord Brougham had a right to avail himself of any fair opportunity of 'taking down' Melbourne, and putting himself in the best position before the public; but that I did not think that he had much improved that position by his letter to the Radical meeting at the Freemasons' Tavern or some other place of the sort, giving in his adherence to ballot, extension of the suffrage, and triennial Parliaments. "Oh, that signifies nothing; he cares nothing about those questions. I see no reason why he should not be Chancellor in any Government to-morrow".

(Hatherton MS.)

Brougham to Lansdowne. [1839]

. . . The late hoax (scandalous and cruel towards Lord Wellesley, whom it nearly killed, towards the Press and the public I care not a pin) has shown me the public and the party in so kind and amiable a light that it confirms if it does not create an intention in me for next session which will tend to terminate hostilities on my part towards old allies.

(Lansdowne MS.)

Lord Hatherton's Diary. February 13, 1844

. . . I sat close to the Woolsack, where Lyndhurst was continually talking to Brougham, who was sitting as usual on the Woolsack by his side. They were continually making interlocutory observations aloud on the speeches, in a coarse and disgusting manner, Brougham frequently spitting between his legs on the fine carpet of the House, and rubbing it with his feet—his common practice—imitated, however, by nobody else.

(Hatherton MS.)

Chapter XII

Brougham to Althorp. Hill Street, Monday

As you had left Althorp before Abercromby had an opportunity of speaking to you upon our Educating Committee which I urged you some time ago to join—we are now about commencing operations—and I enclose the prospectus—but to the list of subjects are to be added some general ones, on History (good Constitutional History of England, for instance, eradicating Hume's errors in ecclesiastical and civil matters), Ethics, Political Economy, Biography, etc., etc. We did not give those among our samples at first—but we are to do so now—and we have added a notice "that as there are various Societies established already for the diffusion of religious instruction, and as we can only give *books to all* by keeping from controversial matter, we shall never sanction the publication of any tracts on Divinity, or interfering with the subject of revealed religion". This we did to prevent misconstruction. At the same time all our scientific lectures are in fact to be largely mixed up with the sublime truths of Natural Theology—without which science cannot be well, any more than fairly, taught. . . .

(Althorp MS.)

Brougham to Lansdowne. Brougham, August 19 [1828]

[*P.S.*] I should like much to have your opinion upon a point that has occupied a good deal of my attention of late—the proper steps to be taken for instructing the agricultural classes—that is, yeomen and labourers. Their dispersion makes it difficult, nor can I see any means but multiplying cheap treatises on subjects which at least *ought* to interest them—such as the branches of natural history connected with country pursuits, and always mixing with the knowledge conveyed its practical applications to those pursuits. Would your

Wiltshire yeomen, for instance, read treatises (very cheap) on the natural history of domestic animals, anatomy, etc.—their treatment, diseases, etc.? Or is there any other subject (likely to enlarge their minds) which they would prefer? Our Useful Knowledge Society, of course, intends to publish regular treatises on all the branches of agriculture as well as science, but some such as I have mentioned, combining parts of agriculture with detached portions of Natural History or Chemistry, appear to afford a more likely means of attracting readers among a very un-reading class of the community, and who might be scared by systematic treatises on agriculture, in which, moreover, practical farmers put little trust.

(Lansdowne MS.)

Brougham to Althorp. House of Lords, Monday

I am very anxious about my Education plans. The Roebuck Committee will do little good except to show how little they know of the question. But that is fixed and I cannot unsettle it. I was very anxious in 1818 on the Education Committee respecting a volume on the Scotch education part of the question, that there should then be a commission of two advocates and a writer sent through Scotland to investigate—because the expense of bringing up witnesses from the Highlands is intolerable, and we were thereby prevented from doing so in 1817 and 1818.

It is melancholy to think that the Scotch, once the best, are now amongst the worst educated in the island. This can only be rectified by a commission of inquiry, and this can cost only £1,200 or £1,500, whereas a committee would cost £5,000 or £6,000 and do little good.

(Althorp MS.)

Robert Owen to Brougham. [June 1835]

The literary Liberal Party (political) in this country and throughout the civilised world look to you to lead them wisely out of the difficulties in which their old learning and principles have involved them. Nor is there any other individual to whom they will listen with the same attention, or by whom they will be so readily directed. It is, therefore, most important that all who desire the permanent improvement of society should assist you to detect those errors and prejudices which retard the attainment of the objects which rational persons have so much at heart. . . .

To you a large proportion of the most active minds throughout the present half -civilised parts of the world look to effect a change from this most ignorant and barbarous state of society. .

(Owen MS.)

1. Only 36 Whigs supported Folkestone's motion on informations *ex officio* for libel, brought forward on March 28, 1811.
2. The regular Party leaders abstained. Folkestone was supported by Romilly and Whitbread.
3. Jenkinson—the family name of the Earl of Liverpool, who became Prime Minister in 1812.
4. The last paragraph of this letter is quoted in the text, p.124.
5. The *Beacon* was an Edinburgh Tory paper of 1821,
6. A contemptuous reference to Sturges Bourne, whom George IV. had originally suggested for the Chancellorship of the Exchequer (August 8).
7. This letter is evidently the reply to Lansdowne's letter of September 6, which is quoted in the text.

Authorities

MANUSCRIPT SOURCES

(i) *Private Collections.*

The Duke of Devonshire's Papers at Chatsworth.

The Marquess of Lansdowne's Papers at Bowood.

The Earl of Ilchester's Papers at Holland House.

The Earl of Durham's Papers at Lambton Castle.

Earl Spencer's Papers at Althorp.

Lord Hatherton's Papers at Teddesley.

(ii) *At the Public Record Office.*

The Pitt Papers.

(iii) *At the University of London.*

Nassau Senior's Account of the Poor Law Amendment Bill Conferences, 1834.

(iv) *At the British Museum.* (Additional Manuscripts).

(*a*) The Papers of Sir Robert Wilson (30095–30144); (*b*) The Place Papers (27789–27859, 35142–35154, 36623–36628, 37949–37950); (*c*) The Broughton Papers (36455–36483); (*d*) The Wellesley Papers (37274–37318); (*e*) The Leigh Hunt Papers (38108–38111); (*f*) The Liverpool Papers (38190–38489); (*g*) The Hardwicke Papers (35349–36278); (*h*) The Huskisson Papers (38734–38770); (*i*) The Napier Papers (34611–34631); (*k*) The Auckland Papers (34412–34471); (*l*) One Volume of Lord John Russell's Correspondence (38080); (*m*) One Volume of Canning's Correspondence with J.H. Frere (38833); (*n*) One Volume of Ricardo's Letters (34545); (*o*) One Volume of Miscellaneous Letters (34079).

(v) *In the Possession of the Co-operative Union, Holyoake House, Manchester.*

The Robert Owen MSS.

(vi) *At University College, London.*

The Bentham MSS.

(vii) *At the John Rylands Library, Manchester.*

　　The MSS Collections.

PRINTED SOURCES

I. Periodicals and Newspapers

The Edinburgh Review.
The Quarterly Review.
The Westminster Review.
The British Quarterly Review.
The Annual Register.
The Pamphleteer.
The Satirist.
The Times.
The Morning Post.
The Courier.
John Bull.
Hone's Register.
Sherwin's Register.
The Statesman.
The Morning Chronicle.
The Manchester Guardian.
The Leeds Mercury.
The Champion.
The Black Dwarf.
The Examiner.
The Gorgon.
Cobbett's Weekly Register.
The Parliamentary Debates.

II. PRINTED BOOKS
(Works marked with an asterisk contain important documents.)

LADY AIRLIE. *In Whig Society, 1775–1818*. London, 1921.

ALLEN, W. *Life, with selections from his correspondence*. 3 vols. London, 1806.

*ALTHORP, VISCOUNT. By Sir Denis Le Marchant. London, 1876.

ATLAY, J.B. *Trial of Lord Cochrane before Lord Ellenborough*. London, 1897. *The Victorian Chancellors*. 2 vols. London, 1906.

BAGEHOT, W. *Biographical Studies*. Edited by R.H. Hutton. London, 1895.

*BAGOT, J. *Canning and his friends*. 2 vols. London, 1909.

BEACONSFIELD, BENJAMIN DISRAELI, FIRST EARL OF
The Crisis Examined. London, 1834.
The Runnymede Letters. With introduction by F. Hitchman. London, 1885.
*Life, by W.F. Monypenny and G.E. Buckle. 6 vols. London, 1910–20.

*BENTHAM, J. *Memoirs of*. By John Bowring. Vols. x. and xi. of complete edition of Bentham's Works. Edinburgh, 1843.
The Black Book; or *Corruption Unmasked*. London, 1820.

BROOKFIELD, C. and F. *Mrs. Brookfield and her Circle*. London, 1906.

BROUGHAM AND VAUX, HENRY, LORD.
An Inquiry into the colonial policy of the European Powers. 2 vols. Edinburgh, 1803.
A concise statement of the question regarding the abolition of the slave trade. London, 1804.
An inquiry into the state of the nation at the commencement of the present Administration. London, 1806
An inquiry into the causes and consequences of continental alienation, written as a sequel to the Inquiry into the state of the nation. London,1808.
A Letter to Sir Samuel Romilly from Henry Brougham, upon the abuse of charities. London, 1818.
Practical observations upon the education of the people, addressed to the working classes and their employers. London, 1825.
Opinions of Henry Brougham on negro slavery: with remarks. London, 1826.
Observations on two pamphlets addressed to Mr. Brougham. London, 1830.

Speeches of Henry, Lord Brougham, upon questions relating to public rights, duties, and interests; with historical introductions, and a critical dissertation upon the eloquence of the ancients. 4 vols. Edinburgh, 1838.

Life and Times, written by himself. 3 vols. Edinburgh, 1871.

Brougham and his early friends. By R.H.M.B. Atkinson and G.N. Jackson. 3 vols. privately printed. London, 1908.

BROUGHTON, JOHN CAM HOBHOUSE, LORD.

A defence of the people, in reply to Lord Erskine's Two defences of the Whigs. London, 1819.

A trifling mistake in Thos. Lord Erskine's recent preface, shortly noticed and respectfully corrected in a letter to his Lordship. London, 1819.

Recollections of a long life. Edited by his daughter, Lady Dorchester. 6 vols. London, 1909–11.

BUCKINGHAM AND CHANDOS, DUKE OF.

Memoirs of the Regency. 2 vols. London, 1856.

Memoirs of the Court of George IV. 2 vols. London, 1859.

Memoirs of the Courts and Cabinets of William IV and Victoria. 2 vols. London, 1861.

BURY, LADY CHARLOTTE. *The Diary of a Lady-in-Waiting*. Edited by A.F. Stewart. 2 vols. London, 1908.

BUTLER, J.R.M. *The Passing of the Great Reform Bill*. London, 1914.

BYRON, LORD. *Letters and Journals*. Edited by R.E. Prothero. 5 vols. London, 1899.

CAMPBELL, JOHN, LORD. *Lives of the Lord Chancellors and Keepers of the Great Seal from the earliest times till the reign of Queen Victoria*. 8 vols. London, 1869.

Life. By Hardcastle. 2 vols. London, 1881.

*CAMPBELL, THOMAS. *Life and Letters*. Edited by Wm. Beattie. 3 vols. London, 1850.

CANNING, GEORGE. *Political Life*. By A.G. Stapleton. 3 vols. London, 1831.

Life and Times of. By A.G. Stapleton. London, 1859.

Some Official Correspondence of. Edited by E.J. Stapleton. 2 vols. London, 1887.

Life. By H.W.V. Temperley. London, 1905

The Foreign Policy of. By H.W.V. Temperley. London, 1925.

Carlyle, Thomas. *Letters of, 1816–36.* 2 vols. London, 1888.

Caroline, Queen. *An Injured Queen.* By L. Melville. 2 vols. London, 1912.

Cartwright, J., Major. *Life and Correspondence.* Edited by F.D. Cartwright. 2 vols. London, 1826.
   The Comparison: in which Mock Reform, Half Reform, and Constitutional Reform are considered. London, 1810.

*Castlereagh, Viscount. *Lives of Lord Castlereagh and Sir Charles Stewart.* 3 vols. London, 1861.
   Memoirs and Correspondence. Edited by Charles Vane, Marquess of Londonderry. 12 vols. London, 1848–53.
   The Foreign Policy of Castlereagh. By C.K. Webster. London, 1925.

Clayden, P.W. *Rogers and his contemporaries.* 2 vols. London, 1889.

Cobbett, William. *Life.* By E.I. Carlile. London, 1904.
   Life. By G.D.H. Cole. London, 1925.

Cockburn, Henry, Lord. *Memorials of his time.* Edited by H.A. Cockburn. Edinburgh and London, 1909.
   Life of Lord Jeffrey. 2 vols. Edinburgh, 1852.
   Coke of Norfolk. By A.M.W. Stirling. London, 1912.

Colchester, C.A., Lord. *Diary and Correspondence.* Edited by Charles, Lord Colchester. London, 1861.

Copinger, W.A. *On the authorship of the first 100 numbers of the Edinburgh Review.* Privately printed. Manchester, 1895.
   The country without a government; or, plain questions upon the unhappy state of the present administration. London, 1830.

*Creevey, T. *Papers.* Edited by Sir Herbert Maxwell. 2 vols. London, 1904.
*Croker, J.W. *Correspondence and Diaries.* Edited by L.J. Jennings. 3 vols. London, 1884.

Currie, James. *Life.* By W.W. Currie. 2 vols. London, 1831.

Delane, J.T. Life and Correspondence. By A.I. Dasent. 2 vols. London, 1908.

Denmane, Thomas, first Lord. *Memoir.* By Sir J. Arnould. 2 vols. London, 1873.

*DUDLEY and WARD, LORD. *Letters to "Ivy"*. Edited by S.H. Romilly. London, 1905.
   Letters to the Bishop of Llandaff. London, 1841.

*DURHAM, J.G. LAMBTON, EARL OF. *Life and Letters*. By Stuart J. Reid. 2 vols. London, 1906.

ELDON, LORD. *Life and Correspondence*. By H. Twiss. 3 vols. London, 1844.

*ELLENBOROUGH, LORD. *A Political Diary*, 1828–30. Edited by Charles, Lord Colchester. 2 vols. London, 1881.

ELWIN, WHITWELL. *Some eighteenth century men of letters*. Edited by W. Elwin. 2 vols. London, 1902.

ERSKINE, THOMAS, LORD. *A short defence of the Whigs against the imputations attempted to be cast upon them during the late election for Westminster*. London, 1819.
   A letter to "An Elector of Westminster", author of "A reply to the short defence of the Whigs". London, 1819.
   The expediency of a property tax, considered in relation to the objections of Earl Grey and Lord Brougham. London, 1831.

FERGUSON, R.S. *Cumberland and Westmoreland M.P.'s, from the Restoration to the Reform Bill of 1867*. London, 1871

.

FRERE, J.H. *Frere and his Friends*. By G. Festing. London, 1899.

GALLATIN, JAMES. *Diary*. Edited by Count Gallatin. London, 1914.
   Government without Whigs. Being an answer to the "Country without a government" and the Edinburgh Reviewer. London, 1830.

GRAHAM, SIR JAMES. *Life and Letters*. By C. S. Parker. 2 vols. London, 1907.

*GRANVILLE, HARRIET, COUNTESS. *Letters, 1810–45*. Edited by the Hon. F. Leveson Gower. 2 vols. London, 1894.

*GRANVILLE, EARL. *Private Correspondence, 1781–1821*. Edited by Countess Granville. 2 vols. London. 1916.

GRAVES, C.L. *Mr. Punch's History of Modern England*. 4 vols. London, 1921.

*GRENVILLE, CHARLOTTE. *Correspondence with Lady Williams Wynn and her three sons*. London, 1920.

*GRENVILLE, CHARLES. *Journal of the reigns of George IV., William IV. and Queen Victoria.* Edited by Henry Reeve. 8 vols. London, 1872.

GREY, CHARLES, second EARL.
    Some account of his life and opinions. By General Charles Grey. London, 1861.
    **Correspondence with Princess Lieven.* Edited by Guy Le Strange. Vols. i. and ii. London, 1890.
    **Correspondence with William IV. and with Sir H. Taylor.* Edited by Henry, Earl Grey. 2 vols. London, 1867.
    **Lord Grey of the Reform Bill.* By G. M. Trevelyan. London, 1920.

HAMMOND, J.L. and BARBARA. *The Skilled Labourer, 1760–1832.* London, 1919.
    The Village Labourer, 1760–1832. London, 1920.
    The Town Labourer, 1760–1832. London, 1920.

*HATHERTON, E.J. LITTLETON, LORD. *Memoir and Correspondence relating to political occurrences in June and July 1834.* Edited by H. Reeve. London, 1872.

*HERRIES, J.C. *Memoir of.* Edited by Edward Herries. 2 vols. London, 1880.

**Historical Manuscripts Commission Reports.*
    Fortescue Papers. Vols. viii. and ix.
    MSS. of the Earl of Lonsdale. 13th Rep. Vol. 27.
    MSS. of the Duke of Norfolk. Vol. 63.
    Manuscripts of the Earl of Rosslyn. 2nd Rep. App.
    MSS. of the Earl of Bathurst.

*HOLLAND, LORD. *Memoirs of the Whig Party.* Edited by his son, Lord Holland. 2 vols. London, 1852–4.
    Further Memoirs of the Whig Party, 1807–21. Edited by Lord Stavordale. London, 1905.

*HOLLAND, ELIZABETH, LADY. *Journal.* Edited by the Earl of Ilchester. 2 vols. London, 1908.

*HOLLAND, fourth LORD. *Journal 1818–30.* Edited by the Earl of Ilchester, 1923.

*HOLLAND, LADY. *Memoir of Sydney Smith.* 2 vols. London, 1855.

*HORNER, FRANCIS. *Memoirs and Correspondence.* 2 vols. London, 1843.

HUNT, LEIGH. *Autobiography*. London, 1885.
  *Correspondence. Edited by his eldest son. 2 vols. London, 1862.
  A full report of the trial of John and Leigh Hunt, 9th Dec. 1812. London, 1812.

HYLTON, LORD. *The Paget Brothers, 1790–1840*. London, 1918.

KENT, C.B.R. *The English Radicals*. London, 1899.

KNIGHT, CHARLES. *Passages of a working life*. 3 vols. London, 1864.

LENNOX, LORD WILLIAM PITT. *Celebrities I have known*. Second Series. 2 vols. London, 1877.
  My recollectios from 1806 to 1873. 2 vols. London, 1874.

LIECHTENSTEIN, PRINCESS MARIE. *Holland House*. 2 vols. London, 1874.

*LIEVEN, PRINCESS.
  Letters during her residence in London, 1812–34. Edited by L.G. Robinson. London, 1902.
  An impartial collection of addresses, songs, squibs, etc., published during the election of members of parliament for the borough of Liverpool, 1812.

*LIVERPOOL, EARL of. *Life and Administration of*. By C.D. Yonge. 3 vols. London, 1868.

LYTTON, EDWARD BULWER, first LORD.
  Life of. By his grandson the Earl of Lytton. 2 vols. London, 1913.
  A letter to a late cabinet minister on the present crisis. To which is added a Letter from Lord Brougham to Mr. Bulwer. London, 1834.

*MACAULAY, ZACHARY. *Life and Letters*. By Viscountess Knutsford. London, 1900.

*MACAULAY, LORD. *Life and Letters of*. By G.M. Trevelyan. London, 1883.

MARTINEAU, HARRIET. *History of the Thirty Years' Peace. (1816–46)*. 4 vols. London, 1877.
  Biographical Sketches, 1852–68. London, 1869.

MEDWIN, THOMAS. *Conversations of Lord Byron noted during a residence with his Lordship at Pisa*. London, 1824.

*Melbourne, William Lamb, Viscount. *Papers*. Edited by Lloyd C. Sanders. London, 1889.
  Memoirs. Edited by W.M. Torrens. 2 vols. London, 1890.

Mill, James. *Life*. By Alexander Bain. London, 1882.

Mill, John Stuart. *Autobiography*. London, 1873.

Molesworth, W.N. *History of England*. Vol. i. London, 1874.

Morley, Lord. *Life of Gladstone*. 3 vols. London, 1903,

*Murray, John. *Lord Byron's correspondence, chiefly with Lady Melbourne, Mr. Hobhouse, the Hon. Douglas Kinnaird, and P. B. Shelley*. 2 vols. London, 1922.

*Napier, Macvey. *Correspondence*. Edited by M. Napier. London, 1879.
  The New Whig Guide. London, 1819.

Oldfield, T.H.B. *A Key to the House of Commons. Being a history of the last General Election in 1818; and a correct state of the virtual representation of England and Wales*. London, 1820.
  The representative history of Great Britain and Ireland. 6 vols. London, 1816.

Owen, Robert. *Life written by himself. With selections from his writings and correspondence*. 2 vols. London, 1857.
  A Biography. By Frank Podmore. 2 vols. London, 1906.

*Palmerston, Lord. *Life, with selections from his diaries and correspondence*. By E.L. Bulwer. 2 vols. London, 1870.

*Palmerston, Lady. *Lady Palmerston and her times*. By Lady Airlie. 2 vols. London, 1922.
  The Patriot Ministry. A poem. London, 1831.

*Peel, Sir Robert. *Private Papers*. Edited by C.S. Parker. 3 vols. London, 1891–99.

Place, Francis. *An authentic narrative of the events of the Westminster Election, 1819*. London, 1819.
  Life, by Graham Wallas. London, 1918.

De Quincey, Thomas. *Life and Writings*. By H.A. Page. 2 vols. London, 1907.

Editorship of the Westmoreland Gazette. Pollitt. London, 1890.
RAE, W.F. *Wilkes, Sheridan, Fox. The Opposition under George III*. London, 1874.

RAIKES, THOMAS. *Journal*. 1831–47. 2 vols. London, 1858.
The Result of the General Election; or, What has the Duke of Wellington gained by the Dissolution? London, 1830.

RICARDO. *Works*. By J.R. McCulloch. London, 1852.
Letters. Edited by Bonar and Hollander. Oxford, 1899.

ROEBUCK, J.A. *History of the Whig Party*. 2 vols. London, 1852.
Life and Letters. Edited by R.E. Leader. London, 1897.

*ROMILLY, SIR SAMUEL. *Memoirs, written by himself, with a selection from his correspondence*. Edited by his sons. 3 vols. London, 1840.

ROSCOE, W. *A letter to H. Brougham on the subject of Reform in the representation of the people in parliament*. Liverpool, 1811.
Life. By his son, H. Roscoe. 2 vols. London, 1833.

*ROSE, GEORGE. *Diaries*. Edited by the Rev. Vernon Harcourt. 2 vols. London, 1860.

ROSS, JANET. *Reminiscences*. London, 1912.

RUSH, R. *A residence at the Court of London*. Second Series. Vol. i. London, 1845.

RUSSELL, EARL. *Recollections and Suggestions*. London, 1875.
Memoirs, Journals and Correspondence of Thomas Moore. 8 vols. London, 1853–6.
Early Correspondence. Edited by Rollo Russell. 2 vols. London, 1913.
Life. By Spencer Walpole. 2 vols. London, 1898.

SANDERS, L.C. *The Holland House Circle*. London, 1908.

SCARLETT, JAMES (first Lord Abinger). *Life*. By P.C. Scarlett. London, 1877.

*SCOTT, SIR WALTER. *Familiar Letters*. 2 vols. Edinburgh, 1894.
Memoirs. By J.G. Lockhart. 10 vols. Edinburgh, 1869.

SCOTT, SIR WILLIAM. *Letter to, in answer to Mr. Brougham's Letter to Sir Samuel Romilly upon the abuse of charities*. London, 1818.

*Seymour, Lady. *The "Pope" of Holland House. Selections from the correspondence of John Whishaw and his friends.* London, 1906.

Sheridan, R.B. *Life.* By Rae. 2 vols. London, 1896.

*Sidmouth, Lord. *Life.* By Dean Pellew. 3 vols. London, 1847.

Stephen, Leslie. *The English Utilitarians.* 3 vols. London, 1900.

Stuart, Lady Louisa. *Letters to Miss Louisa Clinton.* Second Series. Edited by Hon. J.A. Home. Edinburgh, 1903.
  The Talents run mad, or 1816. A satirical poem. London, 1816.
  Tories, Whigs and Radicals. Thoughts on the present state of parties and public affairs, in answer to a letter by E.L. Bulwer. London, 1834.

Walpole, Spencer. *History of England from the conclusion of the Great War.* 6 vols. London, 1890.

Ward, R.P. *Memoirs of.* By E. Phipps. 2 vols. London, 1850.
  The Whig Conspiracy; or, a handle to a broom. London, 1832.

*Wilson, Sir Robert. *Canning's Administration: narrative of formation.* Edited by H. Randolph. London, 1872.

*Wellesley, Marquis. *Papers.* By the editor of the Windham Papers. 2 vols. London, 1914.

Wellington, Arthur Wellesley, Duke of.
  *Despatches, Correspondence, and Memoranda. 7 vols. London, 1867.
  *Life. By Sir H. Maxwell. 2 vols. London, 1899.
  The Duke of Wellington and the Whigs. London, 1830.

Wharton, Richard. *Remarks on the Jacobinical tendency of the Edinburgh Review, in a letter to the Earl of Lonsdale.* London, 1809.

*Wilberforce, William. *Correspondence.* Edited by his sons. 2 vols. London, 1840.
  Private papers. Edited by A.M. Wilberforce. London, 1897.
  Life. By his sons. 5 vols. London, 1838.

Index